Disciplining Germany

Disciplining Germany

Youth, Reeducation, and Reconstruction after the Second World War

JAIMEY FISHER

WAYNE STATE UNIVERSITY PRESS

DETROIT

K R I T I K

German Literary Theory and Cultural Studies
Liliane Weissberg, Editor

*A complete listing of the books in this series
can be found online at wsupress.wayne.edu*

© 2007 BY WAYNE STATE UNIVERSITY PRESS,
DETROIT, MICHIGAN 48201. ALL RIGHTS ARE RESERVED.
NO PART OF THIS BOOK MAY BE REPRODUCED WITHOUT FORMAL PERMISSION.
MANUFACTURED IN THE UNITED STATES OF AMERICA.
11 10 09 08 07   5 4 3 2 1

LIBRARY OF CONGRESS CATALOGING-IN-PUBLICATION DATA
FISHER, JAIMEY.
DISCIPLINING GERMANY : YOUTH, REEDUCATION, AND RECONSTRUCTION AFTER
THE SECOND WORLD WAR / JAIMEY FISHER.
P. CM. — (KRITIK: GERMAN LITERARY THEORY AND CULTURAL STUDIES)
INCLUDES BIBLIOGRAPHICAL REFERENCES AND INDEX.
ISBN-13: 978-0-8143-3329-7 (HARDCOVER : ALK. PAPER)
ISBN-10: 0-8143-3329-X (HARDCOVER : ALK. PAPER)
1. GERMANY—SOCIAL CONDITIONS—1945–1955. 2. YOUTH—GERMANY—HISTORY—
20TH CENTURY. 3. YOUTH MOVEMENT—GERMANY—HISTORY—20TH CENTURY.
4. RECONSTRUCTION (1939–1951)—GERMANY. 5. COLLECTIVE MEMORY—GERMANY—
HISTORY—20TH CENTURY. I. TITLE.
DD257.2.F57 2007
943.087'4—DC22
2007005012

∞ THE PAPER USED IN THIS PUBLICATION MEETS THE MINIMUM REQUIREMENTS
OF THE AMERICAN NATIONAL STANDARD FOR INFORMATION SCIENCES–PERMANENCE OF PAPER
FOR PRINTED LIBRARY MATERIALS, ANSI Z39.48-1984.

CHAPTER 5, "CHILDREN OF THE RUBBLE: YOUTH, PEDAGOGY, AND POLITICS
IN EARLY DEFA FILMS," WAS ORIGINALLY PUBLISHED IN A SLIGHTLY DIFFERENT FORM
AS "WHO'S WATCHING THE RUBBLE-KIDS? YOUTH, PEDAGOGY, AND POLITICS IN EARLY
DEFA FILMS," *New German Critique* 82 (WINTER 2001): 91–125.

For my mother and father

Contents

CONTENTS

viii

Acknowledgments

THIS PROJECT HAS BEEN LONG in the making and I have many, both institutions and individuals, to thank for its completion: they are, doubtlessly, responsible for its felicities, while its shortcomings are entirely my own doing.

The German Academic Exchange Service (DAAD), the Free University of Berlin, and the Einaudi Center of Cornell University supported the project in its early stages, and to all of them I am grateful. In its last phase, the research was sponsored by a Federal Chancellor Fellowship from the Alexander-von-Humboldt-Foundation (AvH), and I would like especially to thank, in addition to the foundation in general, Robert Grathwol, Donita Moorhus, Rebecca Schmitz-Justen, and Iris Fama at AvH for their support and help. During my two stays in Berlin, Gertrud Koch and Rüdiger Steinlein were exceedingly generous with their advice and time. I would also like to thank the staffs at the Library for Publizistik at the Free University of Berlin, the Bundesarchiv-Filmarchiv, and DEFA Spektrum in Berlin as well as the DEFA Film Library in Amherst, Massachusetts, especially Betheny Moore Roberts and Sky Arndt-Briggs, for helping me to secure the images appearing herein.

During the completion of the project, I had the good fortune to be teaching at two universities that offered unusually challenging but also supportive intellectual communities. At Tulane University, Teresa Soufas and George Cummins were more than magnanimous in encouraging me to take up the Humboldt fellowship, and Elio Brancaforte and Allison Mull offered indispensable help and support in the Tulane Department of German. I have had the good fortune to bring the project to its completion while teaching at the University of California–Davis, and I am grateful to my colleagues there, especially Carlee Arnett, Clifford Bernd, Gail Finney, Jeff Fort, Caren Kaplan, Elisabeth Krimmer, Winder McConnell, Susette Min, Gerhard Richter, and Eric Smoodin. Bastian Heinsohn provided indispensable assistance in the final preparation of these pages. A grant from the UC–Davis Office of Research and the guidance of interim dean of HArCS, Patricia Turner, helped the manuscript assume its final form.

I owe many debts of gratitude to individuals who generously acted as guides and mentors throughout the project. Peter Uwe Hohendahl has been involved in myriad ways and at every stage of the project, and to him I am immensely grateful. David Bathrick was invaluable as teacher, interlocutor, and guide to archives and contacts around Berlin, while Geoff Waite offered useful feedback at a crucial stage. I owe a special thank you to Eric Rentschler for advice and guidance on two continents. I would also like to express my gratitude to the following colleagues who offered feedback and support all along the way: Nora Alter, William Brumfield, Barton Byg, John Davidson, Jennifer Fay, Mary Fessenden, Sabine Hake, Michael Hayse, Martha Helfer, Robert Holub, Jan-Christoph Horak, Yasco Horsman, Konrad Jarausch, Manuel Koeppen, Ben Martin, Biddy Martin, Joseph Metz, Tobias Nagl, Gerda Neu-Sokol, Nancy Pearce, Todd Presner, William Rasch, Christian Rogowski, Wolff von Schmitt, Leah Shafer, Robert Shandley, Michael Steinberg, Katie Trumpener, and Wilfried Wilms. Brad Prager and Mike Richardson shared both their intellectual acumen and good humor throughout the many years of the project. An extra debt of gratitude is owed to Sean Forner and Mark Clark, who, at a late stage and on short notice, offered invaluable advice and guidance. Kathryn Wildfong at Wayne State University Press has shepherded the manuscript ably and offered expert advice along the way. I am particularly indebted to Liliane Weissberg, a consistent source of encouragement who demonstrated a tenacious belief in the project without which it would never have reached fruition.

I owe both my work and well-being during my time in Germany to a great number of friends and colleagues, including, above all, Joan Murphy and Uli Nowka, whose hospitality is endless, but I would also like to thank Lutz Artmann, Maria Biege, Jutta Braband, Stefanie

Fronert, Pascal Grosse, Sergei Hurwitz, Angela Jung, Familie Kampmann, Jens Kempf, Karen Ruoff Kramer, Familie Lechner, Franz Neckenig, Leonie Roos, Ralf Saborrosch, Carol Scherer, and Dorothea Schmidt. Special thanks are due to Olaf Schmidt, who generously offered his help and expertise both in Berlin and New Orleans.

Finally, and above all, I have my family to thank. Jacqueline Berman has been not only unfailingly supportive but also, in this as in so many things, a consistent revelation. I feel fortunate beyond words to have found such a rigorous but warm interlocutor. Our son Noah, in his conceptually untainted approach, has taught me to find the transcendent in the quotidian, reenchanting the world each time he touches it. My grandmother Teresa and uncle Corey have provided a bottomless well of support through the years. My brother Joel has shared both his sharp wit and his considerable skills during my work on this project. My father, Randy Fisher, has often volubly remarked that he has no idea whence I derived my curiosity and contentiousness, but I think we both know. My mother, Jackie Fisher, is, intellectually and emotionally, the most patient and giving person I know, and to her I am, and will forever remain, particularly grateful.

Introduction

Youth, Memory, and Guilt in Early Postwar Germany

HITLER'S LAST TROOPS

Adolf Hitler made his last public appearance on his fifty-sixth birthday, 20 April 1945, just ten days before he was to die. The Führer's birthday had traditionally occasioned a prominent pageant of his personal life, parades as well as parties, a celebration straddling the public and private spheres. But Hitler's last birthday began as a muted echo of these earlier festivities: he was received and toasted by many top party and military officials deep inside the beleaguered Berlin bunker, far from the screaming crowd. Despite the mood of impending doom, however, he did manage to fulfill one last public duty: he climbed out of the bunker for a short ceremony in the courtyard of the heavily bombed and increasingly crumbling Reich Chancellery. His last appearance was to be, unsurprisingly, a review of troops, but this was not just any group of war-worn soldiers. The exhausted and stooped Führer hosted a small group of Hitler Youth to be honored and decorated for bravery in defending the teetering German capital. In fact—for reasons historians have either left unexplained or disputed—there were no regular Wehrmacht troops present: this last photo op would frame Hitler, Göring, and Goebbels with a group of adolescents.[1] Nonetheless, as with all of Hitler's public appearances, the event was carefully staged, performed, and documented: his weary clappings on shoulders and tired pinnings of medals were filmed, yielding the last official photographs of the Führer, the last public record of the man who had led Germany for its twelve most infamous years. These images, some of the last of the Nazi regime, frame him with three unidentified Hitler Youths, Germany's remnant Nazis, only eighteen days before the unconditional surrender.

That Hitler would appear for the last time publicly with members of the Hitler Youth—that his last few public moments would be spent with a kind of youth group—corresponds closely to a generational profile cultivated by official Nazi culture. The Nazi cultural, social, and political imaginaries had deliberately developed and exploited a youthful image, their popularity riding a wave of vibrantly juvenile enthusiasm. The photograph visually confirms the central role of youth in establishing and maintaining modern German political and social hierarchies. Such hierarchies must create and constantly enforce social distinctions and differences; an important and underrated axis of such difference in modern society is age, the significance of which has been growing within such hierarchies. Though age has become an increasingly important issue in modern Western societies, the image of youthful Nazis in Hitler's last official photograph underscores the central status of youth and youth groups in Germany's particular modernity.[2] But these final photographs of Hitler do more than look backward to the Nazis' rise to and maintenance of political and cultural power.

This image of uniformed children associated, as the alleged *Stunde Null* (Zero Hour) approached, with the Nazi nation and its nefarious leader proved indelible, in various visual and textual forms, throughout the postwar period. After the war, with Hitler dead but nonetheless requiring repeated exorcism, many postwar intellectuals, authors, journalists, and filmmakers turned to the youthful half of this photograph, the Third Reich's ineradicable final image, to come to terms with the past. This study will trace this repeated and ubiquitous tendency in early postwar culture and society: the consistent reliance on discourse about youth and generation to navigate and negotiate the most difficult questions of Germany's recent history. Youth and particularly youth crises served as discursive sites onto which to displace, and with which to distract from, the wider challenges of coming to terms with Germany's burdensome past.

2

In German studies in particular and cultural studies in general, a growing number of analyses have foregrounded the importance of youth and youth culture in the twentieth century. Recent studies, such as those by Ute Poiger, Kaspar Maase, and Heide Fehrenbach, investigate the role and significance of youth culture in the early FRG and (in Poiger's case) the German Democratic Republic (GDR).[3] Other works, such as those by Susan Wiener and Kristin Ross, have highlighted the importance of youth and youth culture in other Western societies.[4] Almost all of these studies, however, focus on the importance of youth in the emergent consumer cultures of the 1950s: the young were becoming an essential, if not the central, node for the transfer of globalizing, often Americanizing, cultures to western Europe. Although Fehrenbach does address, in part, an earlier moment in the occupational period, she does not attend to discourse about youth as it was inflected through the discussion on reeducation and the past; her investigation carries her through the early 1950s without fully examining discourse about youth as it first appeared after the war.[5] Surprisingly, none of these studies considers at length the transition from the war—largely fought, at least in the cultural imaginary, by young people—to the postwar period, and none of them considers the central role that young people played in Germany's particular cultural history throughout the first half of the twentieth century. In an otherwise intriguing chapter on the debate about generation after the war, Stephen Brockmann similarly does not take up the longer-term importance of youth discourse in German culture or the contingent importance of reeducation in the occupational period.[6] As such, these studies risk reproducing the myth of a radical break with 1945 and its alleged Stunde Null. On the other hand, Thomas Koebner, Rolf-Peter Janz, and Frank Trommler have offered an extensive analysis of the "myth of youth" in the fin de siècle, 1920s, and Nazi periods, though without taking up the fate of this uniquely German discourse after the war.[7] The present study aims to fill the gap left by these works by investigating the afterlife of discourse about youth in the early reconstructive years.

A careful analysis of early postwar discourse about youth can augment previous studies because it will illuminate why reactions in the 1950s to the *Mischlinge* children of U.S. GIs, to phenomena like the *Halbstarken,* and to an increasingly globalized youth culture became so virulent. It was more than, for instance, regressive biases on the part of Germany's social and cultural elites, as Fehrenbach and Maase argue; it was more than anxiety about Americanization as subversive to moral, cultural, and political authorities, as Poiger suggests. The reaction was also so pronounced because, in the first years after the war, discourse about youth played a central role in Germany's coming to terms with the past. Indeed, discourse about youth and reeducation became an essential means by which (adult) Germany narrated its transition from its own, abruptly dubious history; it served as a means that would propel and progress the culture out of the now tainted Wilhelmine, Weimar, and Nazi periods. Early postwar society initiated a deliberate dismantling of conventional youth groups and, perhaps more important, a deliberate abandonment of youth as a unique and celebrated form of life. In his *History of Youth,* Mitterauer highlights the importance of the youth group for youth formation in German culture; it was more important, he writes, than family or school, because discourse about youth—the belief that youth represents not only a stage in life but also a unique Weltanschauung—played a much bigger role in German culture than elsewhere.[8] His expansive declaration, if not quite totally convincing, is still revealing: many German youth groups before World War II were founded on this alleged uniqueness of a youthful perspective—for example, the *Wandervogel* or related reform movements—and they were, from an American perspective, unimaginably widespread. In 1927, 35 percent of adolescents belonged to formal youth groups, an astounding figure when one considers the low participation among female and rural youths. Only twelve years later, in 1939, with the advent of Hitler Youth (Hitler-Jugend) and the Association of German Girls (Bund Deutscher Mädel), 98 percent were involved in such groups. Moreover, the youth movement had long had a substantive impact within adult culture beyond mere membership numbers due to its socially elitist aspects.[9] It seems fair to say that of all the particularities of modern German social and cultural history, the role of organized and celebrated youth is among the most unusual.[10] In the postwar period, the deliberate dismantling of these social forms and their cultural inflections played an important, if not central, role in adult Germany's narration of its postwar trajectory. Only by attending to these years and Germany's particular coming to terms with the past via young people can one comprehend the role of generation, youth, and youth culture in 1950s, 1960s, and 1970s Germany.[11]

This study examines the way in which early postwar culture, particularly the occupational period (1945–49), relied repeatedly on a multifaceted discourse about youth to come to terms with the Wilhelmine,

4

Weimar, and Nazi pasts and some of its most difficult challenges—guilt, German militarism, humanism, the concept of nation, and postwar gender relations. The study analyzes a number of different media, including literary texts, newspapers, popular magazines, academic journals, tracts by intellectuals, radio speeches and lectures by public figures, and popular feature films. In many ways, the most convincing evidence for the central importance of youth is the wide range of environments in which such discourse functions fundamentally, namely, in the realms of both "high" and "low" adult culture, on both the political right and left.

REFIGURING "FORGETTING": SILENCE, REPRESSION, AND REALISTIC RECONSIDERATIONS

> The forgetting of National Socialism should be understood far more in terms of a general social situation than in terms of psycho-pathology. Even the psychological mechanisms that defend against painful and unpleasant memories serve highly realistic ends. This is revealed when those who are defensive point out, freely and in a practical mood, that a too vivid and lasting remembrance of those events could harm Germany's reputation abroad.
>
> Theodor W. Adorno,
> "What 'Working through the Past' Means"

In his much-cited essay, Theodor W. Adorno takes up the relation of Germany's Nazi era to individual and collective memory.[12] In sketching what he elsewhere calls "the effacement of memory" of the recent past, Adorno makes clear that this "forgetting" should not be regarded as an unconscious, or even particularly psychological, mechanism: in fact, this essay, in deliberately dialectical fashion, elaborates a refigured forgetting as a diverse phenomenon that intertwines social and psychological, conscious and unconscious, aspects. Adorno's questions of how precisely one, especially postwar Germans, forgets have returned to the fore as analyses of Germany's relation to its Nazi past have enjoyed a marked revival in the last few years in German studies and German history. In reconsidering questions of *Vergangenheitsbewältigung* (conventionally translated "coming to terms with" but more literally meaning "mastering" the past) or *Aufarbeitung der Vergangenheit* (working through the past), scholars have begun to reexamine how these questions were manifest in the early postwar period, in particular in the 1940s and 1950s. Before this turn, most studies had focused on more recent questions of remembering and mastering the past, for example, on the 1980s *Historikerstreit* (historians' debate) and the 1980s–90s contestations surrounding memorials.[13] Parallel to the recent scholarly turn to the 1940s and 1950s have been the public debates about W. G. Sebald's *Air War and Literature*, Günter Grass's *Crabwalk*, and Jörg Friederich's *The Fire*, all of which similarly aim to amend and revise Germans' relationship to their own difficult past.[14] The present study builds on this recent turn in German studies and history to examine a moment and discourse mostly neglected by contemporary studies: the way in which the late-1940s discussion of youth and reeducation permitted Germans to come to terms with their past, anticipated later debates about youth in the 1950s, and generally helped them ground postwar German identity.

In turning to the past—in self-consciously explaining or casually recalling it—postwar Germans faced what many scholars, including figures as diverse as Eric Santner, Robert Moeller, and Volker Hage, have underscored as a nearly intractable paradox, that is, a contradictory challenge or conundrum.[15] On the one hand, postwar Germans had to acknowledge the war and Nazism, not only (perhaps even less) because it was required by the Allies and the world community but also because it had scarred their own psyches and lives, their homes and their environs, their families and friends. Germans had to confront a political movement that had led to their unmitigated suffering and unconditional surrender. On the other hand, they wanted, understandably or at least predictably, to distinguish themselves as much as possible from history's most nefarious criminals, to distance themselves from history's most horrendous crimes: from the wars of sheer aggression, the unspeakable brutality toward the vanquished, and the all-too-successful extermination of European Jews.

In the first decades after the war, studies of Germany's coming to terms with the past tended to focus on whether Germans, faced with this paradox, did indeed successfully confront this difficult past. In approaching these "whether" and "to what degree" kind of questions, Alon Confino has emphasized how many scholars highlighted the repression of the past by Germans thinking back but wanting, emphatically, to look forward.[16] One of the earliest and most respected figures to take such a tack was Hannah Arendt, who in 1950 highlighted Germans' inability to confront the past, their repression of its most intractable aspects, and silence about its most horrifying crimes:

Nowhere is this nightmare of destruction and horror less felt and less talked about than in Germany itself. A lack of response is evident everywhere. . . . And the indifference with which they walk through the rubble has its exact counterpart in the absence of mourning for the dead, or in the apathy with which they react, or rather fail to react, to the fate of refugees in their midst. . . . This general lack of emotion . . . is only the most conspicuous outward symptom of a deep-rooted, stubborn, and at times vicious refusal to face and come to terms with what really happened.[17]

Arendt tellingly links a lack of reaction to the ubiquitous destruction to an inability to mourn the dead or to confront what happened. Later in the essay, she suggests (probably in a nod to her friend and mentor Karl Jaspers) that twelve years under "totalitarian" rule and subsequent destruction destroyed Germans' ability to speak. Indeed, repression of the past and silence about it are inextricably linked in her very pessimistic account of the postwar period and its prospects.

Arendt wrote her account of repression of and silence about the past in the first years after the war, but a long series of later studies has followed her formidable lead by underscoring Germany's failure to face the past. *The Inability to Mourn* by Alexander and Margarete Mitscher-lich is probably the best-known and most influential study of this kind: the first edition sold over one hundred thousand copies and was even eventually incorporated into school texts.[18] Like Arendt, the Mitscher-lichs underscore West Germans' denial of responsibility for Nazism and the war, though they analyze this tendency in a psychoanalytic mode, attributing to Germans the "inability to mourn." Though they, like Arendt, focus on refusal and denial, their arguments substantively shift the evolving theory of a repression of the past: the highly realistic forgetting of Adorno's account or even the stubborn refusal of Arendt's becomes here an emphatically unconscious defense mechanism, thus a (consciously, at least) more passive agency.[19] According to the Mitscher-lichs, unconscious defense mechanisms protect Germans en masse from the destruction of Hitler and the *Volksgemeinschaft* (national community), from which Germans, through Freudian identification, drew important sources of self-worth. In order to preempt a potentially radical shock to self-esteem, Germans have engaged in all sorts of denial, including the "derealization" of the Nazi period (emptying of it reality by withdrawing libidinal cathexes) and a single-minded focus on economic productivity and material well-being.[20]

The focus within Vergangenheitsbewältigung studies on repression, denial, and silence has continued through the 1980s and 1990s. Accepting and extending the arguments of the Mitscherlichs in his important study, *Stranded Objects,* Eric Santner suggests that children even inherit the psychological structures of their parents' "inability to mourn," such that the unfinished work of mourning (and its ancillary repression/denial of the past) persisted intergenerationally into the 1970s and 1980s.[21] When as prominent and nuanced a scholar as Saul Friedlaender can casually remark that there was a "repression of the Nazis epoch in the German public sphere" and a "massive denial" in the historical work in the 1940s and 1950s, it confirms how much a part of the conventional wisdom these kinds of arguments have become.[22] In the late 1990s, W. G. Sebald's study of the air war in literature manifested the latest, if more nuanced, avatar of this kind of repression hypothesis. He generalizes the kind of denial silence Arendt observed to an overarching German literary condition after the war.[23] Though he makes more modest claims by limiting the repression and silence to German literature, Sebald nonetheless focuses on a refusal to engage the past, a refusal his own text—literary despite itself—pretends to remedy. With these prominent scholars and writers—just some among many—one witnesses the considerable and important afterlife of the tendency to regard Germany's postwar Vergangenheitsbewältigung as a legacy of unconscious repression and psychologically blocked silences.

In analyzing these arguments about the repression of and silence about the past, Y. Michal Bodemann and Alon Confino have underscored how scholars tend to resort to the facile polarities of repression versus atonement or silence versus memory.[24] Despite the often foregrounded forgetting and silence, Germans certainly remembered something, and historians and critics have increasingly started to ask how it was, in the light of the all-too-wakeful consciousness and intertwined conscious and unconscious forgetting of which Adorno writes (rather than the more unilaterally unconscious mechanisms of the Mitscherlichs and others), that postwar Germans could have worked through the past that imposed itself upon them constantly and, one assumes, devastatingly. In an attempt to circumvent these kinds of simplistic binaries, there has been a shift, as Confino remarks, from ubiquitous questions of "whether" and

8

judgmental answers of repression to the questions "What did the Germans remember of the Nazi past, how was it remembered, and who remembered what?"[25] These new questions afford much more complex answers that acknowledge and investigate the complexity of Germans' response to Nazism, World War II, and the Holocaust. Although the conventional analyses have a sympathetic moral urgency, this turn in Vergangenheitsbewältigung studies has galvanized a historically more comprehensive approach to postwar German society and culture.

The public sphere of the late 1940s and 1950s was remarkable not so much for its silence about the Nazi past but, as scholars like Moeller, Confino, and Brockmann remark, for its sheer volume about the past, a fact lost or ignored in a large number of studies, including, most recently, that by Sebald.[26] The discussion about the postwar "rubble film" is a good example: it was only in the 1950s that the films ceased their preoccupation with the past; until that point, there were calls from all sides for German feature films to confront what had happened, which they did with varying degrees of success and conviction. During the 1945–46 *Filmpause*, when Germans were not yet allowed to make feature films, film personnel debated the approach and shape of German cinema in the wake of the Nazi "dream factory." Calls for the films to confront the recent past were both ubiquitous and high profile, as Robert Shandley has outlined.[27] Thus, there was not so much the impulse to keep quiet about what happened but instead the need, after years of surveillance or perceived surveillance, to talk, to write, and to debate. But of course that talking, writing, and debating were highly directed and often diversionary. As Moeller has observed, remembering selectively is very different than mere forgetting.[28] The foremost questions throughout are how such talking, writing, and debating were so directed, why, and what ends they ultimately served.

More recently, scholars have begun to investigate how Germans did partially or selectively confront the past in various political and cultural representations and practices. In this, I would emphasize, they are following the lead of Adorno, although many who cite his essay "'Working through the Past'" do not fully elaborate just how Adorno recast "forgetting" as social as well as psychological, conscious as well as unconscious, or how he cannily recounted the conscious, "realistic" diversionary tactics of those "remembering." Over twenty years after Adorno, Hermann Lübbe thematized and explored the (necessary, according to him) function of postwar silence in the establishment of democracy and thereby probed the repression theory of Germans' relation to the past; his essay is often taken as a starting point by later reconsiderations of Germans' coming to terms with the past, although Lübbe was probably motivated to contest the repression theories for different reasons.[29] In his important and rich study, *War Stories*, Robert Moeller focuses on the way in which the memories of the suffering of the prisoners of war (POWs) and expellees from the eastern territories became important sites at which the early Federal Republic worked through issues of the past and guilt. Other scholars have also charted the fuller political and social trajectory of the two Germanys in coming to terms with the past. In his thorough study of East and West German politics and the "Jewish question," Jeffrey Herf emphasizes how political memory of the Holocaust and other crimes of the Nazis reflected a certain type of Vergangenheitsbewältigung: despite the claims of repression and silence mentioned above, postwar political discourse offers a demonstrable, and differentiated, engagement with the past in the two Germanys.[30] In a similar, if more targeted vein, Pertti Ahonen tracks the impact of the expellee groups on the foreign policies of West Germany.[31] In his important recent work, Norbert Frei has investigated both the kind of repression that was created by amnesties and the sort of localizing of guilt that was possible in the legal pursuit of particular figures.[32] Examining some of the same materials as Moeller, Maria Mitchell analyzes the interpretation of Nazism by the Christian Democratic Union and demonstrates how the specifics of its interpretation—antimaterialist and antisecularist—impacted both the founding of the party and the politics of West Germany through its first decades.[33]

Besides these analyses of society and especially politics in the two Germanys, other studies have focused on specific inflections of memories through remarkable aspects of the late 1940s and 1950s that are often overlooked. Alon Confino has written about the way travel and tourism functioned after the war as a site of collective memory for the war, which had brought many young Germans abroad for the first time.[34] Frank Biess has focused more specifically on the importance of the POW experience and how it was used by both Germanys to negotiate postwar identity.[35] Elizabeth Heineman has argued that the specifically female experience of the war and the early postwar period—including women's disproportionate experience of the bombing as well as mass rape by Soviet troops, of the clearing of rubble and reconstruction, and of (alleged) fraternization with occupying forces—was "universalized" in German national memory, such that they became the experience of Germans in general.[36] In these multiple examples, it becomes clear that postwar Germans did remember, but that their memories were directed, selective, and even self-serving. With this multiplicity of recent studies, a new understanding has begun to replace the traditional arguments about repression and silence about the Nazi, wartime, and Holocaust pasts. Instead of an all-too-homogeneous vacuum of the past, scholars have begun to sketch a dense discursive field of competing narratives that seek to negotiate the past in specific ways, ways that each have their own stakes, repercussions, and consequences.

DIVERSION AND DISPLACEMENT: CONJURING VICTIMS, ORDINARY GERMANS, AND CONVINCED NAZIS

As in these recent studies, the question addressed herein will be how exactly postwar Germans negotiated discussions of guilt and reconstruction, especially how they could paradoxically narrate the past without incorporating overwhelming culpability into postwar identity. In analyzing this circuitous navigation, recent scholars have tended to favor an investigation of "memory traces" or other, more extreme contortions of memory. Bodemann, for instance, though he productively problematizes the conventional emphasis on repression of the past, allows for only "faint allusions, symptomatic traces" to the Holocaust—he goes on to investigate the way in which these can function as a kind of "negative memory."[37] Like Bodemann, many scholars seem hesitant to regard the necessary mechanisms facing this paradox as deliberate diversion and distraction. Following a more Adornian path, I would like to focus on more deliberate and "realistic" mechanisms, that is, on the social context of remembering that can rechannel memory as well as the mechanisms of the all-too-wakeful consciousness bent on the effacement of memory (rather than merely unconscious forgetting). Perhaps realistic diversion and conscious distraction sound too quotidian, but if one considers that there are limited resources in any person, population, and therefore public sphere, limited resources for feeling and thinking, discussing and debating, writing and reading, then focusing on something determinedly else can have an enormous discursive and diversionary impact. There certainly was not mere repression, there was a selective remembering (Moeller and Confino), a type of negative memory (Bodemann), but above all, as I shall argue, deliberate diversion and displacement onto other topics that could defuse the issues of the past and guilt. In "'Working through the Past,'" Adorno suggests such with his prescient critique of the "settling of accounts" via the calculation of dead in the air war. Another prominent example of such diversion and displacement was the debate about "collective guilt," which, although it had near-hegemonic dominion over the early postwar cultural imaginary in Germany, has been shown to be, at least as an articulated policy, largely a myth.[38] Both the creation of such a mythic diversion and willingness to be distracted by it must be considered and attended to as fundamental discursive functions within the postwar political and cultural imaginaries. And in the postwar period one of the loudest and most ubiquitous debates about the past concerned reeducation and problems of the "indoctrinated" young.

A wide range of scholars, in analyses of the early postwar period, has emphasized the persistence of what might be called Germans' ideology of victimhood. Heineman argues that the victimization of women during and after the war was universalized such that it became central to postwar German identity; for Biess, German POWs' victimized and subsequent "survivor" status was central to the way in which West Germans reconstituted themselves in the 1950s—he charts a careful trajectory that Germany itself could follow from victim to survivor.[39] In his *War Stories*, Moeller explores how new forms of victimhood solved the paradox of postwar identity: a focus on the expellees and POWs from the eastern territories allowed Germans to narrate the intractable wartime past while casting themselves as still-suffering victims. In a recent essay, Moeller explicitly takes up the theme of victimization after the 1950s, traces it into the post-1989 era, and weighs its consequences for scholarship.[40] Omer Bartov, in his essay "Defining Enemies, Making Victims" and then in his longer study *Mirrors of Destruction*, takes a longer-term view by emphasizing the importance of this mechanism from the late nineteenth century on: the tendency within German culture to exaggerate or even invent enemies and then to cast itself in the role of victim, a mechanism that aided and abetted, if not produced, some of its most belligerent inclinations.[41] Because this mechanism played such a central role for the Nazis and their propagation of virulent anti-Semitism, Bartov suggests that it persisted into the postwar period, when Germans searched for new enemies of whom they could be victims: "the aftermath of disaster may have fewer devastating psychological and physical consequences for survivors if they can, in turn, victimize their real or imaginary enemies."[42]

12

Both Bartov and Moeller argue persuasively that 1950s Germans understood themselves as victims in order to diminish or circumvent guilt for the extermination of Jews: as Bartov observes, the emphasis on German suffering rapidly eclipsed the suffering of European Jews—their suspiciously common victimization was now ascribed to vague third parties.[43] Both Bartov and Moeller, among many others, have remarked how the cold war would then come to function perfectly within this model for the past and for guilt: with the endorsement of the Western Allies, West Germans found a new über-perpetrator in Stalin, of whom they could be retroactive, present, and future victims. But, as with the youth studies of Poiger, Maase, and Fehrenbach cited above, one sees in this convincing assertion a historical leap into the 1950s. In Moeller's recent essay on victimization, for instance, there is little mention of the operation of the mechanism in the late 1940s, reflecting generally the scholarly trend to subsume these early postwar years under the history of the cold war.[44] What was happening before the cold war made the fixation on "crimes" in the eastern territories more politically palatable? Who could serve as perpetrators for Nazis' crimes in the first years after the war, when, presumably, the crimes would be most present and the Nazi ideology of victimhood, which both Bartov and Moeller argue, most penetrating?

One of the central questions that this study aims to address is against whom postwar Germans could cast themselves as victims, against whom could they define themselves and their suffering while having to come to terms with their Nazi past. While it is clear that once the cold war started to heat up in the late 1940s and 1950s, West Germany could invoke a conveniently familiar "Bolshevik" enemy, the Soviet Union, to define and narrate itself as victim, little attention has been paid to the period right after the war when the mechanism that Bartov defines would have been the strongest but the viable candidates for enemies the fewest. Certainly, throughout the war, the Germans could blame the Allies for their misery, but with the end of the war and the unconditional surrender—which brought with it tight controls on information, the press, and the public sphere in general—they could no longer (at least publicly) vilify either "the Jew" or the Allies.

One solution to this second postwar paradox of coming to terms with the past was to make "average Germans" the victims of "the Nazis," a problematically putative distinction between "ordinary" citizens and "real" criminals. Many Germans, as a number of scholars have observed, though few have traced, emphatically distinguished themselves from ideologically convinced, truly criminal Nazis. It was here, in this deliberate effort to conjure a new enemy of whom Germans could be victims, that young people served most usefully. Many prominent authors, intellectuals, and filmmakers cast young people as the most convinced Nazis, to whom guilt could then be ascribed. Making the young guilty for Nazism and the war proved particularly useful (that is, discursively operable) because it allowed Germans to understand themselves as victims of a group that, in its youth, could nonetheless be—by responsible, anti-Nazi elders—redeemed. In his work, Biess focuses on the 1950s transformation from the POW as victim to the POW as survivor, making the POW a positive role model for West German identity, but I want to argue that the "young," convinced Nazis fulfilled a similar role before many POWs returned: they could be perpetrator and victim simultaneously and then were subsequently, like Biess's POWs, redeemed.[45] By focusing on the young as convinced but redeemable Nazis, discussions of the past shift the site of postwar contestation from difficult questions of guilt to manageable challenges of generational discipline, a discipline that would then also serve as a cornerstone for postwar national identity. Such discursive displacements and diversions became a crucial mechanism within the wider processes of Vergangenheitsbewältigung and, as I shall argue, the production of German national identity.

The guilt of "German youth" has proved a thorny issue, something on which Michael Kater has reflected in his recent book, *Hitler Youth*. Kater's nuanced discussion of guilt and the complicity of the Hitler Youth underscores the complexity of the question. Could a ten-year-old member of the Hitler Youth be considered guilty? Could a nineteen-year-old whose parents put him or her in the group at age ten and who was sent directly from Hitler Youth to Wehrmacht? Both Stephen Brockmann and Kater answer, probably as one must, that young people involved in the Hitler Youth were partially innocent of and partially complicit with the crimes of the regime, but I would underscore how this unavoidable ambivalence toward youth guilt is exactly the remarkable point.[46] This ambivalence, tending all too often to a thoroughly muddled adjudication of juvenile guilt, made it very useful in the early postwar period. It was precisely this complexity, this ambivalence, this muddledness that postwar authors, intellectuals, and filmmakers would instrumentalize in approaching questions of German guilt and the past in general.

It is at the nexus of victimhood, the convinced Nazi, and youth that discussions of "the German young" and the "youth problem" intersected reeducation, probably the Allies' most resonant postwar policy. School and education constitute an indispensable, yet frequently ignored aspect of cultural and social discourse: as scholars like Michel Foucault, Jacques Donzelot, George Mosse, and more recently Ann Stoler have argued, it is precisely at the intersection of family and education that ideological battles about the young are often waged, battles that come to constitute (adult) subjectivities, society, and nation.[47] There have been studies of reeducation and its importance to the occupation—like those of James Tent, Karl-Heinz Füssl, and Hermann-Josef Rupieper—but these studies generally focus on (re)educational policy and neglect the wider public sphere debates about generation and "the German youth" as well as their consequences for German culture and national identity more generally.[48] Conversely, some recent studies of the postwar public sphere, like those by Jeffrey Olick and Stephen Brockmann, do not attend systematically to reeducation, even as they acknowledge that reeducation was an Allied code word for democratization.[49] And finally, although their studies attend to the function of youth within adult society and culture, Poiger, Maase, and Fehrenbach, for instance, generally overlook the ubiquity and depth of the discussion about German reeducation.[50] In the early postwar period, *reeducation* became a catchall term, a synecdoche for the occupation in general, so it is impossible to analyze the role of youth in the Germany of the 1940s and 1950s without attending adequately to the widespread and wide-ranging debates about it.

Reeducation became a last front on which the Germans could fight the Allies, for the education of the young is, as I shall argue, one last sphere of influence that could hardly be denied even a defeated people. One of the still-timely observations of the Mitscherlichs is their emphasis on self-esteem for mourning and identity during and after such mourning. At a time when the Allies subverted German sovereignty on nearly everything—government and society as well as economy and culture—reeducation became a site at which Germans could make a determined last stand in defense of traditional German culture. Before the 1950s—with their returning POWs and economic miracles—the intersection of the young Nazi and German reeducation became a crucial

15

building block for postwar national identity because it offered a solution to the overarching paradox of the past (confronting while distancing themselves from it) as well as a solution to the Allied occupation and the implied infantilization of Germans by the Allies. Coming to terms with the past via discourse about youth and education helped select elements of German culture around which a postwar national identity could be organized; and this very process of selection and emphasis demonstrated that the Germans as a whole were not in need of education. It was, according to them, primarily the young Nazis (of whom they claimed to be victims) who warranted such treatment. For these reasons, among others, discourse about the young and reeducation became a crucial site at which Germans sought to come to terms with the past, with guilt, and with conflicts with the Allies. Solving the myriad paradoxes posed by Vergangenheitsbewältigung, discourse about youth and reeducation permitted postwar German adults to look back as well as forward in certain highly selective ways. Mastering the German past became in large part a disciplining of the "German young."

In the first years after the war, discourse about youth and reeducation played a subtle but nonetheless central role in adult Germany's coming to terms with the past. Although the generationally emphatic rhetoric of the writers associated with *Der Ruf* and then the "Gruppe 47" is well known and documented in conventional literary studies, I will attend to this group only peripherally, because I want to argue for the central role of reeducation and youth in "adult" culture more generally, not just in the often isolated discussions of *Der Ruf,* usually regarded as the troubled poster children of the "young generation."[51] The various media I examine in this study confirm, extend, and complicate the symbolic centrality of discourse about youth in the early postwar period within culture not usually associated with youth and education, such that the debate about youth and reeducation can be regarded as a subterranean current, or even a subtext, of postwar culture generally. For this reason, too, I shall not discuss diaries, memoirs, and so on, as they tended to appear much later than the period on which I am focusing.

In the first two chapters, I aim to trace the continuities as well as ruptures between the Nazi period and the postwar period, many of which have been neglected by studies of youth in the 1950s. First, I analyze discourse about youth within the Nazi imaginary and explain how at least one strain of culture under the Nazis understood the Nazi "revolution" as a youth revolution, a trope that becomes indispensable background for postwar Vergangenheitsbewältigung. In chapter 2, I discuss how allegedly Nazi youth remained at the center of debates about reeducation and how these phenomena impacted postwar culture—for example, in Thomas Mann's *Doktor Faustus*, in which the fin de siècle youth movement serves as a cipher for Germany, nationalism, and National Socialism.

Germany has long been considered the land of *Dichter und Denker* (poets and thinkers), and after the war, there was a flood of publications, lectures, and radio addresses from Germany's intellectuals on how to comprehend the recent past and how to rebuild the country. Chapters 3 and 4 examine the responses of the German intelligentsia to Nazism and the war. Two important authors in the period, Friedrich Meinecke and Ernst Jünger, both associate the young with the most pernicious aspects of Germany's deviant modernity, such that the young become those agents most guilty for Germany's descent into Nazism. As a result, both authors recommend a reconstruction via strict discipline and pedagogy that deliberately resists the Allies' reeducation. Other key intellectuals, like Karl Jaspers and Ernst Wiechert, deploy very different discourse about youth, in which the young are those most isolated from Germany's mangled, maiming modernity. Their versions of reeducation are based on putatively positive attributes of youth, rather than on a strict "disciplining" of the young.

After attending to various forms of "high culture," the study turns in chapter 5 to popular feature films of the so-called rubble-film genre, German films made after 1945 and concerned with the contemporary context and problems of the recent past. In his recent essay on victimization and its consequences for future work, Robert Moeller exhorts scholars to look at the way that mass media, especially film, "mass-mediate" memory, and so I would like to argue that these films offer unique documents for studying the tribulations of postwar German identity.[52] As the most commercially and critically successful films of this period, the early DEFA (Deutsche Film Aktiengesellschaft, the East German film studio) rubble films rely on childhood and young people to represent the recent past and to reconstruct the returning German soldier. Many of these films foreground the plight of a traumatized male protagonist who has lost faith in civilian life and then repeatedly employ parent-child and teacher-student relations to reconstruct both the male subject and the postwar community. After the war, there were many calls

17

to avoid the kind of "dream-factory" filmmaking characteristic of the Nazis, including explicit criticism of the commercially crucial "star system." In the face of much vehement criticism, the first U.S.–licensed film nonetheless cast the biggest male star of the Nazi years, and chapter 6 analyzes how the young were deployed to rehabilitate stars by downgrading their constitutive exceptionalness and individualism. In a short conclusion, I consider how these debates on youth and reeducation would continue and influence the early cold war. Contestations about youth and education persisted and resonated well beyond the early postwar public sphere.

In this analysis, I shall identify how these varied representations and debates among German authors, filmmakers, and intellectuals reveal the myriad ways in which discourse about youth became a filter for leading thinkers to understand the past and to advocate rebuilding Germany. Although these various authors and media represent youth according to their positions vis-à-vis Nazi and post-Nazi Germany, discourse about youth consistently occupies a central position in their narrations of Germany's past, present, and future. It was a Vergangenheitsbewältigung and *Wiederaufbauen* onto which the generations of Germans were constitutively mapped, a disciplining reconstruction from the generational ground up.

1

Hitler's Youth?
The Nazi "Revolution" as Youth Uprising

In investigating Vergangenheitsbewältigung in the early postwar period, it is perhaps most productive to start with the most obvious: the 1945–49 trials at Nuremberg, which provided the most focused and famous forum for exploring culpability for Nazi crimes. At the trials, among the most prominent defendants was the former head of the Hitler-Jugend (HJ), the "Youth Leader of the German Reich" (*Jugendführer des deutschen Reiches*), Baldur von Schirach.[1] In his defense, he declared:

> I raised this generation in faith and trust in Hitler. The youth movement that I built up bore his name. I believed I was serving a leader who would make our people and its youth great, free, and happy. Millions of young people believed this along with me and saw their ideals in National Socialism. Many gave their lives for it. It is my guilt that I have to bear before God, before my German people, before our nation. . . . It is my guilt that I raised this generation for a man who was a murderer a millions of times over . . . and so I bear this guilt on behalf of this youth. The young generation is innocent.[2]

The passage is remarkable, not least because, in contrast to the vast majority of Nuremberg defendants, Schirach openly acknowledges guilt, which he rehearses a surprising number of times in fairly short order. But at the same time that Schirach denounces Hitler—he was, along with Albert Speer, one of the only defendants to do so—he also executes overtly exculpatory maneuvers around his admission of guilt. It is an interesting and indicative strategy. On its surface, the passage reflects the postwar tendency to blame Hitler and his "clique"—to which Schirach undoubtedly belonged—for the crimes committed everywhere throughout Germany and the Nazi protectorate.[3] This strategy proved one of the most effective for confronting and contradicting the Allies' policy of widely defined (if not collective) guilt, still very much in effect in the fall of 1945 when the trials began.

There is, however, something else about the passage that proves particularly noteworthy. As one of the only speeches from Nuremberg to admit guilt, this passage, if read closely, also reveals more subtle mechanisms that I shall underscore throughout this study: Schirach is one of the only defendants who can acknowledge and manage guilt for the past—that is, narrate it, shift it, ultimately mitigate it—in part because guilt is filtered through discourse about the young. For my study, likewise revealing is that the passage is not contesting charges of Schirach's guilt, which he acknowledges and even embraces, but, rather, accusations of guilt among the "young generation." "The young generation" and "the German youth" were, as we shall see, very specific constellations that had to be discursively sketched, characterized, and manipulated as meaningful social groupings. But, as I shall argue throughout, Schirach's response is indicative because it confronts head-on one of the most ubiquitous aspects of the postwar guilt discussions: the debate about the role of young people in Nazism and its criminal excesses. This chapter considers what role youth played in the rise of Nazism and, more specifically, what role it was imagined to play in the culture of the Nazis.

This study focuses on the role that (adult) writings, debates, and other cultural products concerned with youth, especially the "German youth" and the "younger generation," played within the (adult) social and cultural imaginary. Most accounts of youth during the Third Reich focus on the institutional or social history of the Hitler Youth "movement," actually an orchestrated aspect of the wider Nazi Party. The most recent version of these histories includes Michael Kater's *Hitler Youth*, which, although it effectively covers the institutional history of the Hitler Youth and incorporates more recent scholarship on the experiences of young people, still focuses on the youth group itself rather than its place either in the party hierarchy, the wider social context, or the cultural imaginary of Nazism in general. While I will give some background details on the institutions housing youth in the Nazi and postwar periods, I am primarily concerned with how discussion and debates about the "German youth" and the "younger generation" became, within (adult) culture in general, a key site on which to displace questions of the past and guilt for its crimes. Although I cannot hope to offer a full accounting of how young people facilitated the rise of the Nazi Party— a topic worthy of a much fuller study than I can offer herein—I shall demonstrate how at least certain sectors of Nazi culture imagined the Nazi revolution as a youth revolution. This imagined role of the young in remaking Germany provides important background for the rest of my study because it would prove remarkably influential in early postwar narrations of Nazism and, subsequently, in early postwar attempts to come to terms with the Nazi past.

Youth, Hitler-Jugend, and the Nazi Movement

While Schirach suggests that he built up the Hitler-Jugend, it is closer to the truth to observe that he did not lay the necessary groundwork for the movement. This disjuncture reflects the complex relation between the youth group and the Nazi Party, which clouds the common assumption that the young were indispensable in the ascent of National Socialism. There is, in fact, significant scholarly disagreement on the importance of youth for the Nazi movement and for the regime. While most scholars seem to assume that youth played a pivotal role in the movement, scholars like Joachim Radku and Bernd Hüppauf have suggested that Nazism did not rest on the backs of the young as much as widely assumed.[4] In fact, the early organizational and foundational institutional work was done not by members of Hitler's inner circle like Schirach but by others, and the Hitler-Jugend had roots in the independent youth movement of the 1920s and even in the pre–World War I period, rather than in the Nazi Party. As was true of much of German society during these years, the changing character of the Hitler-Jugend—the name it was given only in 1926—reflected the increasing politicization of society during the Weimar period, during which the group was as much youth organization as party branch.[5]

21

Gustav Lenk, the founder of the Youth League of the NSDAP (Nationalsozialistische Deutsche Arbeitspartei), probably intended it to compete with other, nature-oriented youth groups, emphasizing Wandervogel-style hikes and travel, something that would change later with Schirach, who favored the more contained and controllable world of camps.[6] Lenk's successor, Kurt Gruber, was responsible for the first significant growth of the group and headed the organization until Schirach assumed control in 1931. Not coincidentally, however, Gruber kept the group at deliberate arm's length from the party leadership in Munich and maintained a fair degree of independence, even though it was he who oversaw its renaming as the Hitler-Jugend. He maintained his headquarters in Plauen—close to his base and farther from Hitler's—and, perhaps more important, kept most of the financing of the group private and member based rather than party based. The NSDAP was happy with this arrangement, largely because it did not have to fully fund the youth group's mass rallies, organizational costs, and leadership salaries. The subordination of the Hitler-Jugend to the SA (Sturmabteilung) during Röhm's hiatus (1925–30) actually afforded some distance from the party leadership and, as one Bavarian police report suggests, many Nazis were, as late as 1927, hardly enthusiastic about completely absorbing the group into the established party structure.[7] With the 1931 appointment of Schirach and the move of the organization's headquarters to Munich, the party assumed fuller control of the Hitler-Jugend, a shift that did, indeed, pose considerable financial and administrative difficulties for the party.[8]

Although I do not have space to unfold a detailed institutional history of the Hitler-Jugend, these short remarks indicate how complex the questions concerning the role of young people in the Nazi ascent and party prove. The fact that many of the Nazi Party leaders were biologically young in the mid-1920s is hardly a causal argument for the decisive role of "youth"—a very specific notion in Germany at the time. By the time the party came to and consolidated power, many of its leaders were decidedly middle-aged and did not, as Gerhard Rempel observes, manifest any particular propensity toward rejuvenating the leadership.[9] Institutionally speaking, it seems clear, looking at the rise of the party in the 1920s and of the regime in the 1930s, that the Hitler-Jugend was hardly the engine of Nazism. In fact, its trajectory did not guide or steer but rather ran parallel to, or even somewhat behind, that of the party. This kind of more conventional youth group was fundamentally transformed only in the later republic, when German society and politics entered a new crisis phase and party leaders saw unprecedented opportunity in tightening control over various aspects of the party. Leaders instigated these new controls of the Hitler-Jugend in 1926 and completed them in 1931, with the removal of Gruber, appointment of Schirach, and move of the Hitler-Jugend headquarters to Munich. Notwithstanding these reforms, however, the Hitler-Jugend enjoyed the kind of explosive growth usually attributed to it only after the Nazis' stunning successes with German adults in the elections of the early 1930s (1930 and, more important, July 1932). And even with this more rapid growth, through January 1933, the Hitler-Jugend still represented only about 1 percent of all youth overseen by the member organizations of the Reich Committee of German Youth Associations.[10]

If the Hitler-Jugend did not form any radical vanguard for the party in its late 1920s and early 1930s ascent, it seems clear that it was not the core of the Nazi Party.[11] There is instead a sense, as with much of German society in the first half of the 1930s, of the tightening grip of the party and its diligent coordination (*Gleichschaltung*)—in this case, coordination of diverse strains of the youth movement in general (the *Bündische* groups and other parties' youth groups) as well as within the Hitler-Jugend itself. Perhaps most revealing in this regard is the history of the *Streifendienst*, a kind of internal police within the Hitler-Jugend. The Streifendienst's internal reconditioning of the Hitler-Jugend membership reflects the tectonic shifts within the movement in the early and mid-1930s. The Streifendienst targeted exactly the kind of idle and free-spirited youths that had been celebrated by the Wandervogel and the wider youth movement through the 1920s: its mission was not to carry out surveillance only on individuals but also on those other groups still committed to wandering the countryside.[12] Thus, although stereotypes about thoroughly convinced Nazis among the Hitler-Jugend would abound in the postwar period, even the "voluntary" Hitler-Jugend members who joined before compulsory membership (which began officially 1936 and was enforced in 1939) apparently did not quite correspond to the visions of their leaders. The need for such an aggressive police force within the ranks of the supposedly convinced Hitler-Jugend shows how heterogeneous the group actually was.

In light of this evidence, the claims of Radku and Hüppauf about the limited role of the Hitler-Jugend and youth prove, at the level of political and institutional history, convincing. Their arguments about youth's exaggerated role are also relevant to the speeches and ideas of Hitler himself, who seemed only intermittently committed to rhetorics of youth and often contrasted young "show-offs" to the kind of war-hardened toughs he needed.[13] On the other hand, the Nazi movement was highly diverse and contradictory, probably intentionally so, to appeal to as many potential supporters as possible. It is important not to reduce culture between 1933 and 1945 to state and party institutions controlled by the Nazis, as has too often been the case. Although I shall refer throughout this study to "Nazi culture," I do not mean to characterize it monolithically or reductively. It is important to keep in mind that there was a diversity of cultural production and reception during these years and a diversity of relations to the regime.[14] In contradistinction to the institutional rise and hegemony of the party, one important strain of Nazi culture did indeed foreground the fantastical or imagined role of the young in the Nazi movement.

This particular but prominent strain of Nazi culture appropriated and extended a cultural constellation inherited from the fin de siècle and wartime eras: these strains instrumentalized preexisting currents of German culture and linked young Nazis to longer-term discursive trends, such as youth movements and the "war generation." Perhaps most important, cultural works of this stripe connect these longer-term discourses about youth to a number of cornerstone concepts of the movement, including the Volksgemeinschaft, militarism, and the Führer-principle. To explain and establish the role of youth in these sectors of Nazi culture, I examine a 1929 novel by the later Reich minister for National Education and Propaganda (*Reichsminister für Volksaufklärung und Propaganda*) Joseph Goebbels, a 1933 play about the youth of Langemarck, and the 1943 G. W. Pabst film *Paracelsus*. All qualify as "adult" culture but demonstrate how, in at least some sectors of the Nazi imaginary, the young could serve as a linchpin for the National Socialist "revolution."

Each of these narratives stages the Nazi revolution as a transition from one socioeconomic constellation—bourgeois society—to a nationalized, postbourgeois community, and each casts the young as the crucial agents in this wide-ranging transition. The importance of youth in representing this transmogrification of society and polity is not all that surprising if one considers how fundamental the young proved to bourgeois society. As Michel Foucault suggests generally and Jacques Donzelot traces more carefully, the bourgeois family consolidated

24

around the parent-child axis in a radical new way, such that the changing status of the young proved indispensable to the bourgeois dismantling of older domestic orders.[15] An entire regime of discourse around the young allowed the bourgeois nuclear family to emerge, rendering the young, both children and adolescents, the constitutive core of the bourgeois social constellation. It is therefore fitting that at least part of Nazi culture, in depicting a "revolution" in the social order it labeled obsolete, would foreground, deploy, and "liberate" youth from the bourgeois family in its drive to forge a nationalized, postbourgeois community.

This liberation, however, is also highly contained and curtailed: all of these important Nazi texts displace a fundamental political revolution onto a less-thoroughgoing refiguring of society and economy along generational and educational lines. In this regard, these texts realize a conservative revolution via youth: they maintain many of the basic institutions of society while recasting them in a conservative mold.[16] These works deliberately replace class solidarity and revolution in politics with youth solidarity and reform in society, economy, and education. In depicting this conservative revolution as generational transformation, the texts manifest central tropes of more general discourse about youth, including the young as social "other"; the family as transfer point for social norms; the young as border crossers; the young as dual in character (affirming/threatening, passive/active); and youth crisis as crucial in representing and redrawing society. Tropes of this cultural strain would prove revealingly influential in the postwar period, when a wide range of intellectuals and artists would seize repeatedly on this imagined role of youth in Nazism.

GENERATIONAL CONSCIOUSNESS AND YOUTH AS OTHER IN GOEBBELS'S *MICHAEL*

Although Joseph Goebbels was unable to find a publisher for his novel *Michael* for some six years, the work went through seventeen editions between 1929, when it finally did appear, and the end of World War II, an unusually successful run that undoubtedly had more than a little to do with the propaganda minister's name on the cover. The novel has now become, along with works like Hans Grimm's *Volk ohne Raum* and Hanns Johst's *Schlageter,* part of the canon of "Nazi literature" that is much mentioned but little analyzed.[17] Few scholars, however, have observed, let alone elaborated upon, *Michael*'s clearly generational approach to the personal, social, and political turmoil of the time. Although *Michael,* as critics have observed, certainly aims to subvert class and party divisions in favor of a national community (Volksgemeinschaft)—an often-discussed Nazi thematic—the novel relies not only on the imagined community of nation to undercut class but on generational experience and discourses to forge a kind of national-generational community.

The novel, in fact, does more than underscore the importance of generation vis-à-vis class and nation in the post–World War I period; it also intermingles generation with the concept of youth and a "young nation" in a self-serving fashion. As George Mosse and others have observed, youth had served centrally in nineteenth-century nationalism, strains of which regarded the cultivation of the young as an emphatically national project.[18] While the concept of youth had been celebrated by turn-of-the-century culture and aesthetics, by the post–World War I period it was compelled to share the discursive stage with the notion of "generation," especially the "war generation." Goebbels's novel demonstrates the intermingling of these concepts of youth and generation and points to what ideological ends—particularly nationalist ends—they could together be deployed as a linchpin for a transition from bourgeois society to the new postbourgeois, national-generational community. For my argument about Nazi culture, *Michael* also effectively demonstrates how youth became a key form of alterity—a form of constitutive otherness—in overcoming bourgeois society and in forging a new, generational community. Cultures and societies, especially those in transition, are often defined by mechanisms of alterity and otherness: underscoring the otherness of something outside or different helps to offer definitions, draw boundaries, fill out identities. In this narrative of personal and social transformation, the text foregrounds "youth as other" both in its targeting of bourgeois society—especially bourgeois education—and in its subversion of conventional political or class consciousness with generational consciousness.

Over the course of its plot, *Michael* invokes Goethe both literally and literarily: it refers to both the work and life of the famed literary figure as well as to his breakthrough novel, *The Sorrows of Young Werther,* whose basic form and trajectory *Michael* follows. Like *Werther, Michael* traces the travails of a young, itinerant German; similar to *Werther,* the novel is structured as a series of first-person intimate narratives, here diary entries that cease when the protagonist dies and an outside figure completes the work and the life. Finally, and perhaps most important, like *Werther*, *Michael* follows the increasing isolation of its young protagonist from bourgeois society, ascendant in Goethe's time and (allegedly) decadent in Goebbels's. Son of well-to-do parents who hardly appear in the text, the eponymous Michael begins the novel studying in Heidelberg, where he meets and falls in love with a fellow student, Hertha Holk. As a veteran of World War I, Michael is unsure about what to study but concentrates primarily on literature and especially on his own writing. Eventually, both Michael and Hertha move to Munich to continue their studies, but the bohemian lifestyle of sophisticated Schwabing (Munich's university quarter) begins to divide them. Against what he regards as academic decadence, Michael becomes increasingly committed to German nationalism. When Hertha no longer understands him or his new nationalist interests, she breaks with him by abruptly leaving Munich. Devastated and drifting, Michael fortuitously hears a speech by a fiery German nationalist (unnamed, but meant to stand in for Hitler), an experience that, predictably, changes his life. Though he makes one more, short-lived attempt at studying in Heidelberg, he decides to abandon his bourgeois lifestyle altogether and to become a miner. At first his coworkers are suspicious of the bourgeois student-turned-worker, but after a labor dispute that turns violent, they welcome him as one of their own, cementing a *Gemeinschaft* (community) that grounds the formerly isolated student. After a short visit to Munich, Michael switches to a mine in Bavaria, where he is killed by a cave-in that highlights his sacrifice to his fellow miners and the elusive national community toward which their camaraderie points.

In this particular plotting, Goebbels's *Michael* traces the path of "ein[em] deutsche[n] Schicksal" (a German fate) that very much conforms to the normative transformation that the Nazis' revolutionary rhetoric would come to emphasize. The novel deliberately overthrows decadent or empty bourgeois society, aesthetics, and lifestyles for a new, postbourgeois community based on the nation and a nationalized camaraderie of all classes. Michael's literal and personal journey from isolated bourgeois student to politicized mine worker is very close to the message the Nazis would highlight in their antibourgeois "revolution." But in *Michael*, tellingly, generational recasting of class displaces the need for a literal revolution. Above all, the novel depicts the potential of youth to serve as a form of alterity, a social other around which the text can refigure bourgeois society.

During the first half of the twentieth century, the young increasingly defined themselves, and were understood by those around them, as the corrective opposite of the bourgeois constellation. This development confirms the increasing importance of age, especially youth, in modernity: as Norbert Elias, Philippe Aries, and Michael Mitterauer have argued, differentiation according to age has been growing more important throughout modernity.[19] And as Foucault, Donzelot, and Ashis Nandy demonstrate, the young person came to serve as an internal enemy around which to organize and mobilize the emotional, economic, and discursive resources of modern European societies.[20] Especially in Germany, however, this alterity of youth as internal enemy meant that the young had a revealingly double function: they organized familial resources but also constantly threatened to subvert the conventional domestic and social order. As the middle class seemed to be losing vitality in the imaginary of Wilhelmine and Weimar Germany, becoming rigid and dead, "youth" increasingly came to symbolize everything it was not.[21] Mosse suggests that a major component of this development was the discourse about the body, but to a similar end: "The *fin-de-siècle* rediscovery of the body was the most serious challenge respectability had to face. . . . [As part of the rediscovery of the body, the] challenge of youth was . . . disturbing to bourgeois society."[22] Ultimately, this kind of alterity would have more than a cultural or social function. As Frank Trommler argues, writers and other intellectuals deployed youth as a means to disguise their own political weaknesses, a "natural" and "biological" refuge from an increasingly inhospitable social and political climate.[23] In the Weimar context of severe political turmoil, youth functioned as a site to which frustrated or unrealizable political desires accreted. Celebrating the cult of the young was far simpler than starting a revolution. In *Michael*, youth alterity, the rediscovered body, and revolutionary politics intersect to form a constellation that would be central to Nazi ideology and the national-generational community.

This kind of transformative alterity of youth for bourgeois society becomes clear above all in Michael's relationship to Hertha, which occupies the first two-thirds of the novel. Their romance is very much the product of bourgeois society: they meet at the university in a lecture and he impresses her with his aesthetic pursuits: his poetry, his drama, and his interest in art. But these studies and interests eventually leave Michael cold, and as he becomes less and less content with bourgeois society, he begins to regard her as the embodiment of a class that is increasingly obsolete: "Hertha Holk is very middle-class. She does not have the courage to get out of herself, to be herself. . . . This is what we are witnessing today: A class has carried out its historical mission and is about to make way for the creative will of a new, young class."[24] Hertha personifies an increasingly archaic bourgeois class, one that Michael will soon leave behind, but already the filters of generation, of young and old, mark his understanding of both her and historical class.

In sketching its normative transition from the archaic bourgeois constellation to a postbourgeois national community, *Michael* relies repeatedly on an emphatic critique of bourgeois society in the form of bankrupt bourgeois education and the *geistig* (spiritual) violence it does to the young. Along with Michael's aesthetic interests, which other scholars have discussed, the novel positions secondary and higher education as a central pillar of bourgeois society and a—if not the—central target of *Michael*'s critique. Critiques of bourgeois education, especially of the German *Gymnasium* and universities, were widespread during the Weimar period and general debates about educational reform resonated at the time.[25] *Michael* fits into a model sketched by Karl Prümm, in which the antipaternal rebellions of Expressionist works were increasingly replaced by the overthrow of and liberation from schools in autobiographical novels of the 1920s.[26] Though Michael feels initially relieved and fortunate to be out of the war and at the university, he is soon deriding the kind of empty learning that is all the celebrated professors can offer. In a short vacation episode on a Frisian island—in what seems a deliberately moralizing reworking of Mann's *Death in Venice*—Michael befriends but then laments a little bourgeois boy whose entire goal is to study at a German university. By the time of his break with Hertha, Michael is openly contemptuous of the academic life: "In Germany's great schools, they are working hard, but doing little for the future. This is hack work. We can never be saved by academic speculation!" (91).[27] In locating Michael's transformation in urbane Schwabing, the bohemian area around the Munich university, the novel focuses its critique of bourgeois society on the university.

In dismantling bourgeois society via this critique on education, the text deliberately appeals to something beyond the bourgeois class that might help retire and ultimately replace it. The text deliberately subverts class difference by rewriting social differentiations and groupings, such that generational solidarity replaces any kind of class solidarity. Though the text eventually arrives at a nationalized Volksgemeinschaft, from the novel's first pages, the text attempts to establish, as a foundation for this coming community, a generational consciousness via the war. In the first words of his diary, Michael emphasizes his military service and then demobilization, thereby creating a common bond with readers of his generation.[28] As Michael is compelled to face his feelings of isolation at the university and even in his relationship with Hertha, he returns in a more deliberate fashion to the specifically generational experience and crisis: "We young people are groping our way forwards. After the war, we were numb and paralyzed for a while. . . . The war was the beginning of our revolution; but it was not carried through. When the war ended, the revolution was adulterated, twisted, degraded, and that is why the younger generation has lost for the time being" (27). George Mosse and others have emphasized the importance of the myth of war for veterans and for postwar politics in general: I want to expand this understanding by underscoring how the war experience and its veterans intersected the notions of generation.[29]

While youth had become a meaningful concept for social understanding shortly before the turn of century, during and after World War I there was an increasing shift in emphasis to the "young generation."[30] Turn-of-the-century notions of "youth" tended to emphasize the alterity of youth in its aesthetic *Innerlichkeit* and isolation: youth was other to calcified bourgeois society, which had grown rigid and cold. During and after World War I, however, "generation" came to serve a different ideological function, particularly as the cipher for a new type of collective experience and a new form of emergent community. Generation and generational solidarity became, in the 1920s, a kind of counterconcept to class, a concept to balance and even negate class as a meaningful category for understanding and analysis.[31] Perhaps above all, generation, in its allegedly *überpolitisch* and *überparteilich* aspects, circumnavigates traditional politics and parties. The passage demonstrates the revolutionary potential of the times—the much-desired and sought overthrow of bourgeois society—but also how generational discourse, as a kind of conservative revolution, can displace and satisfy such revolutionary impulses. The young generation serves as a site onto which other political and social trends, urges, and impulses can be displaced, such that it substitutes for more fundamental political change. By the end of the 1920s, the "younger generation" was increasingly called upon to provide a "third way" between socialism and capitalism, foreshadowing and facilitating categories like *Volk* (nation) and the Volksgemeinschaft, both of which rested at the core of the Nazi's ideological program.

Although *Michael* manifests the conservative-revolutionary potential of the young generation as other to bourgeois society, it also demonstrates an important discursive shift during the Weimar Republic from "generation" back to "youth." As the Weimar period wore on, this emphasis on generation became, in this text and in Nazi culture more generally, the basis for a reviving and rewriting of discourse about youth similar to one around the turn of the century and one that ultimately helped cultivate the national-generational community that the text is at pains to produce.[32] As the war generation aged, the Nazis needed to recruit the "1902" generation and those younger who did not fight in the war but (allegedly) suffered under its consequences. So, in addition to generation as the basis for its community, youth itself became an emphatic site for the text and Nazi culture more generally. Various authors and intellectuals revived the concept of youth for its own sake, though it looked, in its emphasis on the aggressive remaking of Germany, very different from the turn-of-the-century notion of youth. *Michael* mixes specifically generational experience with generalizations about youth, its allegedly unique characteristics, its positive potential: "The world cannot forget that Europe's youth bled its last on the battlefields for an idea—maybe unconsciously—but each soldier felt this idea: The knowledgeable felt it as faith and the faithful as an inkling. One cannot bury youth in silence" (61). The passage moves subtly from the experience of the war generation to vague shibboleths about "youth." Much as young Hertha is suddenly declared old, "young" and "old" become floating signifiers to make distinctions necessary for the text's overarching trajectory and the social transition it stages.

This increasing intermingling of generational consciousness with a revived notion of youth plays a central role in the novel's climactic transformation. Revealingly, this transformation replaces the revolution Michael discusses at the beginning of the novel. When Michael decides to abandon his bourgeois existence and join the workers, he initially struggles against the physical challenges of hard labor and the suspicions of the other miners. This struggle constitutes the climax of the novel, as Michael abandons his bourgeois lifestyle but has not yet created a "bridge" to the workers. Tellingly, to create this bridge—that is, to overcome class difference and consciousness—Michael relies on both generational experience and the contrast between young and old that he sees growing out of it. Matthias, Michael's foreman in the mine, warns him that miners will not welcome a bourgeois student: they have seen such students before, who they feel condescend to them. But the entire text, of course, has been working against precisely these kinds of indelible class divisions, working to sublate class differences in favor of a generational solidarity and camaraderie. In his rejection of class difference, Michael refers to and relies on generational consciousness that then manifests itself in a general discussion of young versus old.

After Matthias warns Michael that he is ruining himself, that the challenges in the mine and resistance of the miners will be too great, Michael responds initially by referencing his war experiences in order to establish a generational connection to Matthias: they, the generation that suffered during the war, must fight against existing powers that do not care for the workers. A postwar camaraderie among veterans constitutes the initial link, but Michael then commits to this struggle—a struggle that will forge the coming community with the workers—by emphasizing the alterity of youth and the subsequent conflict between young and old: "Some people are impressed only by a fist under their noses. We must be ruthless. We, the young, have the greater authority in history. The old still don't want to recognize that the young even exist. They will defend their power to the last. But some day, they shall lose. Ultimately, youth must win. We young men, we shall attack" (117). Generation inflected through the contrast between young and old comes to constitute a worldview supporting Michael's chosen transformation. At the pivotal moment, when Michael commits to persevering in the mines, the novel devolves into a lengthy discussion of the indelible differences between young and old that eclipses even talk of the nation.

By the last few pages of the novel, this new generational community fortifies the German nation that the text is committed to cultivating. The damage done to the young by the educational system becomes an emphatically national curse:

> I hear the dear sounds of Munich. A young man passes by with a Schwabing girl.
>
> Students come from the university, carrying books and briefcases.
>
> Most of them look thin, pale, and earnest.
>
> Did I not notice this wretchedness in the past?

The stigma on the forehead of the German people?
A hungry, famished, freezing youth. (123)

By committing to a new generational community, Michael helps to realize a "young Germany" for both himself and his community of workers: "I am overcome by a profound peace. I feel an ocean of strength
roaring through my soul. Here young Germany stands up, the workers
who shall forge the Reich. Now they are an anvil, but some day they
shall be the hammer!" (124). Generational consciousness and community now fortify the German nation as young, a creation that is typically
both "peaceful" and at the same time militant.

The notion that a particular nation could be young or old might
strike one as a curious mixing of discursive registers—age with political
discourse—but it had attained, after World War I, considerable currency.
Theories concerning the "young nations" were elaborated, with the
young Teutonic protagonist clearly implied throughout: "The age of a
people is heritage; it is property, it is indulgence; it is exceptional call and
fame. Youth of a people is a readiness; it is expectation; it is right and
prestige. Youth depends on its confidence in itself. Youth is determination."[33] By 1932, at the end of an increasingly nationalizing decade, entire books like *Das junge Deutschland* would appear. In *Michael*, forming the core of this new national-generational community is the triad
that traverses the text: "Soldiers, students, and workers shall build the
new Reich. . . . The new German will be born in workshops, not in
books. We have written enough, we have blithered and blathered
enough" (97–98). Between soldiers and workers, both central pillars of
Nazi culture and society, Joseph Goebbels's novel normativizes the
politicized youth as the key figure in the critique of bourgeois society
and its transformation into a new nationalized community.

Although Goebbels wrote *Michael* in 1923, the novel was not published
until 1929, when Goebbels's rising profile within Nazi circles (as an editor, for example, of *Völkische Freiheit*) helped him finally find a publisher. Since no original manuscript survives, it is unclear what Goebbels
changed and/or added to the text before its belated but very successful
publication, but one can surmise, from the context, that substantive
changes were made that reflected the intervening years.[34] One of the
clearest revisions would seem to come in the novel's published foreword, which, *après la lettre*, emphasizes and encourages the approach to

the text I have sketched herein. In the foreword, the text's intermingling and balancing of generation with the concept of youth tips increasingly in the latter's favor. As I mentioned above, Nazis started to rely less on generational consciousness and more on a rhetorical celebration of themselves and Germany as young, since they increasingly needed to appeal to voters who were too young to have fought in the war. Given this context and the novel's approach, it is not surprising that Goebbels's foreword spends four of its eight paragraphs discussing youth and then ends with a call to the "coming nation": youth consciousness, which Goebbels underscores six years after the initial composition of the novel, should serve as the cornerstone for the national community. The foreword points to and celebrates above all the potential of "German youth today in its Faustian urge to create." The link between the young and Faust might at first seem surprising, in light of Faust's advanced age, but Goebbels is actually connecting the discourse about youth to another important trope of Nazi culture, the "Faustian" as the search for the primordial or primitive, an important theme of Oswald Spengler's *Decline of the West*.[35] This link between the young and the primitive casts youth, in the starkest terms, as other to the bourgeois constellation. The foreword goes on to declare succinctly: "Youth is always right in any conflict with age" (3). As Michael suggests to Matthias in the text, youth is not only different from bourgeois society—it is superior, a superiority that will be reinforced in both *Youth of Langemarck* and *Paracelsus*.

THE "YOUTH OF LANGEMARCK" IN NAZI RHETORIC, RITUAL, AND LITERATURE

Goebbels's *Michael* demonstrates how, in the wake of World War I, the discourse about generation, intertwined with discourse about youth, helped to create a myth of camaraderie that foreshadowed and fostered the Nazis' Volksgemeinschaft. More specifically, the text deploys discourse about "youth as other" to narrate Germany's transition from bourgeois society to a nationalized, postbourgeois community. Although popular throughout the Nazi period, *Michael* also belongs to an earlier cultural moment, one reflecting the kind of collective the text produces as well as Goebbels's own "left-Nazi" leanings:[36] in offering a community of miners the text celebrates ordinary workers. Although such a generational and young community of workers did serve the illusion of the NSDAP as a radical workers' party, it does not foreground the kind of militarism that Nazism favored in its march toward war. In its celebration of militaristic values and sacrificial death for the father-land, Nazism would come to rely on other myths from World War I, myths that would more directly militarize German society. Of course the "stab-in-the-back" legend of the war—of brave soldiers at the front be-trayed by political and economic elites (often coded as Jewish) at home—was probably the most important such myth.[37]

Another of these recurring myths, however, relied upon a particu-lar construction of youth to augment the Nazi war myth. The battle of Langemarck would, like the Marne, Somme, and Verdun, enter the pan-theon of battles that signify much more than transient military engage-ments; it came to symbolize a political and cultural transformation, even a radical break in the political and cultural history of Germany. Lange-marck entered, and grounded in many ways, the German imaginary about World War I and the nefarious "betrayal." Scholars like George Mosse, Herbert Lehnert, and Bernd Hüppauf have outlined how im-portant Langemarck became in the German memory of World War I, but I argue that much of its power at the time and then throughout the Weimar and Nazi periods was derived from its conspicuous emphasis on bravery, duty, and sacrifice as they intersected discourse about youth.[38] In the socioeconomic transition galvanized by the myth of Langemarck, youth again plays a central role, but here bourgeois society is trans-formed by a normatively militaristic order. The myth invokes the fin de siècle discussion about "youth as other" to bourgeois society, remaking it to resonate with militarized values and tropes. In this conservative rev-olution as generational transformation, the young serve not only as other to existing society but also to the bourgeois family that a text like *Youth of Langemarck* sets out to recast in a nationalist-militaristic mode.

The Langemarck Legend

"Langemarck" refers to a series of battles on the (German) western front in late October and early November 1914. By that time—with the fail-ings of the Schlieffen plan becoming clear and the reality of a long trench war settling in—the need for a decisive victory "in the West" was crucial. German generals attempted to sweep through Flanders to the English Channel to prevent further forces and supplies from joining the existing French lines. This series of battles served as the basis for what became, in the German public sphere, one of the most famous and repeated mil-itary bulletins of the war: "West of Langemarck, youthful regiments singing 'Deutschland, Deutschland über alles,' broke forward against the front line of enemy positions and took them. Approx. 2000 men of the French regular infantry were taken prisoner and six machine guns captured."[39] Although the German forces did not achieve their goal of the Channel, and although the war did—against the plans and promises of the German general staff—sink into miserable, nearly intractable trench warfare, this bulletin and the battle of Langemarck assumed mythic proportions.

Key elements of this myth are already clear in the brief bulletin: near a place with the memorable name "Langemarck," the "youthful" regiments were singing a future German anthem about dedication to the nation. The absurdly low total of "six machine guns captured" seems to underscore, in poetic tension with their musical enthusiasm, the modesty and solemnity of these young men. Many of these rhetorically resonant details were the vertiginous stuff of myth, a chimerical veil that obscures unpleasant realities. First, the battles took place closer to Bixchote, which does not have the same monumentally Teutonic ring as "Langemarck." It also seems improbable, as Mosse points out, that the forces could have been singing audibly as they slogged through deep mud and thick forests.[40] Moreover, the forces at and around Langemarck were probably at the most about 18 percent high school or university students or their teachers: in the most detailed study of the Langemarck battles, Karl Unruh puts the number of young volunteers closer to a mere 10 percent.[41] There were, indeed, volunteer regiments, but they were also troops who were probably completely mismanaged, even betrayed, by their superiors. Although they are cleverly glossed over in the legendary bulletin, commanding officers at Langemarck sent these undertrained and ill-equipped volunteers, without an opening artillery barrage, against British regular infantry, many of whom were battle tested and war ready from colonial conflicts. Finally, the modest declaration of their victory was certainly deceptive, since the German volunteers were effectively slaughtered by the British regulars, with an estimated 10,000 dead.[42] The mythic elements of the bulletin seem deliberately duplicitous in light of this mismanaged foray and resounding defeat.

What interests me in particular is why the Langemarck myth exaggerates the youth of the soldiers. Why does the terse bulletin highlight their age? Why not, for instance, emphasize their status as volunteers, a facet certainly figuring in this context?[43] Because, by invoking "the youth of Langemarck," the myth could then exploit the longer-term

36

cultural and social discourse about youth—as a demographic and cultural other—from the fin de siècle, war, and Weimar periods. Even more than Goebbels's *Michael*, the Langemarck myth demonstrates how Nazi culture could exploit existing cultural tropes to narrate and normativize its own trajectory, that is, stage its transformation of bourgeois society into a nationalized postbourgeois community. Ever opportunistic, Nazi culture exploited the Langemarck legend because it, particularly in its emphasis on the "youth of Langemarck," allowed National Socialist rhetoric to instrumentalize fin de siècle and Expressionist trends. These trends made available to Nazi culture such tropes as generational conflict within the fading bourgeois constellation, the idea of nation as a spiritual community, and the requisite militarism to define and defend it. To understand the considerable afterlife and propagandistic value of Langemarck for the Nazi regime, I offer a short overview of its discursive fate as a kind of counterhistory of the war for the political Right and the militaristically minded.

The Afterlife of the Langemarck Myth

Unlike Verdun, Langemarck remained almost unknown to British and French civilian societies, who tended to refer to the same series of battles as the (first) battle of Ypres. But Langemarck maintained a considerable hold on the German imaginary throughout the 1920s. For example, the "Day of Langemarck" (10 November 1914) was celebrated on numerous occasions, including in 1919, 1924, 1928, and 1932. While leftist commentators tended to regard Langemarck as a tragedy in which irresponsible generals had led innocent youths to their slaughter,[44] the "youth of Langemarck" and "Day of Langemarck" remained important for the Right as a signifier of dogged nationalism and subsequent sacrificial death. In the 1920s, some conservatives, lamenting the lack of ritual in the "coldly rational" republic, lobbied for the Day of Langemarck to replace abruptly cancelled holidays such as the Kaiser's birthday or the Day of Sedan.[45] Although an annual Day of Langemarck was not fully institutionalized until the Nazi years, rituals around Langemarck manifested themselves throughout the 1920s and later in speeches and ceremonies—for instance, at the 1932 dedication of the German cemetery at Langemarck, which was overseen by the German Student Union (Deutsche Studentenschaft).

Especially for the Right, Langemarck became an important symbol for the most honorable and noble aspects of World War I: before things started to turn horribly wrong, the bloom of Germany's youth volunteered and sacrificed itself with a nationalist melody on its expiring breath. That the war did, thereafter, go wrong serves as an indispensable aspect of its mythic power: youth sacrificed themselves but were ultimately betrayed by the extinguishing of the "Spirit of 1914." As Wolfgang Schivelbusch, Uwe-K. Ketelsen, and Hüppauf have observed, defeat may be more important than victories for marshaling and cementing identities.[46] Particularly in relation to the nation's young, the fixation on such defeats—such collective wounds—has served to found and ground a new identity. The kind of "youth as other" one sees in *Michael* here serves as a lightning rod for nationalistic memorialization, for a kind of countermemory to other accounts of World War I. It was this kind of countermemory of the "shame of the Reich" or "dead history" that the Nazis, as they did with the stab-in-the-back legend, were able to institutionalize and exploit in their own culture of war. For example, in a speech read at the dedication of the Langemarck cemetery that was also read at universities throughout Germany in 1932, noted Nazi author Josef Magnus Wehner declared: "Before the Reich emerged those from Langemarck *sang*. Those who were dying sang! . . . But with the suffering with which they died, they rose again a thousand times and they will rise again a thousand times until the end of the Reich, and that is—our world."[47] As cultural other to mainline history, the singing of the Langemarck youths contravenes the shame of the German Reich, and it is this singing that resurrects them, keeping them forever remembered, forever present. Rudolf Binding's report on the 1924 festivities marking the tenth anniversary of the battle executes exactly the same discursive maneuver, contrasting conventional, dead history to the young, living myth of Langemarck: "Their deeds [in Langemarck] will be preserved by history and in people's memory. But each event no longer belongs merely to history, where such an event would once have hardened and been buried, but rather the unendingly procreative, the unendingly rejuvenating, the unendingly animated force of *Myth*."[48]

Langemarck would play a particularly prominent role under the Nazi regime, right up through World War II and the "Second Day of Langemarck," when Germans would finally conquer Flanders in 1940. The Day of Langemarck became the day each year when students were inducted into the Nazi Party. In 1933 alone, there were at least three plays about the "Youth of Langemarck," the most important of which I analyze below. Martin Heidegger, Germany's then most important and now infamous philosopher, even gave a speech on the topic to a rally in November 1933.[49] In 1935, the book *The Calling of the Time* (*Berufung der Zeit*) by Eberhard Wolfgang Möller, which won that year's national book award, closed with a chorale dedicated to the youths at Langemarck. By 1936, the year compulsory membership in the Hitler-Jugend was legally mandated, radio stations across the country transmitted celebrations of "Langemarck—Heritage of the HJ."[50] And by 1938, with the war very much in the works, Langemarck was definitively institutionalized by the regime in the everyday experience of the population: the monthly "Langemarck-penny," to be paid by every member of the Hitler-Jugend, was introduced. That year as well the party rolled out a formal educational program, called the "Langemarck-Programm," that would prepare pupils for university study without the requisite Gymnasium attendance.[51] In a route revealingly divergent from the traditional bourgeois path, racially approved pupils were prepared for the university while being educated in the values of "Youth of Langemarck."

Nazism under the Sign of Youth: Zerkaulen's *Youth of Langemarck* as War Memorialization

Even this short overview demonstrates the remarkable degree to which Langemarck played an important role well past 1933–34 and right up through the war.[52] As late as 1944, the National Committee for Free Germany still saw the myth as important enough to publish an article entitled "Langemarck—Truth and Legend" in its *Free Germany*.[53] Because of its emphasis on youth, this persisting link between Langemarck and National Socialism confirms the lasting symbiosis of youth as other and tenets of Nazism. To understand more precisely how Langemarck functioned within Nazi culture—and to illuminate how this culture consistently and fundamentally instrumentalized existing discourses about youth—I would like to offer a closer analysis of the most important of the (at least) three plays about Langemarck from 1933/1934, Heinrich Zerkaulen's *Youth of Langemarck* (*Jugend von Langemarck*).

With *Youth of Langemarck*, the first play of this established folkish-nationalist author, Zerkaulen had one of his biggest successes.[54] As part of the celebration of the tenth anniversary of the Beer Hall Putsch, the play was premiered simultaneously in ten cities (Dresden, Bremen, Kassel, Darmstadt, Halle, Lübeck, Hagen, Greifswald, Beuthen, and Bonn) and was even included in the first *Reichstheaterfestwochen* (Reich Theater Festival) (1934) in Dresden, during which it was showcased as one of ten celebrated works, along with Hanns Johst's *Schlageter*, Friedrich Forster's *All against One and One for All* (*Alle gegen einen, einer für alle*), and Kolbenheyer's *Heroic Passions* (*Heroische Leidenschaften*) as well as classics like *Wilhelm Tell* and *Götz von Berlichingen*.[55] These *Festwochen* demonstrate how, despite much revolutionary pretense and rebellious histrionics to the contrary, culture during the Third Reich continued to engage with bourgeois traditions. In fact, I want to argue that Zerkaulen's *Youth of Langemarck* activates a very deliberate double, or, more precisely, parallel and mutually illuminating sublation of bourgeois society via the young. It engages and then transcends two inherited discourses: bourgeois dramatic theater and bourgeois social forms, especially the social forms of the family and its young. Both of these inherited forms—the theatrical tradition and the conventional formations of family—are invoked, explored, and then deliberately rendered obsolete by way of the young. The play positions itself, like National Socialism, as the complete realization and negation of these inherited traditions: it charts, like Michael's rejection of the university in favor of the mines, a transformative transcendence of older forms via the young. Finally, and maybe most remarkably, World War I is memorialized so that the play not only creates a legend but underscores the very process by which something—in this case youth—becomes memory, memorial, and ultimately myth.

In the first two of its three acts, the play follows the protagonist, Franz Gärtner, the eldest son of a factory-owning family. It opens in Germany at the beginning of World War I, with the young Franz about to break off his studies early and inherit his dead father's textile factory. Since production will undergo a radical transformation with the beginning of hostilities, his father preferred that the son oversee the transition rather than his mother and the managers in whose hands he left the firm. An obvious ulterior motive is to keep his son away from the front by drafting him to serve at home, on the safe home front of military production. At the reading of the will that divulges this paternal plan, however, Franz reveals that he and his entire university fraternity have already enlisted in the army and that he cannot unenlist to stay at home. Against the vociferous protests of his mother and the passive entreaties of his love interest, Franz forges ahead to the front. Act 2 portrays the young soldiers' lives on the front: in a barn in Flanders, Franz and his young comrades debate the war and their role in it, a debate and role I examine below. By act 3, Franz has already been killed at Langemarck, and the action shifts to the humble, dedicated Karl Stanz, a young worker from the Gärtner factory who enlisted and served with Franz's fraternity (though he, as a worker, was not a member). In a short epilogue (*Nachspiel*), Karl is demobilized, and Franz's mother welcomes Karl into their home with the announcement that Franz's inheritance will be dedicated to a foundation (the "Franz-Gärtner-Stiftung") to pay for the university studies of young workers like Karl.

In its first act, *Youth of Langemarck,* like much of culture during the Third Reich, references and relies on the parameters of inherited, largely bourgeois artistic forms, here Expressionist drama. The play's basic conceit of a parent-child conflict that reflects fundamental changes in society is familiar from Expressionist plays like Georg Kaiser's *Gas I* and Walter Hasenclever's *Der Sohn* (*The Son*). Kaiser's *Gas,* in particular, seems the primary intertextual reference here, since in *Gas,* too, a son inherits a factory from his father but has very different ideas about the trajectory of his own life and work. In both *Gas* and *Youth of Langemarck,* the apparent boon of this inheritance becomes a literal and symbolic burden for the son at odds with the bourgeois, materialist values of the parental generation, a clash that recurs in a great number of Expressionist dramas.[56] In *Gas,* the billionaire's son realizes that it is not the engineer's formula but rather the manufacture of gas itself that leads unavoidably to fatal explosions: he comes thereby to recognize that the contradictions in capitalist production point toward inevitable destruction.[57] In *Youth of Langemarck,* the protagonist-son is similarly poised to inherit a factory that is also about to be pulled into a military orbit, but in Zerkaulen's work the familial tensions and bourgeois contradictions are revealingly different. While Kaiser contrasts the bourgeois family to emancipation because of the bourgeois family's affinity for war, Zerkaulen contrasts the bourgeois family to emancipation because the bourgeois family rejects the nationalist war.

Both *Gas* and *Youth of Langemarck* underscore the centrality of the family, especially its particular relation to the young, in the bourgeois social order. Much more than Goebbels's *Michael, Youth of Langemarck* traces the potential of the politicized young to remake the family as the cornerstone of society. It is not surprising that these texts fixate on the family, since the family and the social norms circulating not only around it but also through it form the foundations of bourgeois society. Although theorists and historians like Aries, Foucault, Donzelot, and Mitterauer agree that the bourgeois family consolidated

41

itself in the domestic sphere in a radically new way—literally closing it-self up in the house and closing down older, more open socialities—the family did become open in a new way: it became a key transfer point for modern norms circulating in society at large. It became, as Donzelot has shown, a, if not the, key site at which society exercised its disciplinary functions. As Gilles Deleuze points out in his reading of Donzelot, the family is not, in accordance with conventional thinking, a protected private sphere cordoned off from society and state but instead straddles all of these different arenas, the domestic, social, and governmental.[58]

Throughout the instantiation of modern society in the nineteenth and twentieth centuries, the young and their family life have provided the fulcrum between the conventionally public and the allegedly private. At first the young served as a point of negotiation between the family and the wider society and state, but Donzelot is clear that the family counted less and less as a discrete, institutionalized interlocutor for the society and state; it became instead a "relay, an obligatory or voluntary support for social imperatives . . . so as to link together normative requirements and economic-moral behavior." The young became less a point of negotiation between family and society and state and more of a transfer point: there was no longer a governance of the families, rather a governance through families.[59]

In light of this youth-family-society linkage, both *Gas* and *Youth of Langemarck* cast the young as protagonists in their family-dismantling and society-recasting dramas: like *Gas*, *Youth of Langemarck* aims to govern through the young in order to remake the family, and thereby the entire society, into a postfamilial, postbourgeois community. Similarly to Goebbels's *Michael*, Franz's and then his family's bond with Karl is forged generationally, not economically: instead of the (emancipated) "Workers of Gärtner," the play foregrounds and normativizes the (nationalistic) "Youth of Langemarck." In this pursuit of a postbourgeois community, *Youth of Langemarck* invokes another important work of the bourgeois tradition, one also preoccupied with the fate of the family and postfamilial forms in the wake of it: Schiller's *The Robbers*. Any dramatic work with young protagonists named Karl and Franz inevitably recalls Schiller's classic, but the similarities also include the basic form and structure of the play.[60] Like *The Robbers*, *Youth of Langemarck*, in acts 1 and 2, balances the conventional family with scenes not only away from but deliberately breaking with the family in a new kind of youth collective. *The Robbers* alternates scenes of the Moor family with those of Karl's robber band, while *Youth* balances the Gärtner family with military units at the Flanders front. Both the (youthful) robber band and the (youthful) military unit are explicitly defined against the family as it tries to claim its son and ensure generational continuity and stability. *The Robbers,* like *Youth of Langemarck,* traces the fate of a new postfamilial collective that emerges when a son rejects his paternal inheritance, and both texts utilize the family drama to overthrow the existing society and explore a new one in its place.[61]

In addition to appropriating these discourses about youth to found a postfamilial community, Zerkaulen's play instrumentalizes specific tropes that continue to resonate even after World War II. In a way neither *Gas* nor *The Robbers* does, *Youth of Langemarck* celebrates youth's alleged propensity to militarism. The Day of Langemarck functioned so effectively throughout World War I and the 1920s because it offered a defeat that could, via youth as other, narrate a counterhistory of the war, a kind of countermemory as myth that marshaled a certain kind of identity. In *Youth of Langemarck,* this counterhistory returns to consecrate nationalist war and militaristic sacrifice, defined against the world of bourgeois (that is, draft-dodging) family values, as the highest manifestation of Germany. Considered the highlight of the play, act 2 deploys a specific discourse about youth to depict and justify the war and its warriors. It was the one section of the drama that Zerkaulen referred to as "performed again and again" by the Hitler-Jugend and, less predictably, by SA groups.[62] The entire scene takes place in and around a barn in Flanders where the army unit of Gärtner and his fraternity (and, of course, Karl Stanz) is spending the night. As with Schiller's robber band, the play depicts the army not as a perfectly homogeneous and purely productive organization but as rife with tensions within the ranks, particularly between the older professional soldiers and the younger volunteers.

These generational tensions become an occasion for the young volunteers to discuss their unique contribution to the war and, by association, youth's contribution to the nationalist movement in general. As they consider the bias against them as young recruits, they lament how the older soldiers have families and careers to worry about, concerns that prevent them from trusting the *Rausch* (intoxication) that seized all of Germany in August 1914.[63] The idea of Rausch was a key aspect of Germany's culture of war in the 1910s and 1920s. For instance, Ernst

43

Jünger lauded it in both *Storms of Steel* and *The Attack as Inner Experience*, in which he writes: "[Battle] is an intoxication beyond all intoxication, an unleashing that breaks all bonds. It is a frenzy without caution and limits, comparable to the forces of nature."[64] For Zerkaulen—writing in 1933—the wartime Rausch became the special purview of the young defined against the old. As his young comrades lament the fearful hand-wringing of an older officer, Lehmbruck, Franz argues emotionally: "If only Lehmbruck knew how it is with this intoxication [*Rausch*] and with us—German students! *Rausch*—that comes from rustling [*rauschen*]. Yes, brothers, it rustles [*rauscht*] in us. In me and in you (*more and more feeling*), in us all—all" (162). As with Goebbels's young Faustians, Nazi culture connects the young to longer-term tropes, outside and antagonistic to the staid and fearful middle class. Rausch and rauschen are precisely that which distinguishes not only Franz from his bourgeois family but also his young comrades from the older soldiers and, more generally, from adult worries. The play's positive coding of youthful Rausch is particularly noteworthy because both *Gas* and *The Robbers* manifest a marked skepticism about any kind of Rausch in their new collectives. The association of the youth of Langemarck and Rausch has a long history, confirming the centrality of youthful Rausch for postwar German nationalism and militarism.[65]

In Franz's climactic speech about the advantages of young soldiers over their older comrades, he associates this unique access to Rausch with a specific kind of history and memory that produces the nation.[66] As he considers the possibilities of the Rausch he has just positioned as the special purview of the young, he declares:

> The blood of our fathers from the centuries rustles [*rauscht*] in us. All of those who left their lives for the soil of their home [*Heimaterde*], those from Fehrbellin, from Rossbach, from Leuthen, Jena, those from Sedan—they are with us—in *us*! . . . Children, we have to be there too! We have to attack there. And even if it all goes to hell, children. And even if we get there in the midst of a slaughter. But get there—get there we will! (*Ecstatically*) *We* will then rustle [*rauschen*]—in them! Over the centuries and forward—out of the infinity *we* will rustle [*rauschen*] in *their* blood! (163–64)

This dramatic speech, a discourse about Rauschen that leads Franz to his own "ecstatic" Rausch, underscores the relation among youth as other, Langemarck as war memorial, and counterhistory as guiding memory. History here is bred of a kind of nationalist myth that is referenced, as well as produced by, discourse about Langemarck. The Rauschen links the young of Langemarck to the generations of soldiers who have died on behalf of "Germany," which, for many of the forebears Franz invokes, would have been a distinct nationalist anachronism. The irony in this context is that this Rauschen becomes the basis for a link to the "fathers," something this play and its Expressionism-influenced plotting has been seeking since act 1. Franz will find this connection to fathers not in the bourgeois family but instead in a new sort of national-generational community. The speech demonstrates how the play rewrites not only bourgeois drama but also bourgeois social forms of the young and Germany in general.

That the play is ultimately concerned with this kind of mythic counterhistory of youth itself becomes clear in the final act and the epilogue. Here the play reassembles the now radically reconfigured family and the social norms flowing through it. By the final act, Franz is dead, and Karl, captured by the British, mourns him. With this surprising and abrupt development, the play shifts from the presumed protagonist to a new central character who had, before this moment, been a background figure. The death of Franz makes clear that neither he nor Karl is the true protagonist or even focus of the play—instead, youth itself is. And what persists in Franz's climactic speech in act 2, in Karl's mourning him in act 3, and, finally, in Franz's mother's welcoming Karl as a son in the epilogue, is the memorialization and mythification of youth and all it symbolizes.

In this sense, with its bifurcated protagonist, the play enacts the kind of double process that Reinhart Koselleck has argued marks war memorialization in general. Koselleck emphasizes how war memorials galvanize a double process of identity production: they define the dead as a certain kind of hero while (and thereby) designating the living as the protectors and guardians of this status. This process not only commemorates the dead but also renders survival meaningful in a specific and forward-looking way.[67] War memorialization as a double process— a diametrically opposed but also reciprocally constitutive identification—is similar to what Zerkaulen's *Youth of Langemarck* undertakes in its double protagonist. It first defines Franz as a certain kind of hero and then charges Karl and his family with the protection and defense of this constructed image of Franz as a hero. The play commemorates Franz but also gives Karl, the Gärtner family, and the viewers a specific charge to keep, that is, a normative identity based on this commemoration. The cult of the fallen soldier has been mapped, via the myth of Lange-marck, onto the German World War I generation, the generation that would provide core supporters to National Socialism.

This double process is illustrated not only in the unusual double protagonist but also in one of the play's dramatic highlights. During the epilogue, at the moment the legal advisor and friend of the family reads aloud the dedication of the foundation "to the memory of the student and army volunteer Franz Gärtner," those present hear the cheering and march music accompanying soldiers' returning home from war (190). It is a cleverly theatrical moment that juxtaposes the memorialization of Franz by his family with the return of his comrades, the familial memory coinciding with his chosen generational community that replaced the family in acts 1 and 2. On the one hand, as Koselleck outlines, there is the institutional articulation of the dead Franz in a kind of war memorial—the living claim the dead for their own purposes. On the other hand, at the same moment, both the Gärtner family and the demobilizing soldiers are actually mobilized in a new way, that is, mobilized on behalf of the dead. There is, via war memorialization, the total mobilization (to cite Jünger's useful phrase) of civilian life, of families and of friends. In this way, the play achieves a remarkable denouement: it re-places the war with a type of war memorial that reassembles the family in a militaristic mode and that keeps Franz's generational comrades mobilized and ready to fight anytime and everywhere.

Various scholars have emphasized the importance of death and the death cult for Nazi culture,[68] but I want to highlight the at least equally odd resolution of the play in a tuition-granting foundation. What is particularly remarkable is not only the emphatically young community or the cult of death but also youth's relevance as memory and history that hold both the remade family and the mobilized youth community in their grip. The last two lines of the play ("They died for Langemarck— / We live—for Langemarck" [194]) confirm not only the intertwine-ment of death and life in the Nazi imaginary but also the double iden-tity production of war memorialization, that is, simultaneously and co-constitutively defining the dead and the survivors. And, in a way that Koselleck does not explore, this double process obscures other memo-ries of the war—for example, the mistakes of the German high command at Langemarck and in 1914 in general. It is a spectacular and thereby obfuscating process of memorialization and identification, a literal and metaphorical building that can displace and replace other histories, memories, burdens—as well as a more radical revolution.

The foundation seems a surprising resolution to the play's familial as well as national tensions, a resolution that is, at the same time, quite revealing: it demonstrates how identity in the 1930s would be founded on such defeats and such memorialization of both bourgeois sacrifice and neonational war. The notion of a foundation also points forward to the kind of memorializing and monumental architecture that would prove central to the Nazi project in the 1930s and 1940s.[69] World War I and the defeat felt so keenly left German nationalists rudderless in the choppy waters of the Weimar Republic: there was no longer a paternalistic monarch at the helm. This play offers a solution that not only produces a youth community to replace the increasingly obsolete bourgeois family but also institutionalizes the memory of that community, which will emanate forth at the end of the play from the postbourgeois family, from Franz's comrades, from his foundation. The definition of the dead and subsequent marshaling of identity redefines the existing social configurations, achieving another fundamental transformation without a revolution. The factory, the university, even the family fortune remain intact, all merely remade in a nationalist mode. As the retooled Karl undertakes what appears to be a conventional academic track, he will forever harbor the youthful Rausch within him, a prophetic recasting of bourgeois education embodied in the Langemarck educational program introduced five years later. Like Karl's overdetermined plans at the end of the play, the Nazis' Langemarck program would be built on the bourgeois institutions of education. Rather than utter upheaval, the play dismantles the family and university only to reassemble them soon thereafter such that new norms—youthful-militaristic memories and their burdens—flow through them.

G. W. PABST'S *PARACELSUS:*
FÜHRER FIGURE AS YOUTH LEADER

In its remaking of bourgeois society, the tuition-paying foundation at the end of Zerkaulen's *Youth of Langemarck* fulfills the socioeconomic fantasies of the *Heimkehrer* (soldier returning home) while simultaneously institutionalizing the memory of the Langemarck young. As I argue above, this abiding memory and privileged status of Langemarck

47

for the Nazi imaginary would persist through World War II and its "Second Langemarck." But there is also a different discourse about youth that emerges, or at least comes to greater prominence, during World War II, namely, one that emphasized the special relation of the young to the Führer in waging Germany's losing battles. After arguing (with Goebbels's *Michael*) that the alterity of youth and generation was the basis for the Volksgemeinschaft and (with Zerkaulen's *Youth of Langemarck*) that the dismantling and reassembling of the bourgeois family relied on and affirmed youth as war memorialization, I want to offer a short reading of a film that underscores the privileged and peculiar relationship between the young and the Führer during a time of acute crisis. As I shall trace in this film and then later in the postwar period, the youth crisis serves repeatedly as a discursive site onto which to displace, localize, and contain other, wider social and political crises.

Unlike Zerkaulen's *Youth of Langemarck*, G. W. Pabst's 1943 biographical film *Paracelsus* has had a considerable afterlife in German studies. Most interpretations weigh in on the most prominent question posed by the film: to what degree Paracelsus was meant as a Führer figure and what consequences that would have for judging Pabst's complicity with the regime. In his thorough analysis of Nazi cinema, Eric Rentschler even names his chapter on *Paracelsus* "The Führer's Phantom" and argues that the marketing of the film makes clear that Paracelsus was a surrogate for an increasingly absent Hitler. Rentschler observes that by 1943 and the defeat at Stalingrad, Hitler was seen in public less and less and that this caused problems for a regime that had strategically promoted his personal charisma. Emphasizing the film's marketing as a work of overtly propagandistic content, Rentschler sees the film as part of a concerted effort to keep the *Führerprinzip* present despite Hitler's absence.[70] As Regine Mihal Friedman points out, the casting of Krauss (then nearly sixty years old) to play the thirty-four-year-old Paracelsus confirms the intent to link the upstart physician to the aging Führer (then fifty-four years old).[71] Though the film was a box office disappointment, its status as a prestige production—as part of the 450th anniversary of Paracelsus's birth as well as the work of a celebrated Weimar director—corroborates this deliberate positioning of the film.

Given the considerable scholarly attention the film has garnered, it is therefore all the more remarkable that none of these scholars has foregrounded or even much mentioned the prominent treatment of youth and generation in its narrative. While I agree with Rentschler's basic argument that the figure of Paracelsus, as is the case with many of the Nazi "genius films," is meant as a surrogate for the Führer, I want to explore the surprisingly symbiotic camaraderie between this Führer figure and two emphatically young people in the film. Hardly any scholar, for instance, offers an extended analysis of Johannes, the student assistant of Paracelsus and love interest of female lead Renata Pfefferkorn, even though Johannes is conspicuously present from the first sequence of the film until the last. His ubiquitous presence both demands a reading and underscores, in a different context, the central role of youth in Nazi culture.

In *Paracelsus*, youth as other becomes the linchpin in a time of acute crisis, a crisis that allows for the recasting of social configurations and public institutions even more than in Goebbels's *Michael* or Zerkaulen's *Youth of Langemarck*. *Michael* and *Youth of Langemarck* build on earlier discourses about youth inherited from turn-of-the-century culture, which tended to emphasize the autonomy of youth (as a cultural construct) in its potential to reanimate calcified bourgeois society. *Paracelsus* reflects a later moment—one after the complete coordination of the independent youth groups to the Hitler-Jugend and the Hitler-Jugend to the party—that still emphasizes youth's revolutionary potential but aims to harness such potential for its own purposes under an explicit Führer figure. Within the sociopolitical crisis *Paracelsus* depicts, youth's ability to recognize and follow a superior authority figure resolves the public and private crises central to the milieu of the film. The crises of family, education, and the city as a whole yield new relationships to a clear Führer figure that both refigures the existing institutions and foregrounds the young's role—in emphatic concert with the Führer—in this new order. In contrast to *Michael* and *Youth of Langemarck*, *Paracelsus* relies on the young as the only group that, by way of its symbiotic relationship to the Führer, can lead Germany out of its crisis.

The Co-Constitutive Crises of the Home, University, and the City-State

Unlike in a film like *Hitlerjunge Quex* (1933), in which the socioeconomic problems provide the background tensions, a plague causes the public and private crises in *Paracelsus*, probably a reflection of the shift from the early-1930s depression to the early-1940s war. In the film, sixteenth-century Basel fights a plague that is decimating its citizenry. This series of struggles leads to doubts about the city's university medical faculty and the head of that faculty, the Magister. The mayor and a prominent member of the town council named Pfefferkorn invite the itinerant, charismatic doctor Paracelsus to the struggling city. Paracelsus's performance in an academic debate with the Magister convinces a number of students, including Johannes, the young male lead, to break with the Magister. Once appointed to his dual office of municipal physician and university professor, Paracelsus immediately quarantines the city, much to the annoyance of the merchant Pfefferkorn, who tries to smuggle in wares secretly. After catching the convoy, Paracelsus confronts Pfefferkorn in his home about the breach of the quarantine. There Paracelsus meets Renata, Pfefferkorn's daughter, and praises her beauty. Two visually striking sequences ensue, one in which Paracelsus saves citizens from a plague-induced dance of death and one in which flagellants visit the town.[72] After seeing the flagellants, Renata collapses at home due to a mysterious illness; her father, fearing the plague, eventually has to call his nemesis Paracelsus to cure her. Renata becomes a steadfast devotee of Paracelsus, bringing him money that her father had promised for her treatment and then studying with him. Meanwhile, Paracelsus's other main student, Johannes, runs into trouble of his own making. When a patient of the ambitious but inexperienced Johannes dies, the medical faculty turns on Paracelsus and seeks his arrest. Persona non grata in the city he saved, Paracelsus has to rely on his young followers to spirit him out of trouble. The film's final sequence finds Paracelsus, Renata, and Johannes outside the city in the country where Paracelsus commits to serving the common people.

As this short summary suggests, the film depicts a public and private crisis arising from the absence of productive, competent authorities. A crisis caused by a disease returns the concept of crisis back to one of its earliest meanings, namely, a health crisis that requires an effective diagnostic decision before time runs out. It was from this medical meaning of *crisis* that the notion, in the metaphor of the state as a body, of a political crisis of authority arose,[73] a generalization of meaning that was especially resonant in Nazi culture and its emphasis on the *Volkskörper* (national body). In *Paracelsus*, as elsewhere, the health crisis becomes a zone of social and political trouble, a region in which the presocial or antisocial threatens what has been presumed to be an unshakable hierarchy. Thus crisis, in both the body and the polity, operates as a kind of mobile, manipulatable signifier that disrupts social and political codes, their standards, values, and ethics. The film's first extended sequence emphasizes precisely this symbol-laden medical crisis: the Magister is enthusiastic about an unnecessary leg amputation of a local printer, an amputation Paracelsus races to prevent. This sequence confirms that disease-ridden Basel suffers under a kind of dephalliation, that is, a decentering due to the weakness of (traditionally) key male figures, figures both paternal and political. The diegesis of *Paracelsus,* in fact, rests on three inextricably linked and co-constitutive crises: one in the private home, one in the public institution of education, and one in the city-state as a whole.

All of these crises confirm a central aspect of *Paracelsus* and the Nazi discourse about youth—the youth crisis. The youth crisis has a double and contradictory character: the young are threatened by a social crisis at the same time they create or exacerbate the crisis. The enormous potential for the particular crises of youth becomes clear if one keeps in mind the centrality of the young for modern subjectivities, society, and the nation. Foucault describes how discourse about youth sexuality functions as a kind of devastating yet floating crisis: "One comes to have a society of dangers, with, on the one hand, those put in danger; and on the other those who bear danger: And [youth] sexuality will no longer be a conduct with certain precise interdictions but . . . will become a kind of danger that prowls, a sort of omnipresent phantom."[74] Discourse about youth is a "danger that prowls," a danger based on the young who are put in danger as well as the cause of it. If the crisis area is a site at which the social values and structures are in danger of collapsing, the young, as I argue above, are regularly other to the social order and represent the reiteration as well as the transgression of that order.

In *Paracelsus* the two youthful protagonists, Renata and Johannes, suffer under their own particular youth crises in the form of corrupt authority figures, whom they in turn resist and undercut. The lack of benevolent and effective authority figures in Basel underpins the wider crisis of the film and creates the narrative need for Paracelsus, a Führer figure first and foremost to the young. In the private sphere of Renata's family, the film codes her father, Pfefferkorn, as economically corrupt as well as ethically suspect. In an overtly anti-Semitic coding, Pfefferkorn is hoping to marry off his daughter to a powerful count she does not love, all to economic ends. Johannes suffers under a different kind of authoritative oppression, that of the university, with its own bad authority figure, the Magister, played by perennial spook Fritz Rasp. While *Paracelsus* recalls the critique of the bourgeois university in Goebbels's *Michael,* it also radicalizes it as a genuine youth crisis, one that stands in for the public crisis in general. The Magister, as the embodiment of obsolete education, is more interested in preserving the medical tradition than in teaching students, curing patients, or protecting the city from further infection. When the Magister debates Paracelsus at the university lecture hall, for example, he insists on speaking Latin and on using abstruse classical medical terms; Paracelsus, on the other hand, prefers the vernacular German and simple demonstrations, coding him (conveniently, if anachronistically) as a German nationalist. At the end of the debate, the young students flock, zombielike, to Paracelsus in one of the film's more remarkable shots.[75] The crisis of the university has led the wayward young to Paracelsus, such that the youth crisis becomes the means with which to redraw civic institutions.

Youth as Other, Resisting and Resolving the Prevailing Social Crisis

Amid the crisis of these depraved authority figures, *Paracelsus* depicts its youthful protagonists as economically productive, ethically good, and civically dedicated. Like Goebbels's Michael and Zerkaulen's Franz, Johannes and Renata are fundamentally different from their generational antecedents. The film goes so far as to depict the young as the obvious but untapped solution to the prevailing crises in both the public and private spheres. To a greater degree than either Michael or Franz, Johannes and Renata reject adaptation to the private, educational, or civic institutions around them. Indeed, the crises in these institutions of youth (family, university) and youth rejection of them foreshadow a much more radical reconfiguring of these private and public institutions.

The trajectory of the young out of the familial house and out of the university confirms an important theme in *Michael* and *Youth of Langemarck* and another central aspect of the alterity of youth: that, especially in times of crisis, youth are mobile, capable of literal and metaphorical liberation from bourgeois spatial and social constellations. In terms of the relation between youth and bourgeois spatial figurations, Foucault, Donzelot, and Mitterauer all underscore a radical reformulation of domestic space in the modern world: they outline how this domesticity is founded upon the spatial disciplining of the young person. This disciplining aims to combat the recurring anxiety about youth as border crossers, as floaters, as vagabonds who show no respect spatially or psychologically for adult boundaries or property.[76] Since the emergence of modern social forms relied in many ways on a certain ordering of space—domestic and private as well as communal and public—the spatial context of youth proves equally important and equally ambivalent. The emphasis on travel and mobility in the Wandervogel and other youth movements deliberately invoked this long-term historical association of the young and mobility outside the bourgeois constellation built on their spatial disciplining.[77]

Paracelsus exploits this border-crossing capacity of the young in a manner even clearer than *Michael* or *Youth of Langemarck* because, as a film, it relies constantly on the architectural space of sets and its representational potential. In the wake of the prevailing youth crisis, both Renata and Johannes are liberated, literally and metaphorically, from the film's traditional spaces, the house and lecture hall associated with the film's corrupt authority figures. Initially contained in such spaces, the young prove susceptible to something from the outside despite the boundaries of these conventional spaces. It is a seductive something—a song, an intellectual fascination, a contagious illness—that beckons them to depart traditional spaces and social relations. Generational conflict ensues when the authority figures fight this attraction. The beckoning, however, speaks directly to the youthful essence constructed in the film's discourse about youth as other. They join the youth community that inverts generational hierarchy and interrupts generational inheritance. The new community to which they flock entails a remapping of cinematic/social space in which the significant activity for the young rests no longer in the private house or lecture hall but in a nationalistic, postbourgeois collective. This specifically spatial mobility and remapping in the film undergirds the kind of transitions, the transformation of bourgeois society, that I analyzed in *Michael* and *Youth of Langemarck*.

In *Paracelsus,* enchanting music and built-in youthful fascination beckon to Renata and eventually collapse the walls of the private sphere in order to ground a new, national-generational community. I would argue that the film is structured along a series of what I would term fascination shots that emphasize the attraction of the abandonment of traditional spaces and, by association, subjectivity. Each fascination shot consists of a tracking shot, zooming to close-up, occurring at a moment when a radical new connection replaces traditional, now-obsolete loyalties. Since such an unusual shot derives from a deliberate directorial and cinematographic decision, the subtle but clear recurrence of the shot underscores the links among these liberating moments in the film. The first such shot occurs when Renata hears Johannes serenading her from within the fortified walls of her father's home. At this point in the plot, Renata is being courted by, but resists, one of her father's business interests. At this moment of overt paternal corruption, Johannes beckons to her. The shot resonates with the traditional seduction of the female out of the father's domain, but it is also overdetermined by the wider youth crisis in Basel, that is, the youth community of Johannes and the other students beckoning against the corrupt adults' private sphere.

The next fascination shot occurs when Paracelsus invades Pfefferkorn's house to search for imported goods that might introduce the plague into the city. The camera first finds Pfefferkorn strangling an employee for telling Paracelsus whence the goods came, a high-drama moment during which Paracelsus enters. While Paracelsus is castigating Pfefferkorn, he suddenly becomes distracted. When Renata appears unannounced, the very same tracking-zoom shot finds Paracelsus fascinated by her gleaming image. That Pabst uses the same unusual shot for Paracelsus to look at Renata as he did for Renata to look at Johannes is cinematically and narratively remarkable. With this citation of the earlier shot, Pabst plays upon the traditional romantic economy of film, with its standard privatization of public problems. By deliberately inserting Paracelsus the Führer figure into the series of fascination shots, Pabst shows how Paracelsus can participate in the same romantic economy as Johannes and Renata. As when he attracts the discontented students of the Magister, Paracelsus now founds a generational rather than romantic network in which he, the Führer figure, can partake. The film underscores not only the greatness of Paracelsus—as standard interpretations of the film's "genius" Führer figure have it—but also his relationship to an emergent, emphatically young, national community (Volksgemeinschaft). As in *Michael* and *Youth of Langemarck*, youth is not so much chronological and biological as a constructed social position, one repeatedly central to the Nazis' revolutionary agenda.

A New Social Order Forged by the Youth-Führer Symbiosis

The later sections of *Paracelsus* have been largely overlooked because, I suspect, they do not quite fit either the pro- or contra-Führer figure readings the secondary literature invariably has offered. In *Paracelsus,* the last sequence in Basel depicts Renata and Johannes saving the Führer figure: after seventy-five minutes of liberating the young from their oppressive lives, Paracelsus suddenly becomes passive and lets the young take over. Once the city fathers turn against Paracelsus and seek his arrest, the Führer figure whose genius the film sets out to establish is hunted and helpless. His young followers conceive and execute an elaborate plan to smuggle him out of town safely. In a surprising *juvenis ex machina,* the students of the film take over and accomplish something the proto-Nazi leader cannot: sneak his person out of the hostile town. The last sequence, in which the young save Paracelsus, reflects this generational renegotiation, transpiring in a remapped space that definitively undercuts the traditional private sphere, the university, and even the city-state.

The film concludes with Paracelsus, Renata, and Johannes having created a new kind of collective away from the city. In a set that emphasizes the openness of the structure, they act in concert to care for any of the afflicted who visit their open country retreat. The film thus closes with Paracelsus's open house, which replaces the closed houses of the city councilmen or Pfefferkorn's private house. This kind of open house symbolically explodes the bourgeois private sphere in order to refigure the relationship between the Führer and his followers. For example, the architect Guiseppe Terragni claimed that the famous *Casa del Fascio* materialized Mussolini's statement that "fascism is a house of glass into which all can look."[78] Here, this open house is staffed by the youth community that was victimized by the obsolete system and its inability to respond to the crisis. Unlike in *Michael* and *Youth of Langemarck,* which remake the cult of the fallen soldier in a youth mode by killing off their protagonists, *Paracelsus* is careful to keep its young alive to work for the Führer. Paracelsus relies on these youth as much as they rely on him.

The film's arrival at alternative generational relations not only overthrows the father and patrilineal inheritance as in *Youth of Langemarck* but also radically renegotiates generational relations, subverting not only traditional adult authority figures but also, eventually, the film's Führer figure. In a radical discursive shift, a revolutionary generational symbiosis reigns here, one that has replaced the conventional private house, public city, and general municipality with Paracelsus's open house in the country. This specifically generational symbiosis was intended to point to a glorious National Socialist future: the original script called for a cut from Paracelsus and his youthful assistants to images of modern laboratories, clinics, and medical schools.[79] Ultimately, the film's conclusion points toward a dual depiction of youth, one that oscillates between passivity and activity: the young become both the victims and symptoms of the crisis (passively in need of liberation) but also the en-gines/causes of the revolutionary solution to it (active agents in the new order solving the crisis).[80] It is, indeed, a radical discursive shift from those traditional sites of youth in bourgeois society—family and schools—to a reconfigured generational space in a renegotiated genera-tional discourse.

Like Goebbels's *Michael* and the Langemarck myth, *Paracelsus* depicts the emergent—that is, always suffering and always becoming—German nation as a particular kind of generational constellation in which the young constitute the core of nationalist Germany. *Paracelsus* deploys the young to dismantle the private home of Pfefferkorn and replace it with the open house of Paracelsus, a transformation that confirms the border crossing of the young while realizing the Nazi "revolution." In lieu of a class revolution, Zerkaulen's *Youth of Langemarck* similarly narrates a fundamental transformation by dismantling the bourgeois Gärtner fam-ily and reassembling a postbourgeois family based on memories of the war, while Goebbels's *Michael* transforms a bourgeois student into a postbourgeois worker, replacing fellow students with workers, romantic interests with a political leader, the university with the mine. Insofar as these texts, in the normative transformations they depict, sketch a very detailed discourse about youth and a central role for the young, they foreshadow the postwar period's specific deployment of youth. These narratives manifest central tropes of the discourse about youth that will recur in the postwar period, including the young as social other, the family as a transfer point for social norms, the young as border crossers, the dual character (affirming/threatening, passive/active) of the young, and the prevalence of youth crises in representing and redrawing society.

Whereas these texts depict the Nazi revolution with border-cross-ing youth liberated from the crisis-ridden house or university, I shall next attend to various postwar cultural representations that deliberately attempt to counteract such developments with a trajectory in almost the exact opposite direction. The postwar cultural representations confirm youth's usefulness at times of crisis by deploying youth's status as social outsider, but to entirely different ends. For example, Pabst's *Paracelsus* shows youth as border crossing to remap cinematic/social space from the bourgeois private to a nation inhabited by a youth collective. Much of postwar cultural representation problematized this remapping of the nation and its young, often by reworking the paternal and pedagogical relations these works bring to the nationalist foreground. This history and interpretation of youth and generational discourse demonstrate the ineluctable intertwinement of these various fundamental bourgeois themes too often ignored: of the family as bourgeois private sphere, the school as site of social reproduction, and youth as the social other making both of these conceivable as well as unstable. In the postwar period, all of these would become emphatic sites for authors, intellectuals, and filmmakers to reconstruct Germany and to achieve the coming to terms with the past that was required for it.

2

The *Jugendproblem* (Youth Problem)

Youth and Reeducation in the Early Postwar Public Sphere

On 22 January 1946 Pastor Martin Niemöller, a former inmate of Sachsenhausen and Dachau, gave a guest sermon in the Neustädter church in Erlangen, entitled harmlessly, perhaps deceptively so, "Lecture without a Topic" ("Vortrag ohne Thema"). In retrospect, the title seems either modest or misleading because Niemöller used his time in front of the students to deliver what was considered one of the most important postwar addresses on the question of German guilt (which was known at the time and thereafter simply as the *die Schuldfrage* [the guilt question]). In his encyclopedic cultural history of the period, for instance, Hermann Glaser called Niemöller's lecture a "moral and cultural climax in the efforts of the anti-fascist circles to undergo a mourning period and to bring about an inner change in people."[1] At the time, however, there was a different reason the address became famous besides Niemöller's controversial calls for acknowledging the guilt of all Germans—to include, contentiously, an open admission of guilt to the victims of Germany between 1933 and 1945. In the early postwar period, it was in regard to Niemöller's audience—students—that the sermon was passionately described, discussed, and debated.

Newspaper reports underscored how virulently those students rejected Niemöller's sermon and the strategy he proposed for confronting postwar German guilt. According to the press, as Niemöller argued that all Germans must acknowledge their guilt, he was interrupted multiple times by angry protests from the students; he was able to continue his address only because hosting officials appealed to the sanctity of the venue. When the *Neue Zeitung* published the sermon, it was careful to demark the passages that occasioned the student interruptions.[2] During and after the sermon, students allegedly arose and left the room, provocatively shuffling their feet and slamming the doors. Newspapers reported later that an anti-Niemöller pamphlet espousing Nazi beliefs was found pinned to the bulletin board of the university—though the newspapers were (most likely due to preemptive self-censoring) elusive about the details of its contents, U.S. intelligence reported that it labeled Niemöller a "tool of the Allies." Indeed, Niemöller's argument, like that of the famous *Stuttgarter Erklärung*, that all Germans must acknowledge their guilt—an argument eliding juridical and moral guilt that others were careful to distinguish—did seem very close to the Allies' insistence on broadly defined (if not entirely collective) guilt.

Notwithstanding the sermon's controversial negotiation of the labyrinthine questions of German guilt, the focus of the ubiquitous press reports revealingly remained on the behavior of the students. One report in the *Mittelbayerische Zeitung* segued quickly from a report about the address and its "Schuldbekenntnis" (admission of guilt) to a lengthy castigation of the students.[3] It berated the students for violating one of the basic tenets of democracy (the article recited piously), the "right to be heard." After upbraiding the students for failing Germany's nascent democracy and thereby Germany's future, the report made the obvious connection to Germany's problematic past: the students' protest and rejection of Niemöller was not a surprise, given how many ex-Nazi officers had infiltrated the ranks of the "Studierenden." Other articles, likewise circumventing the murky waters of Niemöller's sermon for the clarity of more sensationalist material, made the same connection to Germany's students and "the German young" (*die deutsche Jugend*) in general. A report entitled "Militaristische Studentenschaft" in the *Frankenpost,* more specific than that in the *Mittelbayerische,* criticized the militarism of the students, "at least 50 percent" of whom, but "more likely 90 percent," were war veterans.[4]

The shocked and concerned response was not limited to Bavaria: the *Frankfurter Rundschau* published a letter to Niemöller from the director of the Educational and Cultural Department of the Jewish community in Marburg that linked the "events in Erlangen" to Marburg, where Niemöller was also scheduled to speak but had to cancel due to the "nonconducive atmosphere" of the student audience awaiting him. The author of the letter, Israel Blumenfeld, said Niemöller's reception among students was not so surprising given the young's unrepentant attitude and invited Niemöller, a "fellow sufferer" of the camps, as Blumenfeld put it, to speak instead to the local Jewish community.[5] Thus, in a remarkable rhetorical move, a Jewish survivor proclaimed unlikely solidarity with the evangelical pastor by casting them both as victims— first of the Nazis and, more recently, of the young. Six months later, a journalist returned to Erlangen and recounted the continuing Nazi attitudes of the students, confirmed by two or three sensationalist quotes.[6] The episode came to be known simply as the *Erlangen Vorfälle* (the events at Erlangen) and was cited even forty years later by cultural historians such as Glaser and Füssl as the revealing reception of this most important speech.[7]

The remarkable fallout from and afterlife of Niemöller's Erlangen sermon seems particularly surprising given a correction that appeared, in the *Süddeutsche Zeitung* among other newspapers, a few weeks later on 22 February 1946.[8] It turned out that rather than the two thousand students who were originally cited, there were probably only twelve hundred present at the sermon, only twenty of whom actively protested Niemöller. Other pieces from later that year also admitted that the events had been exaggerated.[9] Even Niemöller himself disputed the initial news reports, rejecting their vociferous emphasis on "Nazi" attitudes and persisting militarism among the students.[10] Why would this episode, then, draw such attention, evoke such hand-wringing, and enjoy such an afterlife? Because, I would like to argue, it invokes a revealing and repeated discursive displacement, exculpatorily shifting the sermon's engagement with central challenges of postwar Germany—guilt for the war and genocide, Nazism, militarism—to focus instead on one social group—the young.

The reaction to Niemöller's sermon was so pronounced because, in the first years after the war, discourse about youth played a central role in Germany's coming to terms with the past. As one of many such articles about youth put it: "With all the efforts to come to terms with the past, there is always the special challenge to give our young people a way to a better future."[11] In the early postwar period, discussions, debates, and dismay about the "younger generation" and "the German young" were ubiquitous: postwar culture fixated on those strains of Nazi culture that I described above, focusing on the Nazi "revolution" as a youth uprising. Even the constant references to "the German young" invoke, as I described above, a very specific discourse inherited from Nazi culture—which in turn, as I argued particularly with Joseph Goebbels's *Michael* and Heinrich Zerkaulen's *Youth of Langemarck,* relied on longer-term discourses about youth. Postwar culture fixated not only on the role of youth in the Nazi revolution but also on the specific tropes I extracted from Nazi culture, especially the young as other to bourgeois society, the family as the key transfer point for social norms, the young as border crossers, and the dual character (affirming/threatening, passive/active) of the young. Perhaps most important in this regard was the social centrality of the youth crisis: the crisis of Germany's young in the wake of the war became a cipher for representing a general crisis in German culture and society; more precisely, the youth crisis served repeatedly to divert attention from the ubiquitous ruins of German society. At a time when the behavior of Germans in the Holocaust, during the war, and in the occupation period signified major crises in national and personal identity, youth came prominently up on the discursive chopping block to consolidate and contain the wide range of such crises.

INTERNAL ENEMIES TRANSFORMED INTO DISCOURSE: RECONSIDERING REEDUCATION

The attention paid to Niemöller's sermon underscores how Germans were able to locate a new enemy after the Allies defeated them: the young. Newspapers' depiction of students raucously receiving Niemöller distracts not only from the sermon's focus on German guilt in general but also from another trope of the time—Allied reeducation. The central discourse about youth in the postwar period related to reeducation, one of the most important tropes in the postwar cultural public sphere in general. Although their studies laudably turn scholarly attention toward the function of youth within adult society and culture, Poiger, Maase, and Fehrenbach, for instance, generally downplay or even overlook the ubiquity and depth of the discussion of German reeducation. As a number of studies observe, reeducation became the general term for the Allies' goal of democratization, a synecdoche for the occupation in general, so it is impossible to analyze the role of youth in the 1940s and 1950s in Germany without attending adequately to the widespread and wide-ranging debates about how the Allies and the Germans themselves were to reeducate Germany's complicit citizenry.[12] On the other hand, recent studies of the postwar public sphere have largely neglected the substantive content of reeducation and the subsequent controversy surrounding it, even if they, like Jeffrey Olick's analysis, acknowledge its centrality for the Allies.[13] And finally, even in the late 1980s and 1990s, studies that explicitly reconsidered the importance of reeducation—those, for instance, of Tent, Füssl, and Rupieper—tend to focus on the unfolding of the Allies' policies rather than the importance of reeducation and the debates about it for the wider public sphere and for German culture and identity after the war. For instance, these studies did not connect the Allies' policy of reeducation to the German debate about youth and generation.

If discourse about youth and education had long been crucial to bourgeois society as well as to the Nazis' imagined postbourgeois "revolution," then the postwar period would attempt emphatically to reinscribe such bourgeois discourse at precisely this intersection of youth and education. Reeducation became, for the occupiers, a cipher for their ambitious attempts to remake a country deeply compromised by the Nazis and largely destroyed by Allied bombs; it was, for the Germans, also a crucial front, perhaps the last front, on which they could stake a German defense of the German nation. In fact, this reinscription of bourgeois discourse about youth and education became a key means by which German society and culture reconstituted itself when its buildings lay in utter ruins. Youth and education thus became crucial building blocks in postwar German national identity, which had to reconstitute itself on the ruins of tainted cultural categories. In fact, coming to terms with the past via the discourse about youth and education simultaneously helped select and emphasize elements of German culture around which national identity could be constituted in the future.

In an important recent essay, W. G. Sebald criticized postwar German authors for their silence about the air war and therewith about the past in general.[14] Although offering an important starting point, his essay almost entirely ignores the impact of the occupation on postwar German authors and intellectuals; he fails to examine the literal curtailments of the censors as well as the internalized controls of the occupier. As I suggested in my introduction, his essay is the latest in a long series of studies of Germans' silence about, and repression of, the past. Against this particular repression hypothesis, I argue that much of the representation and mastering of the past was displaced—as in the coverage of the Niemöller episode—to discussions of youth, reeducation, and the generational reinscription of German culture. For example, echoing the mechanism I underscored in the Niemöller episode, one politician at the time deliberately shifted attention from the destruction wrought by the air war to the problem of the young (*Jugendproblem*): "What does the detritus of our cities matter next to the rubble of the hope and faith of our misguided youth!"[15] His statement seems an almost direct response to Sebald's argument about silence in the face of the air war: it is not so much silence as it is, as I shall argue throughout this study, displacement and distraction. Almost precisely the same rhetorical move marks other treatments of what the author-editor of *Deutsche Rundschau*, in his title, declared "our most urgent task" (*unsere vordringlichste Aufgabe*): "[For the young], the fall of the Third Reich meant more than the collapse of a world. Both culturally and spiritually, they stand in the midst of a wide field of rubble that matches that in our cities."[16] Foucault and Donzelot write of a massive transformation into discourse of certain sociohistorical themes—of new anxieties, including especially youth—in the eighteenth and nineteenth centuries, and there seems to be a deliberate discursive resurrection of such noise about youth in the early postwar context, a noise to deliberately drown out other discussions of Germany's problematic past.[17] In this period, I would argue, there was a massive transformation of trauma into discourse about youth, which served as a kind of discursive safe haven for a country so compromised by the Nazis and so curtailed by the Allies.

Even a brief look at some of the main issues of German reeducation—which will provide valuable background for the rest of this study—confirms what Foucault and Donzelot have argued: as I suggest above with the Nazi "revolution," discourse about youth always already pertains to "adult" subjects, society, and nation—in fact, it reveals the underpinnings of this multifaceted adult constellation. The early postwar period, a period of limited reform and widespread retrenchment, makes clear how discourse about youth continues to serve as a dense transfer point for ideology, that is, for the disciplining and regulative mechanisms of society; discourse about youth renders visible ideological approaches not only to the young but to "adult" subjects as well as their collective forms. In the postwar period, the emphasis on youth and education overlapped to bring to the fore anxiety about the stability of the patriarchal family, the security of society, and the continuation of culture—all refracted through the tropes I traced in culture under the Nazis. These mechanisms and themes of the discourse about youth and reeducation marked both the public sphere debates about youth and reeducation and the period's most important novel, Thomas Mann's *Doktor Faustus*, which together provide indispensable background for the rest of my study.

REEDUCATION AND THE CENTRALITY OF DISCOURSE ABOUT YOUTH IN THE EARLY POSTWAR PUBLIC SPHERE

Both occupiers and occupied deployed discourses about youth in confronting assorted postwar challenges, be they the debilitating despair of individuals or the ubiquitous ruins of society and the nation. To provide some additional context for this study, which will examine a series of "high" and "low" cultural texts from this time, I would like to offer a brief overview of some of the key issues relating to youth and reeducation. In a manner recalling Nandy's and Stoler's studies of colonial debates about childhood, the debate about reeducation and the young became a symbolic code for both the Allies and the Germans to come to terms with the occupation, for occupiers and occupied to symbolically negotiate the occupation's deeply disputed terms.[18] Although I shall not focus on a comprehensive review of the details of the Allies' reeducational policy—something admirably accomplished elsewhere[19]—I will highlight how some of the policy details did emerge in the public debates, debates that confirm reeducation as a discourse of cultural and political negotiation between occupiers and occupied.

The Allies considered reeducation one of the primary tasks of the occupation, for they regarded it as the key aspect of denazifying and eventually democratizing Germany. One U.S. educational mission that returned home after the summer of 1946 reported: "the re-education of the German people is an undertaking of the greatest magnitude . . . at once the hardest and most important task facing the Military Government in Germany today."[20] The American "Zook" report, which I will examine in more detail below, was likewise clear about the centrality of reeducation and especially school reform for the wider effort of the democratization of Germany: it declared schools the "primary agency for democratization."[21] Indeed, as a number of scholars have confirmed, if democratization was the overarching goal, then reeducation was the key element for that goal, at least until 1949.[22] Various historians attest to the centrality of school reform in other zones, especially the Soviet and the French.[23] This emphasis on reeducation and schools locates discourse about youth at the center of the postwar public sphere—formal reports and casual remarks both invariably foreground generational discourse when discussing reeducation. For instance, Saul Padover, a psychologist accompanying the U.S. forces as they drove deeply into Germany, wrote in his widely circulated report that "Germans in their late teens and early twenties are the real problem. In this age group there are genuine Nazis. Some of them give the impression of being beyond hope or redemption."[24] In a manner reminiscent of Nandy and his telescoping of the lifecycle onto different peoples, Padover generationally maps the young onto the problem of political persuasion and thereby implies an older, less Nazi group. While Nazism had, arguably, had an unusual correlation to young people during its rise to power in the 1920s, by the early 1940s and its most nefarious years, its leaders and membership were decidedly middle aged.[25] And irrespective of the membership's demonstrable biological age, it is far from clear, as I observed in the previous chapter, whether age is useful in analyzing and understanding Nazi fanaticism. Nonetheless, the distinction between young, convinced, fanatical Nazism and older, wiser, less compromised Nazism would be made over and over again by the Allies and the Germans alike.

Discourse about youth pervaded not only the Allies' postwar public sphere pronouncements but also the Germans'. In what seems an exact echo of the Allies' high estimation of reeducation, one editor declared: "Anyone who is seriously engaged with the German people should be clear that today our most difficult problem—whose solution is our mission—is the question of the German young."[26] As this passage indicates, the German discussions about youth and education tended to focus not directly on Allied reeducation—which censorship would have made difficult to strenuously criticize—but on this *Frage der deutschen Jugend* (question of the German young) and das Jugendproblem, both of which resonated, I suggest above, with discourses inherited from culture between 1933 and 1945. This shift from reeducation to youth lodged, as I shall trace below, both implicit and explicit criticism of the Allies. In light of these youth questions and problems, German newspapers consistently emphasized the importance of "regaining" Germany's young, thereby deploying discourse about youth to reconstruct subjects, society, and nation, disciplining and regulating in the manner emphasized above. For instance, one article in the *Badener Tagblatt* characterized the Nazi time as an era of the "incitement" of the young, when young people were won over by false promises and turned against their parents. The accusation articulates the duality of youth alterity sketched above: on the one hand, the young were deceived by the Nazis and warrant protection from their elders; on the other hand, the young, due to this deception, now threaten their own parents. There is, the article asserts, hope because the family is once again the healthy "seed" of the entire *Volk* (people and nation).[27] In this declaration, too, the article's strategy is consistent with the alterity of discourse about youth described above: the young become the means by which Germany will progress out of the Nazi era and into the present. The article reinscribes the familial discourse as the kernel of a new, better collective—it constitutes the core of the family unit that is set to reestablish the nation. The trajectory counteracts that of, for instance, *Youth of Langemarck,* in which the family was deliberately opened up to outside mandates and norms. In its attempts to overcome the past and reconstruct the nation, the article governs through the family, in Donzelot's memorable phrase, instrumentalizing discourse about youth for its postwar agenda.

Articles like those in the *Badener Tagblatt* appeared in many newspapers in postwar Germany.[28] Another ubiquitous postwar phenomenon was published letter exchanges "between the generations" (that is, between one younger and one older person) that underscore the importance of generational confrontations when other types of conflict were forbidden or contained by the Allies.[29] These letter exchanges addressed the alleged widespread desperation of the misled Nazi youth and offered normative replies from their generational superiors. For example, a regular columnist for the *Rheinischer Merkur* asked for help for the disillusioned young: "The problem of the young person has repeatedly preoccupied me these past few weeks. It is, indeed, our problem. We all need to confront it."[30] The column, published around Easter 1946, evoked a flood of responses, often angry, that the paper published over the next few months.[31] On 10 May 1946, to illustrate the severity of the youth "crisis," the paper published a summary of letters that young people had sent in, most of which lamented that they were victims of recurring deceptions: first by Hitler and then by the postwar occupiers, who were not adequately supporting the young. The editor of the paper replied to the youthful despair with a crisp disciplining: everyone is in the same position and all must lend a hand.[32] Such an epistolary staging of generational conflict illustrates how the youth crisis affixes itself to one of the central challenges of the postwar period: the disillusioned despair and skepticism about reconstruction.[33] This kind of despair and skepticism was surely not the sole purview of the young, but by mapping it onto the young—by making the crisis of despair a paradigmatically youth crisis—the newspapers managed the problem through discipline and regulation.

A similar epistolary exchange in *Deutsche Rundschau*, "Solace Letter to a Young Father" ("Trostbrief an einen jungen Vater"), achieves almost precisely the same effect: an old teacher responds with a supportive letter to a former pupil who has become a "young father" but who now despairs about postwar conditions for child rearing.[34] The teacher's words of pedantic encouragement place his former pupil back in the metaphorical classroom to be disciplined: he orders the young father not to lose hope and then segues into a veiled critique of the Allies' (putative) collective-guilt policy, even if this policy was, as Norbert Frei has argued, a myth testifying to postwar Germans' "inventiveness."[35] Perhaps even more indicative of this tendency to manage adults through the young—a governing through the reassembling family—is a 1946 essay in *Frankfurter Hefte* entitled "Not the Young, the Adults!" which lays out three conditions needed to come to terms with the ubiquitous "[c]oncerns about the young." All three pertain to adult behavior and suggest how adults can help the young by stabilizing the political and economic situation, by being good role models, and by listening more carefully. These would be, the unusually pedantic article underscores, the prerequisites for a true "Umerziehung" (reeducation)—as with the "Trostbrief an einen jungen Vater," the encouraging of the young allows a veiled critique of Allied policies.[36] Telescoping generational discourse into this crisis of faith in the bourgeois constellation thus lends itself to a careful management of young and adult psychological crises as well as specific opposition to the Allies' reeducational positions.

This potential for a youth crisis to displace other issues of the occupation is confirmed by another ubiquitous trope in this context—youth crime. There was undoubtedly a rise in youth crime at the time, though it might well have been one small part of an overall crime wave marking the social chaos of the early postwar period. But particularly indicative are the rhetorical moves associated with displacing the general social crisis onto youth crime, moves that also afforded further opportunity to criticize Allied policies. In one strange episode concerning youth crimes, rumors in the summer of 1946 spread in the media that Soviet soldiers were kidnapping hundreds of German children to indoctrinate them in Marxist-Leninist doctrine. It turned out that around eighty were arrested for simple theft.[37] An article in the *Süddeutsche Zeitung* also cites the well-known rise in youth crime but then offers a number of biographies of young criminals as sympathetic case studies. The first two describe two different orphaned boys who fled a home and a camp, respectively, and eventually made their way, through picaresque adventures, hundreds of miles to Bavaria. In both cases, the biographies are remarkable for their stress on the unbelievable mobility and resilience of the young: the article builds sympathy by emphasizing how often the boys had been interned, transferred, and then allowed to escape. Both accounts end with the Bavarian legal authorities taking the boys into custody, but by that time the guilt of the boys has been mitigated by sympathy for their suffering. These first two case studies displace the wider social crisis onto youth crime and then diminish guilt for it with sympathetic tales of tragic orphaning and youthful resourcefulness. The article offers implicit criticism of Allied reeducation as well by suggesting that neither the home nor the camp could hold the boys effectively. The last two case studies mentioned in the article, of girls, are more explicit in criticizing the Allies: the first girl, who had worked for the Wehrmacht news service, is discovered to have a sexually transmitted disease, an implication clarified in the final case, in which a seventeen-year-old girl is kidnapped and raped "nearly every day for a week" by "mehreren Negersoldaten" (several Negro soldiers).[38] The article moves from the social crisis to a specifically youth crisis that highlights youth's traditional border-crossing abilities and dramatically concludes with an explicit, even racist indictment—not of the young but of the occupational soldiers.

THE "NEGATIVE" AND "POSITIVE" PHASES OF REEDUCATION: DENAZIFICATION AND RESTRUCTURING OF GERMAN SCHOOLS

The above overview of Allied and German attitudes toward the young confirms the centrality of the discourse about youth for both occupier and occupied, but I also want to offer background on some of the specific policies relating to reeducation before returning to the public sphere consequences of these policies: these policies and subsequent debates about reeducation demonstrate how important education and especially a pedagogic, that is, teacherly subjectivity would become for postwar German identity. The initial phase of reeducation, usually understood as 1945 and 1946, focused on what was called in Allied circles "negative" educational reform, that is, removing Nazi teachers and

69

materials from the classroom. One of the greatest challenges facing the Allies was the denazification of teachers and educational administrators, a notoriously coordinated corps during the Third Reich. The Soviets were the most radical about changing teaching personnel; by 1949 they had replaced two-thirds of the teachers in their zone.[39] They had even begun a large-scale effort to educate and prepare "new teachers," a program that, rhetorically at least, attempted to swell the ranks of workers and farmers among pedagogues.[40] The other Allies' denazification reflected generally how committed they were to reeducation, determined not only by inclination but also by the financial wherewithal of the particular power. While the British and the French dismissed many fewer than the Soviets, the American denazification of teachers was also notoriously strict, resulting in the dismissal of over half of the teachers in its zone.[41] For all the Allies, the denazification of teachers resulted in severe teacher shortages, which, due to war casualties and prisoners, were already a significant problem.

Denazification of personnel and materials was only a first, "negative" step of reeducation; the Allied forces, especially U.S. and Soviet officials, also anticipated a positive contribution to German education.[42] Because U.S. officials in particular viewed reeducation as the key to democratization, they took an extremely interventionist approach to German education. A long and heated debate about the positive content of educational reforms ensued among U.S. officials and between these officials and Germans. I shall offer an overview of some of the key issues—and their considerable public sphere consequences—as they emerged in what became known as the American "Zook" report, by all accounts the watershed for the American approach to positive educational reform.[43] The report was greeted warmly even by the Soviet authorities because it suggested structural reforms very close to their own.[44] Moreover, its provisions were adopted by all the Allied powers in their joint "Directive 54" in June 1947.[45]

In the summer of 1946, after the early emergencies of physical plant and materials had receded, U.S. forces formed a ten-person committee to submit a substantive report on the future direction of educational reforms. The report became both the foundation for U.S. reeducational efforts in Germany and the basis for a heated controversy, particularly in Bavaria. In this double impact, it anticipates some of the most important and contentious issues of the reeducation program. The report begins with a lengthy evaluation of the current state of youth. In

70

a manner similar to that outlined above, the report deploys another youth crisis in order to warrant its own interventions. Its characterization of youth proves to be typically contradictory: it claims that German youth are confused by the loss of authority and the persisting material emergencies since 1945, invoking an ideology of protection, assistance, and supervision for the young; on the other hand, the report argues that the young were won over by the Nazi regime's aggressive educational policy and therefore were still adverse to forming new, more democratic bonds.[46] This duality approximates the contradictions of discourse about youth, and here, as elsewhere, this contradictory representation then becomes the justification for aggressive intervention in German society, where the young serve as a dense transfer point for power and control.

With its own representation of the current condition of the young, the report justified its most radical reform: a fundamental restructuring of German schools. The crisis of the young, the report claimed, was symptomatic of the most undemocratic trait of the Germans, their tendency toward authoritarianism: the young's dedication to Nazi authority figures resulted at once in their confusion at the loss of authority as well as their loyalty to the authority.[47] The very structure of German schools, the report argued, led directly to this tendency, to the unquestioned feelings of superiority and inferiority necessary for it to function. As in pre-1933 Germany, after the fourth year of *Grundschule* (so at about age ten), pupils were "tracked": about 10 percent of them went on to a high school that might lead them to a university career (*Gymnasium, Oberschule,* or *Aufbauschule*), while the rest went to the *Volkschule* for another four years before learning a trade. Even at the college-preparatory higher schools (*Gymnasien*), an 80 percent attrition rate meant that only 2 percent of the overall school population went on to university study. Moreover, because these higher schools charged tuition and for textbooks, they were generally filled with pupils from middle- and upper-class families.

In another telling segue from young to the nation, the report claimed that this tracking structure led to the authoritarian tendency of the entire society: "This system cultivates attitudes of superiority in one small group and inferiority in the majority members of German society, making possible the submission and lack of self-determination upon which authoritarian leadership has thrived."[48] Therefore, the report argued, the various tracks of the German system should be brought together in one comprehensive secondary school that all pupils would attend. As in the U.S. model, all pupils would attend elementary school for six years, then proceed to a secondary school for another six, where both tuition and textbooks would be free. Such a structure would lead, officials hoped, to a common education and, eventually, a common culture for all pupils that would become the basis for a healthy democracy.

This proposal was by the far the report's most important and, as we shall see, most controversial. Along similar "democratizing" lines, the report also recommended raising all teacher training to the university level, free textbooks for all, a gradual closing of confessional schools, and a core curriculum for all pupils with an emphasis on social sciences and civics. But it was the structural change to Germany's schools that evoked the most vehement response: even various U.S. groups found it too ambitious, and a debate raged within the ranks of the military government about its legitimacy.[49] Despite the Allied acknowledgment of its goals, the report's aims were unevenly realized on the ground: Soviet officials liked the plan because it approximated their own *Einheitsschulen* (comprehensive schools), but British and French authorities, thinking it too radical, never attempted to implement it. I shall offer a short overview of the fate of the proposal in Bavaria, the largest and probably most conservative province, as the Bavarian debate reflects both the fate of reeducation in general and the importance of discourse about youth in public discussion about reeducation and German society in general. It demonstrates how youth and education afforded postwar Germans one last front on which to fight the Allies and on which to stake their identities as Bavarians and as Germans.

BAVARIANS RESPONDING TO REEDUCATION

The specifics of this Directive 54, which adopted the Zook proposals for the four zones, were ultimately pursued only by U.S. authorities: British officials were already relinquishing more and more control to German authorities; the French were more interested in pursuing curricular rather than structural changes; and the Soviets had already passed their own laws in this direction.[50] In the U.S. zone, more than in the other zones, there was a public debate about reeducation, which increasingly became a synecdochal site for other issues of the occupation. U.S. officials regarded Bavaria as the most important and complex of its zones,[51] and the educational struggle there demonstrates not only the challenge to reeducation in the Western Allies' zones but also the manner in which discourse about youth played a central role in the symbolic negotiations between occupier and occupied, particularly in the debate about German sovereignty, in reconstituting traditional social formations like the middle-class family and in affirming conventional German culture.[52]

After the publication of the Zook report in the fall of 1946, pressure grew on the U.S.–zone German governments to adopt its policies. The Bavarian government took particular issue with the report's suggestion that the structure of schools had made Germans susceptible to Nazism. For example, Bavarian officials reminded the United States, the German Gymnasium was admired worldwide as a remarkable institution that offered a particularly rigorous education. Such defenses of the Gymnasium were not limited to Bavaria and demonstrate how important education was to German identity in this period.[53] In Bavaria, however, this pride in the structure of German schools and the Gymnasium in particular veered into open hostility against U.S. plans after a conservative, Alois Hundhammer, was named the Bavarian minister of education in December 1946. Hundhammer had worked for the conservative Bavarian Peasants' Party during the Weimar Republic, but his conservatism and his pro–Catholic Church leanings did not endear him to the Nazis. He had subsequently kept a low profile, as a manager of a shoe shop, during the Nazi regime. In the postwar period, his devout Catholicism led him to resist U.S. efforts to abolish confessional schools and to restructure existing German schools. His conservatism became an issue not only for U.S. officials but also for Social Democratic and Free Democratic politicians in Bavaria who criticized him for his Catholic and "upper Bavarian" biases.[54] The trajectory of the struggle between Hundhammer and reform-minded U.S. officials demonstrates how each side deployed different discourses about youth for its own political project and how discourse about youth was instrumentalized to firm up boundaries of the (re)emerging German nation.

As head of the U.S. military government in Germany, Lucius Clay ordered Hundhammer to submit a long-term plan for the restructuring of schools by 1 July 1947. U.S. officials demanded the reforms suggested by the Zook report, including the comprehensive high school, social studies and civics, universal school attendance until age fifteen, and the dismantling of the extensive confessional school structure. Hundhammer, however, saw education as an area in which the occupying powers had no jurisdiction: he claimed that, by "natural and international law," the Germans should have sovereignty over their young and the schools they attended.[55] So, in response to U.S. demands,

Hundhammer submitted an educational plan that adopted none of the U.S. proposals; when he was asked to revise his plan in accordance with the U.S. reform effort, he responded by submitting a bill to the Bavarian parliament that reinstituted corporal punishment, a flagrant political swipe at the United States.

The gap between Hundhammer's bill and the U.S. stance reflects not only differing views of German sovereignty but also different discourses about youth, competing discourses that resulted in contrasting approaches to the discipline and regulation of both the young and their adult supervisors. The divergent discourses of youth recall the differences between the conservative *Bewahranstalten* and liberal *Kindergaerten* in the nineteenth century, as they have been described by Ann Taylor Allen: the former took an authoritarian, child-as-threat approach to the young, while the latter treated the young as proto-Enlightenment subjects, as inherently good or at least neutral and in need of a fostering, protective rearing.[56] Even some Allied documents problematize the Allies' optimistically "tabula rasa" approach to the child.[57] Similarly confirming these discursive differences, the Zook report includes a section on the German family, in which it forcefully asserts that the conjugal and parent-child roles of the family inclined Germans toward nationalism and Nazism. The report called the traditional paternal role "Prussian" in its authoritarianism and criticized the family's confining of women to "Kueche, Kirche, Kinder" (kitchen, church, children) as "antidemocratic sterilization."[58] Its discourse about youth echoes the Kindergaerten and their liberal tendencies, in which the innately good child was ruined by a problematic familial context. In this context, Hundhammer's reinstituting of corporal punishment was clearly an intentional challenge to the U.S. authorities and their liberal discourse about youth and the German family. In a contrary appeal to the sanctity of the family, Hundhammer even cited a referendum that polled "Bavarian parents" about the appropriateness of corporal punishment, which, according to the government, two-thirds of parents supported.[59] For him and his Catholic backers, children needed to be strictly disciplined by their generational elders, not liberated from authoritarian influences. Of course, the rhetoric in which he cloaked this assertion suggested that Bavarian parents were exercising their autonomy, as he was, against the occupying powers.

The other discourse with which reeducation resonated strongly in Bavaria was the issue of confessional schools and its intersection with

German sovereignty. The role of the various churches in postwar Germany has been widely noted as well as their role in reeducation in particular.[60] Conservatives held Christianity to be crucial to the reconstruction of Germany, and the suggestion that confessional schools be phased out was almost as offensive to the Bavarian government as the fundamental restructuring of schools. U.S. officials, however, were concerned about the overarching political impact of religious figures, who, it was feared, would impede democratization by funneling believers to conservative, Christian Democratic parties.[61] Within this refigured context as well, debates about youth become a central part of the symbolic negotiation between occupier and occupied: it stands in for a central contention between the two parties about religion and German sovereignty. Hundhammer, U.S. officials ascertained, consistently mobilized church leaders (including not only Catholic but also evangelical leaders) against them by deliberately misinterpreting Allied directives.[62] For instance, Hundhammer claimed that U.S. officials' demand for free tuition at all schools—a cornerstone of their democratization of school—would affect confessional schools in the extreme, something U.S. officials denied. Ultimately, Hundhammer was able to convince the cardinal's office to support him in claiming education as an area of unchallenged German sovereignty.[63] In fact, in the end, these religious tensions eventually doomed the U.S. reeducational program in Bavaria, for it became clear that even though Hundhammer did not enjoy enormous popular support, he did have the backing of the Catholic Church in his assertion of German sovereignty in reeducation, reaffirming the role of religion in both the occupation in general and reeducation in particular.

Though he was able to garner the support of the church, Hundhammer had to endure the derisive attacks of many newspapers for his outspoken resistance to reform. Perhaps because they had been unable to criticize government officials during the Third Reich, they delighted in mocking government ministers, particularly one perceived to be provincial and atavistically Catholic. Hundhammer's adamant Christianizing of school reform was criticized by other Germans in the public sphere discussions of education, such that youth became a key site at which to debate Christian influence in the reconstruction of Germany.[64] One article accused Hundhammer of approving a textbook with a militaristic poem about Friedrich the Great and thereby contributing to the Nazi Fredericus Rex cult; another offered a photo of an eight-year-old schoolboy missing half of his hair and laying the blame on Hundhammer's corporal punishment initiative. Even some well-known Catholics criticized Hundhammer's heavy-handed approach. In an article from the *Donau-Kurier* on 21 February 1947, one Catholic educator, Dr. Leo Wiesmantal, lamented: "Nothing at the moment is more dangerous than a reaction in the field of cultural life, which . . . leads the people again toward the same chasm. . . . This, however, has happened in Bavaria."[65] In October of that year Hundhammer used a lengthy radio address to defend himself and his educational proposals: he accused the press of willful distortion of the facts of the school debate and observed that "it is astounding how much space newspapers have available" for these educational matters, a protest confirming their increasing symbolic centrality for postwar Germany.[66] In another radio broadcast in January 1948, Hundhammer reiterated that the occupying powers should not have such power and defended his resistance to the reforms.[67] In counteracting Hundhammer's resistance to the U.S. reform proposals, Education and Religious Affairs (E&RA) officials also took to the airwaves. Certainly, the debate about education—a debate reflecting discourse about the young, the struggle over conservative versus liberal social policy, and about the sovereignty of the nation itself—pervaded and helped shape the postwar public sphere.

Hundhammer continued to resist U.S. educational reforms throughout the rest of 1948 and by 1949, more and more power was handed over to the Germans. The United States increasingly lost the resolve and resources necessary to effect the kind of fundamental change set out in the Zook report. Hundhammer's assertions of German sovereignty in this area were realized: historians have tended to regard the U.S. reeducational efforts generally as a failure, as least in terms of realizing their initial ambitions; in a concluding assessment of them, one prominent history says not only did initiatives fail, they hardly got started.[68] While reeducation may have failed to restructure German schools, the debates about it did serve to negotiate and ground postwar subjectivity, society, and nation. As Foucault, Donzelot, Nandy, Stoler, Mosse, and Allen all suggest, these debates about the young were not limited to discourse about youth; in fact, the young and their "crises" always already pertain to the management of "adult" behavior, to mechanisms of power and regimes of control like the family, gender roles, religion, and the sovereignty of the nation. These various discourses were to become the pillars of reconstruction, and the debate about reeducation and the "problem" of "the German young" provided the very foundation for these pillars. In these debates, competing discourses about youth yielded different stances on family, sovereignty, religion, and the nation; contradictory depictions of youth, youth "crisis," and surveillance were deployed on different sides of the debate.

Rejuvenating to Breakthrough: Postbourgeois Community in Mann's *Doktor Faustus*

Many of these tropes relating to youth and reeducation reappear in the most discussed novel of the early postwar period, Thomas Mann's *Doktor Faustus*, to which I now turn to complete my overview of the early postwar public sphere.[69] As an important part of that public sphere, *Doktor Faustus* confirms the centrality of the discourse about youth and education in the postwar culture on a couple of counts: first, *Doktor Faustus* deploys youth as other to bourgeois society and education to structure its most famous and controversial facet, its political allegory for the rise of Nazism (also known as the *Zeitroman* aspect of the novel). The text appropriates the longer-term cultural currents of "the German youth" that literature under the Nazis also manifested and then underscores how these currents were central to Nazism and its "revolution." More precisely, *Doktor Faustus* absorbs and revisits the narratives of transformation I analyzed above—Nazi revolution as youth revolution—and ends up reflecting on them. This centrality of discourse about youth and education is confirmed in a second aspect of the phenomenon that Mann's *Doktor Faustus* became: the heated reception of the novel confirms and contributes to the debate about youth and reeducation in the postwar public sphere.

Doktor Faustus is a very different type of work than newspaper articles, intellectual tracts, or films, but it also deploys discourse about youth as a core thematic. In *Doktor Faustus,* as in many of the articles examined above, youth crisis becomes a privileged means with which to represent the crises of Germany's recent history and current situation. The novel depicts a kind of rolling, roiling youth crisis that, like Foucault's "danger that prowls," manifests but also displaces assorted crises of bourgeois subjectivities and society from the turn of the century through World War II. I include *Doktor Faustus* in the present overview of discourse about youth in the early postwar period because this novel, as the most discussed literary work of the period, makes a startling connection between turn-of-the-century youth movements and Nazism, a notion that became dominant in the postwar period. This linkage serves as a key aspect of both the *Künstlerroman* and Zeitroman in *Faustus*, but has been, as far as I have been able to ascertain, neglected by the immense secondary literature on the novel.

In developing this connection, the novel unfolds at its core not only a social crisis of youth; it also unfolds, in its famous analysis of Nazism and modern artwork, the role of youth in constituting community, another crucial thematic for the postwar period. Typically for the postwar period in general, *Doktor Faustus* absorbed those themes I traced in the Nazi imaginary above: in its representation of youth and pedagogy, *Doktor Faustus* postulates how youth, if "liberated" from the bourgeois constellation, can serve to found a new community, though that new community is in danger of succumbing to extremes of nationalism and Nazism.[70] In a revealing way, this focus on youth as the core of the new community obscures conventional political analysis—it becomes a central aspect of Mann's nonpolitical, or at least not very political, analysis of Germany's slide into Nazism. Youth serves Mann, as it does in so many such interpretations in the early postwar context, as a central category in an "analysis" of National Socialism. This link between discourse about youth—particularly Wilhelmine and Weimar discourses about youth—and Nazism proves exemplary for the early postwar period in general. This tendency to analyze history and politics via generation was a key mechanism for writers, intellectuals, and filmmakers throughout the occupational period, during which youth moved to the center stage of postwar understanding of "the catastrophe."

A Portrait of Nazi Germany as a Young Man: Youth and Nation in *Doktor Faustus*

In his much-cited 1945 lecture "Germany and the Germans," Mann deploys two key themes, Innerlichkeit (inwardness) and the breakthrough to the world, to link Adrian Leverkühn's art to Germany's national trajectory. Even though Leverkühn himself—typical for Innerlichkeit—is apolitical, his Innerlichkeit allegorizes Germany's aloofness from the rest of the world; his artistic breakthrough parallels Germany's aggressive attempts to reach the rest of the world. For Mann, discourse about youth and generational difference comes to play a central role in Germany's national Innerlichkeit and in its belligerent attempts to break through. In addition to exemplifying the break from artistic and social norms, generational difference acts as a kind of schema or intellectual shorthand for understanding the break from bourgeois political norms. In a way

78

that resonates with the Nazi texts above, the novel represents Germany's political breakthrough by way of generational difference, especially as it is depicted through the continuing narrative duel between Leverkühn, the subject of the novel, and Zeitblom, the first-person narrator. Leverkühn and Zeitblom represent two different perspectives on just about everything, manifesting the two sides of Germany's peculiarities (as Mann comprehends them). Within this narrative duality and duel structuring the novel, I would emphasize that one of the greatest differences concerns discourse about youth and education. Although little is made of it in scholarly studies, Zeitblom writes consistently of his career as a teacher at a Gymnasium and the humanistic ideals that underpin such a position.[71] Zeitblom's career and Leverkühn's rejection of all students underscore the centrality of youth and education in the novel. This undertreated aspect of the novel also points to an important trope in the postwar public sphere and throughout this context in general, namely, the centrality of the teacherly or pedagogical subject position vis-à-vis youth. This subject position becomes the most important normative mode of (adult) subjectivity for this context and for its requisite coming to terms with the past.

An extended and emphatic debate about German youth occurs in *Faustus* as it does in Zerkaulen's *Youth of Langemarck*. In these debates between Zeitblom and Leverkühn, adolescence and turn-of-the-century youth movements become conspicuous categories for comprehending the German nation and its attempts at antibourgeois breakthrough. Generational relations come to frame questions of the nation and its political fate. In two crucial chapters of *Faustus*, adolescents advocate and galvanize nationalism and, ultimately, war. Chapter 14 links the German nation and nationalism to the Protestant Winfried youth group; chapter 30 associates adolescents and adolescence generally with World War I. The text not only understands and codes the war as adolescent but, during the mobilization of Germany, Leverkühn and Zeitblom debate adulthood's relation to youth: they debate the war as a matter of generational collapse of the adult into the adolescent.[72]

Chapter 14 recounts an overnight outing Leverkühn and Zeitblom make with the Winfried youth group, a group, I argue, that invokes the turn-of-the-century Wandervogel group and other, later members of the "independent youth movements." The specifics of the Winfried group resonate not only with the general tenor of these turn-of-the-century movements but also with their deliberately antibourgeois character and their implicit critique of modernity. As the name *Wandervogel* implies, this most famous of the fin de siècle youth groups was founded to offer urban adolescents the opportunity to *wandern* (hike) outside the corrupting confines of the city. As Mitterauer writes, the Wandervogel aimed to escape the "urban milieu and create one's own counter-world elsewhere."[73] In this escape from the modern metropolis, the Wandervogel deliberately mimicked archaic social forms in its activities and hierarchy: its members imagined themselves returning to the wandering scholar tradition of the premodern and early modern world.[74] The group self-consciously defined itself as an alternative to adult society and the kind of compromised youth groups that adults offered. This self-conscious status of youth as other assured that the group, despite its modest size, remained the pacesetter among such youth groups. Like many reform groups at the time, it defined itself against those institutions that differentiated and structured modern society, especially against the school and the family.[75] As "wandering" groups, the movement physically enacted this ideological agenda: the youth fled the confines of schools and family. These *Gemeinschaften* (communities) were to gather only in the absence of teachers and parents—or at least away from the private house and all that it symbolized—despite the constant participation of adults. Their overall style—loose, chaotic, antiauthoritarian (within a hierarchy, of course)—reflected their self-conscious negation of the disciplining controls of the modern school, family, and society in general. Such an antimodern self-understanding was not unique in the fin de siècle period, when the social, cultural, and economic tensions of Wilhelmine Germany galvanized a huge array of such reform movements.[76] But the Wandervogel group was the highest-profile movement to deploy discourse about youth to cultivate its status as other to the prevailing social mores, an alterity critiquing the modern institutions and disciplines (educational, familial, health) that had been largely framed by discourse about youth.

In undertaking its own wandering trip, Mann's Winfried group recalls the Wandervogel in more than their alliterative affinity. Zeitblom writes that only adolescents could have made such an excursion.[77] What type of uniquely adolescent excursion? An excursion of a "temporary style of life" (*intermistische Lebensform*) in which they fled the city and floated around the countryside—exchanging fine feather beds for "sleeping straw" (*Schlafstroh*) (124; 156)—a "simplification" of life that offers a flight from the artificial. In the border-crossing capacity I high-

80

lighted in *Youth of Langemarck* and *Paracelsus,* youth becomes, for Wandervogel and Winfried alike, a liminal space away from the private house that mediates between the bourgeois family and a different, new kind of community. Although the sanctuary of this liminal space was only temporary, the Winfried had deliberately abandoned the "customary and 'natural' sphere of bourgeois comfort" (124; 156). Perhaps even more relevant is the notion that although they are young, the Winfried members are also "prebourgeois" (124; 157), that is, predating the bourgeois and therefore representing, like the Wandervogel's wandering scholars, an archaic mode of life. Echoing the spatial constellation of *Youth of Langemarck,* the choice of the barn for their accommodations invokes an earlier era of medieval youths wandering outside of the restraints of the modern private home.[78] Ironically, modern forms of leisure afforded the young the free time to indulge such archaic temptations, but this contradictory character—both modern and archaic—fits the contradictory alterity of the young as well as their critique of modernity.[79]

The independent youth movement that Mann references here was nationalized by World War I and then again increasingly in the late 1920s and early 1930s, but its pre–World War I links to the German nation were largely resisted as attempts to pull it into adult politics.[80] *Doktor Faustus,* however, anachronistically links fin de siècle discourse about youth to the German nation and its past and future upheavals. Adolescence not only saturates the excursionary endeavor itself: similarly echoing the Wandervogel as well as *Youth of Langemarck,* discourse about youth and generational difference becomes an explicit topic of debate. The de facto leader of the group—revealingly named Deutschlin—argues that youth is a special category, as a specific *Lebensform* (form or mode of life) that is, according to Deutschlin, particularly German:

> The concept of youth is a prerogative and privilege of our nation, of us Germans—others hardly know it. Youth as its own self-conception is as good as unknown to them; they are amazed at the demeanor of German youth, so emphatically itself and endorsed by those of more advanced years—are even amazed at its own garb, its disregard for bourgeois dress. Well, let them. German youth represents, as youth, the spirit of the people, the German spirit itself, which is young and full of the future—immature, if you like, but what does

that mean! German deeds have always been done out of a certain immaturity, and it is not for nothing that we are the people of the Reformation. That, too, was a work of immaturity after all. . . . Luther was immature enough, a man of the people, of the German people enough, to bring about the new, the purified faith. And where would the world be, if maturity were the final word! In our immaturity we shall yet present it with a renewal, many a revolution. (126; 160)

One can see immediately to what degree *Faustus* has absorbed the longer-term themes of the discourse about youth and to what degree this discourse frames the novel's analysis of the German nation and nationalism. At its most literal level, the passage associates the young with spirit, with the future, with powerful immaturity. All these will soon count among the most basic themes of Leverkühn's antibourgeois musical breakthrough and the community that hosts it. Moreover, Deutschlin, the little German, argues that adolescents form the core of what is German, a stark articulation of the emphatic link between youth and nation that I highlighted in Joseph Goebbels's *Michael* and in Zerkaulen's *Youth of Langemarck*. In *Doktor Faustus* as well, this complicated discourse about youth becomes Germany's most defining aspect, explicating, for instance, the Reformation, which Mann himself took as the most indicative as well as dubious German contribution to world history.[81] Mann asserts in his lecture "Germany and the Germans" that Luther's immature revolution typifies Germany's national fate. This conviction resonates with Mann's entire loving, ambivalent, resistant relationship to Germany—and generational difference rests here at its very core.

Is the association of youth with Germany mere adolescent prattle or does it constitute, as I am arguing, one of the foundational aspects of the Zeitroman's allegory of the German nation? The test of whether the link between discourse about youth and nation counts as lasting, even fundamental, would be to investigate it later in the novel. Taking place around ten years and 250 pages later than the Winfried chapter (14), chapter 30 offers the novel's single most elaborate depiction of an overtly national event—the outbreak of World War I in August 1914. While Zeitblom frequently asserts a parallel between Germany's slide into Nazism and Leverkühn's life at the beginnings or ends of chapters—in sentences and paragraphs scattered over the course of the long novel—chapter 30 offers *Faustus*'s most sustained representation of a national political event. It also offers the only lengthy account of Germany's belligerent tendencies in the most discussed literary work of the early postwar period. Like the Winfried chapter, the novel's most detailed chapter on "Was ist deutsch?" (chapter 30) stages a debate about German politics at the surface of the text.

When read in concert with the Winfried chapter, this debate on the war confirms the centrality of discourse about youth for Mann's "political" allegory and analysis. In analyzing the cultural and political atmosphere of 1913 and 1914, Trommler describes how (adult) social and political elites produced a specific concept of youth that could be instrumentalized to found the "nation as fateful community" (*als Schicksalgemeinschaft*).[82] This sense of war (and its "fateful community") as a product of a specific discourse about youth and age structures Mann's most sustained representation of war in *Doktor Faustus*. In chapter 30, the outbreak of World War I is associated not only with youth and its peculiar enthusiasms but with the adolescent overthrow of the adult, particularly the rupture of the specifically pedagogical relation that Zeitblom's inglorious career emphasizes. The teacher learns from and indulges his students, thereby collapsing the generational difference that undergirds the bourgeois constellation. As I suggest above, teacher and education were central metaphors for the postwar period and here help structure the most important novel of the time.

After a brief paragraph announcing the date—August 1914—Zeitblom begins the chapter's second, long paragraph with the abrupt and dramatic announcement "War had broken out" (316; 402). The paragraph pretends to a kind of summary of the atmosphere in Munich and Freising (where Zeitblom is teaching at the time): he writes at length of the "rapture of beginning anew" (*Aufbruchsfreude*) and the "heroic festival" (*heroische Festivtäten*) that greeted the war. As he introduces the reader to the war and asserts his first and last impression, Zeitblom turns to his own pupils at Freising: "In Freising, it meant that my senior students' faces were flushed, their eyes beaming. Youth's lust for action and adventure was united with the expedient fun of emergency final exams and hasty graduation. They stormed the recruiting stations" (316; 403). The passage identifies both actual adolescence and those traits that are particularly adolescent—"lust for action and adventure"—with those who stormed the recruiting offices at the beginning of the

83

war. Moreover, the war assumes a kind of alterity to school. Schools symbolize for Zeitblom and the postwar context generally the kind of pedagogy that tends to social integration. In the next paragraph, Zeitblom generalizes the enthusiasm of his students such that it represents Germany's participation in the war. His assertion confirms this sense of the war as an antipedagogical "event." The war collapses the adult world into the nationalized youth: "Such a 'mobilization' for war, however stony its face and grim its call to universal duty, always feels something like the start of a wild holiday—like casting away real duties, playing hooky [*Hinter-die-Schule-Laufen*], allowing instincts that are not gladly bridled to the bolt—has too much of all that for a staid man like myself to feel fully at ease" (317; 403). As Germany mobilizes for war, it, as might be expected, abrogates normal duties and indulges unbridled drives. But this mobilization, exactly as it was in *Youth of Langemarck*, is also a kind of truancy, a youthful escape from school and the adult social integration it requires. Mann, looking back from the horror of World War II and its aftermath, highlights this (literally and metaphorically) juvenile aspect of World War I.

After introducing and depicting the war as a *Hinter-die-Schule-Laufen* of the young and even their teachers, Zeitblom visits Leverkühn at his rural home in Pfeiffering to bid farewell before departing for the front. Their crucial exchange in Pfeiffering, which includes some of the most famous lines in the novel, becomes a debate about their experiences with the Winfried group, and it underscores, more than any other passage, the parallels between the juvenile breakthroughs of the German nation and the antibourgeois modernist artist. In discussing the pivotal term *Durchbruch* (breakthrough), Zeitblom begs Leverkühn to allow for some participation in the breakthrough of the German nation. Echoing exactly what Deutschlin said sixteen chapters earlier, Zeitblom claims what is transpiring in this belligerent "breakthrough to world power" (*Durchbruch zur Weltmacht*) is primarily psychological, emphatically not "political": it is actually a "breaking out into the world—from its loneliness . . . a thirst for unification" (324; 412–13). Zeitblom's wartime breakthrough, he claims, ought to remedy Germany's national loneliness and Innerlichkeit, which persist throughout the novel in the person and music of Leverkühn.

Although Zeitblom could be writing of the youthful breakthrough of either Leverkühn or Germany, Leverkühn's response, at least at first, does not admit this affinity. Instead, he unmasks the adolescent under-

84

pinnings (literally and metaphorically) of Zeitblom's argument for participating in the war. In response to Zeitblom's politically obfuscating pronouncements about the psychology of the breakthrough, Leverkühn interrupts him with a sudden, sarcastic benediction: "May God bless your *studia*" (234; 413). He begs Zeitblom's pardon for the interruption, but, he says, he slipped back into the idiom of the student because Zeitblom's oration reminded him of the "sleeping straw" (*Schlafstroh*) dispute of their Winfried days. Leverkühn says that as he listens to Zeitblom expound upon the psychology of the war, he hears the old Winfried boys: "*Sleeping straw*—by which I mean, once a student, always a student. The academic life keeps one young and frisky" (324; 413). Throughout the passage, Leverkühn's repeated use of the term *Schlafstroh* underscores the antibourgeois inclination of the youth group insofar as it contrasts the idyllic male order of these trips to the bourgeois family, private sphere, and the modern metropolis. Leverkühn's comments point to how the schoolteacher, by remaining close to youth, risks collapsing into the nationalized juvenile frenzy. The strict generational difference supported by the pedagogical does not seem so stable after all, particularly in light of Zeitblom's frequently feeble resistance.

Zeitblom, in fact, deliberately embraces the adolescence that Leverkühn is problematizing. Zeitblom prefers youth despite his efforts to remain a teacher: "I was only a student, and you may well be right to say that I have remained one. But so much the better, then, if academic life keeps one young, which means: preserves a loyalty to the mind, to free thought, to higher interpretation of the crude event" (324; 413). Zeitblom openly admits that perhaps he wants to remain young—a "reproduction" of youth—because of what the youth discourse might deliver, a continued loyalty to "Geist" and a higher interpretation of worldly events. Incredibly—or perhaps not, in light of Aschenbach in *Death in Venice*, Cornelius in "Disorder and Early Sorrow," and the "Mario" narrator—the paradigmatically *Bildungsbürger* schoolmaster, the personification of the pedagogical relation so important for the postwar context, has now embraced and indulged impetuous youth. A nationalized young occasions this startling collapse of generational difference and hierarchy, a collapse galvanized by (according to *Doktor Faustus*) World War I.

After Leverkühn argues, citing Kleist, that one ought to seek only an aesthetic, not a national breakthrough, Zeitblom delivers the last monologue of the chapter, in which he pleads that one not say "only about aesthetics." Zeitblom begs Leverkühn to generalize the break-through to include the political as well (325; 415). The German nation and its national character, whose very definition is threatened by "the poison of loneliness, by eccentricity, provincial standoffishness, neurotic involution, unspoken Satanism" (326; 415) especially require the break-through, Zeitblom argues. Besides cutting all too close to Leverkühn's personal project via his demonic pact, Zeitblom has insisted that Lev-erkühn generalize his aesthetic project into a national one. Leverkühn never does this—he, like Nietzsche, is a German antinationalist—but therein Zeitblom's complicit function in the allegory of Germany be-comes clearer than ever. It is Zeitblom, after all, who is writing simulta-neously about the two time levels, autobiographical present and bio-graphical past, that together create the Zeitroman out of the Künstlerroman. More revealing of this suspect complicity, it is Zeitblom who is espousing a rejuvenated breakthrough to the war. And it is ex-actly as a juvenile breakthrough to war that many of the postwar period would see the descent to National Socialism and World War II.

Conclusion: *Doktor Faustus's* Youth Discourse in Context

> Germany is free, insofar as one can call a devastated nation deprived of its sovereignty free, and it may be nothing now stands in the way of my returning to my educational career. . . . But ah, I fear that over this savage decade a generation has grown up that will no more understand my language than I shall its; I fear the youth of my country have become too alien to me for me to be their teacher—and more: Ger-many itself, this unhappy land, is alien to me. (529; 675)

So end Zeitblom's last metanarrational ruminations, coming at the end of the first section of the "Nachschrift" (Postscript) and a few pages from the conclusion of the novel. In his last words on his own act of writing, his thoughts reflect much of what I have argued above: he writes that the young have become so foreign to him now that he does not know if he can teach them. Both youth and the German nation have left him behind. The segue from youth to nation is seamless and reveal-ing: the young's relationship to their teacher—the pedagogical relation that should integrate both adolescents and adults into society—reflects the distance of Nazi Germany from the good, if contradictory, *Bürger.*

Teaching and a specifically pedagogical relationship serve here at the end of this mammoth novel—and for the context generally—as the central metaphor for a stable society and productive integration in that society. Though the passage underscores the importance of discourse about youth as nation throughout the novel, these concluding concerns of Zeitblom also anticipate an important and indicative controversy in the notorious reception of Mann and *Doktor Faustus* in the early postwar period. In allegorizing the nation once again, Zeitblom suggests that the young are too distant now to understand his speech and for him to return to teaching. As in the newspapers' intergenerational letter exchanges or in the Niemöller episode, the relation of an older German— here an exile—to the young stands in generally for the nation's postwar struggles. This proved a favorite question to pose about Mann himself in his postwar reception: whether the author who had personified Germany around the world during the Nazi regime could still speak to and for the much discussed and debated "German young," and whether his embodiment of the better Germany as *Kulturnation* still had validity.

In the early postwar public sphere, Mann himself had become, as is well described in the scholarship, a figure of dispute and debate, a lightning rod for the wide range of views and vehemence relating to exiles, "inner emigration," and Germany's cultural figures in general.[83] Though Mann was widely attacked for assuming American citizenship and refusing to move back to Germany after the war, even at the height of the invective, the importance of his work for German literature was rarely questioned. When *Doktor Faustus* appeared in 1947, his work was suddenly no longer so unassailable. Many critics, particularly many critics from the increasingly important quasi-Christian perspective, dedicated large parts of their reviews to describing how they found the novel unsuitable for the "German young" in this dire moment—a seemingly tangential but, I am arguing, revealing criticism given the context. Werner Milch criticized the novel for being "merely" a historical novel without any meaning or relevance for Germany's young.[84] In his analysis of music in the novel, Jürgen Petersen was more forgiving, admitting music as an appropriate symbol for Germany and its decline. But he also criticized the novel's foregrounding of music because it brought with it the temptations of "death in intoxication" and "an ecstatically sought-after nirvana," temptations that were precisely those that the "young generation in Germany," which "wants life and not death," could do without.[85] Another critic, Ulrich Sonnemann, even ended his analysis with a lengthy and impassioned appeal to "Germany's young":

> Germany is laid out on the ground and no one knows what
> will happen to it . . . if it does come back, if there is another
> word to be spoken by it, if the day will dawn . . . when Eu-
> rope no longer staggers from one nightmare to the next, but
> rather wakes up: if all this happens, then a surviving genera-
> tion—that part of the young that is not frozen and dying of
> hunger—will treat the supreme rottenness that we know as
> the work of Thomas Mann with indifference, the kind of in-
> difference that is more fatal than protest. German *Geist*
> [spirit/culture]—what does it have to do with this work?[86]

Such reviews confirm how discourse about youth functioned fundamentally in coming to terms with the past. These critics deploy an ideology
of pedagogical protection—of protecting the young from the "demonic
novel"—to attack a work of art investigating the uncomfortable decline
of Germany, the complicity of the entire nation and its culture in
Nazism. Whatever one thinks of *Doktor Faustus*'s portrayal, the argument that it is not suitable for young people seems tendentious, but
nonetheless recurred in other reviews. Besides reinforcing the centrality
of a teacherly subject position, the novel and its reception confirm the
centrality of discourse about youth and its obfuscating, depoliticizing
potential for handling burdens of the past. It is as if Mann's postwar critics were telling him that Zeitblom's anxieties were justified, that the author himself was indeed too alienated from "the youth of my country"
to have anything to say to them. For both Mann and these critics, youth
becomes not only a vague metaphor but a specific grounding for German culture in general. For both, discourse about youth and generational difference had become a privileged means for writers, intellectuals, and filmmakers to understand the recent past and to imagine
postwar reconstruction.

3

Germany's Youthful "Catastrophe"

Guilt and Modernity in the Early Postwar Period

In a society that was broken literally and metaphorically by the Nazis and their terror state, then by the ravages of war and bombing, and finally by land invasion and occupation, there reigned a great many shortages: shortages of food and coal and housing, to mention but a few. Something of which there seemed to be little shortage, however, was advice, "expert" opinion in the form of intellectual tracts, lectures, and radio addresses on Germany's past, present, and future condition. This veritable flood of publications runs counter to the widespread assumption that postwar Germans repressed and remained silent about the past. Given the highly publicized scarcity of materials like paper as well as the labor to print and distribute written work, the commitment to such an enormous flood of publications to address Germany's coming to terms with the past—from pamphlets to books to multivolume series[1]—seems all the more astounding. Certainly, some kind of remembering was filling the public sphere, but just what kind and to what ends are the questions this study aims to address.

In part because Germans had traditionally looked to their intellectual elite for political and social as well as cultural guidance, in part because this elite had been forced to write, if not for the *Schublade* (drawer), then with Nazi vigilance in mind, the German intelligentsia was happy to oblige this social demand with quick, voluminous advice.

89

Moreover, the lack of a sovereign German state and concerns about the articulation of a German point of view during the occupation led many to look to the intellectuals for guidance. A huge range and number of publications, penned by authors, professors, and other social-cultural elites, offered analyses of the past, diagnoses of the nation's present condition, and prognoses for its future.[2] The irony was that all this activity on the part of established—and usually establishment—intellectuals assured that there would indeed be no Stunde Null, assured that many preexisting and conservative ideas, values, and agendas would be reinstated and restored. In his study of postwar politics and political debates, *Divided Memory*, for instance, Jeffrey Herf has underscored "multiple restorations" in German politics, society, and culture from before the end of war, akin to the kind of conservative continuities that Diethelm Prowe has also emphasized.[3] Among these multiple restorations and conservative continuities, I argue, was postwar culture's attention to the Nazi discourses about youth I sketched above.

In this and the next chapter, I would like to supplement existing cultural histories of these various texts by taking a different tack, one that has been largely neglected by studies of the early postwar period.[4] I have been suggesting that in certain historical moments, usually at times of social transformation and hegemonic instability, youth crises, as kinds of affective panics, become symbolically central aspects of the public sphere: youth crises become an indispensable way to come to terms with challenges facing any society—in this case and in this period, the considerable burdens of the past. Especially in those times when doubts about—or threats to—an established social system emerge, youth crises are deployed in order to redraw old boundaries or explore new ones. Due not only to the recent past but also to the massive social, economic, and political upheaval, the postwar period counts as one of those times. There was a real youth crisis in the postwar period, but the emphatic manner in which the youth crisis was constructed in literature, film, and various texts by intellectuals ultimately outstretches its "real" nature and intersects the central challenge of the time, coming to terms with the past.

Authors deploy discourse about youth and generation quite subtly, and such subtlety necessitates close readings of texts. I would like to elaborate and highlight the mechanisms of generation and youth with a number of case studies that engage prominent authors and texts in a sustained fashion. Such an in-depth approach to authors' backgrounds and their postwar texts not only illuminates how discourse about youth came to play a central role in postwar writings but also connects youth to the important themes that intellectual and cultural histories of this period emphasize, including nation and crisis, catastrophe and guilt, rubble and reconstruction, fall and redemption, the masses and technology. Only by examining some of the details of these authors' backgrounds and the specifics of their textual strategies can one understand the centrality of discourse about youth for this thematic constellation.[5]

The categories of youth and youth crisis were deployed by various authors not only to negotiate the problems of the past but also to assert an agenda for the future. In this and the following chapter, I shall pair two intellectuals—one generally regarded as a "classical" liberal and one as a conservative—who were prominent in the postwar public sphere. In this chapter, I shall concentrate on how two high-profile intellectuals came to terms with one of the central challenges of the postwar period—how to explain the rise of Nazism—by employing discourse about youth and especially the youth crisis. For many intellectuals and authors, coming to terms with the past meant effectively explaining how Nazism could arise in Germany and, by implication, how it could then be overcome. Two of the most important German intellectual figures of the twentieth century, Friedrich Meinecke and Ernst Jünger, deploy discourse about youth in their etiologies of Nazism: both associate the young with Germany's deviant modernity, which eventually yields Germany's national fall to Nazism. Meinecke arranges the uneasy balance of his fundamental binaries by emphasizing the role of a youth crisis in the Nazi "catastrophe"; Jünger connects certain discourses about youth to the most important shift he observes in the Nazis, the radical transformation of combat and the chivalric values that should underpin it. Both authors incorporate youth and generation into their analyses of the recent past by mapping Germany's deviant modernity onto the young: like the colonizer's telescoping of age onto racial difference, these authors telescope youth onto the most problematic elements of German modernity in order to come to terms with the dubious trajectory produced by this modernity. In this way, in a manner similar to that traced by Bartov, Moeller, and Biess, these authors define new categories of perpetrators and victims: they portray the young as the most important agents in Germany's nefarious descent into Nazism while casting themselves (older, wiser adults) as the victims of Germany's deviant juvenile modernity. This displacement of recent history onto the young subsequently structures their understandings of guilt—another of the central aspects of postwar Vergangenheitsbewältigung—for the Nazi regime. Their particular understandings of Germany's juvenile guilt help them then deploy discourse about youth in reconstituting postwar communities, a guilt mechanism that pervades the cultural context of the early postwar period. In both cases, discourse about youth can help explain not only their approaches to the past but also some of the more peculiar aspects of their agendas for the future, including Meinecke's quasi-Christian *Goethegemeinde* (Goethe community or congregation) and Jünger's *The Peace,* an important political text inexplicably addressed to the young.

A Liberal *Wunschbild:* Nipping the Masses in Their Youthful Bud

One of the best-known and most influential German historians of the first half of the twentieth century, Friedrich Meinecke reemerged in the early postwar years as a key intellectual figure. His 1946 tract *The German Catastrophe* counts as probably the most significant of all those I am surveying, those concerned with the causes of and cures for National Socialism and its legacy. For indicative example, in his very thorough *Cultural History of the Federal Republic of Germany, 1945–1948,* Hermann Glaser permits the last pages of *The German Catastrophe* to take over his own text for about two pages, an unprecedented primary source intervention in his lengthy history. For Glaser, Meinecke becomes the liberal voice par excellence, his diagnoses and treatments of German fascism paradigmatic.[6] Wolfgang Wippermann takes the popularity and influence of the book as a given, as the starting point for a discussion of what rendered the book exceptional among the great number of similar contemporary texts.[7] Both Glaser and Wippermann point to the wide, even momentous reception the book enjoyed, occasionally ambivalent but always high profile.[8] Moreover, the *Catastrophe*'s considerable influence would persist well past the early postwar period: an important history of 1950s German culture continues to treat Meinecke and his emphasis on humanism as paradigmatic for postwar reactions to National Socialism and the recent past.[9]

Meinecke and *The German Catastrophe* have also provided some of the most enduring, sometimes derided images of the occupational period in the text's famous climactic "Goethegemeinden" (Goethe communities), which Meinecke describes as an "ideal" or *Wunschbild* (wishful fantasy) for the reconstruction of Germany. Wippermann cites it as the key example of Meinecke's well-meaning naiveté, and Pois openly mocks it as indicative of an archaic and inane political agenda, while Glaser quotes the entire passage pertaining to it:[10]

> To the Goethe communities [*Goethegemeinden*] would fall the task of conveying into the heart of the listeners through sound the most vital evidences of the great German spirit, always offering the noblest music and poetry together. One crisis—namely, the lack of books into which we all fell through the burning of so many libraries, bookstores, and publishing houses—supports this proposal. Who is still in complete possession of his favorite books, his complete Goethe, Schiller, and so forth? Many young people may in the future have their first access to the imperishable poems of Hölderlin, Mörike, C. F. Meyer, and Rilke at one of those regular music and poetry festal hours of the "Goethegemeinden," which we desire as a permanent institution everywhere among us—perhaps weekly at a late Sunday afternoon hour, and if at all possible in a church![11]

Like many scholars, Glaser, Wippermann, and Pois underscore the restoration of Geist, of "bildungsbürgerliche[r] Kultur" (traditional middle-class culture), as the core of the reconstructed nation. While they concentrate on the evocation of Goethe-based humanism, they do not highlight a central aspect of Meinecke's national agenda: Meinecke's turn, in the climax of his sketch for the Goethegemeinden, to Germany's young as the *Gemeinden*'s (and therefore Germany's) future. Meinecke's Gemeinden as national reconstruction are suddenly but revealingly mediated by discourse about youth.

The sudden presence of youth in Meinecke's "ideal," however, proves not so surprising if one reads Meinecke's etiology for National Socialism closely. In the extensive analyses of Meinecke's political-historical studies, critics often underscore his renunciation of a statist synthesis of *Macht* (power) and *Geist* (spirit)—the central categories of his political intellectual history—in the wake of World War I.[12] *The German Catastrophe* expands on this schism between power and spirit by narrating Germany's descent into Nazism as a renunciation of spirit for a pure pursuit of power. This idealized twain between power and spirit meets less and less in Meinecke's account: his post-1800 German history assumes an initially healthy balance that grows polarized, aggravating antagonistic binaries between power and spirit, social history and cultural history, occidental (*abendländisch*) developments and the *Sonderweg* of German modernity. With these collectivist binaries and the force that splits them—primarily the modern masses, which are the liberals' worst nightmare—Meinecke explains Germany's slide into National Socialism.

Within this now-familiar account, however, discourse about youth and generation comes to play a linchpin role in the deviant modernization that leads to this national degeneration. In fact, the youth crisis ends up mediating Meinecke's fundamental binaries: the young serve as that which threateningly exceeds, thereby divides, and eventually polarizes the incipient binaries. This subtle but fundamental status explains youth's memorable reappearance in Meinecke's final liberal, would-be national Gemeinden that try to roll back Germany's aberrant modernity. The national collapse pivots, to a remarkable degree, on a youth crisis and the disruption of healthy generational relations: the young exceed cultural and political borders, so the national reconstruction should commence with a disciplining reeducation to redraw and bolster these boundaries.

The German Catastrophe: Underlying Politics and Pervading Polarities

The German Catastrophe proves so resonant in postwar Germany—and so fertile for my own investigation—because it suggests an eclectic middle way that steers clear of left and right extremisms while simultaneously incorporating, often contradictorily, many of their points. Wippermann, for instance, sees the text falling between studies like Gustav Büscher's *Hat Hitler doch gesiegt?* (*Did Hitler Actually Win?*) (1947) that blame Hitler for Nazism and completely exonerate industrialists, and those like Walter Ulbricht's *Der faschistische deutsche Imperialismus* (*Fascist-German Imperialism*) (1946) that place the entire burden on the shoulders of the capitalist system.

Meinecke's middle way, in which he did cite industrialists and capitalist society as major contributing factors among many, is not really surprising in light of his long-term attempt to steer a conservative-liberal path between political extremes. Meinecke did start out as something of a conservative monarchist, a position to which his education (born in 1862, in Gymnasium and university through the late 1870s and

1880s) would have most likely predisposed him. But already, toward the end of the nineteenth century, he manifested markedly liberal leanings. For example, he showed sympathy for Friedrich Naumann's left-liberal National Social Association and argued for the inclusion of groups that Bismarck's conservative unification of Germany excluded. He remained a nationalist and statist through the first years of World War I; his 1907 *Weltbürgertum und Nationalstaat* (*Cosmopolitanism and National State*), following a Hegelian and Rankean tradition, argued that the state, tending to an ideal mixture of power and spirit, would ultimately provide the necessary spiritualization of society. In a manner reminiscent of Thomas Mann, World War I caused Meinecke to rethink his idealization of the state. As early as 1915 he was arguing for a negotiated peace ("status quo ante," that is, a nonannexationist peace) and by 1916 had started publicist work (of which *The German Catastrophe* would be a much later example), primarily arguing against Germany's aggressive submarine war. Distancing himself from most in his field, Meinecke became a committed *Vernunftsrepublikaner* (pragmatic republican), a member of the elite who understood the Weimar Republic as necessary if not preferable. Though his ambiguous work in Weimar in favor of a *temporäre Vertrauensdiktatur* (temporarily entrusted dictator) tends to contradict his claimed commitment to the republic,[13] he probably thought some consolidation of power in the person of the president was necessary to protect the republic, which he was always at pains to defend. There is, however, no questioning his opposition to the Nazis, who forced him to retire and stripped him of the editorship of Germany's most influential historical journal, *Historische Zeitschrift*. He spent the Nazi era writing more on questions of historiography and on purely cultural topics, distancing himself from the political intellectual histories for which he had become most famous.

In *The German Catastrophe* Meinecke returned to his earlier national intellectual histories of post-1800 Germany and recommitted to the liberal stance to which he had come in the wake of World War I. The book, written at the age of eighty-three and eighty-four, first in the village of Wässerndorf and then finished in Göttingen, was often treated as autobiographical, perhaps because he wrote much of it without the benefit of scholarly materials; for example, when he cites Burckhardt, he is quoting from memory. Perhaps due to this rather free, at points autobiographical form, Meinecke's culturally conservative inclinations persist in his fetishization of Goethean humanism and his nostalgic treatment of Christianity. But the book's basic tenets are certainly liberal—Hermand, for example, takes the book as a paradigmatic explication of Nazism's impact on the (right-)liberal tradition.[14]

In line with these liberal leanings, Meinecke narrates the rise of National Socialism in Germany as successive modern assaults on individuality, some generally occidental, some specifically German. Consistently balancing historical continuity with contingency, human universality with German particularity, he describes Germany's modern fall from the romanticized, idyllic heights of Goethean humanism, Christianity, and political liberalism down to the dark, antihumanist, anti-Christian, antiindividualistic depths of National Socialism. In a strong critique, Meinecke casts the modern masses as the central force in this disastrous development. If bourgeois Goethe—with his free individuality, focus on the human being, and duty toward community—inhabits a liberal paradise, the masses nibble at the forbidden fruit of politically promised collective happiness. According to Meinecke, the masses form the two waves, of nationalism and of socialism, that serve as the text's fundamental dialectic and ultimate crucible for the fall to National Socialism. Modernity's rapid population growth, the expanding role of the masses in politics, and the promise of collective satisfaction—trends Meinecke groups under "masses"—all wreak havoc with the great liberal tradition. In fact, Meinecke describes the masses' direct assault on his beloved Goethe: spreading through the masses like a wildfire (a very apropos natural catastrophe), Machiavelli and power politics replace Goethe and spirit as the (forbidden) apples of the masses' eye.[15]

Parallel to the abandonment of Goethean humanism are modern rationalization and technologization, which Meinecke vilifies in his famous "Homo Sapiens und Homo Faber" chapter. Arguing that humans embody a balance of rational and irrational forces, he asserts that modern life, its rationalization and technologization, threaten this balance— indeed, the synthesis of power and spirit that classical liberals (like himself) used to celebrate has its equilibrium utterly upset by modern life. Life has become too rational, too mechanical, irreparably injuring inner spirit. The damage is, however, both inner and outer: the utilitarianism that rules social life has severed old community bonds without providing meaningful new ones. Apparently most egregious for Meinecke, Goethean higher reason and piety before the individual has withered in favor of a rationality that promises but cannot deliver mass happiness.

The shift from homo sapiens to homo faber has brought the twilight of individualism, that it so to say, the end of his holy trinity of humanism, Christianity, and liberalism.

These trends—toward mass society as well as modern rationalization—have impacted not only Germany but also the "neighboring countries," which Meinecke saw sharing authoritarian trends. Many of Meinecke's harshest critics, for example, Pois,[16] miss the fact that he was balancing this generalized explanation with his own version of the Sonderweg, of specifically German developments that led to Germany's deviant reaction to these modern trends. Much as Meinecke balances cultural (*geistig*) with materialist historical analyses, likewise balancing the long continuity (Goethe's evaporating legacy) with the historical contingency (Hindenberg's growing inefficacy), he also balances general Western trends with Germany's peculiarities. In the most powerful example, the Western trend toward rationality fuses with specifically German Prussianism and its (concomitant) militarism and authoritarianism. Throughout *The German Catastrophe,* Meinecke blames the Nazis on Prussia, its obsessive attention to the army, and its subsequent militarization of the whole society. Upsetting the power-and-spirit balance as much as the modern masses, Prussianism yielded uniquely German configurations like Bismarck's militaristic unification of Germany and the pan-Germany movement, two of the direct predecessors to Hitler's expansionist, racist machinations.

Likewise, in another thematic often overlooked, Meinecke underscores the complicity of the German bourgeoisie in abandoning Goethe's humanism for National Socialism. Even if critics like Giess dramatically accuse Meinecke of being a "shaman for his class," Meinecke explicitly blames this very class, the bourgeoisie, for Germany's precipitous descent.[17] Like Prussianism, the compromising choices of the bourgeoisie play a determining role in Germany from very early on, early on in the history of the nation and in this text itself. Consistently choosing money over cultural or political capital, the bourgeoisie betrayed humanistic principles for a pernicious "national egoism." As with Prussianism, Meinecke cites not only these abstract trends but the specific manifestations of the problem, underscoring the bourgeoisie's participation in both the pan-Germany movement and the *Vaterland* (Fatherland) parties in the 1910s. By the time of Weimar, they were prepared to forfeit the constitution and state, thereby deciding decisively for power over spirit. And the bourgeoisie paid for forgetting their Goethe and embracing Hitler, Meinecke states, with the catastrophe of the war and occupation.

Meinecke's *German Catastrophe* as a Youthful Tale

In his story of a modern fall from humanism, Christianity, and liberalism to National Socialism, Meinecke thus focuses on factors generally Western (mass society, rationalization/technologization) as well as specifically German (Prussianism, Bismarck, pan-Germanism, World War I, the German bourgeoisie). *The German Catastrophe* shared many of these thematics with other texts, though its inclusion of so many rendered Meinecke's text particularly rich. *The German Catastrophe* constitutes a kind of balancing act, indicative of Meinecke's ambivalence toward the constellation that had produced him and his own work. Critics like Pois, Wippermann, and Hermand focus on the inherent divisions and gaps in such a balancing act: Pois points to Meinecke's divorcing of spirit from power; Wippermann underscores the distance between the excellent "Homo Faber" chapter and the naive Goethegemeinden; and Hermand focuses on Meinecke's writing of guilt, but subsequent inability to blame any Germans for the disaster.[18]

In order to augment these interpretations of Meinecke's canonical text, I would suggest that, along with the bourgeoisie, Germany's young become remarkably important figures in Meinecke's story of a national fall. Not only does a youth crisis play a significant role in this series of assaults on the individual, but the young also permit the very balancing Meinecke describes. For Meinecke, the young serve to mediate between those contradictory categories above as Germany oscillates between them and then degenerates. As modern society weakens, the young escape society's disciplines and becomes its excesses. They are a social threat, that which is excessive and perilous to his preferably balanced binaries, because they cause the crisis that destabilizes these binaries for Meinecke: the modern social crisis becomes in large part a youth crisis. Portraying the young as the cause of this social crisis allows the text to transform the social excess, when dutifully disciplined, into a social fundament. One of the highest-profile intellectuals in this period deploys discourse about youth to explicate the national catastrophe as modern youth crisis, casts the young as the guilty but innocent perpetrators, and asserts an agenda for reconstruction that begins with the disciplining and education of the young.

Following Pois, who singles out this section for particular criticism, and Wippermann, who sees it as one of the book's great strengths, I understand Meinecke's "Homo Sapiens und Homo Faber" chapter as one of the book's most important. The chapter describes how, due to rationalization and technologization, modern society injures the "inner soul" and polarizes power and spirit. But Meinecke describes this process not on a social level, as Weber or Adorno and Horkheimer had, but rather by offering a remarkably specific account of youth. In a manner similar to the sudden entrance of youth into his Goethegemeinden-ideal, this chapter focuses on education and youth, thus anticipating Meinecke's surprising and unconvincing Gemeinden. After briefly theorizing what rationalization and technologization can inflict on the inner soul abstractly, Meinecke turns to some concrete specifics. He says that one example of the "internal spiritual damage" caused by "external rationalization" should suffice because it is an "especially typical" case:

> It often happens nowadays, this observer said in the days before the Third Reich, that young technicians, engineers, and so forth, who have enjoyed an excellent university training as specialists, will completely devote themselves to their calling for ten or fifteen years and, without looking either to the right or the left, will try only to be first-rate specialists. But then, in their middle or late thirties, something they have never felt before awakens in them, something that was never really brought to their attention in their education—something that we could call a suppressed metaphysical need. Then they rashly seize upon any sort of idea and activity, anything that is fashionable at the moment and seems to them important for either the public good or the welfare of individuals—whether it be anti-alcoholism, agricultural reform, eugenics, or the occult sciences. The former first-rate specialist changes into a kind of prophet, into an enthusiast, perhaps even into a fanatic and monomaniac. Thus arises the type of man who wants to reform the world.
>
> Here one sees how a one-sided training of the intellect in technical work may lead to a violent reaction of the neglected irrational impulses of the soul, but not to a real harmony of critical self-discipline and inner creativeness—rather to a new

one-sidedness that clutches about wildly and intemperately.
(59; 36)

This single and especially typical case of modern rationalization Meinecke offers in this short but crucial chapter is thus remarkably generational. Discourse about youth and generation suddenly intervenes at the
crux of his national narrative: it underpins the themes of rationalization
and technologization as well as the distortion of the "inner spirit" (*in-
nerer Seele*) and the resulting imbalance. The young come to embody
modern society's excesses: society's overly rigorous and repressing education results in something "growing" inside the young until it bursts
out, intemperate and wild. The passage even deploys youth stereotypes
I described above—waywardness, an ability to float across borders to
any cause—to explicate the impact of such injury. Above all, it is this
specifically generational mechanism that causes the coming crisis of
modernity.

    Moreover, and perhaps more resonant, the passage suggests a gen-
erational rhetoric by which the young are sketched as the (contradictory) innocent perpetrators: while the young threaten stable constellations, their status as menace is no fault of their own. Although they serve
as important agents of these catastrophic modern trends, they are also
susceptible largely because of when they were born: the generational
model grafted onto history renders their susceptibility to maiming
modernity merely the bad luck of birth date. It is this tendency to blame
but then to exonerate the young that I term the youth-guilt mechanism.
Deploying discourse about youth and education in this manner affords
Meinecke not only a cornerstone for his thematic, it also permits him to
balance the various contradictions of his account, for example, explaining how the guilty agents are reeducable, how inner damage manifests
itself in outer politics, how the spiritual trends meet power politics:
youth can connect the poles that Pois, for instance, sees as so divorced.

    Meinecke writes of the *Bedürfnis* (need) of these young engineers,
technicians, and so on that modern society neglects and then has to
later, radically satisfy—it is a term that recalls the general masses of
which he has been warning throughout and whose "needs" he sees
modern society dangerously indulging. In fact, the young, who along
with the bourgeoisie and the workers become the only other major social group he discusses, stand in for the nihilistic modern mass upon
which Nazism preys. Although Meinecke will later describe how the

young played a specific role in Weimar's decline into the Third Reich—
a contingent historical factor—he also emphasizes the young's longer-
term predisposition to modern mass movements. Two decades before
World War I, Nietzsche embodied the contradiction between the golden
Goethean age and the growing influence of power politics in pan-Germanism, and it was the young who were particularly susceptible to this
unholy influence:

> In Nietzsche's realm of ideas, which now began to exert a
> powerful influence over all yearnings and restless spirits, there
> were gathered together almost all the noble and ignoble de-
> sires and self-longings which filled this period—a demonic
> phenomenon in the ambivalence of its character and influ-
> ence. It was predominantly harmful. Nietzsche's superman,
> destroying the old table of morality, guided like a mysteri-
> ously seductive beacon an unfortunately not small part of the
> German youth, guided it forward into a wholly dark future
> which must be fought. (42; 24)

"The German young," a category whose longer-term trajectory I examined above, stand in for the uncontrollable, restless, wild masses that are
no longer grounded in Goethean humanism. Their susceptibility to
Nietzsche and his "demonic" appearance foreshadow the coming disaster in an almost direct anticipation of Mann's association of Leverkühn's
Nietzschean breakthrough with the young.

The "Homo Sapiens und Homo Faber" chapter suggests a more
general Western development, but in the section following the "Homo
Faber" chapter, "Militarismus und Hitlerismus," Meinecke balances the
generally occidental trend with the specifically German. In this chapter he
describes modern Germany's dangerous fusion of rationalization and
technologization with Prussianism, militarism, and Hitlerism. Serving
once again as the pivot between the general Western trends sketched in
the "Homo Faber" chapter and specific German developments is discourse about youth. Though generation was part of a more general trajectory in European modernity, the vagaries of youth were, as described
in chapters 1 and 2 in my introductions to culture under the Nazis and
to the postwar public sphere, especially important in Germany. This discourse intervenes in Meinecke's sketch of Prussianism colliding with rationalization to produce Nazism—in fact, the young become the catalysts

101

of this explosive modern mixture. As with the Goethegemeinden passage or the "Homo Faber" chapter, Meinecke introduces youth to synthesize disparate discourses:

And did one not see that the democratically minded majority was now melting away more and more under the hot blast of the Hitler movement? We must now cast a glance at this.

An intoxication [*Rausch*] seized upon German youth at this time, both upon those who fought in the World War and upon those who had grown up under the debilitating effects of the Versailles peace. On the material side they craved employment, an income, and opportunities for advancement. In the field of ideas they craved something which gave play to feelings and phantasy—to ideals which were worth living for. The Weimar Republic, to be sure, was founded on a great ideal, for which a whole politically ripe nation ought to have lived and fought—the ideal of an established national community uniting both working class and bourgeoisie, the ideal that all groups formerly avowedly hostile to the state should be permeated by a sound national feeling, not exaggerated but embracing all human values. Combined with this ideal in the Weimar majority was the firm determination to throw off, or at least to loosen, one by one the fetters of the Versailles Treaty, by working patiently and slowly through steady though meager compromises with the victorious powers. It was at that time the only politically realistic method possible for gradually doing away with the restrictions. Every other method threatened sooner or later to lead to war, and every war to lead again, as happened later, to a catastrophe for Germany.

Such a program, however, involved too much reasonableness and resignation on the part of the craving youth of 1930. "You have offered us no ideals," they cried out against the Weimar supporters; "you cannot fully satisfy us"—and they meant it . . . in both the material and the ideological sense. There is a national impulse in all youth to form associations which stimulate impulses for speedy action wherever possible. So in the early thirties many young people worthy but wholly unripe politically, began to organize themselves as the Storm Troops (SA, Sturmabteilungen) of the Hitler movement. Hitler, one may say, came to power through a typical but dazzled and blinded youth movement. (70–71; 45)

The passage confirms first of all and most obviously the central role of the young—in Meinecke's analysis, as a meaningful social class for Germany's peculiar modernity. In a manner similar to his overdetermined move from the "typical case" for rationalization to generation and education, Meinecke shifts here from the majority (*Volksmehrheit*) to the young, who were presumably not really (since they could not have been demographically) the majority of the population. Moreover, their tendency to undifferentiated, histrionic demands on society links them to the story's swift and strong undercurrent, the masses. The young represent here the explosive excess of the formerly disciplinable modern masses. Therein they become central villains in his story of a national fall, a story now unfolding, in considerable part, as a modern youth crisis.

In other ways as well the passage deploys discourse about youth which, I argue, becomes so significant in the early postwar period: youth's predisposition to Rausch and aggression, which I examined in chapter 1, contrasts nicely to the coolheaded and idealistic syntheses achieved by calmer, older heads like himself. While he admits that the Weimar Republic, like so many of the young, was given to idealism, it was a healthy, more deliberate idealism—thus asserting a self-serving distinction between young enemies and older defenders of the republic. While some idealism is permissible, the young represent that part of idealism that is excessive, crisis causing, and eventually revolutionary. Such a contrast constructs youthful idealism as the other so as to define, and exonerate, more mature commitment to political ideals. His characterization of youth's role in Hitlerism displaces and obscures socioeconomic factors: the young were left unemployed and armed, but more important, they were also demanding something "fantastical," mythical. In this way, they serve as a social transfer point for modernity's processes but also, in this lightning-rod function, obscure the socioeconomic base of these processes. In their irrational frenzy (*Schwärmerei*), the youth defeat Meinecke's celebrated union of the bourgeoisie and the workers: they represent the pernicious excessive element in the masses that drags down the calmer heads of the defenders of the republic. The young demand—in another cliché from discourse about youth—a revolution,

although I have noted above in what attenuated form a youth "revolution" could and would transpire.

The long passage above makes clear that, contrary to some scholars' criticisms, Meinecke does manage to blame somebody for the disaster of Nazism: in no small part, he blames German youth. Of course,
Meinecke suggests a number of guilty parties, as I outlined above
(masses, Prussianism, German bourgeoisie, and so on), but in perhaps
the passage's, and one of the book's, most remarkable turns, Meinecke
mimics an essentialized youth subject talking to its generational superiors, a suddenly literary device resonating with the ubiquitously published "generational dialogues" I discussed in chapter 2. In the midst of
The German Catastrophe, however, it is a strong, even strange rhetorical
move that suggests a dialogue between discrete interlocutors, thereby
essentializing a putative difference between the Nazi-inclined guilty
young and the republic-defending old. The result of an emphatically described generational mechanism and subsequent youth crisis, this gener-
ation-essentializing conversation yields, as Meinecke dramatically declares, Hitler's rise to power. The Hitler-Jugend hardly played a decisive
role in the rise of Nazism, but Meinecke asserts that Hitler came to
power on the wings of a "youth movement" because the young have
served his particular narration of the past and, as we shall see, the future.

With this understanding of how youth underpins *The German Catastrophe*'s key themes (the masses, rationalization, technologization, Hitler)
as well as mediates the work's contradictory categories (continuity versus contingencies, European/Western versus German, Geist versus
Macht, spiritual versus material), I would like to return to Meinecke's
famous Goethegemeinden. Meinecke's deployment of discourse about
youth in the reconstruction of the nation should no longer be so surprising: generation, in large part, underpins his etiology of Nazism and
will certainly rest at the core of his national cure. The "Homo Faber"
chapter explains how modern rationalization dispelled Goethean humanism and liberally inclined Christianity by casting the young as the
protagonists in a tragic scenario; the Goethegemeinden counteract this
trend by regenerating the nation in churches, which "Gemeinden" obviously connotes and where Meinecke actually imagines these societies
convening on Sunday afternoons. These Gemeinden aim to restore Meinecke's fetishized synthesis of power and spirit: "Rather was it borne
along, as Burkhardt was not quite fully able to understand, by that great

idea of an inner union of spirit and power, by humanity and nationality. Great cultural values emerged for us from it" (159; 109). Not only will this restored unity blend power and spirit, it will also reconstruct the link between Goethean humanism and the German nation that Meinecke posited as a prelapsarian paradise before corrupt modern (juvenile-mass) society.

Meinecke's national agenda for a liberal reconstruction, a restoration of the individual, transpires on the postwar battlefield of the young. Meinecke senses that this kind of discipline and institutionalization, however, contradicts the sort of individual freedom he aims to restore. Given the widespread suspicion toward any kind of organization, Meinecke has to be careful about the type of institution he suggests. He aims, in accord with his liberal approach, to create institutions that will balance an organized cultural legacy with individual freedom:

> Doubts about the certain value of organization begin in connection with the upper schools and the examination system in Germany, where so much that is external comes into play and what is inward may be injured. In Goethe's day the external things retreated very much into the background, so the inward things could develop more freely. We cannot intimate that; we stand too much under the pressure of everything that the external has meanwhile created and organized around us. In order to keep our striving for inner development free from pressure of these organizations, we must ourselves, paradoxically enough, occasionally turn to organizing. (169; 116)

There were many who called for the teaching of classical literature as a panacea for the "catastrophe" and the postwar chaos, as well as some, like Karl Jaspers, who criticized the "cult" around Goethe, but of interest in Meinecke's work is how he deploys the young to negotiate binaries he has arranged conceptually and centrally.[19] The contradiction between private freedom, demanded by all sides, and cultural legacy is conveniently answered in the image of the Gemeinden. The young provide the means to negotiate this paradoxical task, the restoration and preservation of freedom in institutions. They play the convenient guinea pigs for a coercive cultural institution in the service of "liberalism." Since the youth crisis—as the unrepentant excess of modern society—

was the primary cause of the catastrophe, the great violator of liberalism, the young are the first candidates for its disciplining into freedom. If the young are to be the subjects of this coercive education, our reconstructive hero is to be a teacher. For a nation and a national culture preoccupied with its questionable activity and freedom, it is a solution I shall uncover and unfold in other contexts: come to terms with the past, rebuild bourgeois social and cultural constellations, on the contested grounds of youth.

Meinecke Reconstructs via Reeducation

I have argued that the young appear suddenly because Meinecke explains National Socialism as, in large and crucial part, a modern youth crisis. But the disciplining and reeducation of the young, subsequently the central postwar national project for Meinecke, grows clear not only over the long course of his 150-page narration of German history; it also rests in the historical contingency of the Allies' occupation. Like many German intellectuals in the late 1940s, Meinecke was responding to the presence and pressure of the Allies, a fact consistently overlooked by Sebald in his influential essay; also like many intellectuals, Meinecke took a stand on the Allies on a very particular issue, that of educating the nation's youth.[20]

Like many of the journalists I quoted in chapter 2, Meinecke uses the positive agenda for Germany's reconstruction around the young to criticize covertly the Allies' policy of reeducation: education becomes an arena to assert German sovereignty against the Allies, a sovereignty grounded in the realm of the young. Tellingly, in his Goethegemeinden, Meinecke suggests the transmission and reproduction of humanism via youths not in schools but in churches. That he is concerned with and targeting schools, that is, the Allies' reeducation project, becomes clear in the less carefully read portions of his agenda for renewal. Much earlier in the chapter he expresses sympathy for the Allies' project of a new "national education" (*Volkserziehung*) and certainly advocated some (unavoidable, in his opinion) work with the Allies, realized, for example, in his later prominent role in the 1949 establishment of the Free University of Berlin.[21] But at this point and in this famous account of his happy ideal substituting Goethe for a technical training of the young, he positions his Gemeinden squarely against the Allies' reeducational project: writing of Germany's own tradition of humanism and Christianity, he asks, "Is that not a rich comfort for us in our present tragic situation?

We do not need any radical re-schooling in order to function effectively again in the Occidental cultural community" (119; 173). Meinecke wants to regenerate the nation outside the school system to demonstrate and exercise the autonomy of Germany's humanistic tradition, the edenic spiritual heights from which Germany has fallen. The Gemeinden, as nonschool education for youth, become the substitute for a national culture formerly passed on through institutions like the Gymnasium, now controlled by the Allies.

ERNST JÜNGER AND HIS WORD TO THE YOUNG

Kirschhorst, June 16, 1945. The relationship between youth and age is not a temporal-linear, but rather a qualitative-periodic relationship. A few times in my life, I was older than I am today, especially around my thirtieth birthday.[22]

Probably no single German author has been associated more with Germany's culture of war than Ernst Jünger. As much scholarship on the topic observes, however, Jünger's relationship to war is complicated and ambiguous. His early postwar writings reflect precisely this ambiguity. Having written what has been called the most important piece of writing to come out of World War I, *In Storms of Steel* (1920)—which celebrates and aestheticizes combat as one of humanity's highest and most beautiful experiences—Jünger composed a pair of more ambiguous texts after World War II, his diaries, called *Strahlungen* (*Radiances/Radiations*) (1949) and a short tract, *The Peace* (1949), both of which offer an opaque portrait of the ambivalent warrior-aesthete.[23]

The above quote, taken from the "The Second Paris Diary" section of *Strahlungen*, finds Jünger at his Kirchhorst home at a crucial historical moment.[24] The time in which the above entry was penned constituted a watershed in the war and in all German history: it was the moment when it started to become clear that Germany might lose the war; when the bombing of major German cities (including Hamburg and Hannover, close to Jünger's childhood and later home) began in earnest; when word and then evidence of the Holocaust started to spread.

In the wake of all these epoch-making events, the passage—abstract, seemingly oblivious to the maelstrom of political events around him, and above all oriented toward himself—reflects the kind of detachment for which Jünger's conduct during World War II has come under harshest indictment, as Elliot Neaman has carefully traced in his *A Dubious Past: Ernst Jünger and the Politics of Literature after Nazism*. As soon as *Strahlungen* appeared, many of his contemporaries condemned the text as a cold-hearted and callous report on the war from the perspective of a dangerously dulled aesthete. In his review, for instance, Peter Mendelssohn argued that, with his coldness of heart (*Herzenskälte*), Jünger had been more fascinated by the awfulness of barbarity than engaged in upholding humanistic values in the face of it. Mendelssohn was so horrified that he turned his review, entitled "Counter-Strahlungen" ["Gegenstrahlungen"], into a kind of antitext and later condemned Jünger as part of a wider critique of conservative intellectuals after the war.[25] In a most unsettling manner, Jünger moves seamlessly in the diaries from darkly meticulous accounts of devastated west German cities or executions in France to blithely detached descriptions of beautiful flowers— such aloofness in the face of so much suffering breeds, for many readers, contempt for Jünger's privileged wartime assignment in Paris, where he was stationed with top Wehrmacht leaders at the Hotel Majestic. This kind of well-appointed detachment in the face of the suffering surrounding him in Paris seems, for many critics, a synecdoche for his detachment from the crimes of Nazism in general, something that Jünger might have manifested given his clearly anti-Semitic statements before the Nazis' genocidal program came into focus.[26]

The obfuscating passage above, however, also resonates with the particular topic I have undertaken herein. Although I am not interested in passing a final judgment on Jünger, his politics, or even his relationship to World War II, he offers another case of a high-profile figure whose key nonliterary postwar texts rely fundamentally on discourse about youth and generation. These texts, as Neaman recounts in *A Dubious Past*, were central to the postwar rehabilitation of Jünger and to his supporters' ability to attribute to him a persuasive change of heart from his authoritarian utopianism of the 1920s. But I would like to focus on an aspect of these writings that many overlook: the subtitle of his *The Peace* introduces the piece as *A Word to the Young of Europe, a Word to the Young of the World* without explicitly explaining why the text should address the young. This seemingly tangential subtitle has puzzled even the most diligent scholars of Jünger, for example, Gerhard Loose, who wonders in exasperation: "Why did the author limit his appeal to the young people (subtitle of the tract!) as they could not be instrumental in refashioning the world?"[27] Others, like Neaman in his otherwise very careful and convincing account, overlook the puzzling subtitle, simply omitting it from their discussion.[28] Though the seemingly impertinent subtitle might seem yet another case of Jünger's predisposition to abstraction and obscurantism,[29] I would suggest that the book is very much an address to the young because, for Jünger, the young were key agents in Germany's descent into Nazism, and they constitute an instrumental means for refashioning the German nation after the war.

By reading both *The Peace* and *Strahlungen* for their deployment of discourse about youth, one discovers an important pattern to Jünger's detached, often obfuscating approach to politics, to the Nazis, and to their impact and legacy. Writing about the 1944 July conspiracy to assassinate Hitler (about which he knew quite a bit), Jünger went so far as to see *The Peace* as his contribution to the organized effort against "Kniéblo," his nickname for Hitler, the man he saw ruining Germany.[30] Since Jünger understood the text as central to his relation to the war and politics of Germany, its curious subtitle should also count as central: though Jünger is a very different author than Meinecke, discourse about youth and generation also plays a central role in Jünger's account of Germany's recent history. On the one hand, Jünger provides a case of a political conservative deploying discourse about youth and generation to his own ends; on the other hand, this very deployment in such divergent authors confirms the importance of such discourse in coming to terms with the past. Youth functions differently in Jünger and this difference demonstrates the diverse and constructed nature of such discourse, but it still functions centrally. By allowing the intellectual context and its symbolically central discourse about generation to illuminate Jünger's two postwar texts, the function of this discourse, in Jünger's particular kind of antipolitics, emerges.

Jünger at War, Again

In order to elucidate how discourse about youth and generation function in Jünger's understanding of the catastrophe and the postwar period, I would like briefly to sketch the key elements of his analysis of the recent past as they emerge in *Strahlungen*, his voluminous diary during the "Nazis' war" and Allied occupation. Jünger's reactions to Nazism and World War II suggest a marked change from his celebration of combat in dubious classics like *In Storms of Steel* (1920), *The Struggle as Inner Experience* (*Der Kampf als inneres Erlebnis*) (1922), and *Forest 125* (*Wäldchen 125*) (1925). Throughout the late 1920s, he had affiliated himself with conservative movements, writing for such right-wing or militarist journals like *Standarte, Arminius* (which he edited for a while), *Der Vormarsch,* and *Widerstand.* Vesting his hope for a militaristic, right-wing authoritarian government in the rising fascist tide, he at times drew close to the Nazis, including a 1925 gift of three works on World War I to Hitler, one of which Jünger inscribed *Dem Führer* (to the Führer).[31] Despite such social proximity to top Nazis and some journalistic work for *Völkischer Beobachter* in the mid-1920s, he tried to distance himself from the Nazis after 1933: he moved to the country with his family, where he pursued his interests in and writings on nature. Politically conservative, Jünger remained loyal to the ideal of a more traditionally authoritarian state—the Nazis, after all, participated in parliamentary democracy and modern mass politics, both of which Jünger held in absolute contempt.[32]

Jünger's reaction to World War II thus constituted a major shift—but it was not so much Jünger's attitude about combat that changed as, he would underscore, a transformation in the nature of modern combat itself. In *Strahlungen* Jünger highlights repeatedly what he sees as the fundamental and qualitative difference between World War I and World War II: "this second World War is completely different from the first; it is probably the greatest confrontation around autonomy since the Persian wars" (21 December 1942, 1:458–62).[33] Jünger believed that the metaphysically meaningful experience of combat in previous wars had given way to a technologized war in which soldiers not only used new weapons in horrific ways but also internalized modern machines into their psyches. Although he had, in some of his 1920s writings, previously celebrated technology's overcoming of bourgeois society, he now saw processes of automation as yielding a new kind of heartless slaughter, which replaced, for him, meaning-laden struggle and violence: "At the bottom of this ubiquitous transformation into automatism, threatening us as it does, must be a general vice—to ascertain that would be the duty of precisely the theologians we are lacking" (6 June 1942, 1:335–36).[34]

In Paris, Jünger received an important assignment to write a long report on the competition in occupied France between the Wehrmacht and the Nazi Party. It is easy to see how he would have understood such a struggle as that between the Wehrmacht, in which Jünger always celebrated the great Prussian military tradition, and the SS/SD, the "wolves" of Hitler. His diaries are filled with observations on how a war driven by mechanical hatred and slaughter rendered obsolete both Clausewitz's theories of war and the educated and noble Prussian generals who ran it. Subsequently (and self-servingly) he saw the war unfolding between automata, which had literally become killing machines, and the traditional, spiritual powers of the earth (6 June 1942, 1:335–36).[35] Although it was precisely this kind of automata—fighting machines—with which *In Storms of Steel* seemed populated, Jünger increasingly emphasized the "old-Prussian" qualities of chivalry in a conspicuous revision of his formerly favorite themes.

As a consequence of this modern technologization and mechanization, the formerly hierarchized society had become one of amorphous masses. Like liberal-minded Meinecke, conservative Jünger saw modern society's tendency to undifferentiated masses as the key crisis in the "catastrophe." On a trip back to Germany in 1944,[36] Jünger was at first surprised by the *Verkehr* (traffic, intercourse) of people on the street, but then realized that these masses had been a driving current of many recent disasters, including, he claims, the inflation, the "seizure of power," and even *Kristallnacht,* which Jünger later characterized as the radical watershed in Hitler's racist policies. In his harangue against modern mass society—pumped full of the odious modern "Demos," as he put it—he, like many conservative intellectuals, blamed the Americanization of traditional European culture (29 February 1944, 2:226–28).[37]

The deeper social changes manifest in the modern masses and technology were not the only driving force behind the final catastrophe of World War II; they had been the fertile ground on which the demonic Hitler had been able to sow his "seeds of hate and destruction." Like many conservatives who hesitated to ascribe causation solely to structural or economic factors, Jünger combined his antimodern social analysis with a speculative psychologization of the demonic Hitler. Much as World War II represents a disastrous shift from previous wars, Jünger saw Hitler (the "Enemy of the World" [*Weltfeind*]) as a degeneration from Prussian leaders like "der alte Fritz" (Frederick the Great) who, despite early belligerence enjoyed a certain "sympathy for the world." As the war went on, particularly after his late 1943 trip to the eastern front, Jünger mentioned Hitler more and more in his diaries. Such blaming of one demonic figure supported Jünger's fatalistic detachment: under and due to Hitler, the Germans were being frozen in and could no longer, by themselves, free themselves from his grip (28 February 1943, 2:12–13).

These factors eventually led to the so-called catastrophe, as many, especially conservative, Germans liked to call it. Like many of his intellectual colleagues, Jünger often ascribed an apocalyptic quality to Germany's degeneration, akin to a natural catastrophe whose ravages could hardly have been predicted or prevented. For example, Hamburg's enduring the phosphorous bombing that could kill sixty thousand in an evening becomes, in Jünger's account, Pompeii under Mount Vesuvius—an obviously guilt-diluting analogy downplaying both German and Allied agency. As I argue in my introduction, it is not so much, as Sebald suggests, that postwar authors refused to write about the bombing; rather, it was the selective and diversionary manner in which they did describe it.[38] For Jünger, the war catastrophe was self-servingly like a comet, a fire from heaven, an earthquake (27 November 1943, 2:392–93). His favorite reading in the last years of the war reflected his fatalistic posture vis-à-vis these "cosmic" events: he combined biblical depictions of the apocalypse with a lot of morbid readings on shipwrecks. The fate of the *Titanic* and its modern technologized arrogance became an organizing metaphor for the war and the sinking of the German nation: when discharged from the army in October 1944, he wrote that he was simply awaiting the end on a sinking ship (20 October 1944, 2:312–13; again 11 December 1944, 2:339). He spent the winter months of 1944 and 1945 reading accounts of sinking ships, and by 26 January 1945 (2:363–64), he wrote at length about Germany as one of these ships skewered by an iceberg, adrift without wind, or battered by a storm. The fatalistic helplessness vis-à-vis nature abrogates individual agency and responsibility, a position tending to the detached dullness that many critics rightfully underscore in Jünger's reaction to the war.

The "Catastrophe" as a Youth-Driven Phenomenon

Jünger's *Strahlungen* offers important background clues for *The Peace* and the persisting puzzle of its subtitle because it provides the context out of which he conceives and composes his program for peace. A conservative account of the Nazis' rise and reign, Jünger's *Strahlungen* sketches themes—technology, the masses, demonic Hitler, and a (natural) catastrophe—that focus on the modern loss of individual autonomy and therefore a mitigation of individual guilt. But the rise of the Nazis, the execution of the war, and the crimes committed were nonetheless carried out by individuals. In an exculpatory circuitousness, however, Jünger suggests that the German young were those individuals most affected and converted by this modern transmogrification in war: whereas Meinecke analyzes youth and youth crisis in a sociocultural context, Jünger focuses much more on the role of youth and generation in war. Neaman describes a revealing postwar debate between Jünger's supporters, who insisted there had been a significant change in Jünger's perspective on nation and war, and his critics, who emphasized the continuities in his writings.[39] *Strahlungen,* as I argue, does register some changes, at least in his depiction of war. What is telling and problematic about the change, however, is that it is premised on youth's role in it: Jünger deploys youth's alterity to sketch and fill out his notion of a radical transformation of war by modern technology and society. Youth comes to constitute a social alterity whose crisis offers a central means for Jünger to come to terms with the past, which for him means explicating the transformative disaster of modern war and exculpating the elders.

This transformation very much informs *The Peace,* besides *Strahlungen* the key text to come out of the war years and into the postwar debates about Nazism and its legacy. On 27 March 1944 (2:240–42), Jünger wrote in *Strahlungen* that he was rereading the text of *The Peace* and found: "It is correct that many of my views, especially my estimation of war and Christianity and its constancy, have changed" because war had changed so much. One also finds in *Strahlungen,* however, that this technologization of war was not generationally neutral, that the modern crisis in the nature of war transpires primarily among the young. In the 28 July 1942 (1:357) *Strahlungen* entry, Jünger describes a good-natured French pharmacist whose wife was torn from him by the German occupiers:

> Such benevolent characters [as the pharmacist] do not even think to defend themselves. . . . It is horrifying how blind these young people have become to the suffering of the defenseless; they simply do not have the appreciation for it. For a chivalric life, they have become too weak; yes, they have lost the plain decency that prevents one from striking the weak. On the contrary, they see therein their way to glory. . . .
>
> I must never forget that I am surrounded by sufferers. That is much more important than all the fame of weapons and culture and than the empty acclaim of the young, which is pleased by this and that.[40]

Much of the scholarship on *Strahlungen* criticizes Jünger's cold and detached gaze as he witnessed the horrendous crimes of war,[41] but this passage reveals one of the key ways that Jünger could achieve the distance required for detachment—by peering through the filter of generation. He copes with a wartime behavior that he once exalted but can no longer stomach by explaining it as the radical transformation in warfare among the young. Thus, the passage links youth and the youth gaze I elaborated in chapter 2 not only to Jünger's central theme of transformed war but also to the very mode in which he analyzes: the way he looks, describes, and distinguishes himself from unpalatable events, as he is throughout the multivolume *Strahlungen*. The second paragraph of the passage confirms the fundamental, constitutive alterity of youth in Jünger's eyes: the diaries' deliberately detached "I" ("ich") is constituted by a stark contrast with the young who embody the crisis in the nature of war.

A wide array of other entries confirms this view of World War II as a transformed war caused by, as well as ravaging, a technologized youth in another dual representation: the youth cast in this cultural context as those most susceptible (passive) to Nazism and therefore most threatening (active) within it. The young, through little fault of their own, cause the crisis that has maimed the war experience. Jünger offers a great many images of the technologized war, images that very often include the young as the integral agents, the paradigmatic representatives, of a—for Jünger—newly problematized, mechanized humanity:

> From the young troops, it radiated [*strahlte*] thickly the proximity of death, of the glory of a fiery death of the ready hearts.
>
> As the machines withdrew, as their complexity disappeared and they became, all at once, both simpler and more meaningful. . . . And the young sat on top of the tanks, ate and drank, cautious with one another like the engaged couple [*Brautleute*] before the festivities, as they would be at a holy repast. (7 June 1944, 1:277)

This stark and frightening portrait of technologized war and mechanized humanity—once again, intervening in his cold, observant gaze—inextricably links youth with modern technology. The stark association of the young with the modern is made all the more vivid by Jünger's invocation of an archaic image of the young, the atavism of the formerly festive, now distorted Brautleute ritual—as in Mann, the young function representationally as other by signifying both the feared future and the repressed past. The young are, via the parallel construction and syntactical repetitions, indelibly associated with and tied to the machines and constitute the (formerly) human element in the image. As in Meinecke, it is the youth who personify society's excesses and general crisis but, in contrast to Meinecke, the excesses are tied intimately to the nature of modern combat itself. For Jünger and his celebration of war, it is they who embody the crisis and negate the old chivalric order, the older, more wholesome struggle and violence.

Jünger's icy observation of the furious ravages of the war associates the young with technology so intimately because they are the most devout believers in the rhetoric of hate that Hitler feeds the masses. The young believe in the rhetoric of Nazism when their elders know better: "In the afternoon, a conversation with a Captain Aretz, who visited me once as a student in Goslar and with whom I spoke for a long while about the current situation. He thinks that I wouldn't recognize the state of mind of the twenty- to thirty-year-olds, who only believe what's in the newspaper and never learned anything else" (14 October 1943, 2:169–70). In a manner reminiscent of Meinecke's very specific mentioning of ages, the passage offers a generational diagnosis for the nation's crisis. Of course, this realization comes in a conversation between two elders who have "learned something else" (though both are dutiful members of the occupying Wehrmacht). After the war, in the *Years of Occupation* part of the diaries, Jünger similarly recounts how four young people claimed, as late as April 1945, that the Führer would still sweep to a final triumph. Jünger attributes their insistence to gullible regurgitations of desperate radio announcements. Youth serves here and throughout these accounts in a role that demonstrates what I term a constitutive alterity: they, the young, are implicated in the current social crisis in a way that the elders are not.

Jünger's writings during the war implicate German youth in the pernicious transformation of war, but he also, in a manner more directly echoing Meinecke, represents a youth crisis as central to Germany's degeneration into Nazism. In a series of diary entries over five days, Jünger begins each day's writing with the phrase "Provocation and Reply" (28 March–2 April 1946, 2:607–19). It is the only time in the diaries that he uses such a device, and it is clear that he takes these

115

entries very seriously, as they brood on the rise of Hitler and the success of Nazism. As could be expected of Jünger or many other intellectuals, the basics of the explanation include Hitler (usually the one generating the "Provocation"), the masses, and machines (who constitute the socially catastrophic "Reply"). It also includes some rather peculiar moments, including reading Hitler as a moon figure and Mussolini as a sun figure, but generally the explanation is what we have come to expect through the cultural histories like Glaser's or Hermand's.

Echoing Meinecke's analysis of the Weimar period, however, Jünger also rather abruptly turns to the Freikorps as a youth movement. In describing his idealized imagination of and later disappointment by the Nazis, he writes: "It was similar for me with the Freikorps, of which I had an idealized image. The fatherland was in a sorry state after 1806. Back then the enthusiastic youth streamed together. . . . A few years were enough for liberation. Today, that has been possible once again" (28 March 1946, 2:609).[42] Of course, Jünger suggests that things are not at all the same as in glorious 1806: the golden age of Prussian nobility has passed, due above all to a changed youth. The young become an important social group for the crisis of modern Germany and its subsequent slide into Nazism. The young are the most fertile ground for the modern "Reply" to his "Provocation" and therefore created the crisis, the shipwreck-loving Jünger might say, that sank the great German ship.

The "Catastrophe" as Youth Victimizer: Diluting Guilt via Discourse about Youth and Generation

Although Jünger explains the transformation of the war through the young, he does not blame them entirely for all the trouble. In a manner reminiscent of Thomas Mann, Jünger also depicts the ravages of the war through a generational chaos that suggests that a dedifferentiation of discrete ages destroys society. What emerges in Jünger is a kind of no-fault generational crisis—the young are to blame, but they are not at fault for their own problems—and such a position can dilute the guilt that is attributed to the young. If Jünger is always implicitly blaming the young—making them those inextricably connected to the pernicious transformation of war—on the other hand, it is not entirely their generation's fault. Thus runs what I term the youth-guilt mechanism: in an allegedly unflinching analysis of Nazism, a German author accuses the young (as other) such that the ordinary German is not as guilty as the extraordinary Nazi youths—but then the author exonerates the young by way of a prevailing generational crisis, and overall guilt is thereby dissipated.

The guilt that obtains in this disingenuous model is no longer one based on war crimes or crimes against humanity but on adults' failure to maintain the generational hierarchy of society. As I outlined above, Jünger, like most conservatives, tended to de-emphasize crimes against Jews, perhaps to obscure his own pre-1933 anti-Semitic statements. The focus here is instead on the generationally driven degeneration of modern society. In contrast to Meinecke's exculpation of the young, Jünger describes a crisis of discrete generations—the young on one hand, adults on the other, with adults no longer in firm control—a number of times to depict the severity of social destruction. For example, after the phosphorous bombing of Hamburg, he writes of a parade of children with gray hair, "Little old people, aged in the night of phosphorus" (11 August 1943, 2:118). It is not so much that the bombings were never mentioned—it is how they are displaced onto the young. More pointedly, however, he goes on to blame fathers for the generational trouble, citing

> an appalling story from Aix. There was an SS-company there, and they had a young soldier go AWOL to Spain. The desertion was successful, but they caught him and brought him back. The company commander then had him bound and brought before the assembled company and executed him personally with his submachine gun. The deed must have left a horrifying impression: a number of the young soldiers fainted.
>
> The misdeed is hardly believable when one keeps in mind that one, as commander, is also always the father of his people. (24 October 1943, 2:179–80)

The passage manifests the ambiguous relationship between young and old, both inferior-superior and child-parent, evident in the last public photograph of Hitler. Though Jünger does not suggest that desertion is ever justified—the code of the army remains too sacred for that—Jünger renders the potentially political or at least military question one of generation and family. The victimization of the young—not only the executed but also various "young soldiers"—by their elders eclipses the brutality of the youths themselves. Jünger wrote this entry during the

117

composition of *The Peace,* and it demonstrates in part whence a subtitle as curious as that of *The Peace* may have arisen: a generational crisis once again structures his observational and narrative sense.[43]

The beginning of *Years of Occupation,* when the American forces roll into Jünger's hometown, Kirchhorst, is saturated with images and metaphors of generational chaos. Jünger's "memorable" description of the beginning of the occupation reinforces the centrality of discourse about youth.[44] In the very first entry of the occupation, 11 April 1945, the Americans seize Jünger's house and demand to inspect his belongings:

> I see myself compelled to pull the library onto the floor, whereas as the children stand by like a swarm of ants with clothes baskets nearby.
>
> The children are in a good mood: they have snatched a bottle of vermouth, sit furtively together, and sip from it. Apparently they feel the disturbance of the domestic order as pleasant. I heard them say in the past weeks: "If the bombers come tomorrow, that would be great." They would then not have to go to school. (2:405)

At the zero hour of the occupation, the cheerfulness of children highlights the humiliation Jünger feels at emptying his library on the floor for the victors and occupiers. Moreover, the children swarm around the books, enjoying the bombing as a chance to evade traditional *Bildung* and established generational indoctrination. As in Zeitblom's narration of World War I as playing hooky (*Hinter-die-Schule-laufen*) in *Doktor Faustus,* Jünger's war becomes, discursively, a kind of longed-for truancy by the young. The children, outsiders to conventional culture and happy to serve as social threat, are actually enjoying the destruction of traditional bourgeois society, its private sphere and institutions.

The very first entry of the occupation, those paragraphs with which the book-length *Years of Occupation* begins,[45] depicts the humiliation of the occupation as an experience mediated by a crisis in the discrete relationship between the adults and children. A couple of days later, when the Americans move on, Jünger looks back at the experience as if it had made children of them all: "Early in the morning, the Americans pulled out. They left the village half desolated. We are exhausted like children from a carnival with its crowds, shots, shouting, sideshow booths, horror shows, and music tents" (13 April 1945, 2:408). Generational crisis then operates along two axes: the kids romp outside the bounds of their house, in excess of the bourgeois private sphere, while the adults become (agentless, ineffectual) children.[46] The crisis of the defeat and humiliation of the occupation become therein significantly generational. This metaphor, however, also suggests a kind of dilution of guilt, because it is difficult to cast the agentless or agency-diluted child as completely guilty (for example, a crime narrative with a child criminal is usually a social commentary more than a good guy/bad guy story). Jünger's dilution of youthful guilt operates effectively into the occupational period.

The Peace's Generational Message

I began this section on Ernst Jünger aiming to elucidate the puzzle posed by the often ignored, perplexing subtitle of his postwar tract *The Peace*, and I have tried to use his wartime diaries *Strahlungen* to show how a discourse about youth and generation structures Jünger's analysis of the catastrophe as well as his detached literary vision itself. Jünger's description of youth as both those most guilty of the technologized war and those most victimized asserts a circuit for blame that ends up diluting guilt. One final passage from *Strahlungen* in particular sums up this dilution and anticipates themes that will underpin *The Peace:*

On the train, April 3, 1944. Two young officers from the tank corps, one of whom distinguishes himself from the other with a good face. But they have been chatting for an hour about murder. One of them wanted to take one of the local residents suspected after surveillance and, with his comrades helping, make him disappear into a lake; the other takes the perspective that after an attack on the corps, they should put fifty Frenchman on the wall to be shot. "Then it will stop pretty quick."

I ask myself how this could spread so quickly, this cannibalistic disposition—and how this complete malice, this lack of a heart for other beings, could have spread so quickly and how the general denigration [*Vernegern*] can be explained. With such young people it is easily possible that no remnant of Christian morality strikes them, but one could still expect that a sense of chivalry or heraldic honor or old-Germanic decency and conscience could persist in their blood. Because, on their own, they are not so evil, and their short lives do sacrifice willingly, something worthy of admiration. (3 April 1944, 2:245)

The passage reinforces the connection between youth and the war's most brutal attitudes and actions: these two young soldiers come to stand in for the contagious denigration of modern values that has spread through so much of the German population (old and young, one must assume). Jünger also associates the youthful other with the racial other ("cannibalistic" and de-nigration [*Vernegern*]), a mechanism Dick Hebdige discusses in regards to nineteenth-century England.[47] In their racially figured degradation, the young embody the crisis of the older chivalric traditions that, for Jünger, used to make combat such a metaphysically meaningful experience. But despite this almost explicit blaming of the young, by the end of the passage Jünger has also managed to exonerate and respect the young: "short life" invokes the kind of guilt-diluting sympathy at the heart of the youth-guilt mechanism.

Particularly odd but also revealing in the passage is Jünger's turn to Christianity. Despite his reading the Bible (for the first time, he claimed) during the war, Jünger never considered himself a Christian and never seemed much convinced of God's existence.[48] Christianity, however, comes to play a surprising but revealing role in *The Peace* as well, something that made the text palatable to postwar religious leaders who, like many conservatives, were not very interested in reviewing their behavior during the rise and reign of the regime. Indeed, the quote links youth guilt, youth redemption, and Christianity neatly: it is a trinity that forms the puzzling basis of *The Peace*. The passage also connects the circuit of guilt dilution (blame brutal youth and then exonerate innocent youth) with respect for youth's "sacrifice," the only remnant element of the traditional chivalric system Jünger increasingly celebrated. But in this passage, based on their short lives and their sacrifices, Jünger demonstrates a forgiveness of the young; in *The Peace* he highlights their sacrifice as precisely "the seed" for a lasting peace. The puzzle of *The Peace*'s subtitles thus begins to unravel.

Jünger in fact emphasizes precisely this sacrifice throughout the first half ("The Seed") of *The Peace*, in which he explains how such sacrifice and suffering constitutes humankind's first collective work. Such enormous sacrifice must bear fruit, he informs the reader in typically naturalistic pedantry; he then tries to demonstrate that there was indeed a chivalric side even to this odious war. The first half of the text thus reflects those themes—chivalry, sacrifice, youth—that are inextricably intertwined in *Strahlungen*. In the second half of the text, called "The Fruit," Jünger asserts that just as monarchies gave way to nation-states, so nations should give way to supranational empires. Jünger's vision for the peace after the war is founded upon the war's common experience of "sacrifice" serving as a cornerstone for a *Friedensreich* (peace empire) that would replace the merely national.[49] As part of this negation of the Vaterland—Vaterland as Germany drops out of his book in the first few pages—he insists on seeing the war not as a conflict among competing nations but as a kind of civil war.[50] He wants Europe to become the new Vaterland, with the old nations demoted merely to *Mutterland* (Motherland).[51]

In order to arrive at this synthesizing unity, Jünger dilutes the guilt of Germans by blaming and then exonerating the young instead of the general population—what I term the youth-guilt mechanism, here deployed, as in Mann and Meinecke, to constitute a new type of community. On the one hand, the text blames the young for the war crimes that arose from the twilight of the traditional wartime idols Jünger so reveres: "That will remain a blot on our century for all time, and one will not be able to respect anyone who lacks a heart and eye for what happened. This counts above all for the bellicose youth, because the protection of the defenseless and weak will always be the highest instance of chivalry, and no hero can stand before an enemy that does not esteem it."[52] When arguing that shame and guilt must be acknowledged, Jünger turns to the young whom he, in *Strahlungen,* made particularly responsible for the demise of dear chivalric values. The quote, in fact, seems to derive almost precisely from the *Strahlungen* passage about the pharmacist losing his wife: it seems to revisit and reinforce the moral Jünger derived from this generationally oriented anecdote.

On the other hand, much of the guilt laid here at the door of youth then ends up dissipated in other passages that cast them as victims of the catastrophe. In a section on differentiating the victims of the catastrophe, it was the mothers and above all the young, the reader learns, who suffered most: "The young grew up in hells, in realms that demons rather than people would seek, and the children collected their first images in this horrifying world. They heard the cries of the sirens before the tolling of the bells, and their cradle rocked toward fire rather than light."[53] Revealingly, the passage about the victimization of the young also associates them with *Kinder*, smaller children who are more easily cast as innocent than adolescent youth. It is telling that a postwar writer did feel justified in writing of the devastating air war if the victims mentioned and foregrounded are those with whom it is much easier to identify as victims, namely, the young. As is often noted about German victimization, Jünger's "differentiation" of victims, which declares the young the "true sufferers," diverts attention from other victims of the "catastrophe" like Jews, political prisoners, gays, gypsies, and others.[54]

With the war and guilt mediated by the modern youth crisis of the war, Jünger can commence his positive project for the reconstruction of the nation. Unsurprisingly—in a manner similar to but also varying from Meinecke's—Jünger's plan for the nation and its reconstruction synthesizes discourse about youth with the themes brought forth in cultural histories of this period. Jünger emphasizes both inner and outer reconstruction, and *The Peace* relies on important aspects of discourse about youth in both cases. First, in terms of the inner threat of the catastrophe, Jünger focuses on the pervasive dangers of nihilism. Various other authors in the context invoke nihilism as a particular threat to the young[55]—as if such loses of faith leave adults unaffected—and Jünger, like many conservatives, invokes Christianity to combat it:

> The true triumph over nihilism and, with it, the peace will only be possible with the help of the churches. Just as the dependability of the people in a new state is based not on its internationality, but rather on its nationality, the education has to be directed toward commitment, not toward indifference. It has to be acquainted with the homeland [*Heimat*], in the space of the infinity and in the time of the eternal. And this education [*Bildung*] to a full life, to the complete person, has to be rooted in a higher certainty as that which the state constitutes with its schools and its universities.[56]

This passage responds directly to the one in which Jünger observed the two young soldiers on a train discussing murdering French citizens: they lacked any remnant of Christian morality. Even though he himself is far from a faithful Christian, Jünger invokes Christianity here as an educational environment for the youth to whom he addressed *The Peace*. Another key theme, the strengthening of a Christian ethos after the war, comes to be mediated not by Jünger's or other adults' crises of faith but rather by the crisis among the young—the recurrence of *Erziehung* (education) and *Bildung* (education in a broader sense, formation) confirm their subtextual presence. Much like Hundhammer with his confessional schools and Meinecke with his Goethegemeinden, Christianity ought to counteract the consequences of modernity by disciplining the young in a particular—above all, moral—fashion. Though Jünger hardly ever mentions the young in the text, grounding *The Peace* in *Strahlungen* elucidates why his approach to reconstruction is also mediated by discourse about the young.

Jünger's agenda for political reconstruction also relies on specific discourses about youth and generation. For his political project of dissolving the various nations into the great community of Europe, for this refiguring of the national, Jünger relies on the young and their presumed proclivities. His subtitle now comes clearly into focus: if his project aims to dissolve the Third Reich of Germany into a "Peace Empire" of Europe, then he regards the young as those who can best redraw the borders. Although the young serve Jünger's account as the most brutal nationalists, they are also seen—in Jünger, emancipatorily—as those who exceed and transcend (national) boundaries. They are the ones who can form lasting bonds despite adult borders. Jünger emphasizes this overstepping of borders constantly in his plug for the pan-European fruit of the war: "it could not escape the young that they stood in a struggle that pertained to something higher than the borders of the fatherland—that here, in the brotherly war [*Bruderkriege*], a new meaning of the earth was being borne out, and that some of those who were coming to kill were sworn to a higher ideal than the comrades right at the side to whom they had to be true."[57] The motivation for Jünger's argument of the war as a "brotherly" war of the planet becomes therein clearer, as does the target audience for arguing such a war: the youth are those who can form camaraderie above the borders of Vaterland, those who are more likely brothers.

Jünger's Antipolitics of Youth

Paris, 28 October 1943. Discussion of the current situation [with his young friend Captian von Laue] and especially the question of to what degree the individual should feel responsible for the crimes of Kniéblo [Hitler]. It pleases me when

123

young people who have gone through my school get right to the crucial point. The fate of Germany is doubtful if out of its youth, and especially its workers, a new knighthood does not grow. (2:182)[58]

The passage suggests the special relationship that Jünger saw himself enjoying with young people who had "gone through [his] school."[59] It also inextricably connects the nation to the young as a social class: here the young attain a coherent status on par with the workers, a much better-known and often-discussed socioeconomic configuration in Jünger's oeuvre as well as in humanistic scholarship in general. As I traced in chapter 1 with Goebbels's *Michael*, youth replaces class as an analytical category that obscures other, often socioeconomic approaches. I have tried to show how this social class of youth saturates two of Jünger's wartime texts that were published in the early postwar period; in fact, the recurring discussion of youth in *Strahlungen* elucidates why a text like *The Peace*, which explicitly mentions youth only two or three times, would be subtitled "A Word to the Young." As indicated in the passage above, Jünger regarded his relationship to the young as so important that he understands his text, addressed to them, as active resistance to Hitler.

In *Strahlungen* and *The Peace*, youth has exceeded the bounds of the old wars that constituted, for Jünger, the core of the nation. The chivalric order and the aesthetic experience of combat constitute for Jünger the highest moment of life, but both are radically transformed—especially among the young—by modern technology. With these themes of war differing substantially from Meinecke's, Jünger utilizes the modern youth crisis, which transforms a beloved tradition, to elucidate what has happened to the nation and to advocate for a new community to replace it. Likewise different are the ends of their discourses about youth: Meinecke suggests a deliberate reconstruction of the nation in very German Kulturnation-oriented Goethegemeinden while Jünger wants youth's border-crossing tendencies to reconfigure the nation-state altogether. In both cases, however, one sees the tendency, as one does throughout this context, of the centrality of youth, not only for coming to terms with the past but also for creating new (adult) communities.

Even though Jünger ends up with discourses about youth different than Meinecke's, there is at least one recurring strategy they have in common: discourse about youth and a youth crisis leads both of them away from any explicit traditional politics and toward some particular, quasi-pedagogical relation to youth, a tendency I analyzed in my discussion of the German public sphere and Mann's *Doktor Faustus* in chapter 2. Aside from mentioning Hitler and now-obsolete Prussian generals, Jünger does not discuss the specifics of a postwar political order in *Strahlungen*. The following passage is certainly one of the only ones in which he discusses anything as specific as voting rights in a postwar republic:

> The universality of the right to vote would grow even more if, besides giving the vote to women, one also gave it to children, who would be represented by their fathers in the election. Therein there would be greater liberality and solidarity, a dam against the influence of radical, pure spiritual or literary directions to which a married man would succumb much less. The fathers must once again stand up. The rural provinces would also be more effective against the big-city mass-parties, that today have rapidly gone to work. (19 March 1945, 2:386)[60]

This surprising political proposal demonstrates once again the centrality of generation in Jünger's postwar (anti)politics. By giving children and youth the vote, he hopes to stem the tide of modern democracy, against the mass parties and urban politics, an idea also pushed by the so-called Kreisauer Kreis.[61] Like so much in the intellectual and cultural context, Jünger's agenda for the postwar political scene prescribes not universal democratic participation but strong fathers, a move away from the polis and to the private house—specifically, to its young.

It is in within this generational discourse, I think, that *The Peace*, which one critic describes as one of the most important texts for passing political judgment on Jünger, must be placed.[62] I doubt *The Peace*—only about seventy pages, destroyed in its first draft, unpublished for years in its second—is really the single most important text for Jünger's political lifelong profile, but I do think its politics are saturated with a diversionary discourse about youth typical of its intellectual context. In his introduction to *Strahlungen*, Jünger defends preemptively against the charge that *The Peace* was written once he knew that Germany was to lose the war—that is, was meant as a whitewash of his Wehrmacht activities; he answers such charges:

125

There are situations in which one should not pay attention to success; one then stands, of course, outside of politics. That counts also for these [members of the 20 July 1944 conspiracy against Hitler], and thereby they were victorious morally even if they failed historically. Their courage, their sacrifice was of a higher nature than that which they proved on the battlefield: they were crowned not by a militaristic, but rather by a poetic triumph.

I see it as an honor to contribute with my own medium and in this context my writing took the form of an appeal to the young of Europe . . . this piece's purpose is not political but rather pedagogical. (1:13)

After acquiescing to the Nazis, never explicitly criticizing their rise to power, and taking a job in their occupation, Jünger sees the July conspiracy outside of politics. Given his tendency to see war as a higher metaphysical experience, such a position is perhaps not surprising; what is surprising is how he is able to deploy the young in this effort to move outside and (as in the previous passage) against politics. While generals were risking their lives to assassinate Hitler, Jünger felt he managed meaningful resistance by addressing *The Peace* to the young. In a self-serving defense, one familiar from Thomas Mann and the reeducational context in general, he contrasts the "political" to the "pedagogical," a move that would seem ironclad to any objection. What could be wrong with a pedagogical contribution to the resistance? But I hope I have shown how often such a move occurs in Germany's coming to terms with the past and to what diversionary ends.

As two of the most important intellectual figures of the early postwar period, Friedrich Meinecke and Ernst Jünger share some basic mechanisms in their representations of youth, especially by foregrounding the recurring phenomenon of a modern youth crisis as a key element in their coming to terms with the past. In both cases, their analyses of Nazism via youth crisis allow them to contrast constitutively their own projects (constitute alterity) as well as to dilute German guilt for the Nazi "catastrophe." Meinecke inextricably links the young to those developments that yielded the Nazis, especially the growing importance of the masses, changes in the nature of work, and intemperate responses to those two trends. Jünger similarly connects the young to what he saw as the central disaster of the Nazis: their degradation and desecration of the combat experience. By placing youth crises at the center of their respective crises of modernity, Meinecke and Jünger highlight the young as the most radical opponents of the Weimar Republic. Consequently, in Meinecke and Jünger, the young also become the most devout believers in the Nazi message, a message that could be, by constitutive contrast, correctly defused only by adults. The young thus become the most brutal, the most malevolent, the most fanatical of a fatally fanatical movement—all statuses usefully asserted by adults who would not want to assume those roles themselves. As in the victimization mechanisms Bartov describes, these authors create three groups where there seemed to be two, such that the lines between victim and perpetrators can be redrawn.[63] But both Meinecke and Jünger accomplish this triangulation via discourse about youth: now there are the victims (hanging in the background but hardly mentioned), the (young) Nazis, and the average (older, wise) Germans. They associate the young with true Nazis and make the older and wiser—despite their party participation or at least complicity—representatives of the other, presumably not inherently Nazi, Germany. Thus, this splitting of perpetrators into convinced Nazis and ordinary Germans is accomplished along generational lines: generational difference and discourse allow them to localize and neutralize culpability for the past.

As for the present—a present looking back at the catastrophe of the war and (usually merely implied) the Holocaust—the central category of postwar guilt is run in both cases through a kind of circuit that differentiates and mitigates guilt according to generations and their social resonances. Both Meinecke and Jünger, even though ostensibly toeing the Allies' line, are concerned with breaking up the notion of widespread guilt, breaking it down into constituent groups of differentiated guilt. Time and time again, youth prove one of the most useful groups with which to differentiate guilt, both because they were easy to blame and because they simultaneously also seemed like innocent victims. Blaming the young diverted guilt from the writing (adult) subject, who then usually also suggests that the young are victims of no-fault generational confusion. Guilt, via this circuit pushed away to the young, who are then made less responsible for their actions, is therein diluted or entirely diverted.

In terms of the present and looking toward the future, the young became a useful means for describing and overcoming the national political and social crisis. I argued that sensitivity to discourse about youth and generation can explain two of the most peculiar developments in Meinecke's and Jünger's early postwar writings: in the scholarship on postwar intellectuals, Meinecke's ideal (Wunschbild) of the Goethegemeinden is ubiquitously cited but rarely fully explained. Though Jünger scholars underscore the importance of *The Peace* for his elusive politics, its curious subtitle and basic strategy are rarely elaborated. In both cases, highlighting discourse about youth and generation illuminates their coming to terms with the past as well as their reconstructive agendas.

4

Modernity's Better Others

Youth in Jaspers's Postwar University and Wiechert's Reconstructive Agenda

In an essay on Ernst Wiechert that appeared in the *Deutsche Rundschau* in April 1948, Herbert Stegemann begins with what is, for the postwar period, the best-known aspect of the author's career: Wiechert's celebrated resistance to the Nazi regime. This resistance, Stegemann suggests, included first and foremost his "various 'Speeches to the German Young,'" which doubtlessly belong to the "history of the German *Abwehrkampfes* [struggle for defense]."[1] Much as Jünger regarded his *The Peace* as his act of resistance, Stegemann confirms that the young were, at least from the perspective of the postwar period, one of the most important fronts on which "good" Germans fought the Nazis. Although Wiechert's postwar reputation and the kind of optimistic Vergangenheitsbewältigung it suggests also pivot on the young, Wiechert's addresses to the "German young" construct a different kind of discourse about youth than either Friedrich Meinecke or Ernst Jünger. Wiechert, along with another important author from the early postwar period, Karl Jaspers, takes a very different, though likewise emphatic, approach to the German young. As I suggest in chapter 3, Meinecke and Jünger, after depicting National Socialism as a kind of deviation from the German nation, map onto Germany's troubled modernity a particular discourse about youth, telescoping age onto historical processes in a way that anticipates their postwar projects of disciplining reconstruction.

The kind of discourse about youth Jaspers and Wiechert deploy, however, varies significantly from that of Mann, Meinecke, or Jünger in both conception and effect.

Instead of mapping Germany's problematic past onto the young, Karl Jaspers observes the tendency of others to blame the young for the national descent into National Socialism and replies directly to it in his many postwar publicist writings, lectures, and radio addresses on the university, work generally neglected in the considerable scholarship on the famous philosopher. Similarly avoiding the widespread upbraiding of the young, Ernst Wiechert celebrates youth's outsider status as a means to resist the corrupting influence of modern society. In my overview of youth in postwar Vergangenheitsbewältigung, I have shown how youth and Germany's particular understanding of it served centrally in the nation's unusual modernity, especially in the fin de siècle and 1920s–30s periods, which then serve as indispensable background for the postwar period. But rather than playing the central villains of Germany's deviant modernity, as they do for Meinecke and Jünger, the young in Jaspers and Wiechert have the positive potential to hold themselves aloof from the venal vagaries of German modernity. Neither Jaspers nor Wiechert telescopes youth onto Germany's recent history and its nefarious descent into Nazism; rather, the young constitute the best aspects of the German nation, those elements that can counteract modernity's destructive forces and will be able to provide the building blocks, even a cornerstone, for its reconstruction. Instead of blaming the young for Germany's recent history, these authors suggest that the young can remedy it. Although the approach is revealingly different, the young are still a central aspect of these intellectuals' coming to terms with the past: this somewhat different form of alterity nonetheless confirms youth's particular role in German cultural history.

The parallel between Jaspers and Wiechert is politically revealing as well. They were both celebrated in the postwar period as important intellectuals who had been apolitical but who, after the war, decided to become public leaders in Germany's "hour of need." For these apolitical intellectuals turned heroes, discourse about youth—rather than other axes of social/political difference—served most usefully to negotiate the complex questions of postwar Germany. Like Meinecke and Jünger, both Jaspers and Wiechert deploy discourse about the young to reconstitute the postwar community, but this community is not so much based on strict generational difference, disciplining, and hierarchy:

rather, in a kind of progressive pedagogy, they redraw this postwar community around the young's best attributes, in which they locate the future of German nation.

KARL JASPERS'S TURN TO THE PUBLIC AND THE POSTWAR UNIVERSITY

> The German people should not be annihilated, the German people should be educated.
> Karl Jaspers, "Renewal of the University"

A giant among German intellectuals of any time, Karl Jaspers also counts as a leading figure of the early postwar public sphere. His philosophical writings had already made him, along with Martin Heidegger and Edmund Husserl, one of Germany's most famous philosophers; moreover, his unusually uncompromised record during the Hitler regime and the war qualified him to play an important public role in Germany's cultural reconstruction. In 1937 Jaspers was forced into retirement and in 1943 he was banned from publishing; Jaspers and his wife, Gertrud, a Jewish woman he refused to divorce, were apparently scheduled to be deported on 14 April 1945, but American forces liberated Heidelberg just two weeks before that date.[2] In light of his academic reputation and this record, American officials offered to appoint Jaspers as a kind of minister of culture, but Jaspers recounts how, against his great desire, he had to turn the position down for health reasons.[3] Instead, he played a central role in the "Committee of Thirteen" that oversaw the reopening of the University of Heidelberg, became "honorable senator for life" at the university, and cofounder of one of the most important postwar journals, *Wandlung*. Beyond Jaspers's considerable academic reputation, Mark Clark has called him simply "the most recognized and most important intellectual in the Western zones of occupation."[4]

How did an academic philosopher—one who deliberately rejected any kind of political engagements after World War I—become so important for the postwar cultural and political public spheres? Jaspers's prolific and wide-ranging political publications after the war were highly influential—a flood of pamphlets, short essays, published speeches, and radio addresses representing a rather new and therefore all the more remarkable undertaking for the sixty-two-year-old philosopher.

For a prominent figure who is purported to have published some thirty-five thousand pages, Karl Jaspers had a rather irregular publishing

131

history. Appointed full professor at Heidelberg in 1921, he took a break from publishing any major works from 1923 until 1932 (when he was thirty-nine to forty-seven, usually prime publishing years) to steep himself in philosophy and work on his magnum opus, the three-volume *Philosophie* (1932). His timing was unfortunate: just eleven years after he started publishing again, the Nazis imposed their ban on him, such that from 1939 to 1945 only two works—both translations, both published abroad—appeared. This in part explains why, after 1945 and liberation by the Americans, Jaspers published a flurry of philosophical and political works. Some of these philosophical works—including *Of the Truth* (*Von der Wahrheit*), the thousand-page first volume of the incomplete *Philosophical Logic* (*Philosophische Logik*)—became some of the most important of his oeuvre and were clearly the product of years of "writing for the drawer" during the Nazi times. Other works, like his political essays (enormous in number and wide-ranging in subject), were tailored more specifically to the day and represented a significant new undertaking for the already-established philosopher.

Jaspers's dramatic turn to politics in the public sphere marks an important watershed for the philosopher and, in many ways, for intellectuals in the postwar period. In his *In the Shadow of Catastrophe*, Anson Rabinbach has emphasized how remarkable and unusual this development was for a German philosopher, from whom tradition would normally encourage, if not demand, solitude and detachment.[5] Rabinbach interprets Jaspers's postwar work—and especially his *The Question of German Guilt* (*Die Schuldfrage*, 1946)—through this new commitment to public communication in an open and free polity.[6] As Jaspers's friend and correspondent Hannah Arendt observed: "Jaspers is as far as I know, the first and only philosopher who ever protested against solitude, to whom solitude appeared 'pernicious' and who dared to question 'all thoughts, all experiences, all contents,' under this one aspect: 'What do they signify for communication?'"[7] Rabinbach observes how formative this turn eventually proved for the German intellectual tradition, influencing such prominent postwar thinkers as Jürgen Habermas.[8]

Despite the respect, even admiration, given Jaspers for this turn to the political, both Arendt and Rabinbach fault him for not persevering practically in his theoretical commitment to democratic openness and freedom. Both criticize Jaspers's *The Question of German Guilt* for its theological conceptual constellation and Jaspers's broader failure to engage the formal, institutional elements of democracy.[9] Rabinbach, for example, analyzes Jaspers's celebration of public political discourse but notes the philosopher's own failure in that area, as he preferred private communications.[10] Arendt similarly observed that in his commitment to the moral aspects of German guilt and reconstruction, Jaspers neglected the institutions constitutive of modern democracy, like parties, interest groups, and trade unions.[11] In his study of the "Heidelberg Myth," Steven Remy points to a similar contradiction between Jaspers's reputation as a publicly engaged intellectual and his inability to effect significant change in particular postwar institutions, an inconsistency on which Mark Clark has also remarked.[12] Though I do not entirely disagree with these criticisms, there is one social institution with which Jaspers was repeatedly and conspicuously concerned in his postwar writings: the university. As I suggested in chapter 1 on culture under the Nazis, the university had been an important flash point for debates about the "German young" in the 1910s through the 1940s. Generally, considered and revealing attention has been paid to Jaspers's entry into the public sphere in terms of his model for guilt, but very few in the Anglophone world have analyzed in any detail the trajectory of his wide and varied essays on reconstructing the university.[13] In amending the criticisms of Arendt and Rabinbach, I would argue that the university became a revealing symbol for Jaspers's newly developed political engagement and some of its most complex, often contradictory aspects.

Jaspers's vision for the university, sketched over a wide range of publications, demonstrated a novel public concern with an actual public—even political—institution. He was deliberately engaged with the postwar form of Germany's most famous social institution: during the 1947 controversy about Jaspers's winning the Goethe Prize, a controversy exacerbated by his acceptance speech, one critic, Ernst Robert Curtius, complained that he had pretenses to becoming a postwar Wilhelm von Humboldt.[14] On the other hand, as that 1947 Goethe speech demonstrated, Jaspers's commitment to the university and its traditions manifest a marked ambivalence about any radical transformation of German culture. While Jaspers's interest and participation in politics, the public sphere, and social institutions mark an important watershed—and his writings on the university do reflect this new commitment to open and free communication—his commitment to traditional Bildung persisted. In fact, his specific proposals in defense of the university stake out an apolitical stance in a context in which the university was increasingly politicized. Reading his writings on the university carefully, particularly in light of the wider discourses about youth and education at this time, can illuminate the contradiction on which assorted scholars have remarked, that is, the contradiction between Jaspers's reputation as a publicly engaged philosopher and his inability to support fundamental reforms of postwar institutions.

As I have been arguing throughout, an educational institution and a certain notion of youth serve as framing metaphors for German culture and politics more generally, much as they did in the famous Jaspers-Undset episode, in which a discussion of reeducation became a forum for the discussion of guilt.[15] In his writings on the university, Jaspers proposed regenerating the university as a traditional institution, defensively defined by a specific notion of "young students." In Jaspers's postwar university, the image of the youth as student illuminates Jaspers's postwar navigations of German identity and regeneration. The young person, here the student, becomes an indispensable means by which to constitute, to redraw, a formerly flawed but now reemerging community that can redeem German national identity. The university and the young inhabiting it reflect Jaspers's ambivalent engagement with the past and the politics of the present: youth becomes a key means to negotiate postwar politics as well as to avoid advocating for more fundamental political change.

Rebuilding the University after the "Catastrophe"

In a manner probably even more pronounced than with regard to primary and secondary schools, the university became an important node for a wide variety of postwar discourses about the regeneration of German identity. It was simultaneously celebrated as the foundation for Germany's geistig (cultural/spiritual) rebirth and criticized for entrenched Nazism. In a context in which discussions of reeducation cropped up everywhere, such laudations and laments of the university were particularly ubiquitous. None of the major postwar journals, for instance, was without extensive articles on the import of the German university's regeneration for German national identity.[16] In their praise of the university, many intellectuals depicted the institution as the key cultural artifact extant after the "catastrophe" and therefore the core of any cultural regeneration. The prominent Freiburg historian Gerhard Ritter, in what Steven Remy calls the "most influential" early appraisal of scholars' relationship to Nazism, suggested that many of Germany's greatest intellectuals were able not only to survive as university professors but also, from their academic posts, to criticize the Nazi regime, in large part because Nazi officials were too uneducated to realize that they were targets of scholarly disdain. In Ritter's optimistic depiction, the university serves as an island of tenacious resistance for good German intellectuals among the Nazi philistines.[17]

In a subjugated country reduced once again to a Kulturnation—and, after the war, peddling a highly compromised Kultur—many came to regard the university as the core of German national identity: as one of, if not the, greatest contributions of Germany to the wider community of nations. For instance, in a radio address later published in *Neue Auslese*, Karl Mannheim called the German university—in its national function—"the highest expression of the ideal life of the nation."[18] Mannheim compared Germany's universities to the accomplishments of "German composers," "German authors," and "German philosophy."[19] While the university symbolized a better Germany lost in the recent past, it should also provide (for) the nation in the future. In a more pessimistic mode, Hannah Arendt remarked in a letter to Karl Jaspers that the university "[is] the only thing Germany has left."[20] Less well-known authors also regarded the university as a last chance for the German nation to redeem itself or even to survive at all.[21] Despite the obviously problematic link between nation and university in the wake of the Nazi regime, Mannheim even argued that universities should grow more "national" because the task of the universities now entailed vetting, even more carefully and deliberately than before, the national tradition for good and bad culture.[22]

Considerable practical obstacles, however, would impede the universities' glorious return to the forefront of German culture or Germany as Kulturnation. All universities were closed indefinitely by the Allies in May 1945 and faced a wide range of daunting challenges before they could reopen. Located mostly in cities, which had borne the brunt of Allied bombing, the physical plant of many universities was devastated. Although Heidelberg was spared direct bombing, in Munich, for instance, the destruction was so bad that students were initially required to do six months of manual labor on university buildings before they could begin their studies. Despite the labor requirement, it was nonetheless spring 1946, over six months after Heidelberg's first faculty opened, that Munich was able to open.[23]

135

The Allies and many German officials, however, considered the problem of denazification of the university even more urgent than repairing the physical destruction. In fact, one way in which the universities attracted widespread attention was negative: Allied reports regularly regarded education, especially higher education, as the most deficient aspect of the entire military government.[24] As with most educational institutions, the Nazis had been infamously careful to coordinate the universities to the party line, a process Remy has traced in detail in his study of the University of Heidelberg. In the first wave of American denazification in the summer and fall of 1945, roughly four out of ten professors were removed. At some universities, like Heidelberg, where Jaspers was professor, the percentages were even higher: around 60 percent for medicine, natural science, and political science were not permitted, initially at least, to resume their posts.

At many universities, moreover, there were also uncomfortably high-level and high-profile problems with denazification. At Heidelberg, for instance, local labor officials attacked the rector of the university for a book entitled *Race Hygiene* [*Rassenhygiene*].[25] Soon thereafter, the newly elected dean of mathematics and natural sciences was arrested for falsifying his denazification questionnaire.[26] In Munich, it was discovered that professors had formed a "clique" to resist hiring new faculty while any hope remained for rehabilitating recently dismissed professors. In essence, they were stalling until the expected liberalizing of the Allies' policies, which did arrive with the heating up of the cold war. These persisting problems with denazification provoked a movement in early 1946, on the part of some Allies as well as local German authorities, to close the university until all personnel could be adequately tested. These kinds of problems—like entrenched Nazis who might occupy positions as high as dean—attracted a lot of attention in both Germany and the home countries. Although no university was closed once it had been reopened, a second wave of denazification followed in the summer of 1946 after very negative press reports back in the United States added to the pressure on the military government. A second investigation at that time recommended that an additional seventy-two instructors be dismissed at Heidelberg. In these successive waves of denazification, a particularly difficult group to test and categorize were the students. They became, as I shall discuss later, both a favorite target of critics and a rallying point for defenders of the universities, the contested core of the coming community of the universities.

German Guilt, Nation, and Cosmopolitanism
in Jaspers's Postwar University

Though one of the key figures of the *innere[n] Emigration,* Jaspers distinguished himself in a number of important respects from other intellectuals of this period. Jaspers set himself apart not only in his remarkable turn to the public sphere but also in his foregrounding of German guilt for the reconstitution of the defeated nation. Jaspers thought the German nation, as a political entity, had reached its end and could hope to overcome its pariah status only by openly acknowledging and incorporating its unique guilt into any future German culture.[27] Most studies of Jaspers in this period focus on this aspect of his early postwar writings, understandably, since these writings on guilt were, in many ways, foundational for the later, especially post-1960s political culture of the Federal Republic, something that Olick argues persuasively in his *House of the Hangman.*[28] In analyzing Jaspers's writings, many have noted that his ideas about guilt and regeneration tend to an abstract and even religious conceptualization, but I would argue that the university serves as an important institutional site for these leitmotifs of Jaspers's postwar writings. In Jaspers's early postwar writings, the university becomes the privileged institutional setting for working through guilt, its attendant communication, and the future of the German nation that guilt and communication can come to constitute.[29]

In one of his very first public statements after the war, Jaspers took just such a remarkable approach to the political and cultural reconstruction of Germany. Entitled "Renewal of the University" ("Erneuerung der Universität"), the speech was a keynote address he offered at the opening of the Heidelberg medical faculty on 15 August 1945 and thus the first lecture of the reopened university. The medical faculty was the first part of the university to reopen: despite fears of persisting Nazism among the faculty, the Allies reopened it earlier than expected, largely because of the disturbing condition of the German population (sick, undernourished, disabled) and the widespread shortage of adequate medical care. Edward Harthorne, the officer responsible for universities in the U.S. zone, had suggested that Jaspers give the keynote at the reopening ceremony after he read Jaspers's "The Idea of the University" ("Idee der Universität") in manuscript form in July 1945. It was this address, according to Mark Clark, that turned Jaspers into a national figure, undoubtedly one of the most important for the postwar scene more generally.[30]

The speech, later published in the important postwar journal *Wandlung* as well as in English in the *American Scholar*, offers a trajectory revealing Jaspers's approach to coming to terms with the past, especially on the question of guilt. At a time when most addresses at such occasions glossed uncomfortably over the details of the recent past, Jaspers insisted on integrating German guilt—particularly its crimes against the Jews—into any reconstituted postwar German identity.[31] The lecture foregrounds the crimes of Germans before examining how the university might be rebuilt:

> we ourselves are no longer the same as we were in 1933. . . . Thousands of Germans, most of them anonymous, have sought or found death resisting the regime. We, the survivors, did not seek it. As our Jewish friends were taken away, we did not demonstrate in the streets, we did not shout until we, too, were annihilated. We chose to survive on the weak, even if correct grounds, that our death could not help. Our guilt is still to be alive.[32]

Jaspers considered this passage from "Renewal" so important that he quoted it verbatim in the much more famous *The Question of German Guilt*.[33] The passage quickly dispels any hope of simple restoration: Germans—all Germans who survive—are indelibly different than they were in 1933, and the radical divide is the guilt shared by all survivors. Simultaneously foregrounding guilt shared by all and the crimes against the Jews, Jaspers assumed a tack radically different than that of most intellectuals in the postwar period.

Collective guilt of this sort, however, can all too easily exculpate those guilty of more specific, more heinous crimes, and in "Renewal of the University" Jaspers did not circumvent the particular crimes of the medical community to which he was speaking. He discusses the nefarious euthanasia and sterilization programs under the Nazi regime and asks how medicine could have been capable of such pseudoscience and horrors. Medicine should rest on two pillars, Jaspers argues, the search for truth and a dogged dedication to humanity, but: "The image of the human was largely lost and, especially in many parts of the medical literature, spoiled. . . . We have to win back our image of the human."[34] Jaspers's explication and critique of the crimes of the medical community drive conceptually at one of the most ubiquitous postwar themes, that of humanity.[35] To this civilizing end, Jaspers called for the reintegration of medicine into the rest of the university, a reintegration into the tempering influences of the humanistic disciplines like philosophy that could keep physicians close to the "inexhaustible, inscrutable" nature of every human being.[36]

In grounding the medical faculty in humanity, Jaspers connects the university to one of the most ubiquitous themes of the postwar period and demonstrates how the incorporation of guilt into the university should shape its postwar contours. The university also becomes a lightning rod for another of Jaspers's central postwar themes, Germany's pariah status after the war and its prospect for rejoining the community of nations. Rabinbach explores Jaspers's notion of Germany as a "pariah" nation (a phrase Jaspers uses in *The Question of German Guilt*) and how Germany as a Kulturnation might reestablish itself in the world: for Jaspers, culture can conjure the cosmopolitanism by which Germany might reassert its standing among other nations. Rabinbach convincingly demonstrates how Jaspers implied parallels between Germany's pariah status and the fate of nationless, cosmopolitan Jews, a line of thought affirmed in Jeffrey Olick's study of the early postwar period.[37]

Jaspers's political writings in this period also make clear, however, that this interweaving of national and cosmopolitan themes finds a worldly manifestation in the reconstituted postwar university. Like many intellectuals I cited above, Jaspers celebrated the university's central role in Germany's past and future as Kulturnation. For Jaspers, the university survived the "catastrophe" as one of Germany's greatest and most abiding achievements: with the university, he wrote, "It concerns the maintenance, as well as improvement, of something that Germany has not yet lost, something that once constituted Germany's glory, and that could be, even in Germany's poverty and powerlessness, once again its glory."[38] But even more conspicuously than Mannheim or Clemens or Arendt, who saw some, even the last, hope for Germany in its universities, Jaspers underscored the dual character of the university, as both a national and cosmopolitan creation. In fact, for Jaspers, the university could effectively negotiate between these two elements. The university could come to constitute Germany's unique contribution to the wider community of nations, where the university would simultaneously reestablish Germany as a national presence:

with the claim of the idea of the university, we face a characteristically German question. Within the occidental—European and American—universities, the German university was something special. It had the best reputation in the world. . . . The question we now face is whether its origins can provide, once again, the promise of a cultural blossoming, a blossoming that could, even with all the other universities in the world, only bloom in Germany.[39]

The passage reflects how national the question of the university remained for Jaspers: though universities and their search for universal truths tend to the cosmopolitan, they also articulate German particularity ("only in Germany") within the wider traditions of the West.[40] The university becomes therein a key element of Jaspers's concern with the German nation and its future cosmopolitanism, and Jasper's writings demonstrate how the academy can serve to negotiate a problem central to his postwar ruminations. As with open acknowledgment and guilt, Jaspers links those notions that most distinguish his postwar publicistic work not only to some abstract German identity but also to the practical reconstruction of the university.

Existential Idea of the University

> That [renewing the university] is culturally, today, our only chance. Each person has to take the university onto himself, while he listens constantly and searches for communication, such that the idea of the university grows once again.
>
> Jaspers, "Renewal of the University"

> [I admire] this wonderful balance between pure flight and a firm grasp on reality.
>
> Arendt, letter to Jaspers, 9 July 1946

"Renewal of the University" represents only one of a large number of public essays and published speeches by Jaspers in the years after the war. While a number of critics have attended to Jaspers's writing on the guilt question, Jaspers actually published many more essays on the postwar form of the university. Jaspers's postwar vision for the university proves particularly interesting because it connects his new commitment to an open, free polity with many of his longer-term philosophical themes. In fact, his early postwar proposals for the university rest at the intersection of these themes, his newly found political commitment, and his commu-

140

nicative model for coming to terms with German guilt after the war. In terms of his own philosophical themes, Jaspers's "Philosophical Autobiography" argues that universities can foster precisely the kind of free self-development of which he writes in his philosophical work. The notion of freedom, of the free pursuit of truth, constitutes one of the core concepts of Jaspers's philosophy, corresponding neatly to one of the fundamental currents in his existentialist thought, in which freedom becomes the basis for the transcendent *Existenzerhellung* (existence-illumination).[41] Jaspers subsequently articulates an adamant commitment to academic freedom, the cornerstone of the university, as its most important element; freedom is simply, as he puts it in "Nation and University," the lifeblood (*Lebensluft*) of the university.[42] Academic freedom, for instance, obliges professors to teach the truth, "in defiance of anyone outside or inside the university who wishes to curtail it."[43] With freedom Jaspers repeatedly differentiates the university from the school, which follows a carefully preordained route and thereby comprises a completely different kind of undertaking.[44] The university becomes a key location, or "common room," for the highest mode of being.[45]

This emphasis on individual self-discovery and freedom, however, constitutes only the subjective side of Jaspers's philosophical vision:[46] though an existential philosopher, Jaspers long worked against the isolation of any sort of lonely existence, emphasizing instead the shared search for truth. Certainly as early as his 1932 magnum opus, *Philosophy*, communication serves as a cornerstone in the free pursuit of truth, the central undertaking for the individual subject. Communication receives its own chapter in *Philosophy*, immediately following and thereby complementing the chapter "I Myself." Communication was central to the search for truth: "a thought is philosophically true to the extent which its thinking promotes communication."[47] Communication is, for Jaspers, that which defines the "European," which is first and foremost the "depth" of human communication as well as incorporating it into the "will in community."[48] Jaspers, however, was not merely interested in what communication meant in the abstract or for individual subjects. In the postwar period, his prewar philosophical inclination toward communication manifests itself in his turn to the public and the political. Looking back over his life, Jaspers celebrated Nißl's medical clinic in Heidelberg, where he had started his career: Jaspers saw the clinic as an important model for an institution supporting the search for truth, the growth of the individual, in a community of like-minded and talented scholars.[49] In the postwar period, he located such communication emphatically in the reconstructed universities, which likewise realize his basic themes, like the discipline and education of the self, its being, and its relation to the world.

Just as Jaspers's work focuses on the method rather than the ends of inquiry—on the experience rather than content of the search for truth—free and open communication is the fundamental method of the institution of the university.[50] Such a combination of self-realization within a community, of individual freedom with communication and participation within a community, facilitates the experience of the search for truth and therefore existence, for Jaspers the ultimate end of being.[51] The university fosters the systematic development of natural talents by concentrating on the individual's relation to the world and individual creativity in that relation.[52] Communication in general, as Rabinbach has shown, served as a linchpin for Jaspers's postwar thought,[53] but I would emphasize that Jaspers also emphatically located it abstractly in his philosophy and practically in the university. This twain—the intersection of his philosophical insistence on communication and his practical insistence on the university to house it—would go far in explaining his much-discussed relation to Heidegger in this period, something on which I shall remark in more detail below.

Among the most important aspects of this communication hosted by and grounded in the university is the indispensable dialogue between the sciences and the humanities, another perennial theme of Jaspers. Jaspers himself was trained as a doctor, earned an M.D. instead of Ph.D., and even wrote an important textbook on psychopathology. Unsurprisingly given his background, Jaspers argues in his *Philosophy* that one needs both idealism and positivism. Both philosophy and science are required for the search for truth: "Without positivism, the objective and substantial realization of possible *Existenz* lacks a body; without idealism, it lacks scope."[54] In the postwar period, Jaspers was even more emphatic that science as an end in itself is ethically empty, a clear reference to the fate of science under Nazism. Science is "limited to the study not of Being itself, but of its appearances. . . . It is directed toward clearly designated objects, not toward Being itself," and therefore requires philosophy.[55] For a complete self, one needs both modes of inquiry. "The relation of philosophy and science is thus: science without wisdom is meaningless, wisdom without sciences is unreal."[56] Ultimately, both the sciences and humanities suffer under their own limitations—science offers no guidance for individual being and cannot justify its own activity, while philosophy enjoys only dubious claims to universality—and therefore they need each other.

In the early postwar period, Jaspers did not leave this complementarity and unity at the level of abstraction or individual existence; instead, in his postwar turn to the public sphere, he explained how it was intertwined with the history of the university and of Germany. The university again institutionalizes—that is, realizes the worldly manifestation of—one of his abstract themes. The lecture "The Living Spirit of the University" ("Vom lebendigen Geist der Universität") differs from most of Jaspers's writings on the university because it offers a detailed historical account of the modern university, including its fate under the Nazi regime: once again, for a prominent figure of the postwar public sphere, an educational institution provides an occasion to engage with the past. Delivered on 11 January 1946, the lecture inaugurated an evening lecture series for a wider public; it was so popular that Jaspers delivered the very same talk again a week later. Jaspers explains how the first German universities were Protestant universities, intended primarily for the training of clergy, and these were, according to Jaspers, rather dreary places. In the eighteenth century, the classical humanistic university developed the ideal of the Western university, academic freedom, and the supreme search for truth. These ideals produced a university that demanded both research and teaching from its community of scholars.

Over the course of the nineteenth century, however, this university went into decline through overt politicization and positivistic modes of inquiry. Jaspers narrates a story of the fall of the classical humanistic university, which degenerated over the course of the century into a series of technical schools, a frequent target, as Remy recounts, of scholars at older universities.[57] Instead of an education in a range of complementing disciplines, students choose from among specialties in an "intellectual department store." In stark contrast to the unifying whole of the university, these technical schools isolate the sciences from the humanities and subsequently churn out narrow experts instead of educated citizens. The nineteenth-century proliferation of varied professional schools and "technical" universities demonstrates how the old ideal of a unified university was forgotten—instead of a community of free researchers, the university became a mere *Massenuniversität* that ruined effective communication.[58] The Nazis were thus able to prey on what had already grown corrupted: exploiting the lack of unity or effective

143

communication among the disciplines, they turned the already fragmentary university into the many splintered schools of the party.[59]

This tale of specialization and degeneration parallels Meinecke's "Homo Faber" chapter, but fundamental differences structure the two accounts. Meinecke targets—and vilifies—the individual "young" student deformed by nineteenth-century specialization, while Jaspers focuses on the historical trajectory of public institutions, institutions that intellectually maim the individual. As I shall argue below, Jaspers deploys discourse about youth in different ways for different purposes. On the basis of his institutional story of decline into specialization, Jaspers can advocate two of his most specific demands for the reconstruction of the university: the introduction of a new technical faculty within the context of the traditional university and the reunification of the philosophical faculty, which had been split into natural sciences/mathematics and the philosophical faculties. On the former count, Jaspers feared that the burgeoning technical fields would be left—as they largely had been—to specialized schools and separate technical universities, therefore independent of and isolated from the traditional faculties. With the reunification of the sciences and philosophical faculties, Jaspers aimed to promote communication between the sciences and philosophy—in short, reining in the sciences with the humanities. Such a reunification was not simply an anachronistic restoration of a former unity; rather, it was to constitute a uniquely modern, mutually illuminating dialogue between the sciences and the humanities.[60] These specific directives—rare enough for postwar intellectuals—did not remain at the level of rhetoric: when he participated in Heidelberg's original Committee of Thirteen on the reconstruction and constitution of the regenerated university, he called immediately for the creation of such a faculty, a plea that was—like many of his suggestions—ultimately ignored.

"A Few Exceptional Young People": Jaspers's Images of the Postwar Student

Even the few studies analyzing Jaspers's writings on the university, like Remy's or Clark's, tend to focus on the much-contested denazification of faculty. But recent scholars have overlooked a remarkable suggestion Jaspers offered in his proposals for a new constitution of Heidelberg University. It was a suggestion that his colleagues similarly overlooked: that the students themselves should become "primarily" responsible for working on the "common spirit" of the university, which presumably meant including them substantially in the governance of the university.[61] This unusual and then disregarded idea underscores the important role students assumed in Jaspers's vision for a postwar university. That Jaspers would want to include students in this way was particularly remarkable given the widespread and often vitriolic debate about "the problem of the student" in this period, a controversy reflecting and reinforcing youth as a centrally contested site at this time. Throughout the early postwar period, university students became a particularly complex and important locus for denazification and reeducation, something generally downplayed in recent attention paid to Jaspers and the early postwar university. In general, the vast majority of male students were veterans, which invariably exacerbated persisting concerns about Nazism and the young. Specific cases, like students' responses to Niemöller's collective guilt speech, also fueled suspicions about the Nazi inclinations of the young. But after the British declared an amnesty for students born after 1919, the pressure on American officials to do likewise grew considerably, provoking many to defend the students and their putative political tendencies.[62] In March 1946, the American military government started to grant amnesty to those students born after 1919 whose direct Nazi activity could not be established (that is, did not belong to either group 1 or 2 in the denazification classificatory scheme). This did not quell widespread criticism, however, and by June 1946, in response to criticism of the amnesty in the United States, General Clay notified his lieutenants that students were to be denazified more aggressively.

Denazification, however, was only one element of a wider debate about students in the early postwar period, a debate reflecting general concerns about the direction of postwar German society. University admission policies, for instance, were also contested vehemently, since many, especially on the left, believed that the overwhelmingly bourgeois background of prewar students had made them, as well as the social elites they became, fertile ground for Nazi teachings. Looking to the Soviet zone, where Soviet officials had promised to populate the universities with children from worker families, labor union officials demanded vociferously that more worker children be able to study.[63] Some intellectuals, like Theodor W. Adorno, lamented how early efforts had failed to increase the number of working-class students, much to the detriment of the celebrated "democratization of the university."[64] On the other hand, many educational officials, teachers, and professors—products, after all, of the old system—defended the traditional admissions process, with its requisite *Abitur* and the *numerus clausus,* which favored those families that could afford the Gymnasium.[65] Jaspers himself weighed in on the issue of student selection consistently and at considerable length, usually quite conservatively.[66] All sides of this discussion were aware of the obvious stakes: those allowed to study would inevitably come to constitute the postwar social, economic, and political elites. These very public, often histrionic debates about denazification and the selection of students suggested a break between the young and the old, many of whom tended, as I have argued above, to characterize the young as especially committed Nazis.

In this context, particularly in *The Idea of the University,* one of two book-length political statements published after the war, Jaspers sketches a notion of the student that corresponds to and supports his philosophical vision for the postwar university. Like many of his lectures and essays, Jaspers's *The Idea,* which was based on a 1923 manuscript, describes a university that institutionalizes Jaspers's philosophical themes of freedom, unity, and self-development. In *The Idea,* however, Jaspers also sketches a specific image of "the young student" around which this university could be reconstituted. As he begins a description of the university's basic, indispensable activities in "Chapter Four: Research, Education and [Professional] Instruction," a detailed description of the "young student" intervenes in Jaspers's otherwise highly philosophical and abstract book. Though Jaspers is generally more circumspect about essentializing the young than Meinecke, he still appeals to discourse about youth to advocate the specifics of his ideal university to reconstitute the postwar community.

If the postwar university should offer individuals a context in which to realize and develop themselves through unfettered research and communication, then students become the privileged subjects for such processes. Like many liberals, Jaspers normativized the free individual as the diametric opposite of the *Massenmensch,* those followers whose ideas and passions were at the mercy of the mass.[67] For Jaspers— and in contrast to Friedrich Meinecke and Ernst Jünger—the student him- or herself becomes the opposite of the mass: "[Students] are individuals who deepen their individuality through communication. They are not the people as a whole, not the average, not the mass, but numerous individuals who risk being themselves. This is at once reality and a necessary fiction. It represents an attainable ideal and at the same time a challenge to live up to one's highest aspirations."[68] Such an optimistic

146

image of the student, in many ways harkening back to an image of youth more characteristic of the 1920s, stakes a particularly contentious claim in this context, in which many, including their own professors, vilified students as the most miserable dupes of Nazism.[69] For Jaspers, however, the student's natural inclinations tend toward the core functions of his philosophical university. The student and the appropriate reformulated university could overcome the mass, one of the recurring scapegoats for postwar etiologies of Nazism.

The university can support and enrich the student's inclination to free self-development in part because of the unity of knowledge it offers, a unity Jaspers made a cornerstone of his ideas for the university. In *The Idea,* Jaspers makes clear that the university in fact offers such a unity because of the student's "natural" demands: "the university with its aura of tradition represents to him the unity of all branches of learning. He respects this unity and expects to experience it, and through it to arrive at a well-founded Weltanschauung. He wants to arrive at truth, wants to gain a clear view of the world and of people. He wants to encounter wholeness, an infinite cosmic order."[70] In "The Living Spirit of the University," Jaspers narrates a specific history of higher learning that demonstrates how the university degenerated from the classical humanistic unity of knowledge, but here the young and their special predisposition to the university demand the synthesis of all knowledge under its unifying roof. The student makes demands that would result in precisely the kind of unified, philosophically inclined university that can overcome the specialization and technologization that Jaspers regards as the root of many Nazi evils. The student thus stands contrary to Germany's deviant modernity. Although Meinecke and, to a certain extent, Jünger understood German modernity as a maiming process, Jaspers contrasts the inclinations of the young to such a process, whereas Meinecke and Jünger make the young key agents of it. For Jaspers, students can help reconstitute the university deformed by this deviant modernity—the student, as modernity's better others, can help Germany come to terms with its past.

In *The Idea of the University,* Jaspers describes how in addition to demanding unity and wholeness, the young inevitably want more: "Yet even with all this [unity of knowledge], youth is not satisfied. The young person has a heightened sense of the seriousness of life since he is aware of the weighty decisions still ahead. . . . The young person wants to learn either by apprenticing himself to a master, through self-discipline, or through frank discussion among friends similarly motivated."[71] For over two pages, Jaspers describes in a similar manner how youth tends to a unity of knowledge and to the pursuit of the self—and how the modern educational process damages these natural predispositions. For Jaspers, the young are not a tabula rasa: they have inherent, apparently natural, philosophically resonant traits with which Jaspers asserts his vision for the university, the optimal institutionalization for his philosophical vision. This different discourse about youth explains in part Jaspers's well-known critique of the postwar cult around Goethe, which Meinecke, as we have seen, proscribes in stark fashion for Germany's young.[72] Instead of Meinecke's Goethegemeinden, which would school the degenerate youth in German classics, Jaspers deploys a different discourse about youth, a more optimistic one that can form the foundations for his preferred postwar panacea, the university. Moreover, his discourse links his basic philosophical themes—the free search for self, the unity of knowledge, the pursuit of truth and transcendence within it—to the institution with which he was practically and intellectually preoccupied at this time. At the intersection of his longer-term philosophical themes and their postwar institutionalization in the university rests a specific—in this context, contested—notion of the student.

Nation, University, and Politics: Jaspers's Depoliticizing Youth

> Out of trust in the era of Humboldt, we strive for, in the forms of our institutions, no radically new creations; rather, we build them in the sense of a conservative revolution.
> Jaspers, "The Living Spirit of the University"

> One might think of cases of wholly non-political persons who live aloof of all politics. . . . One may wish to make such aloofness possible, yet one cannot help admit to this limitation. We should like to respect and love a non-political life, but the end of political participation would also end the right of the non-political ones to judge concrete political acts of the day and thus to play riskless politics. A non-political zone demands withdrawl from any kind of political activity—and still does not exempt from joint political liability in every sense.
> Jaspers, *The Question of German Guilt*

Jaspers's image of the student provides not only an explicitly self-interested means to advocate on behalf of his ideal university; it also helped resolve one of the most contradictory challenges of the postwar university, its overtly and increasing political character. For Jaspers, who was in the postwar period becoming more publicly political while remaining loyal to the traditionally apolitical university, this question of politics in and of the university proved a difficult challenge indeed. One of his highest-profile appearances in the postwar public sphere, the November 1946 lecture "Nation and University" ("Volk und Universität"), reflects Jaspers's effort to isolate the traditionally nonpolitical university in an increasingly politicized climate, a climate he himself supported in *The Question of German Guilt*. A vigorous defense of the conventional university, the speech was widely disseminated, first broadcast on the radio and later published in its entirety in *Wandlung*. The text proves particularly important in evaluating Jaspers's postwar political writings because it documents how Jaspers responded to the increasingly politicized climate surrounding the university. In a context in which political controversy raged about the denazification of the faculty, the makeup of the student body, and the institutional form of the university, Jaspers responded by depoliticizing his beloved academy. Though by the end of "Nation and University," the university becomes the core of the (future) German nation, Jaspers insists that it remain removed from day-to-day, party politics. According to Jaspers, Germany should remain in the position of a Kulturnation, at a certain remove from the grit of "mass" politics and the messiness of democracy. This proves a particularly contentious stand in an environment in which both labor and state officials had called for more involvement in education in general and the university in particular.

Throughout 1945 and 1946—the years during which Jaspers wrote most of his public declarations on the university—the academy became a flash point for political struggles in the postwar social and cultural order. I have described above how the university became an important node for various discourses about German national and cultural identity in the wake of the war, but the University of Heidelberg was an especially revealing case of the struggle for control of denazification and social influence, as Remy has shown in his *The Heidelberg Myth*. Although Remy's account is both revealing and convincing, he does not fully elaborate how the university became an arena for a struggle between traditional elites like university professors and reform-minded German political activists like local labor leaders.[73] As early as September

1945, shortly after the medical school reopened as the first faculty after the war, German labor officials attempted to organize work councils among some of its clinic employees. Longtime political activist Max Bock, at the time the state director for reconstruction, labor, and society and later labor minister for Baden-Württemberg, led the attempt to organize the university clinic, a move vehemently fought by the new rector, K. H. Bauer, who also happened to be a professor of medicine, the head of the relevant clinic, and a close friend of Jaspers. The attempt to organize such unprecedented councils within the university was a clear effort by Bock to involve the labor movement in the governance of the university, an overt attempt to refigure, if not subvert, the university's traditional autonomy and isolation.

Rector Bauer, with help from the American military government and its suspicions of organized labor, ultimately prevailed, and no councils were formed. Not one to accept defeat so easily, Bock took to the local newspaper and published a number of articles challenging the denazification of the university, including one criticizing Rector Bauer for his book on "racial hygiene." But, by the winter of 1945–46, Bock had changed tactics: in December 1945, he formed a special "Work Group" (Arbeitsgemeinschaft für geistig Schaffenden) which was supposed to help liberate the state and economy from Nazi influences by vetting personnel for assorted professions, including lawyers, architects, and scholars. More generally, the Work Group aimed to secure the labor movement greater influence in postwar social and cultural life. Part of Bock's revised tactics was apparently to shift his focus on the staff of the university to the students: the first public lecture presented by the group was entitled the "The Fascist Attitudes of the Youth Admitted to the University" ("Die faschistische Geisteshaltung der zum Studium zugelassenen Jugend"). At the same time that local labor officials were criticizing denazification at the university in winter–spring 1946, a U.S. CIC (Counterintelligence Corps) officer, Daniel Penham, was investigating and soon criticizing the university's personnel policy. Penham, who was born Siegfried Oppenheim in Bad Hersfeld and emigrated to the United States via France and Morocco, had a sophisticated understanding of German academic culture and undertook an unusually thorough review of various professors' publications between 1933 and 1945. Both Bock and Penham called for the reclosing of the university in the winter of 1946 until a more thorough denazification could be completed.[74]

Bock's and Penham's criticisms were only bolstered by two events at the end of January 1946 that made denazification at the university appear even more dubious. A Heidelberg dean was arrested for falsifying his denazification questionnaire, and the infamous Niemöller episode transpired. As I recounted in my introduction to youth and education in the postwar public sphere in chapter 2, Niemöller was a Protestant minister who gave a sermon on collective guilt for Nazi crimes in Erlangen, during which raucous students allegedly drowned out his call for communal repentance. The event was covered extensively in newspapers and journals, offering another occasion to ponder the vicissitudes of guilt among the young. Penham, in fact, explicitly connected student behavior at Heidelberg to the nefarious Niemöller episode.[75] Although Bock's and Penham's demands to (re)close the university were eventually rejected by U.S. officials, a more aggressive wave of denazification did start in the summer of 1946. During that summer, when Jaspers was composing much of "Nation and University," the attacks on the universities' flawed denazification continued, including the publication of Bock's lecture attacking the fascist element among the students in the *Rhein-Neckar-Zeitung* newspaper, a piece referenced obliquely in Jaspers's speech. Jaspers's letters to Bauer in this period confirm his concern with the very public polemics against the university.[76]

Jaspers's speech "Nation and University" was broadcast on the Heidelberg University radio station on 10 November 1946 as the inaugural broadcast of a program called "The University Hour."[77] Jaspers wrote later that when the military government heard the title "Nation and University," it was immediately skeptical, suspicious of anyone linking the university directly to the nation, with its obvious echoes of Nazi coordination of the academy. When the military government demanded that the university rector turn over Jaspers's text, the rector refused, citing academic freedom and protesting that he had no control over the publications of a colleague. The military government then turned directly to the radio station, which promptly submitted the text, perhaps out of ignorance of the military government's intent, perhaps out of fear for its broadcasting license. Though American officials found nothing offensive or dangerous enough to censor it, they were nonetheless disconcerted that Jaspers had chosen such a resonant title and topic.[78]

What could have made the military government so suspicious of one of the postwar intellectuals it most trusted? It was the appeal to a university in the service of the "Volk," clearly an echo of the relationship between educational institutions and the nation in the Nazi years. Though he had mentioned how a university should serve the nation in the January 1946 "The Living Spirit of the University," Jaspers foregrounded this relationship more emphatically some ten months later. In those ten months came the series of attacks on the university described above. The increasing politicization of the university as a battleground for the postwar German cultural and social order had threatened its traditional form and faculties. The text makes clear that Jaspers felt the need to take the case for the university directly to the German people, to defend it against attacks and advocate for its traditional form. The labor unions were very public in their accusations, and the text responds directly to some of their criticisms about entrenched Nazism at the university.

The opening of "Nation and University" immediately stakes out the university's independence in a political climate in which labor, church, and state officials were jockeying for more control over the academy and its personnel. By advocating contemporary academic freedom and autonomy with principles handed down from the Greeks and the Middle Ages, Jaspers responds to his contemporary political situation with academic ideals of the past. As is often his tendency, he deploys the abstract and idealistic in a very specific political context. The speech engages its own politicizing context even more clearly in the next section when Jaspers strikes an overtly protective tone in defending against apparently well-known and certainly incriminating accusations about the universities. He writes that in the ubiquitous condemnation of the university, no one considers the accomplishments of the self-governed postwar university, and he lists them, including a new constitution, new personnel, and the restoration of the education of the young.

Though "Nation and University" does react explicitly to its political climate, it engages the political context in a deliberately oblique manner, a tendency that reflects the traditional political aloofness of the university and Jaspers himself. This intentional abstraction from the particulars of the political context is confirmed by a text entitled "A Request for Justice for the University" ("Bitte um Gerechtigkeit für die Universität"), which was not published until decades after the controversy.[79] Probably written in August 1946, the "Bitte" demonstrates how Jaspers would have responded directly to public political attacks. It is a draft of a response to the 16 July 1946 piece that appeared in the *Rhein-Neckar-Zeitung* in which Bock's Work Group criticized the denazification of the students. In contrast to "Nation and University," "A Request" directly references and explicitly engages the diatribes that had appeared in the newspapers.

By the time, some four months later, that "A Request" came to constitute the last five pages of the "Nation and University"—perhaps Jaspers's most public declaration to date—he had removed most such specific references to the attacks or the attackers, thereby moving the line of engaged argumentation into the realm of political abstraction. Only after a four-page exposition on ancient and modern ideals of the university does Jaspers explicitly turn to consider the specific criticisms of the university, but though he quotes a phrase or two, including the title of the 16 July 1946 piece, he never gives their sources or directly answers their attackers, as he does in his "Request." Even when wading into the political public sphere, Jaspers seems to be following what would be his own political imperative: the university should remain above the tumult of active, party politics.

Later in the speech, Jaspers makes explicit his intention to remove the university from the political struggle among different interest groups. Though Jaspers wanted the university to play a central role in the regeneration of the Germany polity, he was clear that "party" politics had no place in the university:

> If it is, under the current mission of higher education, especially important to study political realities and to train political knowledge and thinking, we should also warn of a certain confusion. The meaning of higher education excludes active politics from higher education itself. Each student can, when he would like to, belong to a party and be active in it. He can, as a youth, link himself politically to all the other youths of the nation. But as a student with other students, he is not to form party groups within the university. Here he researches the party in a politically windless space. . . no political action will be taken.[80]

In an increasingly politicized environment, Jaspers attempts the difficult navigation between a direct political engagement with the university's critics and the long historical tradition of elevating the academy out of any kind of political messiness. But this passage, in Jaspers's most public statement on the university, is richly revealing because it enacts precisely those conceptual moves Jaspers makes to distinguish the permissible, permanently contemplative politics of the university—which are, doubtlessly, required for the postwar coming to terms with the past—from those politics he banishes from his beloved academic community. Although he would like to foster a new type of education that promotes democratic thought and practices, he continues to be committed to banning active party politics from the university. To negotiate this political contradiction—to solve another conundrum of his particular coming to terms with the past—he suddenly invokes the student: to depoliticize the university in an increasingly politicized climate, Jaspers depoliticizes the student as opposed to the "Jugend."

Jaspers's effort to depoliticize the university by distinguishing the student from the youth is overdetermined by the context's debates on the politics of the student itself. His deliberate depoliticizing of the student here seems particularly noteworthy in light of another element of the debate about postwar students, the widespread criticism of them for being politically apathetic. Any number of essays and articles on the issue problematicized the lack of political interest among students.[81] In fact, U.S. officials saw the political apathy of students as a greater threat to the postwar period than the much-discussed Nazi element among them.[82] But for Jaspers these apolitical tendencies were not to be condemned but rather lauded. In his correspondence with Arendt, he praised his small-seminar students, citing them as "evidence of irrepressible German youth however small their numbers," and he described in September 1946 some students in his philosophy seminar: a "few excellent people" who "have no interest in politics, only scorn and mistrust, but despite that they are extremely well informed."[83] In light of Jaspers's effusive praise of such students, it was left to Arendt to question such attitudes: "What frightens me about your gratifying seminar students is that they, like us in our time—of unblessed memory—are not interested in politics. This lack of interest is part of an overall picture. It is also a false elitism."[84] The false elitism and detachment might have characterized Jaspers himself, though she never says so directly, instead relying on the students to illustrate the dangers of an apolitical stance and academic elitism:[85] for her as well as for him, youth becomes a site onto which to displace politics and political disagreements.

Jaspers's depoliticizing of the university through the adamant de-politicizing of the student is particularly remarkable—even suspect—in light of Jaspers's insistence on academic freedom. At the university, Jaspers repeatedly informs the wider public, both faculty and students have to be free to pursue their interests, wherever they may take them—it is a demand inextricably linking education to the free and unhindered development of the individual, the process of the pursuit of truth in which one can approach *Existenz*. Yet, in this very public passage, Jaspers announces an absolute ban on certain activities at the university. For these contradictory maneuvers with Jaspers's prized freedom, the student serves Jaspers perfectly—at no time, for instance, does he similarly forbid the general faculty from participating in such politics.[86] As in Mei-necke's Goethegemeinden, the attenuated agency of the young solves a problem for a liberal who wants to foster freedom but only within a certain constraining framework. Along these lines, too, I would suggest that one might read Jaspers's contradictory stand on Heidegger's post-war rehabilitation: Jaspers famously advised U.S. officials to support Heidegger's continued philosophizing with emeritus status (and pension) but not to allow him to return to teaching.[87] This contradictory stance is in line, I would suggest, with Jaspers's careful, deliberate nego-tiation of the postwar university. As we have seen in his particular image of the student, the university is to be vehemently protected from what Jaspers defines as any kind of politics, even if that clearly contradicts the premium he otherwise places on free communication.

Attending to Jaspers's writings on the university and especially its deployment of the student/young person, one can see how dedicated Jaspers was to protecting the traditional university, which had, as I have argued throughout, a privileged place in his philosophy. This reading of Jaspers helps to explain the contradiction that others (Arendt, Rabin-bach, Remy, and Clark, as I described above) observe between the en-gaged philosopher who adamantly insisted that guilt become part of postwar German identity and the somewhat detached professor who seemed naive and ineffectual at an institutional level. As happens throughout this postwar and reeducational context, a type of young per-son serves centrally in working through a nearly intractable conundrum for postwar German (adults): the student becomes a kind of intermedi-ate subject, one whose freedom can and should be curtailed, even in an environment where freedom is the "Lebensluft" of a beloved institu-tion.

Ernst Wiechert: The Messianic Poet
as a Youthful Man

In his heyday—the late 1920s, early 1930s, and then again in the late 1940s—Ernst Wiechert counted as one of the most widely read of German authors, domestically and internationally.[88] Despite his widespread and loyal following, his neoromantic *Heimat*-oriented *Kunst* has had a rather muted and dismissive reception among critics and today seems largely forgotten.[89] But notwithstanding this rather uneven staying power, Wiechert's postwar writings and especially speeches—many of which were published as some of those ubiquitous pamphlet tracts—constituted a central postwar public sphere locus. In a critical study of journalistic and literary activity in the occupational period, one journalist has called him "our idol of the years 1945–1950."[90] One survey in the late 1940s ranked him with Hermann Hesse and Thomas Mann as one of the most important German authors.[91]

What turned this broodingly introspective, relentlessly self-oriented, and proudly antisocial poet into one of the postwar's highest-profile intellectuals? Part of it was the publication of writings he had done for the drawer—or, in his case, typically nature-oriented burial in the garden: for example, in 1945 came *Der Totenwald,* a memoir of his three months in Buchenwald, and in 1947 the second volume of *Die Jerominenkinder.* But even more than these literary efforts, his speeches and journalistic activity made him one of the most visible, and later controversial, figures of the time. His speech "Speech to the German Young," delivered in November 1945 in the Munich Kammerspiel, catapulted him to a public renown that transcended both his earlier popularity and the usual professional station of author. *Neue Zeitung* said the lecture made a politician out of the *Dichter* (poet) and then went on to compare the departure of the audience to a congregation leaving a church—thus affording Wiechert, the schoolteacher turned writer, two other, more publicly oriented callings.[92] In a similarly celebratory vein, when the *Neue Tagesspiegel* reviewed a performance of the same speech by Franz Reichert in Berlin's Kulturbund—what was a unique event thus spread around Germany's public sphere, west and east—the reviewer wrote: "Wiechert's words are the most jarring and remorseless testimony that have thus far been offered against the agents of our twelve-year disgrace."[93] Perhaps the most convincing testimony to the public sphere prevalence and power of Wiechert's first public postwar effort comes in a parody, published first in the *Berlin Kurier* and then reprinted in local papers like the *Lüneberger Landeszeitung*. Titled "In the Style of a Well-Known Model: 500th Speech to the German Young, in the Vein of Ernst Wiechert," it was penned by "Hipponax," undoubtedly an ironic urbanite Wiechert would have despised.[94] A more critical satire of the speech appeared in *Der Ruf*, which offered a scathing reply of "the young to their poet" and even foregrounded the ubiquitous redundancy of Wiechert's address by labeling itself "the one and only speech."[95]

Of course, (widely circulated) imitation and satire is also the highest form of (public) flattery, and Wiechert must have been delighted by the attention the speech garnered. Since the late 1920s—already well into his career as a popular writer—he had rethought his lonely, antisocial vocation and desired nothing more than to play the publicly and politically oriented, adored, and above all heeded poet in the service of the poor and oppressed. In this he seems to parallel Jaspers's perhaps humbler decision to become more engaged in the public sphere after explicitly rejecting such public leadership in the Weimar period. Although this seemingly noble mission would sour quickly, in another parallel to Jaspers—ending in Wiechert's 1947 emigration to Switzerland in the face of physical threats[96]—the early postwar period afforded him a unique opportunity. As a former inmate of Buchenwald but also as an artist who had remained in Germany, he enjoyed an unusual authority he was happy to exploit, including most likely mild exaggerations of the dangers to him in the nefarious concentration camp.[97]

Wiechert offers my study of discourse about youth in the postwar public sphere a compelling case because, unlike the other intellectual figures I have discussed, youth had already occupied a central place in Wiechert's oeuvre. After the war, his long-held views on youth became widely known through his relentless postwar publicist efforts. Given his training and early career as a Gymnasium teacher, first in Königsberg and later in Berlin, Wiechert's attention to youth is perhaps not so surprising. But Wiechert's interest in, even dedication to, youth transcends any pedagogical interest. In his work, Wiechert writes repeatedly both of his own romanticized youth in the forests of east Prussia and of youthful alterity to the evils of modern society.[98]

Most fascinating about this neoromantic, Heimat-oriented oeuvre, however, is not its rather predictable idealization of youth but the public sphere resonance of a speech like "Speech to the German Young," in

157

which Wiechert's particular views on society and generation were generalized for public sphere consumption. As I observe above, an essay
about his lifework mentioned his speeches first as what most postwar
readers would have known. Moreover, "Speech to the German Young"
became not only the oratorical phenomenon described above: it later
served as the widely praised inaugural installment of Suhrkamp Press's
Europäische Dokumente, one of the postwar's most prominent series
on the regeneration of German culture and politics. The widely heard
and read speech, however, concludes a trilogy of public sphere efforts by
Wiechert—the other two from the Nazi time—whose strategies and
then trajectory testify to an exemplary understanding of 1930s and
1940s historical events via a very specific recurring discourse about
youth. As Stegemann's 1948 essay on Wiechert suggests, his postwar
speech was often linked to his speeches made during the Nazi era: it is
a conflation that conveniently links the 1933–45 resistance of a well-
known writer to the postwar period, a useful continuity in facing the
challenges of Vergangenheitsbewältigung.[99] In this particular coming to
terms with the past, Wiechert adds yet another kind of discourse about
youth to our growing postwar list: even more than Jaspers, he deploys
the social excess/outsider status of the young to frame his ideal society.
In a more relentlessly positive depiction of youth than in any of the
other writers I have discussed, Wiechert sketches the alterity of youth
such that it assures a mastery of the past, a negotiation of present guilt,
and a reconstruction of the coming nation. His writings return to notions of youth familiar from the turn of the century and the 1920s, the
kind of discourse about youth that many authors explicitly targeted in
their postwar agendas.

Wiechert's Neoromantic Weltanschauung
and Emancipatory Outsiders

One of the disadvantages of the useful cultural and intellectual histories
of the early postwar period, like those of Hermand or Glaser, arises from
their cursory attention to the particular themes or strategies of specific
authors. What makes Wiechert's case remarkable for my study is the coincidence and then confluence of generation in his prewar oeuvre and in
his high-profile postwar public sphere efforts. I would like to elaborate
the thematic that underpins his prewar work and thereby underscore the
central role that discourse about youth comes to play in it and subsequently in his publicist efforts.

Following the logic of the neoromantic and *Heimatkunst* tradition in which he is usually understood, Wiechert's writings focus on binary oppositions between the celebrated individual and corrupting collective, especially between sacred nature and evil society. Our artificial societies invariably maim and eventually kill the natural individual, who should follow the inner law (*das innere Gesetz*) instead of absorbing and obeying social norms.[100] Perhaps somewhat surprisingly given his career, schools play an integral part in this maiming indoctrination: his fiction is filled with confrontations between petty teachers and strong-willed, nature-loving youths. Along similar lines, the man who entitled his first memoir "Forests and Humans" ("Wälder und Menschen") constantly opposes the beauty and spirituality of forests—where he feels people can best achieve their potential according to their own inner law—to cities, which are ruled by the spirit-crushing values of social ambition and competitiveness.

Generally, this fundamental *Welt(scheu)anschauung* yielded in Wiechert's work a literature dedicated to stereotypical German Innerlichkeit, highly abstract and spiritual ruminations on the individual and his (usually his) inner struggles with oppressive social values. But they also provided Wiechert with a political perspective that would be radicalized somewhat in the 1920s and 1930s. Based on the duality of modern society and mass oppression versus human freedom and individual realization, his right-wing politics led him to condemn the SPD (Sozialdemokratische Partei Deutschlands) as a mass party. But he also stood against the NSDAP (Nationalsozialistische Deutsche Arbeitspartei), which he saw as only the latest avatar of modern mass politics. Formative for his right-wing politics was his tutoring in the house of an old east Prussian baron before he began teaching in Königsberg: the tutoring experience taught him to distrust the moral progress supposedly guaranteed by modern society.[101] In a kind of reverse (and therefore pro-) Prussianism, he thought the highest political value was the individual aristocrat's suffering self-sacrifice to the public good—such quasi-religious, silent suffering proved a constant theme of both his literary and journalistic efforts.

In both his literary writings and politics, then, emancipatory subjectivity is best located in the natural outsider, the other to the prevailing social and moral values. Such social values included Christianity, the clerical representatives of which he often depicted as corrupt: for a typical example, in *Die Magd des Jürgen Doskocil* (1932), a quiet, suffering individual who loves nature and his solitude away from the city saves a helpless woman from the rapacious clutches of an evil Mormon priest from Salt Lake City. The recurrence of the antisocial, nature-loving protagonist in his novels seems autobiographical given Wiechert's early attachment to the woods and his long residence at Ambach am Starnberger See. In his 1948 essay, Stegemann observes how attractive the return to the "Forests of Stifter and Eichendorff" would become in the 1939 *The Simple Life* (*Das einfache Leben*), published at the moment that the Nazis launched their brutal wars of aggression.[102] Following one of his favorite authors, Hesse, Wiechert mapped these outsiders onto a series of topographies: besides preferring the margin to society and the woods to the city, they tended to be poor, excluded from the upper classes, to the orient outside the occident. He mapped them as historically other as well, tending to cast them as archaic aristocrats in the mold of the Prussian baron for whom he had tutored. Likewise, he was inclined to romanticize (and essentialize) women characters above corrupt males.

This antisocial topography included as well a peculiar alterity of youth, which has enjoyed only peripheral attention in secondary work on Wiechert. In much the same way the woodsman is outside and above the social, the young remain aloof from the petty and corrupt adult world: they are the celebrated outsiders, in excess of modern society. In his peculiar politics, Wiechert ascribes to youth as other a much more positive valence than one finds in Meinecke or Jünger or even Jaspers. This generational undercurrent to Wiechert's literary thematics emerges most clearly in his public sphere appearances, particularly in the speeches he gave, in "Poet and the Young" (1933), "Poet and His Time" (1935), and "Speech to the German Young" (1945). Wiechert understood these talks as the core thrust of his public effort and certainly understood them as a single series, as he indicates at the beginning of the latter two talks.[103] A cursory analysis of the first two speeches demonstrates how generation mediates the core categories of Wiechert's literary work and thereby occupies a central place in the important postwar publicist "Speech to the German Young." One of the speeches, "Poet and the Young," was republished in the postwar period (1946) as part of Wiechert's public sphere onslaught. Perhaps the central role of generation would not be so interesting for my study if it merely constituted one of his literary themes, but these talks connect his literary-personal understandings to his approaches to the recent past and his resistance to the regime, both of which became important loci for the postwar public sphere.

"Poet and the Young": Bridging the Poetic Personal to the Publicly Youthful

In July 1933, Wiechert gave a speech on the vocation of the poet and his or her relation to the young to the students at the University of Munich. That he would give a speech on youth and the poet to a group of students is perhaps not so surprising, but he uses the forum to connect his own life and work to the young in a special relationship that is intended to subvert the Nazis' deliberate exultation of youth, which I described in chapter 1. The structure of "Poet and the Young" is, given its topic, simple and logical: first Wiechert asks what constitutes youth, then what constitutes the poet, and finally how they relate. In asking (in a rather essentializing mode) what constitutes the young and how this might have changed since the turn of the century when he was young, Wiechert opens the talk with an approach one can hardly imagine in a contemporary context: he offers a generational history that is the product of social upheaval, wars, and economic crises, one that resonates with but fundamentally contradicts that of Meinecke's *The German Catastrophe*. According to Wiechert, all of this led to generational instability and conflict. As I have been arguing throughout, radical, abrupt, or accelerated social change triggers a heightened discourse about youth. For Wiechert, though, a timeless discourse about youth obtains despite the war and the chaotic 1920s—for him all indicative of the assault of modern society on the individual, of the modern "loss of humanity." Although the tumult of the past decades would seem to subvert the forty-six-year-old poet's communication with the young, the ahistorically transcendent character of the young means that Wiechert can still commune with them.

For Wiechert, of course, there is more than a potential connection between the aging poet and the young. In his second section, on what constitutes the poet and his vocation, Wiechert invokes again his favorite outsider, the woods-inclined loner who remains true to eternal values instead of surrendering to the capricious moment. The key conceptual maneuver, embedded in an indulgent long quote of himself, is to affiliate the timeless youth he has just suggested with the poetic, natural outsider. For Wiechert, the poet and the young are natural outsiders, both socially skeptical and negating, lonely, suffering, and introverted.

Wiechert thus suggests a discourse about youth and generation at considerable odds with that in Meinecke and Jünger and one much more in line with fin de siècle cultural currents. With these latter authors, the young, though still other, occupy the center of a society that turned to National Socialism. Wiechert insists, with his likewise symbolically central discourse about generation, that youth are natural outsiders to precisely this catastrophe. No longer the causes of the catastrophic crisis, they are the natural resisters of such degeneration, not its most violent perpetrators.

He confirms such alternative discourse about youth by quoting (for eight pages of the forty-page piece) an essay he published in 1929 in the *Literatur* called "Of Interacting with Young People." The sudden and sustained intervention of this piece, from a pivotal moment in Wiechert's life and work, reinforces the special relation this particular poet had with the young. The years 1928–29, the years in which "Of Interacting with Young People" was conceived and composed, were a watershed time for Wiechert because he was having an affair with a married woman, a liaison that left him even more of a social outcast than usual. His Königsberg school had given him an ultimatum, to cease the affair or lose his job, but—seeing the demand as another inevitable conflict between individual freedom and social coercion—he refused. He spent a couple of years with only his writing, a suffering social pariah, a status cementing his image of himself as a lonely poet. The only individuals to rally to him, besides "a few worthy men," were his young pupils: for Wiechert, their youth inclined, them like the poet, to a defiance of coercive social values. They, like him, exceeded and resisted modern society. His "Of Interacting with Young People" describes their visit and the special connection between their suffering outsider status and his. From a natural loneliness and a deliberate distance from the markets of the day, the poet and the young become the "wise seers," an obvious inversion of the traditional generational hierarchy.[104]

It was out of this 1928–29 period that Wiechert reached his "breakthrough to grace" (*Durchbruch in die Gnade*), when he formulated the poet's task for the rest of his life: to serve as the lonely beacon for the rest of society. The outsider should sacrifice himself to the common good by committing his lonely work to those whom society injured most: the poor, the oppressed, the persecuted.[105] In his breakthrough to grace, Wiechert is obviously preoccupied with redrawing the boundaries of the social, and, to do so, he invokes the outsider figure. As I have been emphasizing throughout, in this historical constellation, the redrawing of social boundaries invoked generation as a central pillar of society as well as the youth as social outsider, with whom the bridge from outside to in could be realized: the social threat of youth can be used as social foundations. But in a manner different than Meinecke and Jünger, Wiechert constructs a discourse about youth as outsider to try to correct or improve the inside. Whereas Meinecke and Jünger define themselves by contrast with the young, Wiechert defines youth as other to the prevailing social order to identify himself with it. In all these cases, constitutive alterity is at work, but in different directions. Youth defines what is to be corrected in Meinecke and Jünger; in Jaspers and Wiechert, youth defines with what to correct. Remarkable for my purposes is that Wiechert invokes these themes in a public talk that attempts, by its end, to come to terms with the advent of National Socialism.

The public and political aspect of this thematic becomes especially clear later in the piece when—once having established their "natural" inclination to the outsider—Wiechert pleads for the young to remain outside the current celebration of youth and rejuvenation of Germany. Meant here is, as I traced above, the Nazis' redundant coding of their revolution as a youth uprising.[106] He laments the ubiquitous "Hymn" to youth and reminds them that the young should be social outsiders, in the stillness of the forest away from the noise of the world: "Gratefulness belongs to those things that should not be subordinated to the transformation of these times. And do not be discouraged—rather, retreat a little bit from the cacophony of the world back to the forests, which belong to all youth."[107] Though the critique remains abstract—he refers to the Nazis' movements as "these times" (*die Zeit*)—the counterargument is clear. In his approach to the public vocation of the poet, Wiechert posits a timeless youth discourse that he claims for his own and then contrasts this lonely, quiet, introspective youth to the mass, loud, aggressive mobilization of youth the Nazis emphatically exalt. He describes the perils of this kind of seduction away from youth's natural inclinations in the novel *Missa sine nomine,* in which a young woman, Barbara, is corrupted by Nazism, but here he has made faithfulness to the putative natural inclinations of youth the core of his series of high-profile speeches.[108]

In his "The Poet and His Present," also delivered at the University of Munich, this time in April 1935, Wiechert escalated his anti-Nazi rhetoric. The talk was regarded as a decisive break with the Nazis by Wiechert himself and by the Nazi authorities: after agonizing about whether he should remain reticent, Wiechert delivered explicit criticisms that provoked regular Nazi surveillance of all of his activities, attention that would later result in his internment in Buchenwald.[109] In conceiving his decisive break with Nazi policy, I would argue, Wiechert chooses to continue his generational thematic and to focus on the young as the battlefield with the Nazis: he clearly conceived of this 1935 talk as a continuation of "Poet and the Young"[110] and then revisited, in slightly more direct language, the same ideas. Though the times have grown worse, the poet is still the lonely messianic figure, and the poet's special relationship to the young is taken once again as axiomatic: only this time as more explicitly public, more openly resistant to the spreading political and social revolution.[111]

After reiterating themes from "Poet and the Young," Wiechert develops an influential image from his childhood: a lonely, quiet fisher providing sustenance for thousands while the rest of the community celebrates a holiday. The figure serves as the latest manifestation of the natural outsider—substituting the forest with a lake—and Wiechert explicitly sketches the fisher as the poet dedicated to providing for the public in desperate need of nourishment. Wiechert's image of the poet also has clearly religious overtones, turning the poet into a Christlike laborer and sufferer on behalf of others, a notion endorsed in the context of Wiechert's work in the postwar period.[112] As in "Poet and the Young," the fisher-poet is meant to remain faithful to the eternal (his work and its values that bring him close to nature, God, the relationship between mother and child) instead of to the times (meaning the loud, decadent celebrations of Nazism). Wiechert unmistakably means the Nazis, as he criticizes their godless deification of the day, their forgetting of the holy past and desecration of sacred traditions.

Wiechert's criticisms of the Nazis do not remain in the metaphorical and implicit register: as he turns to more explicit criticism of the hierarchy of his central binary contingent/eternal, he turns once again to the young. He begins his more explicit criticisms by complaining that the young poets are too obsessed and committed to the contingencies of the day.[113] Wiechert explicitly mentions the ages of those committing these generational crimes: they are twenty to twenty-five but think too

164

far beyond their years, Wiechert informs his listeners matter-of-factly. In contrast to Meinecke or Jünger, Wiechert asserts that the young poets' Nazi-indulging mistake is an early abandonment of youth rather than an indulgence of youth. Moreover, their preoccupation with the present has led them to a valorization of war and death,[114] to a violation of the generational order that prescribes a life-affirming youth. As they sacrifice their individual talents—which for Wiechert should lead them to lonely introspection and presumably to the woods—to benefit the masses, they murder their youthful souls.

In expanding his criticism of commitment to the moment rather than to eternal (natural, divine, maternal) values, Wiechert once again focuses on the impact of education on the young. This pernicious commitment to the contingent and ephemeral marks not only poetry and literary criticism, which measure the artist by political commitment rather than timeless values but affects education above all, a subject on which he expends much more time and care than on poetry or literary criticism. The current reforms are ruining the young because they educate them for heroism irrespective of values, good or evil, noble or vulgar.[115] Such education for gladiatorial glory will be short-lived, only the latest manifestation of the unworthy ephemeral.

The poets, according to Wiechert, believe more than any other social group in the young: their generational progress that will ameliorate maiming, evil modern society. In his particular mode of constitutive alterity, Wiechert believes more than Meinecke or Jünger that youth is the solution, not the problem. As in "Poet and the Young," the young and the poets behave differently than those involved in the loud, belligerent revolution for which they are being educated: the young are for Wiechert actually quiet, pious, humble. A crisis of youth does not cause the Nazi catastrophe—rather, that catastrophe victimizes the young. In this talk, intended to criticize and break with the Nazis, Wiechert fundamentally contests the nature of the young, an argument based on competing discourses about youth and their realization in society, especially in education. The momentous battlefield he has chosen evokes above all the young. When he concludes, admitting portentously that he does not know when he will be able to speak to them again, he asks the young to swear that they will not follow the masses, and he himself promises to help prevent it. They are, like him, to remain in excess of, outside of, the powerful mass currents of Nazi Germany. The forty-seven-year-old author's criticism and resistance rest on his special, reciprocal relation to the young—a very different relation than was seen in the other authors of the early postwar period I have discussed.

"Speech to the German Youth": Cementing the Social with the Social Threat

Perhaps in response to popular demand for more words from the juvenile-oriented oracle, "Poet and the Young," was reprinted in 1946 as one of the ubiquitous pamphlets about German society and culture. Such reprinting demonstrates how the three speeches (two from 1933 to 1945 and one from the postwar period) established a convenient continuity in Wiechert's resistance to the Nazis: they suggest a good German who remained consistently and adamantly opposed to the all-too-effective indoctrination by the regime. In his 1948 essay looking back at Wiechert's work, Stegemann even goes so far as to suggest that these speeches to the young erected a "stronger dam" against the tyranny of the times than any "direct act" of resistance could have. Like Jünger's comparing his *The Peace* to the 20 July 1944 conspirators, Wiechert's speeches to the young displace more engaged resistance. Stegemann also confirms the importance of the three speeches taken together, so my long detour into Wiechert's 1930s writings about the young does resonate against the postwar public sphere.[116] Moreover, because the two speeches bring to light how Wiechert understood and analyzed German society before and during the Nazi time—that is, with the center constituted by the periphery of youth's alterity—they foreshadow the manner in which he came to negotiate coming to terms with the past after the war.

These two main public efforts by Wiechert in the Nazi period (he was not allowed such an address again) form the foundation for his high-profile "Speech to the German Young," delivered first in November 1945. I have already mentioned the speech's wide and positive reception as well as its publication as the initiating volume of the Suhrkamp Europäische Dokumente series, which would run through the late 1950s. In its review of the first publication in that series, *Neue Zeit,* in a surprisingly wholehearted embrace of someone like Wiechert, wrote that one could hardly imagine a more impressive start to the series; the newspaper even lobbied that it be required reading in upper school classes.[117] In its original review of the speech, *Neue Zeit* emphasizes a new Ernst Wiechert who abandons his beloved woods, individualism, and interiority (*Innerlichkeit*) and "steps toward his people, talks to them, and reaches a hand to them, in order to find a shared path out of the guilt and crisis of these times."[118] The newspaper is responding to what Wiechert saw in his "breakthrough to grace" and what I emphasized in the speeches above, a bridge from his personal/literary inclinations to public efforts. Obviously, in a "Speech to the German Young," the postwar bridge would once again be founded, most impressively and fundamentally, as the *Neue Zeit* suggests, on the young.

As the *Neue Zeit* also asserts, Wiechert would have to negotiate the guilt issue to find a communal way out of the labyrinthine burdens of Germany's recent past. Once again, as in Meinecke or Jaspers, youth becomes the means to navigate such difficult challenges of the past, though in a different manner. Wiechert spends much of the essay arguing for a more or less collective responsibility: he suggests that no one could have missed the advent of the Nazi upheaval, no one could have mistaken Hitler or his henchmen for harmless democrats, particularly after 30 June 1934, when they murdered "their own."[119] All Germans saw it, it affected them all, and to deny it would only double their guilt. In assigning blame, he focuses on those factors and groups usually attended to in intellectual histories of the postwar: the masses, technology, the generals and their army and, of course, that most demonic Hitler.[120] In fact, the only notable absences from his litany of causes of German fascism are capitalism, which he implies in the modern mechanization of the masses, and Prussianism, whose values he still held dear.

Wiechert thus spends about two-thirds of his essay asserting a collective responsibility, if not guilt, with which the Allies must have been quite satisfied. But from there, in his normative assertions concerning the regeneration of German culture (politics and society typically do not interest him as much), he begins to dilute such widely spread guilt with the thematic I underscore in his other two speeches: the natural outsider via the poet (that is, Ernst Wiechert) and the young. In both cases, mitigating factors qualify them to become the core of a regenerated, healthier culture and society. Wiechert thus invokes, as in his earlier speeches, the poet and the young as peripheral figures who can nourish the rotten core of society—he invokes, in another instance of constitutive alterity, the poet and the young to redraw the boundaries of his reconstructed society. This discourse about youth is quite different than Meinecke's or Jünger's: they saw youth as guilty of Nazism and in need of special rehabilitation, the social threat disciplined into social cement. For Wiechert, the timeless discourse about youth qualifies them as the constitutive margin of society, a margin crucial to his navigation of postwar guilt.

167

Wiechert segues from his lengthy collective guilt section to one in which he emphasizes the mitigating subtleties of his own and youth guilt. His own emerges in his tendency to underscore his persecution, his time in Buchenwald, and the Nazis' ban on his writing. But just as conspicuous in this essay—and linked to his own exculpation via the connection between poet and youth he has argued at length—proves his celebration of the young. He emphasizes that the "most decisive development" (*entscheidendste Aufgabe*) of the last twelve years was the ripping of love from the hearts of the young.[121] Weichert's assertion confirms the young as a central preoccupation for the postwar period: as I suggest in my introduction to the postwar public sphere in chapter 2, phrases like "most decisive" and "most urgent" were often associated with the young. Wiechert's most decisive task suggests (against Meinecke and Jünger) a natural inclination toward love in his particular youth discourse and asserts that the young were the key victims of the last twelve years—Jews and other persecuted groups, remarkably, get no mention in his speech.[122] The young become a key locus for the displacement of other issues of Vergangenheitsbewältigung, here for a diversion from its most severe victims. Wiechert's theory provides a pretty convenient "most decisive development" by highlighting something like the ripping of love from youth's hearts, which can always enjoy a sudden conversion, that is, a change of those hearts. Wiechert also gives special attention to soldiers, and he likewise downgrades their guilt if they were fulfilling their soldierly duty: once again their youth proves useful, because who could "judge the youth" for their dedication to their youthful camaraderie?

Perhaps the most clever and subtle exculpation arises near the end of the speech, however, when Wiechert outlines how the young should now conduct themselves in society in light of Germany's complicated past. Wiechert says the last and hardest task left will be for those who encounter someone who followed the Nazis, that is, who was not necessarily a criminal but someone committed to them. Unsurprisingly, he relies on youth to restore the community, on its constitutive alterity to redraw the boundaries of the social: "Maybe there will be only a few, maybe there will be many. And they will look over to you like children who have been knocked out of a game. And if you believe that there is a newness in your hearts, then do not hit them back!"[123] The exonerating moves of the speech become clearer than ever here: if you in the audience went along with Nazis, did everything short of something directly criminal, then you should be considered a child against whom we should not strike back. Not only is the speech, read throughout Germany and published as a text, addressed to the young, it renders the presumably complicit adult, the fellow traveler (*Mitläufer*), an innocent child.

Embedded in this telling passage is another recurring phenomenon of the generational discourse I shall discuss in the rubble films, the child's gaze. This look of the child to a dubious social agent— especially to a soldier returning home (*Heimkehrer*), whose commitment to society is questionable—adds to the agent's humiliation in such a way that he (usually he) will be encouraged to act in a socially affirming manner. Another form of constitutive alterity, the child's gaze acts as a unique form of social regulation in an environment with decimated social norms: it pushes the subject toward the social without seriously threatening it. As I observed with Jünger, youth's alterity becomes constitutive as it functions to entrench the normative subject in his or her position. After World War I, in which he fought, the Heimkehrer problematic became paradigmatic for Wiechert: the Heimkehrer's ambivalent relationship toward society mirrored the poet's distance from and distaste for the same society. In terms of marriage and marital problems, a constellation recurring in many rubble films, Wiechert writes of the discomfort with women he experienced when he returned from the war; by the late 1920s, this discomfort grew to the poet's open antagonism toward his marriage and the social expectations governing domestic sexual relations.

In "Speech to the German Youth" this child's gaze is invoked at times to mitigate guilt and at other times to reintegrate troubled youth back into the social order: once again, generational mechanisms are invoked dually, to restore and affirm the social. Once he has effectively exculpated youth, whose victimization was "the most deciding task" of the last twelve years, he has to assure their successful social integration. Like so many other key figures in the postwar period, he guarantees this with a restoration of the generational hierarchy:

> Do not ask where and how you should begin with love. You
> have a seed to sow and the field is waiting for you. A haggard
> people is waiting for you, and for the poorest of this people,
> you have gone through the fiery ovens, for their children.
> They have no roof over their heads and no bread to eat, they

have no Bible and no fairy tales. Over their childhood years presided the idols of the desert, and the fiery Moloch stretched glowing arms toward them. They are the only field that is left to us now, the only and precious treasure that we possess. The forest has been cut off, but from the deepest foundations of the nation shoot out new forces: the future, the only future, and it is laid in your hands. Once you would have been educators or preachers, would have been doctors and judges, and a few of you would have raised the comforting light of art before the hungry eyes of the people. But then think about how no new earth will blossom up without your filling them with your love.[124]

As I argue in chapter 2, the loss of faith in the social should be met with the reminder that the children need adults: youth serves, as it often has, to manage adults. In the urge to abandon a society that has victimized them, Wiechert's young should be reminded of the truly innocent who need their help, which should therefore drive them back to the social order. Wiechert's commitment to the young supersedes even his usually foregrounded affinity for nature: now, with the forest (those beloved forests yet again) gone, the children are the only natural treasure left. The context's focus on youth, its reliance on generation to restore social and cultural identity, becomes therein all the clearer: it is the only remaining cornerstone. Its constitutive alterity should therefore regularly define us.

    Not the mere presence of the youth, but its looking at the young and able-bodied should convert the doubting social outsider. Wiechert invokes the child's gaze at a couple of other pivotal points in the speech. Returning to his theme of saving the poorest of society, he writes: "you should go to the poor of our people, and where a child raises his disconsolate eyes to you, you should bend down and with full certainty utter: 'Come, we promise to rescue you from this deepest sorrow.'"[125] The look of those eyes should invite a sworn oath to the social order, the very task of the socially distanced but committed poet Wiechert sees in himself. Likewise, in the concluding lines of the speech, in which he quotes from his poem "The Death Mass," he describes thousands of children whose *Tränenkrüge* (jugs full of tears) highlight their sorrowful gaze turned up to the remaining adults.[126] This look, the child's sad and lost gaze, should exhort us to commit to emptying the jugs of tears, to get behind the social plow, to offer bread and lots of mercy to the fellow members of a formerly despised social order.

CONCLUSION: YOUTH WORKS AND INTELLECTUALS

> All the suffering seems to flow right to this poet or to
> draw him close to itself; a certain primal accord with
> the suffering appears to have formed itself in his soul.
> Reinhold Schneider

In his celebration of Ernst Wiechert's sixtieth birthday, published as "Melody of Suffering" in the *Süddeutsche Zeitung* newspaper, Reinhold Schneider asserts, in overtly theological language, that Wiechert plays the role of savior and redeemer for those who have suffered under the catastrophe.[127] As I have argued above, however, this particular kind of savior and redeemer, who became so grandly exalted for this context, relied on discourse about youth and generation to come to terms with the recent past. As with the three other prominent figures of the postwar public sphere, generational difference provides a pivotal form of alterity for Wiechert to navigate the considerable challenges posed by Nazism and its aftermath. For him, as for the others, such a deployment of generation requires that youth be discussed as a social class in a manner similar to traditional socioeconomic classes, that it become a discursive option in the understanding of such events. In discussing generation instead of class, they were invoking and elaborating on discourse about youth inherited from the fin de siècle period through the 1940s. In postwar Germany, these four authors demonstrate that youth constituted just such an analytical category, in a way that is hard to imagine today, where it attains no such status. In a way on par with gender or national alterity, a great number of prominent intellectuals use generational difference, that is, society's relationship to its youth, to come to terms with the past and to set an agenda for the future.

Although discourse about youth and generation is equally central to their early postwar writings, Karl Jaspers and Ernst Wiechert depict the young very differently from Meinecke and Jünger. Jaspers scholars often neglect Jaspers's extensive writings on the form of the university, but these writings demonstrate a deliberately practical side to Jaspers's thinking: despite the common criticism that he remained at too much of a remove from the practical world even in his public philosophizing, Jaspers was directly and intellectually very concerned with the institutions that might best house his philosophy and processes its emphases.

171

His work shows a self-conscious awareness of the manner in which other writers construct an emphatic, self-serving discourse about youth. Wiechert takes a very different tack from any of these other authors: as he had been consistently claiming since the 1920s, Wiechert, too, sees youth as other, but—for those youth who resisted the temptations of Nazism—as the emancipated other to modern society's ills. Wiechert deliberately cultivates youth's outsider status in order to valorize a subject outside its historical context. Wiechert had been celebrating youth in this mode since his early work before 1933, but what remains remarkable for my study is that this approach and its emphasis on the young as the outside core of society became so popular in the postwar public sphere. This popularity confirms the relevance of the longer-term cultural currents around youth for Germany's coming to terms with what had "tragically" transpired.

All of these inflections of discourse about youth and generation add to the sense of youth as social other. From the station of society's other, the young were used to define and redraw society's boundaries. In a manner similar but contravening that which I traced in culture under the Nazis, youth alterity is constitutive for the society these intellectuals wanted to assert: because youth had exceeded society, run outside its borders, the intellectuals' exploring their excesses afforded a unique opportunity to redraw those same borders. The nation was to be refounded, its metaphorical borders redrawn, by either disciplining or incorporating this youthful other: Meinecke—who wants to discipline youth in his Goethegemeinden—and Jünger—who wants them to synthesize obsolete national states into a supernational empire—discipline the wayward young to redraw the borders of the nation. In a different vein, Jaspers and Wiechert want to reconstitute the core of society and the nation as young.

These youth agendas were national programs that seemed safe in a time when there could be almost no national agenda of Germans' own making: in a similar but more subtle vein than Alois Hundhammer's declarations of German sovereignty in the areas of youth and education, the youth agendas of these intellectuals provide a subtly political position at a historical moment when politics had become in many ways taboo. As I sketched in chapter 2, teacher/parental subjectivity became the widespread normative means for adults to overcome nihilistic discouragement at all that had happened. Such a program based on youth also offers what appears to be an antipolitical project—precisely what transpires in Jünger—at a time when there was both a mistrust of and a disenfranchisement from politics. To understand the peculiar politics of Jünger's detached observations or his obscure *The Peace* or Meinecke's Goethegemeinden or Wiechert's celebrations of youth, one must foreground the importance of discourse about youth and generation. In different but revealingly similar manners, Meinecke, Jünger, Jaspers, and Wiechert all use youth to move beyond conventional politics in an age in which politics, as they had known them, must have seemed intractable.

5

Children of the Rubble

Youth, Pedagogy, and Politics in Early DEFA Films

In the 1920s the German film industry was among the most successful in the world; in fact, Germany was probably the last nation whose industry could seriously compete with Hollywood's products in the world market until Hollywood's hegemony was made certain by the advent of the sound film in the late 1920s and early 1930s. During the Nazi period, especially after the 1940 ban of U.S. films, the German industry developed a Hollywoodesque, sophisticated, and slick style that proved immensely popular and that has now been described in a number of scholarly studies.[1] The end of the war changed all of this: the unconditional surrender effectively ended what had been one of the world's most vibrant, creative, and popular, if suspiciously compromised, film industries. So the end of the war and the unconditional surrender would also necessitate, for German filmmakers and films alike, a coming to terms with a squandered past and a mastering of a problematic complicity.

The next two chapters trace this coming to terms with the past as it was depicted in the first films after the war, typically called "rubble films."[2] Similar to Mann's *Doktor Faustus* and intellectuals' tracts, lectures, and radio addresses, these films deploy the young to solve a num-

175

ber of challenges—here representational challenges—facing postwar Germans. If the German rubble films—that is, German feature films made between 1945 and 1951 pertaining to the recent past or present— were charged with coming to terms with the difficult past, the young appeared again and again in these scenarios to negotiate and navigate opaque situations. Before moving on to the specifics of these filmic representations, I would like to give an overview of the discursive field surrounding the film industry after the war, since it was somewhat different than those sketched above, though the solutions to the challenges it posed would prove nonetheless dubiously similar.

It is no historical accident that Gerhard Lamprecht and Wolfgang Staudte—the directors of the first two postwar German feature films— both appeared at a 22 November 1945 gathering in the Hotel Adlon. Until that date German filmmakers had had little official opportunity to begin work on new productions or even to meet. Hosted by the DEFA precursor Filmaktiv and endorsed by the Soviet authorities, the event and its early date stand in stark contrast to the other Allies' icy policies toward German filmmakers at the time. The advertisement for the gathering was so out of line with other Allies' policies that it was not even taken seriously by the Germans themselves.[3]

The SMAD (Soviet Military Administration) was much more willing than the other Allies to entertain the idea of Germans making a feature film at that early date. The SMAD would in fact approve and support—through the fledgling DEFA studio, officially founded in May 1946—the first two postwar German features. Staudte had originally floated his treatment for *The Murderers Are among Us* (1946, DEFA, Soviet license) to British and then American officials, only to have it rejected by both; one American official informed him that it would be "twenty years" before the American authorities would again allow a German to make a feature.[4] What led to such divergent policies among the Allies toward German films and filmmakers? The SMAD's more reconciliatory cultural policies were in no small part due to its lack of conviction about the official doctrine of "collective guilt." This skepticism was informed by Stalin's idea of "two Germanys"—that is, the Germany of the "Hitler clique" was to be distinguished from that of the workers.[5] Such notions, underpinning the Soviet and KPD (Kommunistische Partei Deutschlands) policy of antifascism, yielded a much quicker rehabilitation of German filmmakers. The Soviets' and subsequently the

KPD's notion of "two Germanys" certainly helped fuel the "groundswell of antifascism" the KPD claimed to detect in its sector,[6] one that led to an emphatic commitment to a unified *Volksfront*—an expansive grouping including not only proletarian artists but also "bourgeois" filmmakers like Staudte and Lamprecht.

These brief remarks demonstrate how the wide range of discourses I have been tracking thus far in my study also intersects the institutional history of early postwar German film: themes like collective guilt, nation, national identity, reconstruction, humanistic reeducation, fascism, and antifascism informed decisions about what and when films were licensed and ultimately produced. As with the other media I have been analyzing, however, the traditional discourse around coming to terms with the past has hindered insight into one of the most significant and symptomatic thematics of the early rubble films:[7] the recurring image of the young. While a number of film critics from the late 1940s regarded the foregrounding of youth as significant—underscoring it as one of the most important, if contrived, aspects of the films' much-celebrated realism[8]—later scholars have never undertaken a sustained look at the pivotal role of youth, both children and adolescents, in early rubble films. In a great number of rubble films between 1945 and 1949, youth figures as a key aspect of the films' Vergangenheitsbewältigung, confirming youth's symbolically central place in the immediate postwar historical and cultural context.

Despite the political and bureaucratic differences noted above, filmic content in the various sectors did not significantly differentiate itself in the first years of the occupation. In his book *DEFA, Artists, and SED—Cultural Politics*, Thomas Heimann is quite definite on this count, asserting that there was little thematic difference between the zones until 1948—Heimann suggests that *The Murderers Are among Us* could have been made in the West; other, less DEFA-friendly authors confirm this commonality.[9] A close reading of youth in some early DEFA features suggests both this commonality and its slow erosion: while *Somewhere in Berlin* (Gerhard Lamprecht, 1946, DEFA, Soviet license) demonstrates the relatively depoliticized centrality of youth in many early DEFA rubble films, Staudte's *Rotation* (1949, DEFA, Soviet license) highlights the role youth comes to play in the increasingly politicized films of DEFA.

CHAPTER 5

EARLY POSTWAR GERMAN FILM:
SOCIAL AND CINEMATIC CRISES

Although my study asserts the general importance of the young throughout this cultural context and in a variety of media, the filmic manifestation of youth occasions theoretical consideration due to the particularities of the cinematic medium. Youth and youth crises figure prominently in many rubble films for an assortment of reasons. Since these films attempt to depict their context realistically, they deploy the youth crisis as a key element of the wide-ranging and conspicuous social crisis. In addition, these films also faced something of a cinematic representational transition or even crisis. They attempt to brush against the fantastical grain of the Ufa-*Traumfabrik* (big-studio dream factory) of the 1930s and 1940s: they demonstrate a new commitment to realism and often depict a decimated, lacking central character. In this cinematic crisis, youth becomes an overdetermined presence—not a mere mirror of social problems but a recurring, favored device—because of the films' narrative and formal strategies and the representational opportunities that youth afforded such strategies.

It is precisely these strategies and opportunities within the dual social-cinematic crisis that I shall be investigating. Youth becomes the diegetic and formal foil for the returning soldier, the Heimkehrer, whose struggle with Vergangenheitsbewältigung stands in for an assortment of postwar challenges—the Heimkehrer's (re)socialization comes to parallel the youth's, such that the films recurringly stage a double, complementary (re)socialization. While affording the films an obvious element of the social context they explore, youth crises also offer the solution to a number of representational problems arising in the midst of this cinematic crisis. Similar to the way in which the young serve to negotiate the contradictory challenges of coming to terms with the past, youth crises in these films serve to solve the contradictory challenges of "realistically" but reconstructively representing the postwar context.

By the end of World War II, German society had faced two major recent upheavals, the 1933 National Socialist "revolution," which, as I argue above, imagined itself as a decisive break with bourgeois society, and the 1945 defeat of that society at the hands of the Allies. Given these momentous historical breaks as well as the material emergencies in the wake of the war, German society was certainly suffering from a social crisis. This crisis, I would like to argue, manifested itself in an analogous cinematic crisis of dispersion, that is to say, the weakening and blurring of formerly firm cinematic relations and hierarchies. This blurring of hierarchies created a context in which lines had to be redrawn and hierarchies reestablished, and, as with the authors discussed above, the young served especially well in reconstituting selective social groups.

The figure that these films invariably follow across the desolate postwar landscape was the Heimkehrer.[10] The Heimkehrer, however, does not correspond to the desiring male usually postulated in fiction films or psychoanalytic film theories.[11] Such a unified, desiring male in denial of lack dominates traditional cinema and film theory, which often describes how gender difference is deployed to prop up the male, to help the male deny castration and lack. But the Heimkehrer constitutes a passive, marginal, not active or central male and ends up complicating, often inverting, differences that traditionally serve the male's privileged social status.[12] In these early postwar films, this sociocinematic shift requires a rethinking of the male protagonist, a rethinking that will now include generational along with gender difference.

The Heimkehrer serves my analysis as the marginal male Kaja Silverman describes, though his marginality, in contradistinction to that described by her theory, plays out by a subversion of generational (as well as gender) difference.[13] The Heimkehrer sports a persistent lack of belief in the bourgeois social order—productive labor outside the house, patriarchal relations inside it—which the films set out as necessary for coming to terms with the recent past. The trauma of the war and its humiliating aftermath make it difficult for the male subject to reintegrate into the family as well as into the society and nation that the family underpins. There reigns instead the sense that the Heimkehrer is now superfluous to the society whose center he once occupied—and without this traditional center, the films depict a weakening of traditional social relations. This weakening undermines the traditional logic of filmic narrative to create what I term a cinema of dispersion.

For Gilles Deleuze's dense and philosophical film theory, the war marks a radical cinematic break that is parallel to the postwar gender crises Silverman describes. I have discussed Deleuze's theory and its relation to gendered social crisis elsewhere,[14] and so I shall mention only a few of his observations that are important for my analysis of youth and youth crises in early rubble films. For Deleuze, the postwar representational transition is essentially one from a cinema of agency to a cinema of passivity.[15] The core of the historically (and commercially still) dominant cinematic image is the (I would argue) masculine action image, which highlights a character's power and control in regard to his cinematic environment (adversaries, love objects, sets, props, and so on). The action image is based on a duel: on a confrontation between the character and this cinematic context, in which the character usually prevails. Crucial to this kind of image is the controlling, desiring gaze of the (usually male, invariably masculine) protagonist, the gaze foregrounded in much feminist psychoanalytic film theory that reifies and subdues both people and objects around the protagonist.

Deleuze argues that the postwar neorealist films usher in new cinematic images in which the formerly active character becomes passive, meandering, observing. Such a development represents the subversion of the masculine subject and his action image, now rendered obsolete by the simultaneous social and cinematic crisis. Instead of a character confronting and changing his environment in a duel, one finds a dispersive social and cinematic situation in which the sides are not clearly drawn and conflict becomes oblique. Much as the dispersive situation brings the twilight of the clear duel, it also wreaks havoc with the controlling, desiring gaze of the (masculine) protagonist: instead, one finds an uncertain and lacking gaze of the masculine subject, one that merely observes and absorbs the environment rather than confronting and dominating it.[16] For example, shots of the rubble, at which these Heimkehrer stare blankly, serve as the opposite of scopophilic images of women, and signal the twilight of the active, desiring male subject.

Many early DEFA films drop the Heimkehrer into this double crisis of a social and cinematic dispersion, that is, the weakening of formerly stable social and cinematic/specular hierarchies. On the one hand, the Heimkehrer, as the exemplary postwar German subject for rubble films, suffers from a dispersive social crisis highlighting the lack, inadequacy, and castration of the male subject bearing the burdens of recent history. On the other hand, this social crisis corresponds to a dispersive representational crisis in cinema, one that presaged a different relationship between protagonist and setting that underscored the twilight of the ideal, exemplary protagonist's dominance over the setting.[17] Instead of effectively acting on a situation, the Heimkehrer protagonist now stands quietly staring and passively reflecting before it.

THE YOUNG IN THE POSTWAR
SOCIAL AND CINEMA CRISES

In light of this transformed situation—in which both society and cinema struggle with the burdens of the past—these films deploy the young to reconstitute both social and cinematic constellations. The rubble films displace these social and cinematic crises sketched above to a youth crisis that the film and its protagonist Heimkehrer can more easily manage. The young and youth crises afford a number of representational opportunities: the young person is inserted into psychoanalysis's active/passive, male/female binary as a third, intermediate term that chiasmatically connects male to passivity and female to activity. Though the young also represent such a threat to adult women, in most of these films, the young, both children and adolescents, are repeatedly aligned with the returning soldier.[18] The young feel less at home in the world than the traditional protagonist who, in the cinematic system, more often arranges it and dominates it: the youth crisis becomes a means for the film to depict a powerlessness, a threatening lack with which viewers can at the same time identify. This threatening young crisis, however, is only part of the story, only half of the duality of generational alterity I have elaborated. The young simultaneously inhabit the core and the borders of the social order and thereby play a contradictory role in patriarchy and masculinity—that is, they represent a contradiction reflecting the paradoxical representational responsibilities of these films.

The youth duality described above in the context of literary texts also has a specifically filmic articulation:

The youth crisis as social and representational threat. In my discussion of cultural representations of youth during the Nazi period in chapter 1, I argued that children and especially youth or adolescence can manifest exemplary resistance to bourgeois society.[19] In the rubble films, in a similar mode, these youths initially subvert masculine specularity posited by traditional psychoanalytic film theory: they often become an integral part of the dispersive cinematic situation that Deleuze describes, that is, the alien setting at which the traditional protagonist has to stare blankly after the war. These out-of-the-house and out-of-control youths—that is, youth in crisis—are often shot in the middle of the menacing clichés of the postwar context: amid the rubble or in the black market. Both settings subvert key moments of the bourgeois constellation, that is, they undercut both the private house and traditional productive labor. They are alien to and threaten to overwhelm the weakened, now lacking male protagonist. Very often, in fact, the editing connects shots of the rubble to a shot of an adult male looking at a socially lost, menacing young person who personifies the dispersion of traditional social relations. There is a deliberate visual displacement of the past and its destruction onto the youth in crisis.

In such images, the Heimkehrer appears to surrender to his environment, to forfeit that mastery and domination that used to be part and parcel of the ideal, whole male subject. The image counts as what Silverman terms an "ego-unbinding shot," what Stephen Shaviro and Gaylyn Studlar see as a masochistic gaze, one that gives up a formerly privileged patriarchal position[20]: it is the visual manifestation of the despair and desperation I foregrounded in chapter 2. As in the articles I discussed, the despair and desperation are repeatedly displaced onto the young and its putative crisis. Sometimes these socially antagonistic youth manifest open rebellion and hostility against the traditional social authority, as they do in *Ways into Twilight* (Gustav Fröhlich, 1948, Junge-Film-Union, British license), *Birds of Passage* (Rolf Meyer, 1947, Junge-Film-Union, British license), *And We Find Each Other Again*, or *The Last Illusion* (Josef v. Baky, 1949, Objektiv-Film, U.S. license). Sometimes they are oblivious to the role the traditional authority used to play, as in *Somewhere in Berlin, 1-2-3 Corona* (Hans Müller, 1948, DEFA, Soviet license), and *And the Heavens Above* (Josef v. Baky, 1946, U.S. license). In all cases, their relation to paternal figures reflects and displaces the general social crisis: they tend to misrecognize and then ignore the good father, which in turn provokes an ego-unbinding gaze back at the youth. In *Before Us Life* (Gerhard Rittau, 1948, Stella-Film GmbH, U.S. license), for example, the male protagonist, Jürgen, a grounded sea captain, walks out and absorbs an image of ruins after he realizes he will not be able to resume sailing.[21] Jürgen then passes a child on his way into the bar, where he will drink himself into oblivious self-abnegation. With the wide-ranging social crisis displaced to a youthful agent over whom males should have control, this ego-unbinding shot becomes all the more menacing.

Disciplined youth as social and representational affirmation. In contrast to the youth crisis that symbolizes the dispersion of the social order as well as the despair and desperation pervasive in it, the young can serve as the pillar of the bourgeois constellation: they are the cornerstones of the private house and the motivation for productive labor. As with gender difference, generational difference also acts to shore up bourgeois, especially masculine, subjectivities. In contrast to the socially threatening youth and youth's menacing crisis, these young recognize and demur to the father. In the early postwar films, east and west, their successful (re)socializations serve as a model for male Heimkehrer struggling with the past. In their skepticism about social relations, Heimkehrer are childlike, but they, like a maturing youth, (re)develop into adulthood. In this maturation trajectory, however, they are led not by adult superiors but by their own children. In a context where one of the main challenges was the integration of the past, the disciplined young rehabilitate the past as they fortify male subjects and help them overcome the widespread crisis of dispersion.

Cinematically, when adults look at youths in this register, the gaze is not threatening but rather ego binding, subject constituting. This look at the obedient, loving child compensates for, and obscures, the lack and castration the Heimkehrer has endured. This ego-binding gaze counts as the generational parallel of a psychoanalyst's desiring gaze, with which difference and desire for it shores up, instead of threatens, masculine subjects.[22] When the adult male is recognized as the father, his identity is firmed up, not threatened. For instance, in *The Murderers Are among Us*, Susanne's work on a sign, "Save the Children," symbolizes her socially committed and productive activity; Mertens first rediscovers his productive action image when he operates on a sick little girl. In *Before Us Life*, the son shores up the fraying generations and is looked at lovingly in the film's reconstructive conclusion by the formerly irreconcilable father and grandfather. Both moments show how a disciplining deployment of discourse about youth affirms the male subject and his place of privilege.

YOUTH'S DUALITY DEMANDS THE GENERATIONAL DUEL

Precisely this recurring dual representation of youth, as youth in crisis and disciplined youth, structures a great number of the early DEFA films. The task facing these films recalls the conundrum of all Germans that I emphasized in the introduction: to acknowledge and confront the past while distancing one's self from it. In the wake of this conundrum, these films set out to represent struggles with the recent past and the subsequent lack of faith in the traditional social order while pointing toward reconstruction. Youth became the prefect stratagem for this paradoxical challenge. On the one hand, due to the border-crossing tendencies I described earlier, the young could easily be imagined outside the house: the youth crisis becomes the most moving and convenient synecdoche for the horrible social crisis. As in *Doktor Faustus*, the young stand in for and indulge, but also simultaneously isolate and defuse, the obvious adult temptation to abandon an already tenuous bourgeois society. On the other hand, youth's border crossing cuts the other way as well: they were mobile socially and cinematically, and so by the conclusion of the films they end up disciplined and inside the house, the object of an adult supervisory gaze, the ego-binding gaze that assures the reconstruction of the traditional protagonist and the continued existence of the social order. The young as both social outsiders and insiders reflect the basic conflict in the Heimkehrer, who had to face the past while reintegrating himself into civilian life. In this way, these films counteract the narratives I traced in texts under the Nazis, which pried open the family and schools with the border-crossing young in order to reconstitute society as a generational Gemeinschaft.

To galvanize this socializing trajectory, many early postwar films arrange a series of generational duels that recall the letter exchanges between the generations I described in chapter 2. Deleuze notes that the transition from action image to dispersive situation diluted the core form of a cinematic duel.[23] The beginnings of early postwar films often lack a clear duel: the opaque, diffuse, dispersive duel is that between the Heimkehrer and a (deliberately obscured) past. In this opaque situation, the films deploy youth crisis and generational struggle in place of confrontations that the films have to avoid, for instance, a soldier confronting his former Nazi commander[24] or the Heimkehrer confronting Allied officers. As with many of the texts above, the early rubble films arrange a generational duel, one that provides conflict without a politically difficult confrontation. The duel between generations served these films' contradictory task particularly well because it created conflict without any real (that is, adult) loser—all while deflecting attention from the real challenges of Vergangenheitsbewältigung. The lacking, worn, and weary Heimkehrer has scenes where he looks at the socially menacing youth and despairs exactly as he does in rubble-shots. Because the young and youth crises come to represent the loss of faith, the resistance to the restoration of the social order, they come to assist the film's depiction of the postwar social and cinematic crisis. But, via these generational duels, the lacking man is activated once again to rejoin the social order and the action image—he is restored to his privileged and active position in social and cinematic relations via his encounter with, learning from, and then supervision of the youth in crisis. We will analyze how exactly this mechanism works in two early postwar DEFA films.

SOMEWHERE IN BERLIN: THE HEIMKEHRER MEETS THE MISRECOGNIZING CHILD

As only the second feature film of the postwar era—and with a festive premiere in the Berliner Staatsoper on 18 December 1946—Gerhard Lamprecht's *Somewhere in Berlin* counted as something of a cultural event. It enjoyed enormous publicity and attracted much laudatory attention from film critics. They often compared the second postwar feature to the first one, *The Murderers Are among Us,* and approvingly emphasized *Somewhere in Berlin*'s shared realism, its similar attention to the contemporary social context, its "simple materials and serious topics," all while avoiding the adoration of any film stars.[25] Singled out for particular praise was Harry Hindemith's Heimkehrer Iller, who "shared a postwar fate with millions of others."[26]

Critics, however, also indicated how *Somewhere in Berlin* improved on *The Murderers Are among Us,* even if they avoided judging which was better. One critic contrasted *The Murderers Are among Us* to *Somewhere in Berlin* precisely because the latter engaged a "collective" problem, "the lives of our youth."[27] These critics recognized *Somewhere in Berlin*'s basic strategy—one that I argue is telling for the early rubble films. *Somewhere in Berlin* elaborates elements only hinted at in *The Murderers Are among Us,* elements that then come to constitute core themes of many early postwar films—namely, realism, youth, and Vergangenheitsbewältigung. The key conflicts for the protagonist Heimkehrer are not confrontations with the past or the challenges of reconstruction; these are displaced to generational duels. In contrast to the scholarly fate of *The Murderers Are among Us,* later critics have never lavished much attention on *Somewhere in Berlin*—they usually discuss merely its rubble clichés[28]—but I want to argue that *Somewhere in Berlin* is richly typical of the early rubble films for its obvious but generally neglected theme of youth.

Although *Somewhere in Berlin* seems an explicit echo of Lamprecht's earlier *Emil and the Detectives* (1931)—for example, Fritz Rasp's character steals a wallet and exploits children—the significant differences shed light on youth's specific coding in the dispersive postwar

185

social situation. The key and telling difference between *Somewhere in Berlin* and *Emil and the Detectives* rests in their respective approaches to a youth community away from authority figures. In *Emil*, this youth community becomes the lawful hero of the film, the one happily restoring the private sphere by helping reclaim the stolen wallet and thus fight crime and the antisociability that can transpire in the absence of the father figure. *Somewhere in Berlin* attempts almost the diametric opposite, that is, to dismantle the youth community that has caused a crisis and to code parents' disciplining their children as the socially productive solution.

 Somewhere in Berlin tells the tale—at times heartwarming, at times bizarre—of a friendship between two fatherless boys, Gustav Iller and Willi. Gustav's dad has yet to return from his POW camp, while Willi has lost both of his parents in the war. Both situations are overdetermined for children in the postwar social crisis since both cases constituted common social problems of the time. For the first twenty minutes of the film, the boys resist the disciplining efforts of the responsible adults around them: they tend to an antisocial youth community and follow ersatz fathers who also symptomatize the dispersive postwar crisis. From there the boys' paternal fates are split: Gustav's father, Iller, returns—physically haggard and ideologically fatigued—to face reintegration into the bourgeois social order, while Willi's situation under a bad ersatz father, Birke, grows even worse. Willi, deciding to help Gustav's father obtain food (Iller is literally and symbolically always hungry), steals it from Birke and is thrown out. Fatherless and on his own, Willi is taunted as a coward by the other boys, so much so that he decides to climb a ruined building, from which he falls and eventually dies. With the distraction of youthful friendship—and the antisocial youth crisis—out of the way, Gustav reconciles with his father, and the two turn their energies to reconstruction.

 Somewhere in Berlin, I argue, arranges a confrontation with the past by way of generational conflicts. At a moment when conflict had become problematic—what enemies could Germans fight after the disastrous war?—its central narrative tension, like the postwar letter exchanges, rests in generational conflicts. To rehabilitate the wayward Heimkehrer, the film arranges a series of generational duels. The film deploys the first of these duels to depict the ravages of the contemporary social crisis, which is displaced here to a youth crisis. In the last of the duels, the Heimkehrer actually learns from a child who, even before

186

the Heimkehrer, becomes a firm believer in reestablishing traditional social roles within a reconstructed family. Willi, Gustav's friend, represents precisely the youth duality I describe above: his presence as an overactive orphan reflects the socially dangerous aspect of the young, but his ultimate faith in the family props it up. The second postwar film relies on generational discourse, particularly the duality of the young described above, for its central narrative tensions and its ultimate resolution of coming to terms with the past.

Social Crisis as Youth Crisis:
The Dispersive Anarchy of Ersatz Fathers

In staging a social crisis that the generational duel will have to resolve, *Somewhere in Berlin* spends its first twenty minutes representing the youth crisis into which the Heimkehrer will venture. The film represents the wider crisis via the youth crisis and the duality of youth that I underscore throughout this context. Contemporary critics took the two boys as a paradigmatic contrast of the two types of youths, and Lamprecht himself confirmed this youth duality as deliberate.[29] On the one hand, there is the tendency of the young, both children and adolescents, to cross borders, a tendency that relocates, as in *Doktor Faustus,* the young from the private family house into a violent and threatening youth crisis outside the home. On the other hand, there is the capacity of disciplined youth to submit to a paternal agency and adhere to the private house, which metamorphoses in the postwar into the youth crisis of a false father.

The first and most important in a series of ersatz fathers for fatherless boys is Waldemar, played by perennial spook Fritz Rasp. The film opens with Waldemar's being chased through the city ruins because—revisiting a theme from *Emil and the Detectives*—he has stolen a wallet: his active facility at navigating the rubble and evading his lawful pursuers will contrast starkly to the meandering voyage of the Heimkehrer. Waldemar becomes an explicit ersatz father when Gustav finds him in the cellar of his father's garage and invites him to the family dinner table, which has long lacked the biological father. In even more heavy-handed symbolism signifying that Waldemar has replaced the absent father, he puts the wallet he has stolen at the market behind the photo of Gustav's father, respectfully placed above the kitchen table.

Like Gustav, Willi suffers from a false father figure who lives at the fringes of public law. Because his parents are dead—a ubiquitous cause

187

of the postwar youth crisis—Willi has been adopted by Birke, who runs a paper shop as well as a black market business on the side. Birke harnesses the children's resourcefulness for his own antisocial designs: he exploits not only his own adoptive child, Willi, but also a number of Willi's friends, including Gustav. Birke exchanges fireworks—which the children want for their war games—for food, which he goads the kids into stealing from their parents. In Waldemar and Birke, as with Brückner in *The Murderers Are among Us,* one finds figures who have in the postwar context too easily reasserted themselves into the new social order without acknowledging and working through the crisis of dispersion and the contradictions of Vergangenheitsbewältigung.[30]

This anarchy of paternal subjects, entirely lacking in an organizing or dominant paternal agency, undercuts the traditional private sphere and creates a dispersive youth crisis. This lack of a masculine center in the film leads to a decentered youth community; in the depoliticized *Somewhere in Berlin,* however, these young stand in not for the 1933 National Socialist political revolution but for the recent war only hinted at in the ubiquitous rubble. They link the present context to the past war while also representing those active in the war itself. In their war games, which echo the *Volksturm* (national home-defense militia), the young stand in for the men's experience of war—an experience that undercuts the private sphere and men's traditional social roles (photo 1).

The scene of the feral children is among the most memorable of the movie because it achieves what Rentschler terms "striking atmospheric touches" reminiscent of the strange *Stimmung* (atmosphere) of the opening of *The Murderers Are among Us*—that is to say, it constructs, via the youth crisis, an alternative relationship between setting and action.[31] The scene is initiated by the children's literal break away from the conventional family constellation, with Gustav's running from his mother and another ersatz father, a policeman. Gustav's mother is commenting on how hard it is to keep a child under control when, on cue, Gustav runs off to join his comrades' war games. As the children shoot rockets around the rubble and the camera cuts crazily, almost incomprehensibly, among the different groups, what emerges among the ruins are the young's anarchical war games, their indulgence of the death drive of war—a parody of adult wars that shows their anticivilized, antisocial essence, one half of the youthful duality. This particular sequence confirms the visual association of rubble with the youth crisis:

1. Feral children ruling the postwar rubble in *Somewhere in Berlin*
(Courtesy DEFA-Spektrum)

both serve antisocial ends in some of the most memorable images of the film.

After twenty minutes of social crisis marked by deranged paternity and an anarchical youth crisis, *Somewhere in Berlin* introduces the figure whose absence has been ubiquitously felt, the father. The biological father as Heimkehrer first appears as a startlingly castrated, weak, passive figure—his appearance is not a lightning bolt of phalliation (gendered hierarchization)—rather, just another aspect of the wider social crisis. As indicated in various contemporary reviews, Iller as Heimkehrer is very much a recurring type in this filmic and sociohistorical context.[32] The initial visual depiction of Gustav's father matches the rubble-shot I discussed in theorizing the cinematic role of youth images: the male protagonist is shot among the rubble, which fascinates him, on a voyage

189

2. Iller looking at the rubble; the postwar Heimkehrer's lacking gaze in
Somewhere in Berlin (Courtesy DEFA-Spektrum)

3. Iller and children in the rubble in *Somewhere in Berlin*
(Courtesy DEFA-Spektrum)

where he is overwhelmed by—falls prey more than predator to—the cinematic context (photo 2).

Upon encountering his son, he demands no generational recognition befitting the father—he sits miserably on the rubble, overcome by the generational overthrow and dispersion. The combination of youth crisis and rubble highlights the patriarch's lack and castration all the more (photo 3).

The next day, when he returns a stolen wallet in hopes of getting a reward, Iller brings his son along—here, too, the father's claim to power is subverted, parodied, in front of the very child who is supposed to inherit the paternal project. The father is left dumbly staring at a revue show: everything has become alienating and therefore fascinating—he stares and ruminates but cannot act. When, on their way back, Gustav asks to go to the park, the father says, in an apathetic rejection of his paternity and the bourgeois order, "Nothing matters anymore." His articulated attitudes reflect precisely the loss of faith in patriarchy and work and the male's position in the bourgeois social order that I described in my introduction to the early postwar public sphere in chapter 2.[33] As much a cliché of the social crisis as the wayward children, he is a Heimkehrer in desperate need of a jump start—which he will receive in the duels with the young.

Cinematic Duels Solving Social Dispersion: *Somewhere in Berlin*'s Climactic Generational Confrontations

Somewhere in Berlin stages three generational confrontations: the first and the last, in a kind of failed paternity before and after the crisis outlined above, concern the father's confrontation with his biological son. The middle one—the rubble-scaling center of the plot—galvanizes a wide-ranging transformation in the father's attitude, that is, reignites his faith in the bourgeois social order. In the first of these duels, the Heimkehrer walks directly into the antisocial youth community that has replaced a centered, privately grounded patriarchy. As much of the dialogue in the film's first twenty minutes anticipates, Gustav fails to recognize his real father, a common situation at the time, since many children had not seen their fathers in years. This first encounter with the son—a key postwar confrontation—only reinforces generational disruption and the failure of the father. This initial generational interaction and its deliberate visual combination of youth crisis and rubble highlight the Heimkehrer's lack.

191

Despite Gustav's faith in his father, it takes more than a filial believer to restore the castrated male subject to the social order. What it will take generates much of *Somewhere in Berlin*'s narrative tension: the film requires the rehabilitation of a child, Willi, who is initially antagonistic to the social order but who, by film's end, comes to believe in the family. Gustav's friend Willi therein embodies the duality of youth: on the one hand, his very presence threatens the reestablishment of the bourgeois family, but on the other hand, he eventually believes, supports, and sacrifices for the family. This trajectory offers a model for Iller, once he, as we shall see, consciously adopts it.

As the key protagonist of the youth crisis, Willi poses a threat to the bourgeois generational relations in a few ways. First, as a central figure in the war games scene, he represents the break from the traditional social order to the belligerent youth mob. More particularly, Willi threatens to distract Gustav from his biological family, the family the film deliberately engineers. Finally, because Willi is parentless, he becomes easy prey for the predatory false father, Birke. As the film's paradigmatic representative of youth—that youthful liminal space resistant to the bourgeois social order—Willi highlights the father's lack because, in contrast to Iller, he represents active and effective agency but remains unhoused and undisciplined, the poster child for the wider youth crisis.

Despite what his presence represents, Willi comes to believe in helping the family: he decides to help feed Iller, the lacking father. The film ties the father's general ideological fatigue and specific discomfort in his old suits to his symbolic and literal hunger. After Gustav has recognized his father, Willi decides to restore the father, to reconstruct the patriarch, by stealing food from his ersatz father, Birke. He prepares a huge package of precious foodstuffs and leaves it for Gustav to give to his father—a foreshadowing of Willi's ultimate sacrifice to the family. Willi becomes therein the provider, the active agent, while the father mopes, with "no more energy."

Willi's legacy for the castrated patriarchal agency grows clearest in the film's second significant generational confrontation, which begins with the painter's domestication of the orphaned boy and ends with an incredibly strange and stylized scene when Gustav's father visits Willi on his deathbed. After Willi steals food from Birke, Birke chases the boy from the only postwar home he has had. Eckmann the painter takes him

192

4. Willi's alternative rubble-shot contrasts to the adult man's passive gaze in *Somewhere in Berlin* (Courtesy DEFA-Spektrum)

in for a night, but Willi's precocious resourcefulness—the same one that led him to correct the lacking gaze of the patriarch—will not permit him to assume the role of passive son. His climbing the rubble in the next scene demonstrates that the child's resourcefulness seems to overstep the limits of the traditional social order. As the other children mock him, Willi looks up at the rubble in a remarkable shot underscoring the precarious and radically different relation of character to setting in this environment (photo 4).

As I suggested above, an orphaned child, visually paired with the rubble, underscores the vulnerability of the young when jettisoned from the destroyed house. But, in contrast to Iller's passive gaze, Willi is all too determined to conquer the rubble to prove himself to the youth community. This kind of vulnerable agency—orphaned but overactive— highlights the social dispersion underpinning the film, a dispersion dis-

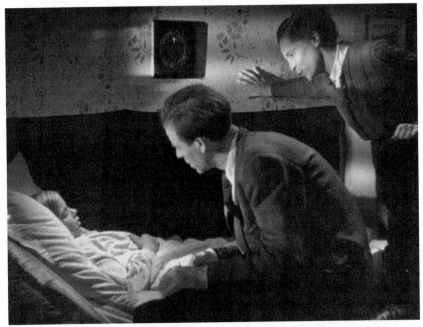

5. Iller with Willi on his deathbed—the return of the prodigal father
in *Somewhere in Berlin* (Courtesy DEFA-Spektrum)

placed to the youth crisis. Because his youthful resourcefulness parodies the (absent) passive male, the traditional social and generational order, the film deems Willi dangerous and eventually kills him.

The film's watershed generational duel arrives in a bizarre variation on the father-son reconciliation scene when Iller goes to Willi on his deathbed (photo 5). Whereas in the clichéd scene, the prodigal son is reconciled to the father and inherits the father's productive project—traditional social order neatly reinscribed—here the despairing and faithless father inherits the steadfast belief of the overactive child. Visually, the image of the now-caring father bending over the now-weakened child revises Iller's first rubble-shot, when children amid the youth crisis were as menacing as the rubble.

Willi's position as devout as well as active believer in bourgeois social relations at first threatens and then corrects the castrated father. Iller tells Willi he appreciates what he did—recognizes it—and that now "we'll build it back up again." In this second generational duel, Gustav's father inherits faith in the traditional social order from the dying Willi in another world-upside-down generational inversion: the man of lack learns from the resourceful child of the youth crisis.

This contradictory depiction of the child in the second postwar film, I would argue, was not just another social cliché among many; discourse about youth proves particularly useful for the contradictory challenges of realistically depicting both a social crisis and its (reconstructive) resolution. *Somewhere in Berlin* sets up the paradigm of a lacking Heimkehrer in a youth crisis standing in for a wider social crisis and then confronts this exemplary postwar figure with a contradictory youth discourse. The youth crisis is not a mere reflection of the social crisis—though it is that as well—it is portrayed by a particularly useful, mobile figure with whom viewers can unproblematically identify in the contradictory resolution of narrative, formal, and social crisis. For the film's adults, the young help bind the ideologically fatigued adult to the past without really engaging the problems of the past; they live out the temptation to unbind and resist the traditional social order but in the end shore up the adult subject in a kind of Vergangenheitsbewältigung that deflects and avoids its most difficult challenges.

ROTATION's History of Masculine Rubble: Paternal Pedagogy against Nazi Family Dispersion

Endless Rotation versus Progressive Education

Wolfgang Staudte's third postwar film, *Rotation* (1949), returned to the contemporary antifascist themes of *The Murderers Are among Us* after a detour through a 1947 remake of his 1944 comedy, *The Man Whose Name Was Stolen.* Enjoying a much-heralded double premiere at the Bablyon and Kastanienallee cinemas in Berlin on 16 September 1949, *Rotation* became a landmark in DEFA film history: up until then the most expensive DEFA film made, it counted as probably the most popular of its antifascist films. Contemporary critics lauded the film as one of the most important postwar films; moreover, unlike *Somewhere in Berlin,* it has also enjoyed a happy afterlife in German studies and film historical scholarship.[34] Returning to the Weimar tradition of proletarian films,[35] *Rotation* emphasized the inadequacy of the individual who tries to hold him- or herself above the politics of the context—an altogether convenient lesson for the Soviet authorities with their antifascist agenda as well as for viewers interested in diluting their own guilt.

Though two-thirds of the film's ninety minutes comprise a flashback from its 1945 present, *Rotation* engages a number of techniques and themes conspicuously connecting it to its contemporary context. In fact, its narrative strategies, particularly those relying on a specific deployment of the young, link it directly to rubble films like *Somewhere in Berlin*. The similarities include not only its contemporary themes but also its narrative and technical strategy for coping with the dispersive challenges of the past. The film's goal, as described by Staudte in an interview, was to galvanize resistance in the average German.[36] Incredibly, however, the film's normative assertion concerns not the (traditional) political engagement of the male subject—what one might expect after the film's debates about the political responsibility of the individual— but rather a contradictory renegotiation of generational relations. Despite the sympathetic depiction of a communist agitator and resister (Hans's brother-in-law, Kurt), Hans is not encouraged to participate in organized politics but rather to be a good father.[37] As in *Somewhere in Berlin,* the film stages confronting the past largely through generational (re)negotiation.

Rotation extends the youth stratagem I described in *Somewhere in Berlin* by emphasizing a symbolically central generational discourse in addition to paternity: pedagogy. In much of the contemporary and later reception of the film, *Rotation* is praised for shifting the postwar films' political emphasis out of the private house into a more public forum, particularly for thematizing the public sphere and the various media constituting it. In fact, the title refers to the rotation of the newspaper printing presses at the Nazi daily *Völkischer Beobachter,* where Hans eventually takes a job. Though *Rotation* does elaborate a theme of the public sphere and its various media (newspaper, leaflets, radio), the film nonetheless ultimately continues to rely on a contradictory generational discourse as constitutive for these other themes. As *Rotation* pretends to public political discourse, it arranges pedagogy as a political form: the problems with the past still grow out of generational confusion—out of a youth crisis—but now this confusion involves not only the private house but also schools. From its more public engagement of political problems—but still in relative accord with *Somewhere in Berlin*'s paradigm—*Rotation* returns to the domestic, to paternity and a paternalistic pedagogy, as the key relationships in that private sphere. *Rota-*

tion deploys youth in a contradictory fashion, though that contradiction is expanded to include not only the social/antisocial contradiction elucidated above but also that of the public and political versus the private and familial.

This argument about *Rotation* pivots on the film's thematic and formal parallel between scenes that emphasize the passivity, hesitancy, and ineffectiveness of Hans's politics and scenes that underscore the passivity, hesitancy, and ineffectiveness of his parenting and teaching. In their emphasis on the political and historical participation of the individual, critics, then and now, have pointed to the same political scenes, such as the famous collage of graphically matched bars, the teakettle scene that results in Hans's throwing an ashtray at the *Führerbild* (picture of the Führer), or the resigned jostling of prisoners between the defeated Nazis and the seizing Soviets.[38] While these scenes do indeed assert *Rotation*'s critique of political passivity, the film also inextricably associates—thematically and formally, from the beginning of the flashback—this political passivity with Hans's passivity as a father. By relying on the paternal-pedagogical disciplining of the youth in crisis, the film limits the horizon of its antifascist message. It ends up preferring the politics of paternity and pedagogy to those of the public sphere.[39]

In its depiction of National Socialism and its aftermath, then, *Rotation* approaches Vergangenheitsbewältigung through the relation between a passive or inadequate male subject and a threatening youth tied directly to the Nazi nation. In this respect, the film also takes up a fairly direct dialogue with the 1933 Nazi propaganda film *Hitlerjunge Quex,* which also depicted the crises of the late Weimar period and the rise of National Socialism as a youth affair, as the story of a son's flight from the father's private sphere into a youth public sphere. Though the two films resemble one another as revisions of the Weimar working-class genre, no one to my knowledge has mentioned the link. Like *Hitlerjunge Quex,* which it seems to quote a number of times, *Rotation* focuses on the dual character of youth, especially adolescents, as a prime mover for Nazism and as a cure for a past clouded by National Socialism.

Rotation's Heimkehrer: Political Acquiescence as Powerless Papa

Many early postwar films offer some sort of rubble-shot, a scene offering a lacking masculine gaze that concretizes the Heimkehrer's experience of the war: foregrounding the rubble from the air war, these

6. Visual leitmotif of Hans in front of the wall—another postwar rubble-shot, another lacking male gaze in *Rotation* (Courtesy DEFA-Spektrum)

sequences usually become a metaphor for the contradictory challenges of the problematic past. Although not ostensibly a rubble film, *Rotation* offers a remarkably similar—and similarly central—image of a passive male gazing at and ruminating on the sets. This particular instance of Hans's lacking gaze offers the guiding image for the entire film: viewers see Hans standing in a dark cell, staring at a brightly lit wall with his back to the camera, arms rigid at his side, face starkly front lit (photo 6).

The shot is cut into a sequence that includes images of violent and desperate street fighting between the Nazis and Soviets and shots of S-Bahnhof Potsdamer Platz, where thousands of German refugees were about to be drowned by the Nazis. This intercut sequence depicts the overwhelming crisis and constructs dispersion as a sociological cross section and collage in a manner similar to *Somewhere in Berlin*. As the film cuts to the prison, the shot of Hans seems particularly quiet because the shots preceding it scream the tumult of besieged Berlin.[40] The peculiar, low-key lighting permits viewers to read the graffiti on the prison wall, which announce the dates and times of the executions of the former inhabitants of the cell. Hans, viewers realize, is being held to be executed while he stares blankly at his predecessors' final messages.[41] Viewers watch the back of another immobile, passive male about to be overwhelmed by what are normally docile, cooperating sets. The editing also underscores this shot as the opening's (and the film's) most important: in the dense sequence of intercutting, it is the only shot to which the editing returns, and it is the one from which the 1945 sequence fades as the nondiegetic "It began 20 years ago!" appears to reopen the narrative in 1925. When the flashback ends near the conclusion of the film, the film deliberately dissolves back into this same image.

The film thus opens with and thematizes a memorable image of male passivity and lack. Much as Hans refuses to become an active political resister, I would like to highlight how he fails to become an active parent, that is, to play his role in the generational hierarchy that supports the traditional social order. The connection unfolds not only in the plot concerning his paternity and his politics but also in the technical genesis of this single prison image. As we shall see, the diegesis of the film links this shot inextricably to the young: the crisis of the adult German becomes a youth crisis. Reading *Rotation* for Hans's lacking gaze, a look that suggests male passivity and dispersion, reinforces what becomes the central aspect of this inadequacy: Hans's repudiation of active fatherhood.

When, near the beginning of the hour-long flashback to the 1920s, Hans first learns that Lotte is pregnant, he greets the news quietly and uncertainly, wandering aimlessly around the room and then ending up in front of a wall (photo 7). The film protocol emphasizes Hans's moments of indecision and Lotte's searching inability to read his elusive, hesitant expression. Suddenly this hesitancy explodes into enthusiasm, a sudden leap from passivity to action that will be problematized later in the film. Here, the scene ends in Hans's renewed indecision and hesitancy when, once his enthusiasm has almost injured Lotte, she scolds him for potentially hurting the baby. Though from that initial moment of indecision he remains excited about marrying Lotte, this moment of paternal indecision and dispersion will recur.[42]

A few minutes later, the birth sequence ensues, which Staudte shoots in a similarly peculiar manner best explained by associating politics with parenting. While Hans waits for the midwife to come out of the

7. Hans in front of a wall in his apartment—the second instance of staring at the wall in self-doubt in *Rotation* (Courtesy DEFA-Spektrum)

bedroom, he busies himself cleaning the kitchen. The deliberately odd blocking of the sequence emphasizes Hans's body before the context: he is shot in front of the bedroom door from straight on, facing the camera in an unusually direct shot. The camera cuts then to his point of view of the curtained door as he awaits the birth of his son: the parallel depiction of a peculiarly direct look at his son will recur and eventually be linked to his reading the prison wall. Confirming this sense of the shots, the film protocol underscores Hans's lack of control of his gaze, an important element of Iller's lacking gaze in *Somewhere in Berlin* and in an assortment of other early DEFA films, for instance *The Buntkarierten* (Kurt Maetzig, 1949, DEFA, Soviet license).[43] While Hans stares passively at the door, we get a close-up of his eyes, another shot that recalls the prison cell and that will recur and emphasize his passive watching, his inability to assert himself over the cinematic situation. The scene, wrought with passivity and hesitancy, provides Hans's first uncertain duel with his son, the first of a number of pivotal father-son duels that, until the very end, link paternal to political dispersion.[44]

National Socialism as Youth Crisis

In *Somewhere in Berlin*, the unruly youths' rubble games obliquely stand in for the war; a more historically precise film, *Rotation* radicalizes *Somewhere in Berlin*'s merely vague association of youth with the recent past by depicting youth's primary role in the Nazi movement and its war. In a manner reminiscent of many early rubble films, *Rotation* deploys one half of the contradictory youth duality—antisocial border crossers—to create the film's crisis; subsequently, the core of the film's crisis becomes the dispersion of the stable family into a kind of youth crisis. *Rotation*'s recurring and well-noted media theme depicts Nazism as it seeps into the house through radio, wall hangings, and newspapers. But the film, in a series of scenes, is careful to show that it is ultimately Helmuth the son who betrays his own family. As in *Hitlerjunge Quex*, Helmuth's loyalty to the family is eclipsed by a dual inclination to National Socialism: on the one hand, toward its false paternal figures, often implied in propagandistic images of some father ideal; on the other hand, in a manner reminiscent of *Doktor Faustus* or Jünger, toward a youth community— here educational—that constitutes the heart of the Nazi movement. Staudte's *Rotation* responds clearly to those strains of culture under the Nazis that I sketched earlier.

Well before the viewers see images of Helmuth outside the house and as part of the national-generational community, he serves as the weak link through which the Nazi nation infiltrates the private house. As in *Youth of Langemarck*, he becomes the means for the regime to remake the family: the regime governs through the family by way of its young. When Lotte's communist brother, Kurt, stops by to say good-bye before fleeing to Czechoslovakia, Helmuth sings an HJ song in the background—a clarion signifier for the insidious encroachment of Nazism. The song, sung by the child against the parents' wishes, quotes a scene of *Hitlerjunge Quex* in which Heini sings an HJ song only to have his father, Völker, slap him into submission. Both songs, as in *Paracelsus*, represent a beckoning from outside the private sphere, a beckoning that seduces the border-crossing young and eventually causes the collapse of the private house.[45] Here Lotte scolds her son for singing the song too early in the morning and, in contrast to *Hitlerjunge Quex*, it is the parent who breaks down weeping, not the child.

201

In the next domestic scene, Hans calls Helmuth from cutting out Nazi images from cigarette packs, a similar interruption in the youth's absorption of Nazi ideology. Throughout the film, the mise-en-scène frames characters with pictures, particularly images of heroic icons, to imply their identification with these ideals. For instance, at their wedding party, Lotte and Hans sit below a still life of foodstuffs; after they realize this dream of domestic plenty, a Nazi official pressures them to hang a Führerbild above the table. At the beginning of this scene with Helmuth, Hans is framed below the newly purchased picture of Hitler, thus below the masculine ideal of the Reich; the camera locates Helmuth not only surrounded by Nazi icons on the walls but also pasting images into a book, a more active absorption of nationalist propaganda. As the scene progresses, the sense of Helmuth as the domestic weak link grows: in the only scene in which the entire family—Helmuth included—is seen happily together, the son peels away from their playful wrestling. A second later he cries from the window, "What's that?" Hans and Lotte come over to watch the Salomons, their Jewish neighbors, being loaded into a truck and deported. Hans sends Helmuth—the one who spotted the transport—to his room and locks the open window. Hans, the former locksmith, tries to lock out the political events, an effort undercut in his own life by his own son, now nationalized.[46]

In this series of scenes, as in *Doktor Faustus*, Helmuth becomes the weak link in the conventional private sphere: much as Donzelot describes, he is the conduit through which National Socialist norms pour into and flood the private family and house. The next sequence pushes the film's youth discourse outside the private sphere to the Nazi public by contrasting Hans's weak paternity to strong National Socialist pedagogy, such that Nazism becomes a kind of antifamilial youth crisis. This crucial sequence opens up with full Nazi flags waving and a singing column of young men, shot at low angle, marching by—an image invoking *Triumph of the Will* and quoting the end of *Hitlerjunge Quex*. The link of Nazi cinematic images to youth becomes all the clearer in Staudte's initial plan to intercut footage from Riefenstahl's *Olympia* between Helmuth's looking out the conjugal bedroom window and his absorbing ideology in school. While Riefenstahl's *Triumph of the Will* and *Olympia*—both prestige productions of the Nazi regime—do link youth to the party, Staudte, by editing in this manner, has elaborated this linkage considerably. Youth and the crisis of traditional paternity prove once again the key vehicle for postwar discourse about the Nazis and their media.[47]

Rotation's first classroom scene is startlingly dissimilar from any other in the film and introduces the nationalized youth community, in which Nazi ideology is imbibed and its solders trained. With the sound bridge of the brigade leader's voice, the film fades from the juvenile marching column to a completely *gleichgeschaltet* (party-coordinated) classroom, with Nazi banners and a huge, full-body portrait of Hitler framing the teacher's desk at the head of the classroom. After class, the students practice grenade throwing, to which the film links (with matches on action and graphic matches) real grenades on the battlefield and then an honor list of dead German soldiers.[48]

The film's editing thus connects the Nazi classroom directly to the Nazi war, while making those fighting the war primarily the young. Radicalizing *Somewhere in Berlin*—in which the unruly children scene stood obliquely for the war—*Rotation* makes its point explicit: that the young stand in for Nazis. The original classroom scene, as described in the film protocol, actually offered an even fuller anticipation of the school's role in the war against the Allies.[49] The sequence taken as a whole replaces the father-son thematic with a general sociohistorical statement about Nazism as a youth phenomenon, not least because Helmuth is never actually shot in the marching column, in the classroom, or (not yet) at war. It constitutes something of a narrative meandering into the sociological context, the kind of dispersion in a coherent plot that Deleuze emphasizes in neorealism: the camera generalizes the indoctrination process into a Nazi collective and will later locate Helmuth within it.[50] The scene affirms the depiction of a Nazism I traced in my introduction: functioning as the Nazi "revolution," the youth revolution "liberates" the young from an already degenerating private sphere into a nationalized community. In the youth crisis of conventional paternity, what used to be an environment based on generational difference now rests in the hands of the young and a Nazi false father. At the core of *Rotation*'s depiction of Nazism, then, the pedagogical and paternal discourses intersect and conflict: traditional generational relations grow dangerously dispersive, cause the youth crisis, and so foreshadow the film's resolution via the repair and reconciliation of pedagogy and paternity.

At this point, however, Helmuth still serves as the lightning rod for the most convinced Nazi ideology to enter the private house. Though

8. Staring at the wall now overtly politicized: Hans looking at the picture of the Führer in *Rotation* (Courtesy DEFA-Spektrum)

the Nazi officials suspect Hans and Lotte are sympathetic with, perhaps even assisting, Lotte's communist brother, Kurt, their investigation makes no headway until they get the help of young Helmuth. Communist Kurt has returned in disguise to Berlin around the time of the first bombing raids, and after berating him once again for his political apathy, Kurt convinces Hans to help repair a printing press so that the resistance might print literature exhorting "End the Insane Hitler-war!" In yet another linking of youths to the oft-mentioned media theme, Helmuth discovers one of pamphlets hidden in the family's encyclopedia, a discovery mocking bourgeois Bildung and Hans's failed pedagogy in the age of National Socialism. Fleeing traditional Bildung seated in the private sphere and opting for the pedagogy of the generational-national collective, Helmuth sneaks out of the house without bringing the pamphlet to the attention of either of his parents and turns it over to the Nazi authorities. The next sequence intercuts two interrogations, one of

Hans and one of Lotte, and ends in Hans's denouncing his brother-in-law and, for the first time, saying "Heil Hitler!" Hans's commitment to a counter–public sphere media (one contrasting to his job for the party organ *Völkischer Beobachter*), that is, his commitment to political resistance, fails in and along with his paternity.

Shortly thereafter, in one of the film's most powerful sequences, a close-up pans and tilts over Kurt's death certificate to cut to a steaming teakettle and then to Lotte's oblivious, hollow expression as the teakettle screeches. In the living room, Hans stands immobile and passive, back to the camera, arms at his side, face front lit and staring at the Führerbild above the father's place at the dining table (photo 8). The shot echoes not only the opening lacking gaze within the prison but also the pregnancy and birth sequences, as a sudden close-up of his eyes confirms.

In front of the *Führerbild,* the paterfamilias is facing the Nazis' paternal ideal for the society, much as in *Hitlerjunge Quex* father Völker looked at the brigade leader in the garden. Helmuth comes into the kitchen to turn off the kettle and then enters the dining room to see his father pick up an ashtray and throw it at the Führerbild. As in the pregnancy sequence, the transition from Hans's radical passivity to sudden, futile action problematizes his inability to balance passivity with activity, to play the effective agent politically or paternally or pedagogically. Helmuth runs out of the private sphere and eventually to his teacher's apartment, where he announces, while framed with a picture of a Hitler Youth, that he never wants to go home again.

Rotation's Generational Conflict: Denouncing and Reconciling

I have underscored how in *Somewhere in Berlin,* the dispersive social situation of the lacking postwar male resolves itself in a duel between the generations, thus making a generational confrontation the key conflict in a generally conflict-centered medium (at a historical moment when conflict was problematic). Though *Rotation* is supposed to galvanize political resistance, it nonetheless echoes this duel between generations. After depicting the same two contradictory figures—the lacking male in a memorable dispersive social situation and the overly active Nazi youth—*Rotation* stages a remarkably similar generational duel and resolution. *Rotation,* like *Somewhere in Berlin,* reduces the problems of the past to the dispersion of generational relations, to negligent parenting and/or generational overthrow.

205

9. The mystery of the wall solved: dissolve from Helmuth to wall at which Hans stares, underscoring the link between youth and politics in *Rotation* (Courtesy DEFA-Spektrum)

Presumably the day after Hans throws the ashtray at the Führerbild and Helmuth flees the house for good, Hans is called into the office of a *Sicherheitsdienst* (intelligence service of the SS) official. This finely dressed Nazi questions Hans again about the pamphlets. Beethoven's Fifth plays on the radio in the background: the diegetic music links this scene to the pregnancy and birth scenes and thereby underscores the film's operation along a series of generational duels in which Hans always ends up passively looking. After the Nazi interrogator rings for Helmuth, the film cuts between tense close-ups of the father's and the son's eyes, recalling the close-ups of Hans's passive gaze in the opening cell sequence, the birth scene, and the throwing of the ashtray. At first there is a struggle between their gazes: between a supervising gaze that subdues the youth and a rebellious gaze that overthrows the elder.[51]

After a conspicuous struggle of gazes that is tellingly interrupted by a cut to the Nazi official—the intruder in the generational relation, the false father like the teacher and the Führer—Hans yields and looks down passively, reiterating the failure of the lacking male gaze in relation to generational juniors.

"That's enough," announces the Nazi smugly, and the film cuts to Helmuth proudly staring his father down—proudly as well as actively, in contrast to the dispersive situation of the first cell shot, that shot to which the frame now dissolves very slowly. In this remarkable dissolve, the graffiti wall replaces Helmuth's gaze so that viewers understand the gaze—that of the youth toward his elder—as the writing on the wall at which Hans passively stares. This dissolve, which ends the hour-long flashback, visually endorses the idea that Hans has ended up in the post-war dispersive situation because of a type of youth crisis (photo 9).

As in *Somewhere in Berlin,* one half of the youth duality—youth crisis as social threat—rests at the basis of a lacking masculine gaze. The dispersive distortions of generational relations and paternal inheritance were key causes, legacies, and symptoms of National Socialism—an overt politicization of *Somewhere in Berlin*'s oblique association. While a powerful evocation of betrayal and loss, this sequence also comprises a stunningly reductive argument, one obscuring the complexity of Nazi and German crime and guilt, all the more astounding for its clarity in a single image of a youth dissolving to the epitaphs of the executed.

Back in 1945, the postwar challenge for Hans rests in, so to say, reading the writing on the wall, much as reconstructing the Heimkehrer's gaze requires that he look at and comprehend the ruins of Germany (such lessons abound for Iller in *Somewhere in Berlin*). The overriding answer is the same: fighting not a political or psychological but rather a paternal and pedagogical duel. The film reaches its second climax in the postwar duel between father and son, when Helmuth manifests the other half of the contradictory youth discourse: he returns to the private sphere he fled to confront, and ultimately affirm, the father he has betrayed.[52] Helmuth rings and Hans opens the door and invites him in. Helmuth reenters the abandoned apartment (photo 10), but Hans—faced with the son who betrayed him—hesitates at the door, his back to the camera and face front lit in another echo of the opening cell shot: it is the passive gaze in which he is rutted and that he will have to resolve with his son.

207

10. Hans at the door, same blocking as cell shot in which Hans stares at the wall in *Rotation* (Courtesy DEFA-Spektrum)

11. Reinvoking the same cell shot above: Hans's back is to the camera, arms at side, staring ahead in *Rotation* (Courtesy DEFA-Spektrum)

12. Progressing out of passive staring, Hans turns sideways in *Rotation* (Courtesy DEFA-Spektrum)

13. Leaving the passivity behind, Hans finally turns to his son and hugs him in *Rotation* (Courtesy DEFA-Spektrum)

Once he returns to the kitchen, where he was drying dishes, Hans pauses without saying anything for an uncomfortably long time, indulging once again the paternal hesitancy I underscored in both Lotte's announcement of her pregnancy and in the birth scene.[53] The lighting and positioning of his body also recall yet again the opening prison shot—his back is to the camera and he is front and side lit. Moreover, Hans is facing the place on the wall where the Führerbild once hung, made clear by its residual dusty outline (photo 11).

This connects this postwar generational duel to both the opening prison shot and the climactic Führerbild sequence. Once again, Hans seems the passive, hesitant father. Helmuth begs him to say something, and Hans turns so that his side now faces the camera, a slow progress out of the back shot to which we have grown accustomed (photo 12). Finally, he breaks out of his trance and embraces Helmuth (photo 13).

The father and son do not even really talk about what Helmuth did wrong (for example, embracing Nazi ideology, denouncing his father, fighting the "Insane Hitler-war"). Instead, the postwar solution rests in the father's taking the son back into the patriarchal house and in teaching the son the lesson the father has learned. The specific deployment of generational differentiation of paternity against youth as social threat— now youth as social affirmation—now also calls for a revised pedagogy. In a very wooden and heavy-handed dialogue, Hans imparts to his wayward son the lesson he learned from reading the wall: he recognized on the wall an international community that wanted to and should leave behind a more beautiful world in which there is no danger or need. This lesson recapitulates Kurt's speech at the wedding banquet, but Hans has been able to learn this international lesson only from the ruined wall at which he stared, from his dispersive social situation that teaches primarily generational lessons.

The message fits the emphatic humanism of the postwar period as well as the internationalist emphasis of the Soviets, but the point here is the form of the lesson itself. If Nazism was staged in the film most conspicuously as a Nazi classroom and school graphically matched to the war, then the film's proposed solution is a kind of homeschooling by the reeducated father. Given the few scenes Hans has with Helmuth, during none of which does he talk with the boy, the lecture seems all the more conspicuously symptomatic of a new model for fatherhood. The teacherly posture is the last one in which we see Hans, the film's protagonist: it is the solution to the dispersive situation in which the film first

210

and recurringly located him. The duel between old and young resolves that image, and the pedagogical undertaking of the patriarch restores the lacking male. As in *Doktor Faustus* or any number of newspaper articles I analyzed above, German sovereignty and agency are normatively located in a teacherly subject position.

The significance of *Rotation*'s paternal-pedagogical answer to Vergangenheitsbewältigung becomes all the more pronounced and peculiar given that it seems the only operable solution the film offers: once again, the contradictory depiction of youth is deployed to navigate the contradiction of public and private resistance. Despite the widely cited themes of individual agency and political responsibility or various media in the public sphere, the film does not agitate for Hans's engagement in any kind of political organization. In fact, it discourages it: the bars montage implies that Hans's public protest against unemployment is just another in a long series of incarcerations, while Kurt's mode of resistance hardly seems either plausible or effective for someone like Hans. Kurt and Hans's publication of leaflets, after all, killed Kurt and had Hans well on his way to execution. Because the film suggests that the essential problem rests with antisocial youth and its relation to adults in a youth crisis of generational dispersion, Kurt's resistance does not end up mattering. *Rotation*'s clarion political solution echoes those abounding in early rubble films: the resistance of the parents remains useless as long as the house is not in order, as long as the young remain out of adult control—a specifically generational control on which the whole postwar period seems to pivot.

6

Reconstructing Film in the Western Zones

Stars of Youthful Sexuality

The Film Star and Its Discontents in the Early Postwar Period

After the war, the Allies did not permit German feature film production for almost a year, a period that came to be known in the once-vibrant industry as the *Filmpause*. During the Filmpause, many German filmmakers and film industry executives turned to other media to speculate on how to resurrect German cinema in this radically changed context. Although these film personnel may also have been aiming to demonstrate their progressive political credentials to Allied authorities, the first postwar feature films, like *The Murderers Are among Us* and *Somewhere in Berlin,* did indeed conform to many of their proposals, which generally advocated an emphatic break from cinema made under the Nazi regime. For a prominent and much-cited example, in a lead article for the British-licensed trade publication *Film-Echo,* director Helmut Käutner espoused a new cinematic commitment to realism that he termed in the article's title the "Demontage der Traumfabrik" (Dismantling of the Dream Factory). An artistically successful filmmaker whose work the Nazis had frequently banned, Käutner called for the final destruction of the dream factory that had dominated film production throughout the Third Reich. The "dream factory" referred to Hollywood studio–style productions that generally relied on a likable hero, clearly drawn conflicts, and a happy ending. According to Käutner, the biggest obstacle to the transformation of postwar cinema was the German audience, which, although visiting the cinema more than ever, yearned for distraction from, rather than engagement with "problems of the German yesterday, the German today, and the German tomorrow."[1] With this dream factory and the audience conditioned by it, German filmmakers and films had their own particular challenges in their self-conscious attempts to come to terms with the past.

Other articles opining on the direction of post-Nazi German film proposed a similar break with the Nazi/Ufa tradition and, although many took issue with Käunter's vilification of the audience, they also advocated filmic realism explicitly engaged with the recent past.[2] Many such critics were more specific than Käutner in isolating the compromised elements of the Traumfabrik to be dismantled and replaced. One such article in the Soviet-sector *Neue Filmwelt,* presumably searching for appropriate models in other countries, praised the realism of postwar Italian cinema while attacking the standard Hollywood fare. The piece segues quickly to criticizing western-sector German films that returned to Hollywood models, recounting with horror how these productions had even started to cast stars in leading roles.[3]

What is it about film stars at this historical moment that could have provoked such antipathy to one of the cinema's most popular and marketable aspects? Why would coming to terms with its past have turned the film industry against its most recognizable faces? Certainly part of it was the deliberate deployment of a star system under the Nazi regime, which, as Eric Rentschler has made clear, self-consciously imitated a range of Hollywood practices, especially after Germany banned U.S. productions in April 1940.[4] But, I would argue, there is also something in the nature of the star system itself that rendered it contrary to what most critics considered a productive approach to the recent past. Although western German films did indeed prove more willing to cast stars as their movie protagonists, three such high-profile productions demonstrate how the contingencies of the postwar period and the demands of Vergangenheitsbewältigung sparked a fundamental renegotiation of the conventional film star. In fact, all three films—*And the Heavens Above, Ways into Twilight,* and *The Last Illusion*—depict a thorough disciplining and reconditioning of the star in many of its constituent aspects. This disciplining of the star occasioned, as it did throughout the early postwar time and context, the deliberate deployment of young people as a key aspect of the films' narrative strategies. Before elaborating how these Western-sector rubble films instrumentalize the young to discipline the conventional film star, I would like to consider why and how the star system could have been so antithetical to postwar representational strategies as they attempt to come terms with the past. As a pertinent case study for the postwar period, Hans Albers illustrates this phenomenon perfectly: perhaps the greatest German star of the time, Albers found himself after the war cast in an altogether different role in an altogether different context.

The Film Star in Context: The Stardom of Hans Albers

Scholars like Richard Dyer, Richard deCordova, and Paul McDonald, among others, have theorized the function of film stars and the star system within their wider social context, and I would like to submit that some of the general operations of the star system illuminate precisely why the star might have been at odds with the postwar rubble film.[5] The film star, argue both Dyer and McDonald, has a fundamentally contradictory relationship to the prevailing social order. On the one hand, stars articulate and embody the values of that social order, the socially endorsed good that must, by film's end, overcome any challenges or obstacles. In this sense, stars personify the status quo and seem decidedly conservative: they are rarely revolutionary and generally affirm the prevailing social order after some dramatic narrative disruption. On the other hand, however, stars do not have to conform to the very social norms that they otherwise embody and enforce. Although they may ultimately affirm those norms, they embody myths of extreme individuation against their immediate social environment. Stars thus embody the success of social values to such an extreme that they simultaneously transcend their immediate social surroundings. They articulate norms without obeying them: that is, they offer the contradictory myth of transcending the social context while simultaneously preserving the social values that make them so transcendently great.[6] This fundamental contradiction between the exceptional individuality of the star and the star's conservative function within the social order reflects the contradictions and dissonances of any social order and helps explain why stars are "popular," that is to say, widely known figures who can mobilize enormous cultural and financial capital.

215

This contradictory relationship to the prevailing social order and its dominant fiction manifests itself in both filmic and extrafilmic discourses about stars.[7] Such contradictory discourses inside and outside the film include the stars' mythical relationship to luck or magic and their relationship to their own performance. Stars enjoy a kind of conforming success that brings them conventional fame and wealth, but they usually unknowingly or unintentionally back into this radical distinction: stars are suddenly, surprisingly "discovered" by film experts who reveal that the given star is "graced" with talent. As McDonald observes, the familiar "rags-to-riches" trajectory is crucial to obscuring the wider system of economic and social exploitation: the success of the star conforms to conventional social norms and values, but its magical path proves the star's fantastical exceptionalness and individuality.[8] Inside the film as well, the exceptional success of stars contributes to their privileged yet conforming navigations of—above all—economic and sexual systems: stars enjoy the favor of fate and coincidence, not least in terms of sexuality, where conventional partners (physically attractive, heterosexual) always, by film's end, succumb to stars' advances. Second, the anecdotal observation that stars constantly play themselves (that is, their offscreen personalities persist in their films) is in fact a general rule: part of the fantasy of individuality that transcends all contexts entails that stars not completely adopt roles written for films.[9] There is always a trace, a residue, of their offscreen personality—itself discursively constructed and cultivated—in any film role they might provisionally adopt. Thus extrafilmic "individuality," which still conforms to prevailing social values, obtains within the filmic context, just as the stars triumph conventionally in whatever context they might find themselves. In fact, great acting ability—the chameleonlike quality of losing the self in a scripted role—would almost seem an obstacle to the fame of a star. In each case, be it economic, sexual, or artistic, there is remnant individuality that transcends the social context yet still conforms to and affirms the values that underpin it.

These myriad aspects apply amply to Hans Albers, whom the press constantly labeled Hans im Glück (Lucky Hans) and whose indomitable *Hoppla, jetzt komm'ich* (Whoops, here I come!) attitude made every adverse circumstance seem irrelevant or at least ephemeral.[10] Though an enormously popular star throughout the Third Reich, Albers's widely cited relationship to the Nazis articulates the star's contradictory relationship to the prevailing social order perfectly. While he was praised for

14. Hans Albers, greatest film star of the Third Reich
(Courtesy Bundesarchiv-Filmarchiv)

not having abandoned Germany—and thus for conforming to the regime—he was also famous for his antipathy toward the Nazis, for example, in refusing to have his picture taken with top party officials.[11] In the postwar period, critics liked to observe that his popularity protected him from the Nazis, an explanation confirming a contradictory social fantasy in the new context of Vergangenheitsbewältigung: it distinguishes him from the more complicit *Mitläufer* (fellow travelers) while obscuring how his popularity relied on, and was supported by, the Nazis he allegedly despised.[12] Similarly, Albers was famous for his performance of himself—what I am terming his transcendent individualism—rather than the scripted character of any given film. Many criticized his inability to subordinate his extrafilmic personality to the specific film role, though one perceptive critic isolated this as a crucial feature of his (as well as others') stardom.[13] The press never missed an opportunity to mock his inability to remember lines, or how he jovially called himself the *Negerkönig*, after the *Neger*, or off-camera chalkboards that cue actors who have forgotten lines.[14] The implication was, it seems, that his considerable and unique personality overpowered any role he might adopt, just as it overpowered the compromising context of Nazism.

Two other aspects of stars affect their specifically filmic deployment—though both also retain a certain validity for the extrafilmic discourses about stars. First, stars serve very specifically as a kind of spectacle within the film frame itself, such that viewers' attention is focused on images of their bodies (rather than merely the active gesticulation or spoken words of those bodies).[15] Films invariably fetishize the bodies of stars—or, more precisely, parts of their bodies—as exceptional in how they conform to dominant corporeal aesthetics of their historic moment.[16] In Albers's case, his blond hair and ice-blue eyes were mentioned ubiquitously, probably more than his acting ability. As McDonald observes, "bodies act as key signifiers of cultural beliefs," and the fetish value of these "Aryan" attributes was clearly overdetermined in Nazi culture.[17] Second, stars' exceptionalness, especially their fantastical negotiation of the economic system, entails a privileged relationship to other spectacular elements of the film, like elegant costumes, luxury goods, or exotic landscapes: stars enjoy enchanted access to coveted material aspects of their environment, both filmic and extrafilmic.[18] This aspect of stardom likewise confirms the conforming but transcendent individualist sketched above: stars affirm the ordinary materialist values while also enjoying extraordinary access to the material goods. Albers's

15. Hans Albers's fetishized blue eyes (Courtesy Bundesarchiv-Filmarchiv)

self-indulgent relationship to fashion and the "good life" was also an indispensable aspect of his stardom: an astonishing number of articles mention not only his fine clothes but also how he offered the interviewer a cognac—and of course always availed himself of one—before they commenced the interview.[19] Though a seemingly minor detail, the ubiquity of the cognac reference is clearly part of Albers's performance of his individuality and becomes part of the discourse about Albers and his unique relationship to fetishized material objects. Given the precarious state of German consumer goods throughout the mid-1940s, this function of the star became even more important during the war: as the bombs were falling during the 1944 shooting of *Große Freiheit No. 7*, for example, it was widely reported that Albers regularly managed to secure fine cognacs, celebrating his privileged access despite the miserable material conditions of the day.[20] Both of these attributes—stars as filmic spectacles as well as their privileged relationship to the material world—manifest the dream of a uniquely contradictory relationship to the social order: the exceptional individual that transcends his or her social context in a radical realization of very conventional norms and values.

HANS ALBERS STARS IN THE RUBBLE FILM

Hans Albers counts as probably the greatest male star of the Third Reich, but the decision to cast him in the first U.S.–licensed film drew harsh criticism: the criticism, however, was motivated not so much by Albers's work during the Nazi period as by the casting of a star in a rubble film.[21] In casting a star as its Heimkehrer, *And the Heavens Above* took the rubble film in an altogether different direction because Hans (Albers's namesake character) stands in stark contrast to the recurringly fatigued Heimkehrer-type familiar from the early DEFA rubble films (Mertens in *The Murderers Are among Us*, Iller in *Somewhere in Berlin*, Hans Behnke in *Rotation*). Stars seemed inappropriate for the depiction of the Heimkehrer's struggles, because, as I argued above, the postwar Heimkehrer figure is based on a complicated, compromised masculinity who has an altogether different relationship to his social environment than is usually the case with a star. The compromised masculinity of the Heimkehrer prevents him from fulfilling conventional social roles: he fails to play the traditional male, a struggle that threatens to destabilize the social order that the star invariably upholds. The Heimkehrer's compromised masculinity experiences the gap between itself and the conventionally dominant role of men as lack, as inadequacy, as humiliating.

220

This humiliating gap between self and social role stands in stark contrast to stars' distance from the social order, in which the transcendent individuality distances itself from the social context while simultaneously affirming the values and norms of the social order. In the case of the Heimkehrer, the gap between his subjectivity and the social order serves as the destabilizing challenge to be defused—not, as with the star, to be constitutively celebrated. The gap between the Heimkehrer and social norms arises from a lack of faith in that social order that results in passivity and fatigue on the part of the Heimkehrer; the gap between the star and the social order arises from the star's exceptional success, which contributes to a fantastical individualism that these rubble films, in reconstructing the social order, sought to overcome.

Due to these differences in character, Hans Albers as Hans Richter in *And the Heavens Above* requires not the ideological jump start of the standard Heimkehrer sketched in chapter 5 in the early DEFA films but rather a severe downgrading of his ambition and activity, that is, the tempering of his star-based exceptionalness that distances him from the humble role society affords. In their coming to terms with Germany's recent history, these controversial star vehicles realize the diametrically opposite trajectory for their protagonists than that manifested in the DEFA films' Heimkehrer: in the DEFA films, the fatigued and overwhelmed Heimkehrer must be inspired to return to his conventional social role, whereas these western-sector films downgrade the stars' exceptional overactivity to a new kind of humble productivity. In order to moderate the exceptionalness of the star for the postwar context and its requisite Vergangenheitsbewältigung, these films nonetheless also deploy young people, but here to diminish the star's indefatigable optimism and his transcendent individuality. More specifically, the films utilize the duality of youth—as both socially affirming and socially threatening—to depict the humiliating and humbling trajectory of their stars. Though they are deployed in an altogether different context, young people once more help Germans come to terms with the past by reconstituting both bourgeois subjects and social constellations—especially in their ability to firm up the prevailing social order after destabilizing it with a youth crisis.[22]

At first, *And the Heavens Above* problematizes the star and his individualism by associating Hans and many of his exceptional star attributes with the kind of antisocial youth and youth crisis that abounded in this postwar cultural context. As I have already observed, images of children and adolescents loitering unsupervised on the ruins of the private house or public school offered some of the most powerful postwar symbols for the failure of society and the bourgeois ethos that served it as a cornerstone. *And the Heavens Above* and the other early western star vehicles use the antisocial youth crisis to problematize the star's most fundamental aspect—transcendent individuality and exceptionalness. The star protagonists also struggle with the challenges of the postwar context because it is so radically different from those contexts on which stars relied and in which they thrived—they, too, struggle to come to terms with the recent past, although they, in their extreme individualism, require downgrading, not uplifting trajectories. In fact, the films discipline unruly youth as a means to discipline the star, that is, to recast and adopt the star's transcendent individualism for important postwar institutions in light of this recent past, including economy, education, and government. These early postwar star vehicles displace the typical but suddenly problematic transcendent individualism of stars onto the young so that they can defuse such exceptionalness, manage it, discipline it. Youth serves here as well as a site onto which to displace challenges arising from the recent past, although those challenges with the star are revealingly different. For example, much more than the DEFA films, there is a deliberate manipulation of gender and a disciplining of the protagonist's sexuality, a development linked to the star's privileged access to sexual economies. In each of the three cases discussed here, the male star is romantically associated with a much younger woman, an amorous involvement the film codes as generationally transgressive and therefore socially counterproductive. The nexus of age with gender provides the terrain on which these films renegotiate the star in order to overcome his transcendent individualism and incorporate the subsequently humbled self into the social institutions of the reconstructive era.

Like that of many other rubble films, the plot of *And the Heavens Above* traces the postwar return and domestic reintegration of a Heimkehrer. When ex–crane operator Hans Richter returns from the war and a POW camp, he finds his Berlin home in ruins, a recurring synecdoche for the psychological challenges posed by the recent past. Upon his arrival, however, he learns that his son, Werner, is also on his way home. Ecstatic that his son is returning soon, he goes to work on the apartment, arranging a tidy domestic space that impresses a widowed neighbor,

Edith. A friend from the POW camp offers to employ Hans and his horse, Florian, to haul some unnamed items to the "Haiti bar." Hans does the job, but upon delivering the goods to an outpost of the black market, he realizes that he has trafficked in contraband. Hans cunningly demands more money from his shady customers and then is slowly pulled into their *Schieber* (black market) enterprise, as is his young, pretty neighbor, Mizzi, another frequenter of the Haiti bar. To this suspect situation returns Hans's son, Werner, who has been temporarily blinded in the war. At first Werner's blindness prevents him from seeing the rubble or his father's criminal profession. Once his sight is restored, however, he witnesses in full horror the ruinous condition of his city and his family. Werner confronts his father about his black market activities, and the rest of the film unfolds in the conflict between father and son, wrong and right, corruption and redemption in postwar Germany.

The film opens by locating the star in an unfamiliar context, that of the postwar rubble film: its first images of Hans emphasize the challenges facing the Heimkehrer in reintegrating into the family and private sphere, a sequence that associates *And the Heavens Above* with other, non-star-driven rubble films of the time.[23] In one of the film's first major sequences, Hans is alone at night flipping through family photo albums. A pan over the pictures triggers a series of three flashbacks that alternate with Hans's looking around the domestic space of his apartment: the flashbacks suggest Hans's struggles with a now-lost past, but they also all correspond to different stages of his son's maturation. Telling is how much this paternal relation eclipses Hans's wife, about whom viewers learn nearly nothing.[24] Though paternity repeatedly served as a key means for the rubble film to represent the Heimkehrer's postwar struggles with the past, it is remarkable that the renowned "blonde[r] Hans" (Blond Hans—one of Albers's popular press monikers) is cast as a father: by Albers's own count, this was only the second time in his long and diverse film career he had played a father.[25] In their outsider status, stars were usually cast as single and often sported only an uneasy relationship to the humbling social integration of family life. The film's casting of Albers as a father demonstrates the changed cinematic and social environment in which stars were then operating: from the very first sequence, conventional star status has been refigured by Hans's relationship to paternity and youth.

This series of flashbacks gives way to images that follow Hans through the rubble of his home, underscoring the tension between his stable star masculinity and the destruction wrought by the recent past. Newly returned, Hans passively absorbs and reflects upon a panorama of sociologically revealing images that highlights the postwar ruins not only of buildings but also of families. He hears Frau Burckhardt yelling for her daughter, Mizzi, to come and then sees Mizzi among the ruins with her angry, despairing boyfriend, Walter. Mizzi wants to escape and "enjoy youth," but Walter retorts, "We'll never get there." Next Hans observes an old couple, the teacher Heise and his wife, who has a stomach ailment and desperately needs better food than they can afford.[26] The open question of *And the Heavens Above* is how the Heimkehrer as star will react to these ruins of the conventional family and the entire bourgeois social constellation. At the end of the sequence, the spectator understands that the famous Albers will, despite the rubble context, play himself: with a glint of his well-known blue eyes, Hans picks a flower and smiles, an optimistic response viewers would expect of the famously indomitable star. Critics focused on this image, his eyes sparkling amid the rubble, as the moment viewers know that the old Albers is back.[27] The opening of *And the Heavens Above*, then, asserts a different kind of Heimkehrer in the rubble context, a star whose transfilmic optimism and transcendent luck means his masculinity and indefatigability are hardly compromised, his exceptionalness and individuality hardly undercut.

Bad Girl, Good Boy: The Gendered Juvenile Lessons of Rubble

While the first sequence asserts the star's individuality and exceptionalness, it also begins to associate him with a teenage girl, Mizzi, whose attitude toward the prevailing social crisis will parallel Albers's but ultimately prove much less happy or healthy. More than the DEFA films analyzed above, these three western star vehicles deliberately deploy the gender of their young people to negotiate postwar subjectivity: as the opposite of the idealized *Trümmerfrau* (rubble woman), Mizzi functions as the most dynamic and interesting character in the film. Though she has received scant scholarly attention, the reviews at the time singled her out for particular praise.[28] In her flight from the ruined private sphere to youthful indulgence, she counteracts the flat and obviously normative depictions of female characters in other rubble films, including Susanne in *The Murderers Are among Us,* Frau Iller in *Somewhere in Berlin,* and Frau Behnke in *Rotation.* She much more resembles Edmund's sister in Robert Rossellini's unflinching *Germany, Year Zero,* a

16. Hans Albers, film
star as postwar worker in
And the Heavens Above
(Courtesy Bundesarchiv-
Filmarchiv)

strong female who demonstrates and acts upon both sexual desire and economic ambition. In this regard, she embodies a threat to the endangered masculinities of the film because she asserts herself in so many conventionally masculine ways.[29]

Particularly intriguing in *And the Heavens Above* is that the film locates this threatening individualist in a woman who is also a young person. In this historical context, the (adult) rubble woman was engaged in those roles conventionally ascribed to men: repairing homes, providing for the family, even carousing outside the private sphere. All the adult women in the film, however, tend to be unidimensional, unthreatening, idealized domestic women who fulfill the conventional feminine role that had been so radically undercut by the war. By rendering Mizzi a young person, the narrative defuses potentially explosive gender relations by displacing them onto generational difference: it makes the ubiquitous gender crisis a youth crisis. If Mizzi had been an adult love interest of Hans, she might have threatened the precarious social system in general; but by depicting her as a young person, the film is, as I shall show, able to instrumentalize her—as Foucault's danger that prowls—as a malleable threat, ultimately in order to manage the adults around her and so to shore up conventional social roles, hierarchies, and constellations. Mizzi's trajectory from good daughter to black market escort parallels Hans's eventual reaction to the social crisis, and therein helps to represent and guide Hans's own suspect decisions. Viewers never hear Hans's rationale for giving over to the dark forces of the black market— as a star who was famous for the Schieber type, his tendency to work outside norms of society is a given.[30] But with Mizzi as the protagonist of the film's youth crisis, viewers hear the narcissistic attitudes behind such antisocial behavior, such that she articulates the suspect foundation of the star's exceptionalness and individuality: the problematic aspects of his stardom are thus displaced onto the youth crisis. Mizzi's early association with Hans links their similar losses of faith in the prevailing social order and its values of hard work and humility. The film's association of transcendent individualists underscores the suspect, ultimately juvenile underpinnings of Hans's star-based exceptionalism.

In order to negotiate and revise the star's now problematic individuality, the film associates his exceptional optimism with a juvenile-feminine response to challenges of the recent past. Early representations of Mizzi highlight her as the only other character in the film's sociological cross section who demonstrates an energetic, optimistic response to the rubble context. Despite her boyfriend, Walter's, despair,[31] she insists on enjoying youth, going dancing, forgetting everything—the individualist, indulgent half of the youth duality that, in various cultural forms, also conveniently manifests the star's resistance to conventional social roles. The editing associates this attitude from the start with Hans: in the opening sequence described above, she is the only character to whom he repeatedly looks, and when he watches her in the ruined bourgeois apartment, the soundtrack crescendos as the camera finds her as awake and restless as he is. Both recalcitrant young woman and determined star scheme about how to overcome the postwar challenges and escape the decimated regime of conventional social control.

Mizzi's and Hans's reactions to the precarious social order resemble each other more and more as the film moves through its first half an hour. In one sequence, for instance, when viewers are cued by Hans's musical theme to expect to see him belting out the tune, the camera instead finds Mizzi softly whistling its melody, sunning and grooming herself with a mirror amid the complete wreck of an apartment building. By way of narcissistic cultivation, Mizzi again distances herself from the ruins of the decimated context and the burdens of the recent past. Walter, however, indulges in an angry tirade against suggestions that he somehow normalize his life, search for work, start to socialize again. Unlike Walter, Mizzi copes by ignoring the ubiquitous ruins and by focusing on her clothes, her image in the mirror, her desires; with rubble all around, she constantly looks at herself in mirrors and doggedly works on her dresses. Such overtly narcissistic images of the body problematize the gap between the self-possessed individual and the social order: it underscores the apathy of certain exceptional subjects toward their social context. Such narcissistic self-grooming proved particularly problematic in a context that, as I showed above, normativized a specific way of looking at the rubble and absorbing the widespread destruction. By emphasizing Mizzi's obliviousness as narcissism, the film undercuts the care and performance of the body required for the fetishized images of the actor's—especially the star's—body, which seem completely inappropriate and indecorous amid the widespread social destruction. The rest of the film deliberately and misogynistically associates this young and female narcissism with the socially problematic aspects of Hans and his star status.

While the film codes Mizzi as both youthfully and femininely narcissistic, its plot and editing continue to associate her with Hans's reaction to the rubble and his decision to join the Schieber band. Shortly after the scene described above, Hans finds Mizzi waiting in his apartment: her dress finally finished, she wants to hold Hans to his promise to take her out. Her angry and skeptical boyfriend is unable to offer the access to privilege and luxury she demands, and she realizes that Hans is a comrade in corrupt materialism and individualism. Hans gives her some of the coveted black market foodstuffs he has brought back and tells her to get out, but then he looks at her again with overt sexual desire. He reaches into his bag, gives her some chocolate—like Albers's cognac, a precious and rare commodity in this context—and steals a kiss from her, a kiss sealing their common fate. The kiss is the only moment of overt sexual desire manifested by Hans in the film, and as Edgar Morin has observed, the kiss was crucial to the star's image not only because it centered its desire but also because it offered the fetishized face

227

of the star in an act of love.[32] But by kissing Mizzi, Hans is not only engaging in tried-and-true star activity; he is also breaking generational barriers, such that an older man's overactive desire for youth is coded as individualistically indulgent and socially threatening. Both are antisocial generational crises that localize the wider postwar social crisis.

When Hans accepts the illegal hauling job that his friend Fritz has offered him, it is Mizzi who brings him the details of the job, effectively sealing the problematic alliance between the exceptional star and juvenile femininity. After he completes his haul and earns his first illicit pay, he finds Mizzi cavorting in the same Haiti club. He tells her that she should have been home long ago, and she replies, "I have no home," confirming her similar loner status and her distance from the conventional private sphere. Recognizing an outsider comrade, Hans curiously accepts Mizzi's reply, forgoes paternalistic concern for the young woman, and sits down to have a drink with her. His new illicit job has distracted him not only from legitimately productive work but also from the purer pursuits of paternity, and they now share the intergenerational camaraderie of the black market after fleeing the rubble.[33] Their shared fate is sealed in one of the film's most memorable shots, when viewers watch the individualistic domestic exiles enjoying a drink together at the bar. After shooting the two together, the camera tilts down to their reflections in the bar, and it pans from Mizzi's mirrored reflection in the bar to Hans's right next to her, underlining their individualistic, youthful affinity. The film has problematized Mizzi's mirrored reflection as a narcissistic response to the social crisis—underscoring the care of self as fetishistic image—and now definitively associates this reflection with Hans the eternal *Einzelgänger* (loner). A parallel constructed thematically and formally, their association underscores Hans's reaction as both generationally and gender suspect.

At the very moment that the film definitively associates the fetishized face of the star with young Mizzi's narcissism, Hans's son, Werner, the socially affirming rather than threatening youth, makes his entrance. The film dissolves from the bar scene to a friend guiding the blind Werner home through the rubble.[34] In direct contrast to Mizzi's feminine obliviousness to and distance from the ruins, Werner comes to personify the compromised yet socially committed masculinity the film is at pains to produce.[35] He demonstrates a more deliberate, balanced response to the rubble than Mizzi's, a lesson that takes the past—since, in his blindness, this is all that he can see initially—into greater and more deliberate account when looking at the present ruins.[36] The film suggests that Mizzi's narcissistic and individualistic femininity aggravates the social crisis, while Werner's humble masculinity will overcome it. The good male child therein serves as the link to the past—but here a linkage possible only when Werner sets out to break the connection between Hans and the feminine and individualist juvenile.[37]

In his first blind experience of the rubble of Berlin, Werner has to imagine the rubble and tends to see the city as he remembers it: whole, ordered, bustling with everyday metropolitan activity. At the same time his blindness subverts the usual potency of men's looking and reiterates the precarious state of masculinity: in short, it anticipates the productive rubble gaze that will incorporate lack and inadequacy into the star's traditional male gaze.[38] When Werner regains his sight a few scenes later, the film deliberately restages his looking at the rubble. Werner walks out of the doctor's office optimistic about seeing his beloved Berlin again, but his hopeful gaze is shattered in a way neither the star's nor Mizzi's ever is. Unlike their individualistic responses to the rubble, Werner's reaction acknowledges and incorporates the social crisis. As Werner walks into the rubble, the film cuts from his looking to documentary shots of ruins, wounded and maimed bodies, Trümmerfrauen laboring atop mountains of rubble, and then cuts back to Werner's reaction shot—a horrified, passively pensive response. The moment echoes those in *The Murderers Are among Us, Somewhere in Berlin,* and *Rotation* in which the male learns to assimilate the lessons of the rubble by looking in an altogether different way at the context. Because Werner has a more mediated relationship to the past and to the rubble, the film stages his drawing more effective lessons from it than Mizzi. These rubble films consistently emphasize the importance of understanding, here personified in Werner, rather than merely acting, as personified in both Hans and Mizzi. Werner's radically different perception of the social crisis, his positively coded rubble gaze, provides the film with its basic conflict: between this humble approach to the devastation and Mizzi's narcissistic obliviousness to the rubble that distances her from productive social roles that Werner will help reconstruct. The film displaces its basic conflict onto this youthful duality, that is, the tension between Mizzi's "feminine" ignorance of the rubble and Werner's complicated masculine absorption of it.

229

Infecting the *Draufgänger* (Daredevil) Hans
with a Humbler Masculinity

The first half an hour of *And the Heavens Above* associates the famously individualist Hans (Albers) with the narcissistic young woman, but then, at that point, introduces the socially affirming youth who can condition the star's antisocial tendencies. A revised relationship to the rubble and the social crisis it represents will transform the star's transcendent individualism into the humble masculinity that the revised star vehicles, in this context, are compelled to produce. When Werner returns from his trip around the rubble to confront his father at home, he brings his humbler relation to the recent past back to the private sphere, to the dinner table, where the paternal provider normally reigns. When Hans comes in, Werner looks at his clothes scornfully, a direct echo of his disapproval of Mizzi's narcissism when he saw her in an elaborate dress. Hans is wearing a fine and meticulously tailored suit that befits his star status, but that was certainly a rarity in those meager times.

Hans asks if Werner has had a look at their old Berlin, and Werner retorts that he has seen the new Berlin: the son, due to his blindness and the flashback, has a better sense of the present mediated by his memory of the past. But his father responds that they cannot complain about Berlin's misery as long as they have something to eat; Hans responds, in other words, by defending the exceptional privilege that distinguishes the star within the film and in society at large. Both Hans's modish suit and fine foods, like Albers's familiar cognacs, confirm his privileged access to the material world, but *And the Heavens Above* problematizes the kind of individualism that underpins such star-generated excess. Angrily, Werner accuses his father of taking food from others, who hunger and work while Hans and his family enjoy the fruits of those others' labor. Werner insists things can be done differently, "honestly," that is, modestly, and that he will prove it to his father—the son will teach his father the lesson of how to productively, not corruptly, overcome of the past.

When the newly determined Werner flees the dining room, Hans looks for the first time defeated and humiliated: being contradicted by his son and embarrassed in front of his family evokes from him a look of lack unlike the usual representation of a star. Edith leaves Hans alone in his lavish dinning room, a man now completely humiliated and brooding.[39] As the music climaxes, Hans finds himself in front of a mirror, staring at a finely coifed reflection in expensive clothes that would be, in other film contexts, completely unproblematic for such a star. Mirrors were, in fact, associated with a couple of well-known extrafilmic rumors about Hans Albers the star: one journalist recounted how Albers would often kiss his reflection in the mirror in his dressing room, asking, "Am I not a beautiful person?" (*Bin ich nicht ein schöner Mensch?*); another rumor had him regularly looking in the mirror declaring, "There is only Albers, and I'm him! (*Es gibt nur einen Albers, und der bin ich!*)[40] In *And the Heavens Above*, however, both the star and his narcissistic reflection have a different, much more problematic coding: the dissonant music on the soundtrack signals Hans's sense of an uncanny double in the standard star image. Up until this point, the film has associated mirror reflections with Mizzi and her youthful narcissistic individualism, ignoring the rubble context and indulging antisocial desires. Hans's reflection becomes dubious, as if the film were foregrounding the fetishization of the star's body as a topic for rumination: Hans considers his own privileged access, his own exceptionalness, and how it was earned. Unlike Mizzi, however, Hans is graced with a generational redemption: in the mirror's reflection, as he stares at and examines his changed self, is a photograph of Werner, tucked into the edge of the mirror. Unlike Mizzi's feminine look into the mirror, where her own image eclipses the widespread collapse surrounding her, Hans finds his reflection in his son as well as in his own person. Though it was a rarity for Albers the star to play fathers, this revised mirror image underscores why his newfound paternity is crucial for the rehabilitation of the star: while Mizzi's is a purely narcissistic youth crisis, Hans is afforded an intergenerational redemption. By foregrounding fatherhood, the film can refigure the narcissistic, self-absorbed gaze of Mizzi and Hans, incorporating into it the humility and integration attributed to paternity. The son, the male side of the youthful duality, can teach and change Hans—that is, revisit and revise Hans's star-based, overly individualistic relation to the social crisis around him.

In the next sequence, Hans retraces his steps around the ruined landscape and relearns the lesson of the rubble. As he wanders around in a majestic overcoat and smart fedora, he quietly takes in the rubble and those toiling away at it. Some critics found this image, of Albers in full star regalia among the ruins, the most memorable of the film.[41] An explicit echo of the film's opening panorama—to which Hans responded with unabated Albers optimism—this collage drives home the enormous scale of the rubble and the burdens of the past. From Werner, Hans has finally learned to integrate humility into his extreme individualism. In his meandering through the rubble, he arrives at a complicated masculinity that integrates lack—metaphorically the widespread rubble and specifically the difficult past—into his exceptional personality.

On his wanderings, which humble him who was the greatest star of the Third Reich, Hans eventually finds Werner at work on a crane, trying to unload a barge. Hans says, "Now I come to you and we have to forgive one another": after the son's rubble lessons for the father, Hans takes the controls and teaches his son how to maneuver the crane. In accepting his role as crane operator, father, and teacher, the star has renounced Mizzi's narcissistic (here feminine and juvenile) perspective and surrendered the youth crisis she represents. Renouncing the individualism and exceptionalness that the film displaces onto youth, he resumes his paternal-pedagogical role as well as his old profession and the humble toil crucial to reconstructing the postwar economic order. A final sequence in which Werner pretends to be involved with the black market and Hans hauls him out of such illicit circles confirms the reinstallment of Hans as the humble and attentive father. After these corrective confrontations with his son, the star takes off his elaborate costume and returns to the humble work clothes with which he started the film. It is a rags-to-riches-back-to-rags story that refigures the usual graced ascent of the star by way of young people.

The reconstructive project of the film transpires primarily in a generational negotiation, which *And the Heavens Above* also codes in gender-specific ways. The film associates the star aspects of Hans with the antisocial "feminine" half of the youthful duality and her youth crisis but then corrects his overactive individuality with the good male youth from whose compromised masculinity Hans will learn. Before its happy ending, however, the film dispenses with the problematic half of the youthful duality. Spurred into crime by Mizzi's materialism, her boyfriend, Walter, is arrested and commits suicide in custody. Apprehending Mizzi in the Haiti bar, the police inform her of his death and then arrest her, marginalizing her from the film's happy and restorative denouement. Viewers never learn the nature of her crimes, but they hardly matter since the source of them is clear: her allegedly "feminine" preening, individualism, and materialism—all constitutive aspects of stardom, all condemnable offenses in the context of Germany's social ruins. Mizzi did not do anything more illegal than Hans did, but he, before a different kind of mirror, learned lessons of humility that diminish his star-driven exceptionalness. The first postwar star vehicle tells the story of a

Heimkehrer who triumphs not in his transfilmic optimism or irrepressible individuality but rather in his learning a compromised masculinity by negotiating generational and gendered axes.

FRÖHICHE OHRFEIGE (CHEERFUL SLAP)? WAYS INTO TWILIGHT'S CIVICS LESSON OF GENERATIONAL DIFFERENTIATION

Unlike Albers, who worked in relative theatrical obscurity for years before his *Blue-Angel* breakthrough in the early 1930s, Gustav Fröhlich became an international film star at an unusually young age. At twenty-four, while a member of Piscator's theater group in Berlin, he was cast by Fritz Lang as the male lead in his monumental *Metropolis*. *Metropolis* counts as one of the best-known silent films of Ufa, when Ufa's reputation as the most sophisticated studio in the world made it Hollywood's main competition. Fröhlich was one of the few silent stars to make the transition to sound film without any perceptible professional decline: he became one of Germany's most popular cinematic heartthrobs throughout the 1930s, second only to Willi Fritsch. (Albers's popularity stretched through the 1940s but, cast most often as an average or even Schieber type, he was less of a *gallant* than Fritsch or Fröhlich.)

Part of Fröhlich's continued success in sound film surely arose from his theatrical talents, which would have afforded him not only the appropriate voice training but also the newly requisite ability to memorize dialogue. Throughout this period, his stage work was also well known and widely admired: for instance, he played Max Reinhardt's last Prinz von Homburg in 1932 to widespread acclaim before Reinhardt departed from Germany in the increasingly inhospitable political climate of the early 1930s.

As with Hans Albers, the 1930s and 1940s stardom of Fröhlich was revealingly co-constitutive with his alleged anti-Nazism. Fittingly for Fröhlich's reputation as a suave cavalier and international star, these anti-Nazi credentials comprised amorous as well as transnational intrigue. It was widely rumored during the war, and reported publicly after, that Fröhlich had slapped Joseph Goebbels for Goebbels's more than professional interest in Fröhlich's second wife, Lida Baarova. Details varied with the version, but in almost every story Fröhlich caught the famously womanizing minister of propaganda flirting with Baarova, a well-known and widely admired Czech actor. The story usually involved Fröhlich's luxury villa, out of which he allegedly saw the minister come in suspicious haste.

17. Gustav Fröhlich, matinee idol of the 1930s
(Courtesy Bundesarchiv-Filmarchiv)

The gossip about the confrontation was so widespread that in 1947 Fröhlich felt compelled to call a press conference to address the rumor. It was true, Fröhlich confirmed, that he had caught Goebbels flirting with his wife and that he verbally abused the minister, who remained stonily silent. Fröhlich then raised his hand to slap Goebbels, but then "it occurred to me that I'd like to live a little longer." Though he resisted the considerable temptation to execute the *fröhliche Ohrfeige* (cheerful slap, a pun on Fröhlich's last name), he was nonetheless soon thereafter banned from acting (*Berufsverbot*) and subsequently drafted.

Similar to Albers's reported relations with the Nazis, Fröhlich's reputation manifests the star's contradictory relation to his context in a time of great political and social complexity. On the one hand, of course, Fröhlich as a star had relied on Goebbels's ministry and his *Reichsfilmkammer* to become one of Germany's leading men. Fröhlich's villa was even close to Goebbels's house in Berlin, a proximity that seems, after all, more than merely geographical. The unspoken subtext of the slap was that Fröhlich and Baarova must have been on some sort of social terms with Goebbels for the episode to reach such (soap) operatic proportions. On the other hand, the public could indulge the fantasy that, despite Fröhlich's complicity with the coordinated culture industry of the Nazis, one of their beloved matinee idols was actually a resister of the government that was, literally and metaphorically, harassing the country. The rumor that Fröhlich had slapped Goebbels, it was reported later, spread through Germany rapidly, providing some celebrity-conjured comfort to those who felt oppressed by the regime. As with Albers, the public forgave (or overlooked) any hint of Fröhlich's complicity with the Nazi regime, including his readiness to let his earlier Jewish companion flee the Nazis while he remained in Germany to become a leading star. Apparently, the political credentials of the fröhliche Ohrfeige and his wartime service sufficiently demonstrated the sincerity of his resistance. The star thus served a contradictory political function for the wartime public: part exceptional success in the general economic and political system, part active resister of the overtly corrupt system itself. Like Albers's antipathy to the Nazis and his access to cognac in the midst of the bombing, the star's wartime fate served clear ideological purposes for a public suffering under the regime and the war: celebrities provided a means for the popular imagination to navigate not only the difficulties of society and economy but also the complexities of politics.

At the same press conference Fröhlich called to address this rumor of the slap, he not so coincidentally also announced his plans to return to film-making as well as his dream to own and run a production company.[42] Given the political nature of the widely known anecdote about him, it is fitting that his first postwar film, which he directed, should cast him as the mayor of a small town diligently committed to reconstruction. Such a casting choice would seem to fulfill star-based political fantasies indulged during the war: the widely celebrated star who embodied Germany's "better" years during the early 1930s and who resisted the Nazis in the 1940s becomes a postwar political leader who promotes political, social, and economic reconstruction. In a manner similar to Fröhlich's unintended heroism in the Goebbels incident, Fröhlich's character, Lukas, is a publisher who happens to be forced into a position of postwar political authority, although he has little ambition of his own.

Given that Fröhlich had been a matinee idol since the late 1920s, it is both surprising and revealing that he cast himself in *Ways into Twilight* (*Wege im Zwielicht*) as an older, disabled man suspiciously involved with his younger secretary, Edith. Perhaps Fröhlich himself had insight into the problematic nature of his heartthrob star status in this postwar context: as with Albers's Schieber activities in *And the Heavens Above*, Fröhlich's first postwar role simultaneously invokes his pre-1945 stardom and acts to subvert it. The device for coming to terms with the star's problematic past seems remarkably similar: the reconstructive activity of the star is invoked but also tempered by a generationally transgressive love affair. As with Hans in *And the Heavens Above*, though the postwar exceptionalness of the star is crucial to reconstruction, the film also sets out to discipline and harness the star's excessive optimism and problematic overactivity. The film performs this disciplining by displacing such conflicts of optimism and overactivity onto the conflict between the generations. In contrast to *And the Heavens Above*, however, *Ways into Twilight* consciously associates the negotiation between the generations with the literal law of the municipality and its police. The film depicts a dual law, that of the municipality to which the recalcitrant young must reconcile as well as the law between the generations to which the exceptional star must reconcile. The municipality was the first political entity over which Germans were allowed any sovereignty, so it is telling that the film would apply the issues of reconstruction and generational struggle to the administration of a small town.

18. Gustav Fröhlich in postwar glamour (Courtesy Bundesarchiv-Filmarchiv)

The Star-Heimkehrer as Mayor

While many rubble films open with establishing shots that situate viewers in the widespread devastation, *Ways into Twilight* commences with a long-take close-up of a worn and weary male face. The unusual opening invokes the status of the film as a star vehicle: the close-up plays a crucial role in the career of a star, particularly of a well-known heartthrob like Fröhlich.[43] This close-up, however, consciously deploys a familiar face as the terrain on which the war has registered its ruin—the self-conscious star vehicle traces the recent past in the scars left on the familiar face of the well-known star. Despite the close-up standard for the star, the codes of postwar male lack are all there: the deep crevices of his face, the unsteadiness of his gait, the glasses with an eye patch subverting the male gaze usually instrumental to the effective assertion of men over cinematic context. Like many a Heimkehrer trying to come to terms with the past, Lukas is searching for something, something intimate and long gone—his wife, missing since the bombing in Rostock. When the viewers finally see a reverse-shot point-of-view, they realize that Lukas/Fröhlich is one among the homeless masses in the rubble of a train station. As with Hans in *And the Heavens Above,* the film opens by self-consciously invoking the star's status, but it also deliberately locates the celebrity in the same struggles with the past as the viewers.

In *And the Heavens Above,* the sparkle of Albers's famous eyes negate the lack the film initially establishes in the ruins of his apartment building. In *Ways into Twilight,* despite the rough looks of Lukas and the fruitless search for his wife, the star likewise transcends the context in a way the everyman Heimkehrer of *The Murderers Are among Us, Somewhere in Berlin,* and *Rotation* never could. More like *And the Heavens Above, Ways into Twilight* realizes the exceptionalness implied in the opening close-up: viewers soon learn that despite his lacking looks, Lukas is the mayor of a small town. After his opening rubble sequence, Lukas walks back to town with a boy and is hailed—literally and figuratively—as mayor by a local farmer asking about the reconstruction of a bridge. Even more heavy-handed is a subsequent three-shot of Edith, the boy, and Lukas with signs announcing the *Bürgermeister* (mayor) and *Polizei,* both framed conveniently between Lukas and Edith and above the boy. Once inside the town hall, Lukas is again framed with signs trumpeting his Bürgermeister title: the film makes abundantly clear that the star is playing, even amid the postwar rubble, an exceptional individual. More remarkably, the star's exceptionalness is

238

not only individualistic here; the film is careful to locate him at the center of his community, at the center of the town's symbolic system, a clear echo of Fröhlich's function as idol of political resistance during the war. Such a symbolically central position would be unimaginable for the common working-class Heimkehrer of *Somewhere in Berlin* or *Rotation* or even *And the Heavens Above;* even in *The Murderers Are among Us,* in which Mertens is a doctor, he starts the film unemployed, having fallen from any privilege that medicine could have afforded him. With *Ways into Twilight*'s Heimkehrer type as a mayor, viewers find themselves in an altogether different type of cinematic context, one that celebrates not only the transcendent individualism but also the social centrality of the star.

Youth Crisis as Veterans out of Control

In the pan mentioned above, Lukas's point-of-view shot falls on a group of young war veterans playing cards and selling cigarettes. Realizing he has none left, Lukas decides to purchase some from these obvious black marketeers. This initial interaction between the lacking male star and the young establishes one of the film's recurring motifs, that is, the overdetermined exchange of cigarettes as intergenerational transaction. Many rubble films—for instance, the early DEFA films—depict how postwar society, due to the rubble of conventional paternity, lacked a phallic center. The ubiquitous exchange of cigarettes in *Ways into Twilight* and in other films represents the currency of phallic exchange in a context in which the adult men no longer enjoy easy access to the well-known phallic symbol. Richard Klein has written about how cigarettes appear in moments when phalliation is imperiled, and the circulation of cigarettes in this and other films reflects the precarious and fluid status of phallicity for the lacking male subject.[44] Instead of a traditional masculine center, a black market for cigarettes/phallicity/power has emerged, often controlled by young criminals.

The sale, however, is interrupted when the youths hear that one of their black market nemeses has resurfaced. The gang of youths, led by Stefan, Peter, and Sepp, now quickly corners their prey, Fleck, in the neighboring ruins of an enormous church. The terrified Fleck cautiously backs up on a rickety plank until it collapses, and he falls to his apparent death in a crater that serves as an open grave. Sending the gang on their flight from the police, Fleck's accident establishes one of the film's fundamental tensions: youth crisis as the opaque relation between Germany's young and postwar law. As I discussed in my evaluation of Jaspers in chapter 4, the denazification of the young was a contentious issue after the war because of their unclear status as adult agents; their age complicated the already murky issues of guilt in the context in general. Though the gang of youths is implicated in the crime, this particular staging of the inadvertent crime complicates guilt and therefore the relationship of the apparently guilty to the law. On the one hand, they seem to be like any criminals on the lam: the police come to investigate and the young have to flee; Stefan even escapes with handcuffs around his wrist. The young men turn renegade and actively flee the rule of law, preferring the band of youthful brothers to the acceptance of an ambiguous guilt and reconciliation with bourgeois law. On the other hand, the episode and, above all, Lukas's witnessing of it demonstrate the tenuous culpability of the young. As in Meinecke or Jünger or *Rotation,* in *Ways into Twilight,* this ambiguously guilty group, belonging neither to the transmitters or inheritors of German bourgeois society, is immediately and thereafter associated with the war and its crimes. They still wear tattered military uniforms, and one of the most memorable shots of the film depicts them fleeing through an airfield full of grounded military planes until an (off-screen) U.S. officer admonishes them to stay away from the implements of war. The youth crisis—here of young veterans—serves as a site onto which to displace the war and crimes.

As in many of the rubble films, this unintegrated gang of youths asserts a liminal time in life between childhood and adulthood, a time between (the child's) subjection to the paternal law and (adult) harnessing and control of that law. The youthful flight from adult authority recalls the Deutschlin episode in Mann's *Doktor Faustus:* in both cases, Germany's current social crises are depicted as a youth crisis that threatens the bourgeois social constellation of economy and society. But more than other films, *Ways into Twilight* maps this liminal developmental stage and its liminal cinematic spaces onto explicitly criminal guilt and lawlessness: the youth are chased throughout the film by the literal law, by the Hannover police, and pose a consistent problem for the municipality, to whose reconstruction Lukas is committed. Two subsequent confrontations between Lukas and the gang will thematize the rebuilding of the town and the youths' reconciliation not only with the metaphorical law of the father but also with the literal law of the municipality. The night after their wanderings, Stefan, Peter, and Sepp are forced to seek shelter in the clock tower of the town's church. The setting underscores their quasi-crime of "murder" as well as the importance of this second confrontation for the town: it transpires in the church's steeple and clock tower, the very phallic core of the town, its religious, historical, geographical—thus, symbolic—center.[45]

When Lukas finds them in the clock tower, the optimistic star confronts the renegade youth who have lost all faith in the dominant fictions of society. To Lukas's suggestion that they go home and resume their studies, they retort sarcastically that he should try applying to the overcrowded universities. Stefan suggests to Lukas that "you" (in the informal plural, *ihr*) be quiet, in order to think back and contemplate (*zurückdenken und nachdenken*) what you have done. Now clearly meaning the older generation, Stefan accuses "you" of knowingly (with seeing eyes [*sehenden Augen*]) running the country into the ground, and now you sit in the mayor's office. The intergenerational tensions recall the letter exchanges I described in chapter 2, in which such exchanges stand in for other, more troubling conflicts. The delivery of the diatribe and the manner in which it is shot underscore it as the central exchange in the film: Fröhlich uses the cramped space and staircase to shoot Stefan at very low angle, simultaneously building sympathy for him and visually supporting his interpretation of the recent past. Lukas is shot in a starkly contrasting high-angle shot, such that he looks pathetic and small in his plea for Stefan to see things differently. As with Albers in *And the Heavens Above,* the film deliberately stages the humiliation of the star before and by the young: Lukas's confrontation with Stefan leaves the well-known star in a position rare for his individualism and exceptionalness. As when Werner accuses Hans, young Stefan's accusations associate the individualistic star with some larger, culpable social group. The telling difference between the films rests in the setting for this degradation of the star: for Albers and *And the Heavens Above* it transpires in the private sphere, which the film aims to rebuild; for Fröhlich and *Ways into Twilight,* the town's church steeple and clock tower foreground the municipality and its precarious laws.

Given the symbolic centrality of Lukas—it is, after all, the clock tower of the town of which he is mayor—the deliberate humiliation of him might surprise viewers. But also as with Albers, the film deliberately draws the star back from the brink of utter lack: the severe camera angles recover to more on-level shot/reverse-shots as Lukas and Stefan continue to converse. Lukas assures Stefan that "mistakes will be forgiven"

241

and there is no reason now to ask who is guilty, an obviously exculpatory declaration for young and adults alike. They have to start anew, all have to begin over again: "Who doesn't even begin will never finish" (*Wer nicht anfängt, wird nicht fertig*), he says, now shot at a slightly low angle, displacing Stefan from this flattering camera position. With this statement he also lends the generational reconciliation to the municipality a motto: later, Peter will paint a sign for the bridge with just these words of the dominant fiction. By reconciling these generationally coded camera angles, the film deliberately stages the narrative's negotiation between the young and the humiliated star. In Stefan and the low-angle sympathy for him, the film gives his sharply skeptical, slightly despairing generational position credence and sympathy. From there, however, in the dialogue and in its shifting angles, *Ways into Twilight* favors Lukas and his attempt to convert the young to the reconstructive project. The camera techniques anticipate the *Versöhnung* (reconciliation) of the youths to a public works project here at the phallic core of the town. Lukas informs them of a bridge that has been unusable since 1945, and in the next scene, the gang approaches the bridge from the rubble, a normative trajectory from social crisis to public works. The bridge, of course, serves metaphorically as a bridge from the 1945 past to the 1947 future, from the unemployed and wandering to the working and productive—but, above all, it represents a bridge between the old and the young as they turn to municipal reconstruction.[46] The subsequent exchange of cigarettes likewise reinforces the newly reconstructed relation between old and young: now the cigarettes flow from adult to young, provided to the boys by the mayor and the town at large. The reconciliation among the generations heals the wounds of the past.

The End of Stefan's Adolescence

The first generational confrontation reconciles the old and young through narrative compromise and visual negotiation: Lukas the star accepts some lack in acknowledging his complicity, and the young submit to the law of the figurative father and convert (in a church) to the reconstructive project. But the gang of youths has yet to come to terms with the police and the literal law of the municipality. The rest of the film treats Stefan's reconciliation to the father's law as an important first step toward his surrender to the rule of state law. Lukas can protect them from the murder accusation temporarily (various scenes depict him fending off police detectives), but ultimately Stefan must face the police

242

and their suspicion he is a murderer—in short, the (overdetermined) criminal past. The double reconciliation, to the law of both the father and the state, transpires through generational conflict and differentiation in the last third of the film, when the law finally and completely subjects Stefan. But his reconciliation with the public law also demands a concomitant sacrifice on the part of Lukas: as in the first generational confrontation, the progress of the young also requires a reciprocal surrendering of the star's exceptionalness.

After the accidental drowning death of the youngest of his gang, Stefan finally decides to turn himself in to the police. The death of the boy provides the second metaphorical bridge between Stefan and the public law, but the boy's demise also signifies the end of Stefan as rubble child, as wayward youth with its liminal black market existence. But Lukas and Stefan's second argument concerns not only Stefan's surrendering to the police but also their mutual love interest in young Edith. When, shortly before, Stefan argues with Lukas about whether to turn himself in, he attacks Lukas's relationship with Edith. Stefan screams that she tolerates Lukas only out of pity and that if Stefan asked her to go with him, she would. The argument is surprising—an abrupt diegetic reversal of fortunes—because it suddenly problematizes a hitherto unremarkable aspect of Lukas. With both his star status and his consistent cinematographic point of view, the film has until now fostered viewers' identification with the well-known star. But suddenly viewers hear an emotional critique of Lukas's liaison with a much younger woman. Confirming the legitimacy of Stefan's attack is Lukas's violent reaction to it: in the face Stefan's accusatory tirade, Lukas strikes him, knocking the young man to the ground and also his own glasses off. The camera cuts dramatically to a close-up of the dead scar tissue of Lukas's damaged eye, interrupting identification with Lukas by underscoring his lack and evoking disgust in Stefan's point-of-view shot. If Stefan was criticizing Lukas's generationally transgressive relationship before this image, the obscene shot of Lukas's mutilated eye completely undercuts his involvement with the young and innocent Edith. The cinematic apparatus has turned against the star in one of its most constitutive aspects: the revised close-up of the star's face subverts his amorous conquest. At precisely this moment of disgust at the famous heartthrob, Stefan and Lukas hear of the boy's death and run off: thus, the death seems to teach Stefan to surrender to the police and Lukas to surrender to the laws of age.

243

When the police decide that Stefan was not legally culpable and release him, Stefan asks Edith if she will accompany him to his studies in Essen and she lovingly accepts. As Stefan rewrites himself back into the social order, he replaces his young friends with a wife, his youth community with the heteronormative bourgeois private. But the police intervention restores generational order not only by ending Stefan's youth but also by tempering Lukas's exceptionalness that resulted in generational transgression. It is a kind of reverse Oedipal law of the father that works here against Lukas, who has enjoyed the romantic attentions of someone too young. He agrees to release Edith to Stefan in a rather typical male traffic in women, handing over the woman as he might have the phallic cigarettes—thereby relinquishing the star's amorous claims to her, thereby acknowledging the transgressive behavior and his symbolic generational crime that he had engaged in to compensate for the loss of his wife.

THE LAST ILLUSION'S REEDUCATIONAL PEDAGOGY: FRITZ KORTNER'S "B-LINE FOR THE RUBBLE"

Exiled from the Rubble Film

After *And the Heavens Above* and *Ways into Twilight,* other rubble films from the western sector began to cast stars as their male leads. For instance, Josef von Baky's *The Last Illusion* (*Der Ruf*), the first postwar film released in both German and English versions, celebrated the triumphant homecoming of one of Albers's biggest pre-Nazi rivals, Fritz Kortner. Vilified by the Nazis for being Jewish as well as for his politically engaged theatrical and film work, Kortner left Germany in the early 1930s for England and then the United States, where he worked from 1933 to 1949 with relative success. *The Last Illusion* was closely identified with the real-life exile of Kortner, deliberately made to be a star vehicle based on his extrafilmic experiences.[47] One critic observed that with *The Last Illusion* von Baky was continuing the trend started with *And the Heavens Above: a Starfilm* of international caliber.[48] Kortner plays a Jewish professor, Mauthner, who returns to Germany to resume his academic career after his comfortable California exile. His German university had ousted him, but Mauthner insists, perhaps overly optimistically, on helping to rebuild both his own institution and Germany in general, a commitment confirming the link between education and nation that pervades the early postwar period. Lending the film its parallel familial

19. Fritz Kortner, film star as great actor (Courtesy Bundesarchiv-Filmarchiv)

tension is Mauthner's separation from his gentile wife, who remained in Germany, subsequently marrying and raising their son with a Nazi general. To compound the romantic tensions and familial permutations, Professor Mauthner returns from the United States in the company of his assistant and romantic interest, a much younger American woman named Mary.

Unlike many rubble films examined above, *The Last Illusion* deploys discourse about youth to examine the challenges posed to a German returning not from the war but from exile in a country appreciative of the exile's presence, a case that recalls a number of prominent figures, including Thomas Mann, Bertolt Brecht, and Alfred Döblin.[49] The focus on an exiled star offers another insight into the parameters of stardom in this context: the film permits viewers to identify with the persecution of one of Germany's most respected actors, lending this star, like Hans Albers and Gustav Fröhlich, a specific ideological function. Despite this foregrounding of the political persecution of the star, the film nonetheless parallels the other two star vehicles discussed above by severely downgrading the star's transcendent individualism and exceptionalness. As with Albers and Fröhlich, a well-known star plays a postwar German male who is exceptional in a peculiar way: the Kortner character, again like Albers's and Fröhlich's, proves overly optimistic about overcoming the devastation of Germany. More than in *And the Heavens Above* or *Ways into Twilight,* however, *The Last Illusion*'s star-exile becomes a transfer point for (*Kultur*)national identity, a node with which the nation can identify and through which it can operate particularly. In his classical training and his commitment to high German culture despite the Nazis, Kortner and his character can help the national community, in Anderson's memorable phrase, to imagine itself.[50] Perhaps because the star comes to play such a nationally central role, *The Last Illusion* radicalizes the humbling manifest in *And the Heavens Above* and *Ways into Twilight.* It traces Mauthner's trajectory from optimistic activity to an utterly failed masculinity. *The Last Illusion* deploys intergenerational relations to discipline and normalize the star-exile returning from abroad by downgrading the problematic exceptional individualism, manifested here in an explicitly pedagogical project. *The Last Illusion* confirms the centrality of the parent-child and teacher-student subject position for this context—and the inoperability of conventional stars in those positions.

American Dreams of the Heimkehrer in Exile

In the five postwar films analyzed so far, the opening scenes offer images of rubble as a succinct symbol of social and cinematic dispersion. In stark contrast to these usual rubble-ravaged openings, however, *The Last Illusion* begins with an image that, for this context, proves far more startling: establishing shots of an efficiently operating modern city and an intact, handsome bourgeois home surrounded by a white picket fence. The image corresponds to the stereotypical image of life in exile, which for many was actually severely impoverished and generally miserable. Besides appealing to German stereotypes about the comfortable life of exiles, however, *The Last Illusion* also deliberately invokes Kortner's status as an exiled star in America, locating its protagonist in sunny Los Angeles and confirming, in his domestic well-being, the link between the film star and private luxury. As Jackie Stacey has observed, images of American stars among luxurious material goods served a particularly important function for war-impoverished European populations.[51] Echoing *And the Heavens Above* and *Ways into Twilight*, *The Last Illusion*'s opening contrasts its star protagonist to the typically despairing Heimkehrer: even when Albers returns to his wrecked home and missing family, the sparkle in his eyes negates the despairing rubble gaze; here Kortner's domestic and professional success likewise locates the star-protagonist in a very different postwar terrain.

Material well-being is not the only privilege Mauthner enjoys: these opening sequences represent the persisting coincidence of the star with the conventional masculine function, which serves to organize the cinematic image and the community of characters populating it. In open love and respect, Mauthner's students and German-exile friends have gathered at his home to celebrate his successful fifteen years in the United States. His privileged relationship to his context recalls Fröhlich's office of Bürgermeister more than any of the unknowns playing the humble DEFA Heimkehrer. Mauthner, however, has been hiding something from both his students and his friends: he has received an invitation, a call (*Ruf*—the German title of the film), back to his university in Germany. Fränkl, another exile from Germany, declares Mauthner crazy for considering a university that suspended him and eventually forced him to flee. Mauthner counters that he has a duty to the young of Germany to return and that he is committed to helping them. The discussion between Mauthner and Fränkl stages what must have been a

CHAPTER 6

constant dispute in postwar exile communities, debating the ethical duty
of exiles to Germany, the security of life abroad, and collective guilt. In
The Last Illusion those larger questions of coming to terms with the past
are, as they are throughout the context, displaced onto questions of
youth and youth crisis. Fränkl is clearly skeptical that returning would
help anybody, whereas Mauthner remains optimistic about changing
Germany through helping its young. In this tenacious insistence on his
own agency despite and against the overwhelming contextual challenges, Mauthner articulates a star-based optimism, here concerning
German youth and (re)education. As with Albers and Fröhlich, the star-
protagonist embodies exceptionalness by manifesting doggedly optimistic attitudes about reconstruction and his contribution to it, an optimism that, in *The Last Illusion,* explicitly mirrors U.S. optimism about
reeducation.

The debate, however, also anticipates the perils of the star's exceptionalness by linking Mauthner's optimism to generational sexual transgressions also familiar from both Hans and Lukas. When Fränkl brings
up Goethe and his infatuation with a nineteen-year-old, the dialogue
makes clear that he is problematizing Mauthner's affair with his much
younger assistant, Mary. The importance of the debate rests not only in
the parallel between Goethe and Mauthner as embodiments of Germany's classical humanism tradition and Germany as Kulturnation but
also in their mutually suspect behavior, which comes up three times in
the California sequence.[52] Though some advance press materials tried to
obscure this theme of an intergenerational love affair,[53] this sequences
makes abundantly clear the romantic overtones of Mauthner's relationship with his assistant. Fränkl recommends that Mauthner, when he harbors illusions about Mary, look in the mirror. Mauthner responds that
he is able to delude himself into thinking that he is a much younger man
than he actually is.

When Mauthner reveals that he is considering returning to Germany, however, Fränkl immediately asks how he can leave Mary. Mauthner chides his friend for changing his mind about her so quickly, but
Fränkl retorts: what is an aging man in love compared to a madman
wanting to return to Germany? Revealingly, Mauthner himself connects
the two: they are both love affairs, he says—indeed, one might add that
they are love affairs of youth, naiveté, and optimism, all symptomatic of
the star's exceptional status within the filmic context.[54] The debate
about Goethe's/Mauthner's age and paramours Ulrike/Mary makes

248

20. Kornter as Mauthner in exile comfort in *The Last Illusion*
(Courtesy Bundesarchiv-Filmarchiv)

clear that not only reeducational optimism but also Mauthner's own relation to age and generation undergird his star-driven optimistic approach to reconstruction. When Mauthner insists on returning to Germany to reeducate the Germans—in a manner invoking his American stardom—the film simultaneously subverts his overactive optimism with his relation to generation. This star-exile enjoys the material and professional exceptionalness standard for the American-based star but, because his sexuality transgresses generationally, his exceptional behavior also foreshadows imminent trouble. As with Albers and Fröhlich, a rubble film codes the star's standard sexual success as generationally violative, a deviation that is, in this context in which youth is so emphatically charged and carefully managed, ultimately doomed.

Reeducation as Pedagogical Youth Crisis: The Father without a Son, the Teacher Who Couldn't Teach

Mauthner's generationally transgressive affair hints at trouble to come, trouble that arises as soon as Mauthner arrives in Berlin to search for his lost wife, Lina, and son. In Berlin, the film conspicuously undercuts the effective agency one would expect from the protagonist played by the star. His ability to navigate and control situations—the key to the star's exceptionalness and individualism—is repeatedly undercut by the logistical obstacles created by the postwar breakdown of the social order. For example, on his search for Lina, Mauthner visits an old friend to whom he sent care packages for years, assuming that his friend was forwarding them on to Lina, only to learn that his friend kept all the packages for himself and does not even have Lina's address.[55] As a frustration of the star's normal agency, this search sequence offers a dispersive sociological cross section common to almost all rubble films, rendering Mauthner's comfortable Californian accommodations and accomplishments an increasingly distant memory.

The symbolic confusion and dissonance of the returning exile grow even greater when Mauthner finds his ex-wife. Lina attacks Mauthner for an affair he allegedly had while still teaching at his German university, but Mauthner protests that the university invented the affair to oust him, an ouster that led directly to his exile. These surprising divulgences reveal the heretofore secret motivation in Mauthner's return: despite the apparent wholeness and plenty of exile, Mauthner wants to return in part to reassert himself in the family milieu from which he was banished—a standard Heimkehrer trope. The film thereby slowly, delib-

21. Ambivalent reunions in postwar Berlin in *The Last Illusion*
(Courtesy Bundesarchiv-Filmarchiv)

erately interweaves his star-based reeducational optimism with the broken family theme—above all, an alienated son—familiar from other
postwar narratives. The images of the haunted, obsessed Mauthner contrast starkly with the cheerful, blithe professor viewers see in exile:
though the film foregrounded his exceptionalness in his exile in California, it also underscores the banality of his postwar lack. The surface ve-
neer of the happy exile and star has been worn away to expose the lacking underside of masculinity in the wake of the war, an underside
pivoting on family and especially paternity. Despite the exceptionalism
of the star, Mauthner's negotiation of exile and reeducation will mean
coming to terms with his past by way of coming to terms with his family: as with Albers and Fröhlich, locating the star within a broken family,

251

as precarious patriarch, downgrades the star's conventionally privileged status.

After the film's plot reveals the hidden familial aspect of Mauthner's exile and return, it cuts back to his other reason for returning, his optimism about reeducating German youth. In its approach to this interwoven thematic, *The Last Illusion* deploys the dual representation of youth I have been tracking throughout. Interestingly, *The Last Illusion* maps its youth duality onto the topography of exile by way of the youth-nation link: the affirming youth are, by and large, U.S. students who know Mauthner from his very successful exile, while the threatening youth will be German, including his own son. The opening sequences in Mauthner's Californian exile, in which the male protagonist is still embedded in stable social and generational relations, show one half of the youth duality. According the professor the obedience, respect, and love that underpin his identity in exile, Mary, Elliot, and Spencer affirm the teacher-student relation and the stability and wholeness it affords.

Whereas these good U.S. youths serve as the cornerstones of Mauthner's happy life in exile, the dispersive situation back in Germany introduces the other half of the youthful duality: youth as social threat tending to an antipedagogical attitude familiar from the images of youth in Mann, Meinecke, and Jünger. In addition to the recurrence of this youthful duality, *The Last Illusion* confirms a trend articulated vaguely in *Somewhere in Berlin* and then more clearly in *Rotation* and *Ways into Twilight:* in displacing Vergangenheitsbewältigung onto the young, the film casts as the convinced Nazis the rebellious, antisocial youth, effectively replacing or at least obscuring the adult perpetrators of Nazi crimes. Much more than the harmless Lina or untenured lecturer Fechner, the German students, including Mauthner's own misrecognized son, Walter Heck, come to represent persisting Nazism: its aggression, its violence, and especially its anti-Semitism.[56] As in *Rotation,* the film establishes a close link between youth and the Nazi nation, one that both threatens the adult male protagonist and decouples him from the fallen nation. Perhaps most important, the young embody bad nationalism so that others may articulate a commitment to a "better" Germany, here Germany as Kulturnation located conspicuously in the Heine-quoting Mauthner. One critic observed how moving it was to hear Mauthner/Kortner declare, despite all that had transpired, his longing for his *Heimat:* as a Jewish professor played by a Jewish star,

Mauthner is allowed to articulate how much he loves Germany; he asks, "May I say the sentence" (*darf [den Satz] sprechen*) that would express the depth of his feelings for Germany.[57] But the film cannot, in the dubious light of the Holocaust and the war, simply evade a more problematic, even pernicious nationalism: this kind of nationalism has to be manifested somewhere in a film where the protagonist remains so remarkably committed to Germany and the Kulturnation. Faced with this postwar dilemma of the burdensome past, *The Last Illusion* deliberately locates this bad nationalism to the German young.

At the same time, the young in *The Last Illusion*—as they are in the work of Meinecke or Jünger—are only weak perpetrators of nationalist and racist evils: casting the young in this dubiously central role dilutes their status as racist or nationalist criminals. They end up, as in *Rotation* or in Jünger, led into crime and vice by a false pedagogy that also stands in for National Socialism. Rather than straightforward guilt, a failure to effectively teach children and adolescents displaces and obscures the crime that itself displaces the Nazi crimes: but this is a sin ultimately forgivable. Although he is the most important character to articulate anti-Semitic attitudes, Walter has moments, especially an amorous association with Mary, that redeem him. Moreover, viewers learn early in the film that he has been led astray both by his mother, who hid from him who his true father was, and even more by Fechner, who becomes his corrupting teacher.[58] As I suggested in my discussion of Meinecke and Jünger in chapter 3, the young invariably suggest an element of passivity, of victimhood, conveniently constitutive of discourse about youth. When *The Last Illusion* associates the young with the Nazi nation, it renders adult guilt and responsibility, like agency generally, highly opaque.[59] The young become Hitler's willing—but innocent—executioners.

The climactic confrontations between old and young occur when Mauthner arrives at his home university. Less like the DEFA films and more in the vein of *Ways into Twilight, The Last Illusion* deliberately engages and refigures important postwar social institutions, especially American-style and star-driven reeducation. In the first such reeducational encounter with the young, Mauthner delivers the reinaugural lecture on which he has been working for most of the film. The topic of the lecture constitutes the film's single greatest articulation of reeducation and its attempts to reconstruct the university out of the intergenerational crisis: Mauthner exhorts the German students to forget war and embrace reeducationally minded cleansing of their studies.[60] Von Baky lets the lecture go on for five minutes, as the camera consistently cuts between the faces of the old and the young, underscoring the film's heavy-handed commitment to discourse about reeducation and youth.[61] This generational confrontation, however, does not conclude with the successful reconstitution of the teacher-student relation, which the spectator might expect from the star professor (literally and metaphorically). The lecture ends not in a rousing reception but rather in the audience's silent protest and exit from the hall. A few of the students knock on their benches in approval, but Mauthner, as viewers learn afterward, was fortunate to escape an outright rebellion and an antipedagogical youth mob.[62] Mauthner's chilly reception seems to reference the infamous postwar episode I described in chapter 2, Martin Niemöller's 1946 sermon whose topic of guilt and penance provoked stomping and booing by students—indeed, the link to the Niemöller scandal was made by film critics at the time.[63] This first confrontation between old professor and recalcitrant students fails to resolve the generational tensions at the core of the film—the young remain antipedagogical, rebellious, and antisocial.

The second, more dramatic generational confrontation pits Mauthner against a more extreme youth mob. The encounter that seals Mauthner's paternal-pedagogical fate—and puts an end to any hope the film held out for a star-driven Vergangenheitsbewältigung by reeducation—comes in a pub brawl. At the *Bierstube* reception for Mauthner's (re)inaugural lecture, untenured faculty member Fechner incites a debate among the students, first by speculating on the nature of Mauthner's "mysterious" relationship with Mary and then by suggesting it would have been better if Hitler had finished the genocidal job he started: Mauthner's generationally transgressive relationship becomes fodder for the local rabble-rousers. The actual fight, however, is caused only indirectly Fechner: a melee erupts among the decentered, dispersive, dephalliated student mob between those for and against his position. The unruly student mob in *The Last Illusion* invokes two youth themes I have underscored above: first, the archaic, alternate sociabilities of the young (here, a bunch of rowdy students in a Bierstube); second, the youth mass on which Nazism allegedly rode to power, as in Mann, Meinecke, and Jünger. Indeed, when Elliot informs Mauthner of Fechner's racist epithets, Mauthner tellingly never attacks Fechner himself: instead, he leads a wedge of the older academics into the youth mob and pedagogically berates the students for defending what Fech-

22. Reeducation as beer hall rebellion in *The Last Illusion*
(Courtesy Bundesarchiv-Filmarchiv)

ner said. The expected duel between Jewish Mauthner and anti-Semitic Fechner is displaced, like so much in this context, onto a generational duel: the confrontation toward which the film has been driving, between the Jewish exile and anti-Semitic inciter, shifts to a duel between the father/teacher and the youthful mob resisting restoration of paternal/pedagogical hierarchy.

In this second climatic generational duel, Mauthner's ultimate pedagogical/paternal efforts fail utterly: when he wades into the melee to castigate the students—to reeducate their rebellion—he is confronted by his own unrecognized and unrecognizing son, Walter. Walter rebels explicitly, aggressively against the father he mistakes for merely an exiled teacher. The film has also been driving toward this conflict between the star and the Nazi, the American exile and the German veteran—but these conflicts are tellingly displaced onto a confrontation between old and young, teacher and student, father and son. When Mauthner thunders at Walter, "Go home or else," Walter retorts, his face inches from

255

Mauthner's, "Or else what? Or else what?" The viewers witness a stunning overthrow of Mauthner's paternal and pedagogical aspirations as well as of the star's exceptionalness and individualism. The face-to-face confrontation and humiliation of the star turned father recalls the fate of Hans when Werner confronts him in *And the Heavens Above* and Lukas when he encounters Stefan's anger in *Ways into Twilight*. Mauthner steps down, a final defeat on the journey started back in California, a journey started on behalf of the German nation and driving toward those very young who act to defeat him here. Elliot grabs Walter, and Mary and Emma wrap Mauthner in a coat and spirit him home.[64] The next time we see Mauthner, he is lying sick and immobile in the bed where he will die. The double defeat in this climactic generational confrontation—as would-be father and as teacher—has effectively killed the star, his overly optimistic return from exile, and his reeducational efforts, leaving the future of the Kulturnation he embodies suspended in murky uncertainty.

The Final Duel: The Star Dissolves before His Son

Mauthner's peculiar death highlights how discourse about youth and an intertwined paternity and pedagogy mediate the star's exile, his reeducational efforts, and his return to Germany. Since the fight in the pub, the melee that undercuts everything the well-intentioned professor tried to teach, Mauthner has been sick in bed. He tells Lina, without a hint of irony or self-reflection, that the illness is high blood pressure brought on by the flows and struggles of young blood that now bursts his old arteries. No rubble film offers a more telling diagnosis of the generational conflict at the root of coming to terms with the past, because none has gone as far in tracing the degeneration of the male subject: this star vehicle underscores how the conventional privilege and exceptionalness of the star no longer fits the male body.

The Last Illusion differs from almost all rubble films because it concludes with the death of its Heimkehrer, providing a very pessimistic perspective on the return of a star-exile, on U.S. efforts to reeducate Germany, and on the future of the Kulturnation embodied in its "better" Germans. In this death sequence, *The Last Illusion* deploys the ego-unbinding youth gaze to finish off the exile-star: the trajectory of the film has been toward, not away, from this shot, which recurs in a large number of rubble films. When Walter unexpectedly sees his mother at Mauthner's side, Walter asks the obvious question: "What are you doing here, Mother?" At this Mauthner awakens, opens his eyes, and asks, "Did someone say 'Mother' to you?" The shock of realizing that his own son was the mob's worst anti-Semite triggers a highly expressionist sequence, one that enacts all the ego-unbinding tendencies associated with youth as threat. As his eyes are opened to see youth for what it is— namely, both the violent rebel and his own son—Mauthner's life begins to disintegrate before his and the viewers' own eyes in an extended internal point-of-view sequence that correlates details of the room with Mauthner's emotional, even unconscious responses to his newly discovered son. In this dense collage sequence, the youthful, ego-unbinding gaze winds Mauthner back to a dream image of his wayward son as a baby in a uniform—a compression of generation realized in one stark image at the film's climax. Mauthner fantasizes a triumphant homecoming to California, a glorious fulfillment of his star function in the first sequence, only to realize that he cannot stay in the United States, that he must go "home"—and at this point he dies. In an internal diegetic point-of-view shot rapidly transformed, the camera pans from the spacious and bright California living room to the cramped, dark German apartment in which Mauthner now lies dead. Viewers have been swept out of Mauthner's point-of-view shot as his star-invoking California abode turns into a German family coffin. The film compresses the star's experience of exile and the Heimkehrer's experience of home in one pan, killing him by the end of it. As with Werner's reeducation of Hans/Albers and Stefan's of Lukas/Fröhlich, the son has opened the father's eyes, forcing him to acknowledge and incorporate into his overactivity and optimism both lack and inadequacy. This ego-unbinding dreamlike sequence is overdetermined in this rubble film context, locating Mauthner in a post-traumatic stress disorder company including Mertens in *The Murderers Are among Us*, Hans-Otto in *Somewhere in Berlin*, Hans in *Rotation*, Georg in *Birds of Passage*, and others. It is not, however, the war that causes Mauthner's trauma; his return from American exile, his ill-fated attempts at reeducation, and the recognition of his son are the events that definitively refigure both his reconstructive optimism and his status as star.

Conclusion: Reeducational Optimism out of Generational Bounds

The Last Illusion charts a trajectory from exile to home: surprisingly, this trajectory arches from the exile's starlike and star-based popularity with his U.S. students to Germany's social crisis of generational chaos, which ultimately subverts Mauthner's paternity and pedagogy as well as his star-based exceptionalness. Many DEFA rubble films, which deliberately cast unknown actors as their despairing protagonists, stage the generational and pedagogical differentiation of the male protagonist from the young, a development that leads to his happy reconstruction and relocation at the center of the grid of bourgeois intelligibility.[65] But the films discussed here, all remarkable as star vehicles, downgrade their well-known protagonists to overcome not their despair but rather their excessive reconstructive optimism. In *The Last Illusion,* in almost a direct echo of *And the Heavens Above,* the moment of family reunion in the private sphere humiliates (rather than reconstructs or reassembles) the father figure played by a star.

For the characters Hans, Lukas, and Mauthner, such differentiation means relinquishing the sexual transgression of an aged man who behaves too young. As Foucault and Donzelot have described, the generational hierarchy entails not so much the coercive oppression of the young but rather the positive assertion of noncoercive norms that differentiate adult from youth roles. Mauthner should, *The Last Illusion* implies, surrender the beautiful young research assistant and instead play the modest father and humble teacher; Walter, in fact, is redeemed by his love for Mary, such that the rebellious youth's sexuality, as with Stefan and Edith in *Ways into Twilight,* serves to correct the father figure's generational transgressions. As this youth matures into sexuality, the star-father figures should adjust their reeducational agenda appropriately to the changed postwar situation. That mixed metaphor, generational transgression and reeducational/reconstructive agenda, is the key nexus of these films: the disciplining of the star's sexuality is co-constitutive of the disciplining of his exceptional reconstructive behavior. Though these films, against proscriptions of the time, have cast stars in their lead roles, they nonetheless assert that Albers, Fröhlich, and Kortner should dilute and disperse their optimism with postwar realism, tone down their ambition and avoid the youthfully naive resumption of their Schieber activity, gallant ways, and old lectures, respectively. The struggle with their own prewar stardom and successes is effectively disciplined by and along with the young.

Conclusion

Mobilizing Youth for the Cold War

THE POSTWAR UNIVERSITY AS COLD WAR FRONT

The star vehicle films *And the Heavens Above, Ways into Twilight,* and *The Last Illusion* echo the kind of discourse about youth that I elaborated in the introduction. In my introduction to youth and reeducation in the early postwar public sphere in chapter 2, I argued that in postwar newspapers, in the Niemöller episode, and in policy debates, both Germans and the Allies displaced central challenges of the past—including former and persisting Nazism, anti-Semitism, and guilt—onto reeducation and other conflicts between the generations. In this wide range of media and in diverse contexts, a parental and especially pedagogical subjectivity becomes normative for this environment in which the operable subject positions available to Germans were radically curtailed by the war and the occupation. In addressing questions begged so obviously by the recent past, both authors and filmmakers turned to discourse about youth and education to represent and negotiate issues that had become nearly unworkable.

Already by 1948, however, reeducation in general and the universities in particular were becoming sites contested not so much between Allied occupiers and German occupied as between the Soviets and the Western forces. The year 1948 was a watershed in which "Trizonia," as the loose alliance among the U.S., British, and French zones was informally called, congealed around the June 1948 currency reform; the subsequent blockade of Berlin hardened polarized positions and provoked open aggressions between "East" and "West." Given the prominent role reeducation and the university in particular had played in early postwar discourse, it is not surprising that the university became, in this context as well, a political, social, and cultural flashpoint for these variegated tensions. If the Niemöller sermon and a film like *The Last Illusion,* as well as writers as diverse as Mann, Meinecke, Jünger, and others, underscore the centrality of discourse about youth before the 1950s, then the 1948 controversy about Berlin universities and a film like Gustav von Wangenheim's controversial *48 All Over Again* confirm how important the university and the young would continue to be within wider German culture as they became important fronts in the coalescing cold war.

Wandering Students and the Vagaries of German History

As Gustav von Wangenheim's first film after the war, *48 All Over Again* was, like Kortner's *The Last Illusion,* taken to be a major statement by an important cultural figure bringing all his exile experience and insight to bear on Germany's postwar plight.[1] Like *The Last Illusion, 48 All Over Again* foregrounds the relationship between students and history, a relationship that provides the film with its overarching conceit. *48 All Over Again* comes to terms with a more distant past to overcome the burdens of recent history: it follows a group of students that has been hired—at a time of radical unemployment and underemployment—to serve as extras on a film about the 1848 revolution. The film opens with the shooting of this film within a film, which treats the events of the famously aborted revolution as comic absurdity. *48 All Over Again* subsequently proceeds on dual temporal tracks, cutting (occasionally panning) between 1848 sets and those of the postwar ruins of Germany in a fashion that was heralded as "dialectical" by Soviet-zone critics.[2]

During the shooting of the 1848/1948 comedy, one of the student extras, Else Weber (played by von Wangenheim's wife, Inge von Wangenheim), disagrees vociferously about the nature of the 1848 events, taking to task both the film's director and the apathetic students who are blithely happy to supplement their incomes by appearing in the film. One medical student, Heinz (played by Ernst Borchert of Mertens

260

fame in *The Murderers Are among Us*), resists Else's "progressive" interpretation of the 1848 events, agreeing with the director that they were politically absurd. *48 All Over Again* thereafter not only traces the students' performance in the film within a film, it also stages a historical debate between those students dismissive of Germany's history (and by implication politics) and those engaged with and committed to the nation's progressive traditions. The film thus offers a more politicized and polarized kind of Vergangenheitsbewältigung that comes to terms with the past by debating longer-term historical trends.

In this emphasis on students and history, *48 All Over Again* relies, like many of the texts I have analyzed, on a dual representation of youth, with the historically and politically committed youth Else contrasted to the problematically apathetic Heinz. As I have argued, at a time when it was difficult or discouraged to represent the postwar period's most obvious conflicts—between Nazis and better Germans or between the Nazis and the Allies or even between returning soldiers and their wives—the conflicts between generations and among young people served usefully and often paradigmatically. More precisely, in a cultural context in which it was essential to represent politically compromised characters but also to redeem them, the negatively coded young person served perfectly: as I also underscore above, the public sphere was full of self-serving critiques of the young, but the young are malleable, educable, and above all capable of rehabilitation, just as they prove to be in this film.

Like many of the texts examined above, the plot of *48 All Over Again* is structured around the confrontations that this dual representation of youth yield. After Else's opening critique of the film within the film and her argument on the set with Heinz, the other dramatic highpoints of the film are a cabaret scene, in which she sings to the skeptics about the events of 1848, and later an academic showdown at high noon, that is, a disputation between her and Heinz about the events of 1848. By that time, of course, the good and bad—that is, the socially productive and threatening—young people reconcile in a shared interpretation of what has happened. As in *The Last Illusion*, in which American and German students are ultimately drawn together by Mauthner's death, the good and bad students of *48 All Over Again* ultimately unite in a shared interpretation of what has transpired not just in the film but in the historical past.

POLITICIZING POSTWAR UNIVERSITIES

In discussing the motivation for making their films, both Kortner and von Wangenheim were careful to mention the ruptured relationship of the "German young" to Germany's historical tradition.[3] In both cases, this ruined relationship becomes a synecdoche for German culture's more general coming to terms with the past in the postwar period. But the differences therein—reestablishing the tradition of German Bildung versus faith in the revolutionary potential of Germany—were growing increasingly resonant in the political and cultural events of late 1947 and 1948, when *48 All Over Again* was shot and released. Events in the Soviet and Western zones exacerbated political and cultural tensions such that *48 All Over Again* reflects these rapidly emerging discursive changes, changes that would soon harden into the ossified positions of the cold war.

For the first few years of the occupation, the Soviets had been careful, like the Western Allies, to acknowledge the traditional autonomy of the German university. Just as in the Western zones, the Soviets considered the university instrumental in their efforts to remake Germany, particularly in their articulated goals to produce a new German intelligentsia, and so they were careful to honor its traditions.[4] In the early years of the occupation (1945–47), this respectful attitude was intertwined with a more general tolerance for things German as part of the "German" (that is, non-Soviet) road to socialism, a peaceful and expansive path Soviet officials hoped would attract Germans from the other zones.[5] But by late 1947, the Soviets were growing increasingly dissatisfied with these policies in general and with the university specifically. Reports from the end of 1947, in fact, display an increasing frustration with the effectiveness of the S.E.D. Party (Sozialistische Einheitspartei Deutschlands, the main communist-socialist party of East Germany) in the university with either students or faculty. Some accounts told of student members of the S.E.D. being beaten up; others complained primarily about these party members' apathy in recruiting other students to the party.[6] In the context of the debate about the "German student" sketched above, these worries resonated with general concerns about students' political indifference but also reflected the growing conviction that more aggressive political persuasion within the university was called for. At the end of 1947 and the beginning of 1948, there was to be increasing cultivation of the German university as a resource for the S.E.D. Party, which itself, in the twilight of the policy of "national" roads to socialism, was being recast in a more Soviet mold.[7]

Not coincidentally, it was in the spring of 1948 that these issues came to a head with the Western Allies, who were already piqued by the Soviets taking unilateral control of the famous Berlin University on Unter den Linden (later the Humboldt University).[8] Suspicions about the co-option of universities were spreading rapidly among both Soviet and U.S. officials: the Soviets were convinced that U.S. "agents" among their students were impeding S.E.D. recruitment, while U.S. officials were convinced that the Soviets had turned the university into a "breeding ground of hatred of the United States."[9] In light of their concern about an S.E.D.–dominated university, U.S. officials had already initiated discussions on founding a new research university that would circumvent both the academy's traditional autonomy as well as more recent S.E.D. control.[10]

The mutual suspicions and reciprocating tensions exploded, unsurprisingly, in Berlin, where—besides the obvious symbolic centrality of the four-power capital—the ability of students from the Western zones to study at the Berlin University exacerbated matters. Berlin, of course, was a four-zone city in the middle of the Soviet zone, which meant that Western-governed Germans there could study at the Soviet-governed university. On 16 April 1948, the S.E.D.–controlled Berlin University expelled three students for "publication activity [that is, political pamphlets] which acts counter to the good manners and dignity of a student," an action that cut at the traditional political autonomy of the university and its population.[11] Large student protests followed a week later, and U.S. officials quickly capitalized on this groundswell of student discontent to call for a new, "free" university in their own sector of Berlin. Even as the Berlin University (and therefore the S.E.D.) made "extraordinary efforts" to satisfy the students, U.S. officials continued to exploit the initial student criticisms of the Soviet-sector university.[12] James Tent observes that the founding of the Free University was unusual in that its founders were "students, politicians, journalists, and businessmen" rather than faculty or academic administrators.[13] Against the wishes of the Soviets and the initial misgivings of the British, the United States encouraged and ultimately enabled the founding of a new university. Military governor Lucius Clay himself put aside the equivalent of 2 million deutsche marks (after the June currency reform) for the new Free University of Berlin, a shot across the Soviet reeducational bow subsidized and fostered, if not entirely initiated, by the United States.

It was against this tense political and cultural backdrop that *48 All Over Again* was shot and released: in fact, the week it premiered in Berlin was the same week in which the Free University celebrated its official opening, astoundingly a mere seven months after the student protests. These events, particularly the S.E.D.'s commitment to recruiting more students, help explain the general conceit of the film, namely, a history student who insists on persuading disillusioned and apathetic students around her. The early cold war context also illuminates more subtle aspects of the film, for instance, the film's historical interpretation of events in 1848, its deliberate critique of the film director within the film, and the casting of Ernst Borchert in the role of an apathetic medical student.

   In his account of Soviet cultural policy between 1945 and 1949, David Pike describes how the "doctrinal" changes of late 1947 and 1948 galvanized (and instrumentalized) a new interpretation of the historical past.[14] Foremost was a new interest in the revolution of 1848, particularly the complex relations between bourgeois and working-class elements in the ill-fated events. The topic became so important that the S.E.D. offered evening courses on the "Bourgeois Revolution of 1848"; also revealing were sudden discussions of Marx's *Communist Manifesto*, whose class-emphatic approach had been avoided in the "national unity" years of 1945–47. As I noted above, these wider discursive changes dovetailed with evolving policy on the university, in this case as Soviet and German officials were taking much more seriously the threat of "bourgeois" elements to effective recruitment within the university.[15] In this light, it is telling and revealing not only that *48 All Over Again* utilizes 1848 as a means for student recruitment but that Else comes from a working-class background and that her historical interpretation highlights, against the conventional historical wisdom, the active role of students rather than the bourgeoisie in the revolution of 1848. The general plotlines, the specific character backgrounds, and the peculiarities of German history all resonate with new S.E.D. efforts to recruit students and faculty the organization had found surprisingly obstinate in their independence.

264

This new stance regarding "bourgeois" elements informed the film's position not only toward the academy but also toward filmmaking. Earlier in the occupation (1945–47), in fostering a "national unity" front that would rehabilitate artists from a diversity of backgrounds, Soviet and later DEFA officials had been willing to recruit "bourgeois" directors long before the Western Allies.[16] This openness helped Soviet-licensed filmmakers and crews produce the first postwar feature, *The Murderers Are among Us,* well before any U.S.–licensed feature. As I noted in chapter 5, U.S. officials had told Wolfgang Staudte, the director of *The Murderers Are among Us,* that it would be twenty years before a German was again allowed to make a feature film.[17] *The Murderers Are among Us* reflects this broad definition of "national unity" both in the political and economic background of its director, Staudte (who had acted in Ufa productions before 1945), and in its content (a protagonist who is a medical doctor). *The Murderers Are among Us*'s bourgeois protagonist was in fact implicitly criticized when later DEFA films more committed to working-class milieus (like *Somewhere in Berlin* and *Rotation*) were released. By the time of *48 All Over Again,* class perspectives were hardening, such that Else's disagreement with a bourgeois film director seems a deliberate departure from, even critique of, the early years of DEFA. Revealing in this context, too, is the curious casting of Ernst Borchert as a medical student insulated from progressive interpretations of German history. Borchert was one of DEFA's best-known actors for his portrayal of Dr. Mertens in *The Murderers Are among Us,* but his role in *48 All Over Again* offers what seems a deliberate reprisal and revision of his most famous character: here he is an apolitical and apathetic medical student who learns lessons of Germany's progressive history from a working-class fellow student at the university. His comparisons between German history and human anatomy on his medical exams actually raise his exam grades and, presumably, improve the memorably morose Mertens from *The Murderers Are among Us.*

CONDITIONING THE GERMAN STUDENT FOR THE COLD WAR

Among the thoroughgoing political changes in 1948, Soviet and S.E.D. officials made a new commitment to reforming the "student type." Paramount among these changes was a determination of what kind of student would be admitted to the university. As I noted above, Soviet officials had declared early in the occupation that they would admit more students from worker and farmer backgrounds, but the numbers of such students had remained relatively small (albeit much higher than in the Western zones).[18] In 1947–48, Soviet and S.E.D officials became more determined than ever to admit more students from such backgrounds because it seemed, increasingly, a mistake to have admitted so many, as Naimark puts it, "representatives of the bourgeoisie and petit-bourgeoisie," of which *48 All Over Again*'s Heinz is certainly one.[19]

Both the film and the publicity materials used to market it heralded the new type of student Else represented. At the moment Berlin was being polarized by the blockade of provisions and the hardening of positions—a city polarized, as one article put it, in politics, in press, even in filmgoing audiences—Else was rolled out as the perfect representative of "this side" of the growing political and cultural gap.[20] Doggedly working her way through her studies while supporting her sister and her nephew, maintaining a *Gefühlskälte* (coldness of feeling) over the loss of her own husband and child, Else is an engaged student committed to becoming a teacher. Her pedantic posture throughout the film and professional ambitions reinforce once again pedagogical subjectivity as the preferred subject position in an environment of severely limited options.

At the end of December 1948, at the conclusion of this tumultuous political and cultural year, a guest column in the Western-zone *Tagesspiegel* celebrated "the Berlin student" as the paradigm for the new Berliner. Not only had Berlin students been compelled to share the hardship of all Berliners during the blockade, but they had even rejected the tempting traditions of Berlin University, where studying would mean inevitable service as a "Soviet mouthpiece."[21] Almost three years after the Niemöller episode, German students were still at the center of political and cultural debates, confirming the continuing symbolic centrality of universities and students for this context in general. In this evolving environment, however, new battle lines were rapidly being drawn. No longer did students serve within the project of Vergangenheitsbewältigung as a convenient constitutive contrast to the wise elders embodying a better, lost *Bildungsbürger* or Christian Germany. Discourse about students and higher education was landing in an altogether different place: in late 1948 and in the middle of the Berlin university crisis, critics in the Western zones attacked the propagandistic use of the students and universities in *48 All Over Again,* to whose defense Soviet-zone critics quickly rose.[22] One "Eastern" critic claimed that *48 All Over*

Again was the only postwar feature to represent the "new academic youth," but this study ought to make clear just what a discursively contested site the postwar student was.[23] Young people had figured prominently in coming to terms with the recent past and German guilt, and now students were deployed on the front lines of the coalescing cold war.

Even before the advent of the cold war, however, discourse about youth and generation had been a dominant and recurring trope in the early postwar period. Cultural and historical studies of the early postwar period share a remarkable coincidence of themes: the mastery of the Nazi past, the current social crisis, future reconstruction, humanistic reeducation, and the history and fate of the German nation. In this study, I have attempted to augment this thematic matrix with another category, that of discourse about youth and generation. Discourse about youth and generational difference—namely, adults' imagined relation to youth and the discursive operations around it—helps adults to make sense of themselves as subjects, as societies, and as nations. Especially at times of social transformation and/or instability, discourse about youth and generational difference can become an important facet of the cultural and intellectual public sphere. In various early postwar media, including intellectual tracts, feature films, and major literary texts, children and adolescents become privileged means with which to represent the past as well as the current social crisis. In fact, the challenges of coming to terms with the past were often displaced to one particular aspect of that wider social crisis, the youth crisis.

These various postwar texts deploy discourse about youth to probe and to reinscribe traditional social relations, especially the bourgeois social order and its concomitant grid of bourgeois intelligibility. Theorists like Foucault, Donzelot, and Mitterauer have elaborated how discourse about youth is constitutive of modern society's milieu in both its individual and collective forms. At least certain strains of culture under the Nazis fixated on this core aspect of bourgeois society to remake the bourgeois constellation into a postbourgeois (national-generational) community: often this recasting along generational lines stood in for and obscured any potential economic or political revolution. In its attempts to come to terms with the past, postwar culture responded repeatedly and emphatically to these strains of culture under the Nazis: the varied and variegated postwar media reinscribe a bourgeois discourse about youth and generational difference such that this society can reconstitute itself. In this way, discourse about youth serves as a transfer point for ideology at which the disciplining and regulative mechanisms of the society become startling clear. Analyzing discourse about youth can not only uncover the ideology underpinning the young but also unveil what undergirds the "adult" subject as well as its collective forms. It becomes an indispensable means by which to manage modern adult subjects. For example, in the early postwar period, the debate on youth and Bildung reveals the deep anxiety about the continuation of German culture in general.

The abstract operations of this discourse invoke concrete themes, including the floating youth crisis, constitutive alterity and the dual character of discourse about youth as well as the link between youth and nation. The youth crisis becomes a privileged means for displacing other postwar crises because it permits a controllable localization of such instabilities. The youth crisis becomes a manipulable zone of social trouble, a region of the grid of intelligibility in which the antisocial youth threatens a formerly stable hierarchy, but in an ultimately innocuous way. Youth crises came to stand in for, symbolize, and defuse the postwar problems in German society, of the recent past, and of the future reconstruction. As I suggested in my introduction to the postwar public sphere in chapter 2, youth crisis even served to distract from the ubiquitous results of the devastating air war. On the one hand, a collapse of stable generational difference between adult and young conveyed the depth of the general social instability; on the other hand, generational trouble is, as many of the narratives revealed, inherently manageable where other social problems may not be. For example, in intellectual tracts and the rubble films, the immense weight of the past reduced many of their conflicts to those between generations. Meinecke's "German catastrophe" becomes in many ways a generational history of German modernity while Iller's Heimkehrer trauma in *Somewhere in Berlin* is also localized in his unrecognizing and unrecognized son. Ernst Jünger understands the decisive modern degeneration of these years—in the technologizing transformation of combat—as a youth crisis. Thomas Mann depicts Adrian's artistic dilemma, an allegory for Germany's place in the world, largely along generational lines. There are radical differences in these various discourses about youth, but in each case the youth crisis serves as a manipulable symbolic disturbance that intellectuals, filmmakers, and authors can deploy to come to terms with the past. There was a real youth crisis in the postwar period, but the emphatic manner in which the youth crisis is constructed in literature, film, and intellectual tracts outstretches its "real" nature.

This youth crisis helps to defuse one of the core tasks of the early postwar period: assuming responsibility and therefore guilt for the recent past. Faced with the overwhelming challenges of recent war and the (usually merely implied) Holocaust, many important authors and filmmakers differentiate and therefore mitigate guilt according to generation. In a wide range of representations, the young, especially adolescents, become those agents most responsible for the rise and success of National Socialism. For example, in *Rotation* and *The Last Illusion,* the obedient soldiers and violent anti-Semites are primarily young people who have fallen from healthy generational relations, fallen under the spell of false fathers or corrupting teachers. Both Meinecke and Jünger depict the young as the most guilty of Nazi crimes, both because they are easy to blame and because they simultaneously seem to be innocent victims. Blaming the young diverts guilt from (adult) subjects, who then usually also suggest that the young are victims of no-fault generational confusion. Even the most guilty young person, due to his or her age, could not be judged as harshly as an adult, as the debate about youth amnesty confirmed. In both *Rotation* and *The Last Illusion* as well as in Jünger's *The Peace* and Wiechert's speeches, young Nazis repeatedly back away from the fascist brink to offer beacons of reconstructive-redemptive hope.

In the deployment of youth crisis and guilt, it should be clear that both children and adolescents offer a form of constitutive alterity to the bourgeois social constellation. Discourse about youth and generational differences provides an internal "other" to the normative bourgeois adult subject, one that helps constitute that subject as well as its collective forms. Drawing generational lines stabilizes and therefore defines the boundaries between parent and child, teacher and pupil, public and private as well as between society and its margins. For example, in the Winfried chapter of *Doktor Faustus,* the adolescents and their antibourgeois sleeping-straw excursion highlight the artificial character and borders of the bourgeois constellation, its private houses, and its disciplining manners. In *Somewhere in Berlin,* when Gustav Iller runs from his mother and a friendly policeman to the war games of the feral children, the spectator observes the disciplining law of the family as well as its limits.

As these examples imply, discourse about youth provides a particularly useful form of alterity because it represents a fundamental duality: the disciplined core of bourgeois society as well as its rebellious outsiders. Alterity is often marked by deep contradiction, perhaps the most obvious being that of the simultaneous inclusion and exclusion of the other as socially defining. Depictions of youth are relentlessly contradictory, representing a binary that itself articulates fundamental contradictions in the culture. In both modes, the young help define the character and boundaries of the grid of bourgeois intelligibility. In this sense, I have tried to elaborate a richness of the representation of youth in a way Foucault, Donzelot, and Mitterauer do not fully draw out. In describing modern social forms, these authors focus on the disciplining of the young as a constitutive function of bourgeois society; in examining cultural representations, I have focused not only on a disciplining but also an indulging approach to the young. As the young rebel against society, they represent a dangerous but also a desired resistance to the bourgeois order, as Mann's Zeitblom and Leverkühn make clear in *Doktor Faustus*. As in *Doktor Faustus*, this dual representation of the young inside and outside the bourgeois social order offers many of these texts their dynamism. Many of the rubble films follow a boy in his trajectory from social outsider, even antagonist, to obedient, loving son. In Meinecke's *The German Catastrophe*, the young are both the greatest threat to staid liberalism and the foundation for the longed-for Goethegemeinden.

The rubble films clarify one of the key functions of this dual discourse about youth: the disciplining and managing of adult subjects who have doubts about the prevailing social order and its dominant fictions. Conventional feature films tend to focus on the travails of an adult male protagonist, and many rubble films thematize a Heimkehrer and his postwar trauma. In stark, realistic images of social ruin, many early DEFA films foreground the lacking, inadequate masculinity of the Heimkehrer protagonist. Though he has returned to the home context, the Heimkehrer still feels displaced by the trauma of the war. Through the representation of youth, the DEFA films encourage the Heimkehrer to reassert his social position positively after he has returned physically. In the Western zones, against the calls of many film critics, filmmakers cast known film stars as Heimkehrer whose exceptionalness threatened the social orders in an opposite manner. Nonetheless, these films also deploy youth to manage and condition adult protagonists. These rubble films, East and West, manage and regalvanize the Heimkehrer's faith in the bourgeois social order by arranging a duel between the Heimkehrer, who no longer believes in his social station, and a boy, often a son, who threatens and then helps him. These films deploy youth crises of false fathers or of antisocial youth communities to stand in for the challenges of both present and past.

In the managing of such subjects, the constitutive relation of youth to bourgeois society grows clear. For example, the young play a significant role in bourgeois spatial relations: the young constantly cross borders, often abandoning the private house, which was increasingly organized around the parent-child axis. In a cultural constellation in which many private homes were literally exploded and "the street" had acquired a special social significance, this function was especially resonant. When the child or adolescent has abandoned the house, the key duel in a generally conflict-oriented medium becomes that between the generational superior and the youth. What I have termed the youth gaze also defines and manages the social position of adult subjects. In line with the duality of youth, a young person looking at an adult can be both fatally threatening (as in *Rotation,* when Helmuth renounces his father by staring him down) or foundationally affirming (as in *Somewhere in Berlin,* when Iller's gaze is met by his son hammering away at the rubble of his old garage). Similarly, when Ernst Wiechert implores young adults to behave themselves, he begs them to think of younger children literally looking to them for guidance. This image, delivered many times in his ubiquitous "Speech to the German Young," manages the behavior of adults, disciplines it in a constitutively normalizing manner.

Discourse about youth can also manage or regulate collective forms in the bourgeois social order. Such discourse provides a cornerstone not only for the bourgeois subject and the private sphere but also for bourgeois society and one of its favored forms, the nation. The young, in fact, became a key conduit for collective forms to enter, often assault, the private house; they serve as an interface between the family and the wider social and/or national community, including that developed and exploited by the Nazis. For example, Meinecke and Jünger connect the young to collective moments, especially the modern "masses" that, they claim, gave rise to Nazism. Therein arises one of the key differentiations in discourse about youth: children are usually seen as familially affirming or detracting, whereas adolescents can self-consciously join some sort of national-generational community that yields the Nazi nation, antagonizes the private home, and threatens the entire bourgeois constellation. For example, in the Winfried chapter of *Doktor Faustus*, the adolescents flee, and define themselves against, the bourgeois house and consider themselves the heart of the "young" German nation. In *The Last Illusion*, the returning exile's lost son, Walter, connects his father to a secretly anti-Semitic group that targets his professorship and eventually kills him. In *Rotation*, adolescent Helmuth becomes the conduit through which Nazi ideology enters the household. Eventually, after he is nationalized, Helmuth inverts the bourgeois order by policing his own parents on behalf of the nation: one can hardly imagine a more terrifying "governing through the family," as Donzelot puts it.

In both *The Last Illusion* and *Rotation*, a key tension emerges between the youth as obedient son and the youth as recalcitrant pupil of a depraved teacher. Such representations of the young underline the importance of discourse about youth and pedagogy in the postwar period, a time marked by widespread and controversial debate about reeducation. Though most studies of children or youth focus on parent-child relations, Foucault and others make clear that the child also serves centrally because of pedagogical regimes of control, which have a hold on the family and its individual subjects. These cultural texts of the postwar period underscore this aspect of discourse about youth: in Meinecke, Jünger, and Jaspers, and as in *Rotation, The Last Illusion*, and *Doktor Faustus*, pedagogy and the teacher-pupil relation become key axes for understanding the recent past and reconstruction. The ubiquitous debate about reeducation also demonstrates the widespread and loud discursive noise on this issue. In all these cases, the link between the young, especially adolescents, and the nation becomes a key moment for working out questions of Germany, especially Germany's recent past and Germany's future national identity.

Why does discourse about youth come to play such a significant role in the early postwar period? In the case of Thomas Mann, for instance, his artistic and intellectual inclinations suggest a revealing reason, a reason that one can perhaps generalize to this postwar context. As has been noted, perhaps most adamantly and eloquently by Lukács, Mann's works never go beyond their bourgeois context.[24] They are keenly sensitive to its contradictory demands, to its instability and even impossibility, yet in understanding it and representing it, they never go beyond its parameters. Instead of attacking bourgeois subjectivity and society from the outside, his writings tend to ironize and parody from within. His ironic, parodic, yet ultimately traditional style and formal tendencies reflect this, especially when one contrasts him to other modernists.[25]

I would suggest that a central aspect of this thinking within the parameters of the bourgeois constellation, of critiquing from within, would be a heightened discourse about youth and generational difference. As I described in the introduction, the young serve paradigmatically in part because they constitute an internal or "intimate" enemy, as Nandy has written.[26] They are a constitutive but also constantly destabilizing element in the bourgeois social order; likewise, they can be a core element and a faraway outsider, a cornerstone and an external threat to the bourgeois milieu.

In this way, Mann's discourse about youth is typical for the wider postwar context in general. Given the collapse of the bourgeois republic into Nazism, writers and filmmakers could have looked outside for a new social/political order. Some did, but many prominent thinkers and artists relied on discourse about youth as a privileged means for representing and coming to terms with the past within the symbolic codes in which they were already operating. Even the Soviet occupational zone, with its particular "German" road to socialism, did not, in the first three years after the war, insist on a radical revolution in the fabric of society. Cultural figures like Thomas Mann, Meinecke, Jünger, and Wiechert, as well as the rubble films, subsequently sought an internal enemy and cast the young as both a central reason for their fall and an essential means for reconstruction. Discourse about youth allowed them to attribute the rise of Nazism to something other than themselves—and thereby dilute guilt—but also still to blame something potentially within their control. As in the Bavarian case elaborated in chapter 2, this dual coding of youth ran right into the Allies' project of reeducation and galvanized massive resistance to it: instead of wanting to reform schools and culture, many prominent Germans, including Jaspers, looked backward within the parameters of their tradition. And this battle was one they were permitted to fight by the occupiers, not least because of the indisputable sociocultural intimacy of discourse about youth.

Such youth agendas were national programs that seemed safe at a historical moment when there could be almost no national agenda of Germans' own making. They provided a subtly political position at a historical moment when politics had become in many ways taboo.

273

Teacher/parental subjectivity offered the widespread normative means for adults to overcome ideological discouragement at all that had happened. Such a program deploying discourse about youth also offered what appears to be an antipolitical project—precisely what transpires in Jünger and Jaspers—at a time when there was both a mistrust of and a disenfranchisement from politics. In different but revealingly similar manners, Jünger, Jaspers, Wiechert, Staudte, and Meinecke all use youth to move beyond conventional politics in an age in which politics, as they had known it, must have seemed intractable. But I hope I have shown how often such a move occurs in the postwar period and to what diversionary ends. Discourse about youth reveals not only the underpinnings of the adult subject and its collective forms—as a lightning rod for wider operations of control, discourse about youth and generation also reveals their veiling political mechanisms.

Notes

Introduction

1. In his classic account of the last days of Hitler, Hugh Trevor-Roper suggests that there were no regular soldiers present because they did not want to overshadow the young fighters. *Last Days of Hitler,* 110. But in his *Hitler's Children,* 240, Gerhard Rempel suggests that there were no regular soldiers there because Germany had come to rely almost entirely on its young people.
2. See, for carefully documented evidence of this intersection of German youth and modernity, Detlev Peukert's *Weimar Republic,* 89, 93.
3. Poiger, *Jazz, Rock, and Rebels;* Maase, *Bravo Amerika* as well as his "Establishing Cultural Democracy"; Fehrenbach, "Rehabilitating Fatherland" and her "Of German Mothers and 'Negermischlingskinder.'"
4. Weiner, *Enfants Terribles;* Ross, *Fast Cars, Clean Bodies.*
5. In a number of recent essays, Fehrenbach has analyzed the discussions about *Mischlinge,* in this case, children of U.S. soldiers and German mothers, as a site of remasculinization as well as reconstruction of German national identity. Her investigation is rich and revealing, but she does not address the ways in which German youth and children were already charged sites of contestation after the war. The present study will attempt to provide background for the treatments of the young in the controversy about the Mischlinge (addressed in Fehrenbach's work) and the *Halbstarken* (young rowdies of the 1950s) (in Maase's and Poiger's work). It is my hope that this study will help explain why the young came to play such central roles in the materials analyzed by those scholars. See Fehrenbach, "Rehabilitating Fatherland" and "Of German Mothers and

"Negermischlingskinder.'"
6. While I applaud Brockmann for moving this discussion to the center of a literary study of this period, he does not fully investigate the stakes and interests in the claim that Nazism was a youth movement, which should not, as I argue below, be accepted prima facie. Brockmann's study also does not explore, as this analysis will attempt to illuminate, how the discussion about youth and generation served postwar Germans in coming to terms with the past. See Brockmann, *German Literary Culture at the Zero Hour,* esp. chapter 6, "A German Generation Gap?"
7. Koebner, Janz, and Trommler, *"Mit uns zieht die neue Zeit."*
8. "[T]he specific characteristics of youth can best be seen in this social form [the youth group]." Mitterauer, *History of Youth,* vi. Both Trommler and Mitterauer are clear that central Europe, esp. Germany and Austria, had a particularly emphatic discourse about youth, in part because "youth" tended to last much longer in central European countries. "In West, Central, and Northern Europe, then, one belonged to the category of 'youth' for longer, and this category made up a very large proportion of the total population, the number of 'older' youths among them very high. Consequently . . . , autonomous youth organizations had great importance in these areas." Mitterauer, *History of Youth,* 21. "Dennoch besteht kaum ein Zweifel daran, daß in Deutschland und Österreich bestimmte Faktoren dazu beitrugen, daß man hier die 'Herstellung' von Jugend als komplimentärsphäre zum Industriealltag wesentlich intensiver betrieb als in anderen Ländern und daß der neue, von der Industrialisierung geschaffene und zugleich von ihr eingeschüchterte Mittelstand diesem Konzept ungewöhnlich viele Hoffnungen entgegenbrachte." Trommler, "Mission ohne Ziel," 16.
9. "The groups under the umbrella of the Free Youth Movement included only a very small percentage of young Germans, but their ideas, their style, their outward forms, their new activities and group structures all sent out ripples which had an enormous impact on the group life of young people in much wider circles." Mitterauer, *History of Youth,* 215.
10. Blackbourn and Eley, *Peculiarities of German History.*
11. Although she does an admirable job of describing discourse about youth and youth riots in the 1950s, Ute Poiger (*Jazz, Rock, and Rebels*) does not really attend to the longer-term trends of which these riots certainly seem part. Though she cites how the phrase *Wilde Cliquen* is revived from the 1920s, she does not analyze, at any sustained length, discourse about youth through the Nazi regime or in the early postwar period, both of which provide indispensable background for the generational histrionics of the 1950s.
12. Adorno, "What 'Working through the Past' Means," 117. This essay, and

this passage in particular, has become quite important for the reconsideration of *Vergangenheitsbewältigung*. It is quoted, for instance, by Jeffrey Herf, Robert Moeller, Alon Confino, and Alf Lüdtke. There has been some disagreement among translators about the title of Adorno's famous essay (in German: "Was bedeutet: Aufarbeitung der Vergangenheit"). Timothy Bahti and Geoffrey Hartmann's translation, the most cited in the secondary literature, does not do adequate justice to the title because it renders "Aufarbeitung der Vergangenheit" as "coming to terms with the past" (the conventional, if also inadequate, translation for "Vergangenheitsbewältigung"), whereas Henry Pickford's recent translation of the essay ("The Meaning of Working through the Past"), although closer to the original, alters the nonnominalizing structure of the title. Since nominalizations of verbs are quite common in German, Adorno's avoidance of one ("Was bedeutet" rather than "Die Bedeutung") seems worth retaining, so I prefer "What 'Working through the Past' Means."

13. There is a very large literature on this subject, but two important examples are: Maier, *Unmasterable Past* and Evans, *In Hitler's Shadow*. A work continuing this line of inquiry is Niven, *Facing the Nazi Past*.

14. These three works are probably the key texts in reigniting the debate about Germans as victims during and after World War II. Sebald's lecture and subsequent essay suggest that there was silence about, if not outright repression of, accounts of the bombing of Germany in early postwar German literature. The effects of the air war and more especially the bombing of German cities is more extensively detailed, documented, and depicted in Friedrich's account *The Fire*. Grass's *Crabwalk*, a fictionalization of a historical event, recounts the sinking of a ship, the *Wilhelm Gustloff*, full of German refugees. The sinking killed thousands and is considered the single greatest maritime disaster ever.

15. See Santner, *Stranded Objects*, 45; Moeller, *War Stories*, 3, 5; Hage, "Erzähltabu? Die Sebald-Debatte: Ein Resümee," in *Zeugen der Zerstörung*.

16. See Confino, "Traveling as a Cultural Remembrance."

17. Arendt, "The Aftermath of Nazi-Rule."

18. Lifton, preface.

19. Mitscherlich and Mitscherlich, *Inability to Mourn*, 27.

20. Ibid., 23, 9, 13, 25.

21. Santner, *Stranded Objects*, 37.

22. Friedlaender, quoted in Bodemann, "Eclipse of Memory," 60.

23. Sebald starts by quoting a U.S. postwar writer describing the context and then confirms her outsider (as a non-German) observations about the silent Germans: "Through [the city's] clogged streets," the passage continues, "trickles what is left of its life, a dwindled population in black and

with bundles—the silent German people appropriate to the silent city." That silence, that reserve, that instinctive looking away are the reasons why we know so little of what Germans thought and observed in the five years between 1942 and 1947. "The ruins where they lived were the terra incognita of the war." Sebald, *Air War and Literature,* 31.

24. Bodemann, "Eclipse of Memory," 80–81; Confino, "Traveling as a Cultural Remembrance," 98.

25. Confino, "Traveling as a Cultural Remembrance," 92.

26. See ibid. and Brockmann, *German Literary Culture at the Zero Hour,* 6.

27. Shandley, *Rubble-Films,* 20–24.

28. Moeller, *War Stories,* 16.

29. A number of scholars, including Bodemann, Confino, and Moeller, cite Hermann Lübbe's essay "Der Nationalsozialismus im deutschen Nachkriegsbewusstsein" as one of the very first self-conscious breaks with the scholarly tradition of a repression thesis about Germany's Vergangenheitsbewältigung. Lübbe was indeed one of the first to dispute, explicitly and directly, the conventions of the repression hypothesis (588, where he declares it simply "falsch"). He does so, however, for very different reasons than those advanced by later scholars, though they, curiously, usually do not remark on it. Lübbe's attack on the repression hypothesis seems largely motivated by a critique of the 1968 generation, which, in his argument, highlights the repression hypothesis to distinguish itself, problematically for him, from the early FRG. For Lübbe, the early FRG did engage with the past (584), even if there was a "certain silence"—that is, a forgivable one—that allowed for the rehabilitation of subjects who had been compromised by the Nazi regime (585, 587). For Lübbe, unlike many of the other scholars cited, the FRG was productively engaged in the past, even if it was quiet about it. This unusual argument lets him, against the grain, read the response to the Holocaust TV series not as an example of widespread return of the repressed (as it is usually understood) but instead as a reconfirmation of the FRG's productive engagement with the past (597–99).

30. Herf, *Divided Memory.* Herf's major contribution differs from my approach in a couple of ways, perhaps most importantly in his focus on "political memory," for example, in his attention to forms of government (West versus East Germany) as well as to political parties. Herf discusses such political topics as the early political debates recovery, political integration with Western allies, and relations with Israel. My approach is more cultural and will focus on literature, intellectual debates, and films; Herf, for instance, makes no reference to the four writer-intellectuals I shall examine (Friedrich Meinecke, Ernst Jünger, Karl Jaspers, and Ernst

Wiechert), though they were verifiably among the most discussed in the period.

31. Ahonen, *After the Expulsion*. Ahonen calls the problem of the expellees "the crucial link between the internal and external levels of West German politics" (8).

32. Frei, *Vergangenheitspolitik*, translated as *Adenauer's Germany and the Nazi Past*. Frei's groundbreaking work concentrates on the early 1950s and the early West German government rather than the early postwar period that is focus of the present study.

33. Mitchell, "Materialism and Secularism."

34. Confino, "Traveling as Cultural Remembrance."

35. Biess, "Pioneers of a New Germany" and "Survivors of Totalitarianism."

36. Heineman, "The Hour of the Woman." The essay appears as well as a chapter in her book *What Difference Does a Husband Make?*

37. Bodemann, "Eclipse of Memory," 80–83.

38. See, for example, Frei, *1945 und wir*, esp. his chapter "Von deutscher Erfindungskraft: Oder die Kollektivschuldthese in der Nachkriegszeit," 145–55.

39. Heineman, "The Hour of the Woman," 355, 360. For Biess, this is a central part of his analysis of the German prisoners of war who returned to Germany after the war. See, for example, Biess, "Survivors of Totalitarianism," 58.

40. Moeller, *War Stories* and "Germans as Victims?"

41. Bartov, "Defining Enemies, Making Victims," 811. The essay appears in a revised form as a chapter in Bartov's *Mirrors of Destruction*.

42. Ibid., 776.

43. Ibid., 788–90.

44. See, for example, Gimbel, *American Occupation of Germany;* Gaddis, *The United States and the Origins of the Cold War;* Zink, *United States in Germany.*

45. See Biess, "Survivors of Totalitarianism."

46. Brockmann, *German Literary Culture at the Zero Hour,* 181, while Kater concludes with this question of youth guilt in his *Hitler Youth,* 263–65.

47. Although I do not have space herein to elaborate at length, all of these theorists have underscored how children, youth, and pedagogical discourse figure centrally in the emergence and constant reconstitution of modern European society. Though his historiography is famously suspect, Foucault's generalizations have been filled in to a large degree by Donzelot and Mosse. See Foucault's *History of Sexuality;* Donzelot, *Policing Families;* Mosse, *Nationalism and Sexuality.* Mosse confirms many of Foucault's assertions en route to pushing Foucault much further in terms

of sexuality's role in the middle-class collective conscious as a nation. In her most recent work, *Carnal Knowledge and Imperial Power*, Ann Stoler also focuses on discourse about children, families, and schools and explains how they reflected and impacted (adult) identity, nation, and race. See her chapter 5, "A Sentimental Education: Children of the Imperial Divide," 112–39.

48. Tent, *Mission on the Rhine;* Füssl, *Die Umerziehung der Deutschen;* Rupieper, *Die Wurzeln der Westdeutschen Nachkriegsdemokratie: der Amerikanische Beitrag, 1945–1952.* All of these studies can be taken as a reconsideration of the importance of reeducation after the largely negative work in the 1960s and 1970s that highlighted it as a failure, irrelevant to Germany's democratization (cf. the essays in Heinemann, *Umerziehung und Wiederaufbau,* which reflect this critical assessment). These studies of the late 1980s and 1990s reconsider the role of reeducation in the significant changes in German political culture after the war, but they still focus on the unfolding and transformation of the Allied policy more than German responses to it, its importance to the German public sphere, and so on.

49. Olick, *In the House of the Hangman;* Brockmann, *German Literary Culture at the Zero Hour.* These are two recent studies that continue the trend to overlook or downplay reeducation during the occupation. Stephen Brockmann does not really attend to reeducation even though his study is at its best when he does take up the dialogue between Germans and Allied officials. Olick acknowledges the centrality of reeducation in his introduction and observes that it was a term that stood for the Allies' denazification and democratization project generally, but, in his otherwise sophisticated and thorough study, he tends to return to the traditional headings of postwar history, with chapters about Nuremberg, guilt, and so on.

50. Poiger, *Jazz, Rock, and Rebels;* Maase, *Bravo Amerika;* Fehrenbach, *Cinema in Democratizing Germany.*

51. Brockmann has an extended section about *Der Ruf* (*German Literary Culture at the Zero Hour,* 186–92), and Olick offers a similar interpretation (*In the House of the Hangman,* 189).

52. Moeller, "Germans as Victims?" 181.

Chapter 1

1. Baldur von Schirach actually ended up with two titles as head of the HJ: *Reichsjugendführer* (as he was called in 1931 when he replaced Kurt Gruber) as well as *Jugendführer des deutschen Reiches* (he was appointed such on 17 June 1933). The two titles might not seem all that different, but

the latter was intended to imply a much wider purview than just leader of the HJ. Schirach was thereafter in charge of all youth and their activities outside of the private home and school. Klönne, *Jugend im Dritten Reich*, 47–48. Typically, however, Schirach referred to himself only with the narrower title, as Reichsjugendführer, in this defense.

2. This speech was quoted at length and then discussed in von Zahn, "Verrat an der deutschen Jugend," 34–38. The speech was also widely reported in newspapers at the time. For example, the front-page story "Baldur v. Schirach nennt Hitler einen 'Millionenfachen Mörder,'" *Frankenpost*, 24 May 1946. Although he confessed his work for the Nazis, Schirach claimed he also promoted the Weimar classics to the Hitler-Jugend and that the group was primarily a cultural organization (he cited how much they subsidized visits to the theater).

3. The *Hitlerclique* or even *Verbrecherclique* were favorite targets for those seeking someone to blame. For example, "Forum der Jugend," *Deutsche Rundschau* 69, no. 2 (May 1946): 145. Lüdtke analyzes the exculpatory nature of these characterizations in his essay "Coming to Terms with the Past," 561–62.

4. Radku argues that the Nazi rhetoric about youth was much more pronounced than its actual impact. "Die singende und die tote Jugend," 117–19. In his essay on the youth of Langemarck, Hüppauf underscores the importance of such youth discourse in the 1920s but identifies during the Nazi regime a discourse about Verdun that valorized hardness, experience, and age instead of youth. Hüppauf, "Langemarck, Verdun, and the Myth of a New Man," 86–87.

5. Klönne disagrees (*Jugend im Dritten Reich*, 18, 13, 45); he regards the organization as completely dependent on the party from the beginning. He does, however, pay only modest attention to the organization pre-1927. Both Rempel's and Koch's histories are fuller and, in this regard, more convincing: before the deliberate coordination, the HJ was more youth group than mere party branch. Rempel, *Hitler's Children*; Koch, *Hitler Youth*.

6. Rempel, *Hitler's Children*, 60. Part of the reason was, undoubtedly, the kind of more narrowly militaristic training one could undertake in camps rather than on free-form hikes.

7. Quoted in Koch, *Hitler Youth*, 73.

8. Ibid., 81–82.

9. Rempel, *Hitler's Children*, 4.

10. Koch, *Hitler Youth*, 94, confirmed in Rempel, *Hitler's Children*, 10 and Klönne, *Jugend im Dritten Reich*, 20.

11. Perhaps its most important function, at least politically speaking, would be to serve as a personnel resource for the party and some of its most effi-

281

cient aspects, including, above all, as a recruiting source for the SS. Even in that special relationship, however, the SS complained constantly about the quality of recruits it gained from the Hitler-Jugend.

12. Rempel, *Hitler's Children*, 55, confirmed in Klönne, *Jugend im Dritten Reich*, 31.

13. For example, "People must know that troops like the SS have to pay the butcher's bill more heavily than anyone else—so as to keep away the young fellows who only want to show off. Troops inspired by a fierce will, troops with an unbeatable turn-out—the sense of superiority personified." Hitler, *Hitler's Secret Conversations*, 177–78. Radku traces the superficiality of Hitler's comments on youth and his halfhearted interest in youth issues. "Die singende und die tote Jugend," 114–18. Hüppauf also points out that Hitler's remarks on Langemarck in *Mein Kampf* seem halfhearted and abbreviated. "Langemarck Verdun, and the Myth of a New Man," 82–83.

14. Ketelsen makes this point convincingly in the introduction to his *Literatur und Drittes Reich*, 16–18.

15. This is an underrated aspect of Foucault's *History of Sexuality:* "The family cell, in the form in which it came to be valued in the course of the eighteenth century, made it possible for the main elements of deployment of sexuality (the feminine body, infantile precocity, the regulation of births, and to a lesser extent no doubt the specification of the perverted) to develop along its two primary dimensions: the husband-wife axis and the parent-child axis" (108). Donzelot traces this more carefully throughout his study, including, for one example, how nineteenth-century philanthropic societies employed new discourses about the family and especially child-parent relations to convince fathers, who had been prone to carousing outside the house, to refocus on the domestic sphere. Such efforts aimed not only at adults' emotional resources: the emphasis on new savings plans similarly refocused their economic means on the family. *Policing Families*, 65–66.

16. I have in mind here two aspects of the much-mentioned conservative revolution. First, that it preserves ("conserves") more social, economic, and political institutions than a Marxist or working-class revolution; second, that it installs "conservative," right-wing politics rather than radical, left-wing politics. Conservative revolution via youth achieves both: it leaves in place many existing institutions (for example, economic institutions) but also gives cover to the hegemony of right-wing politics. On the conservative revolution, see, for two of many examples, Herf, *Reactionary Modernism;* Stern, *Politics of Cultural Despair.*

17. For example, in his *History of Modern Germany*, Tipton sees the novel as especially typical for the time and the Nazi movement and analyzes pas-

sages from the novel at two points in his otherwise primarily political and economic history (323–25, 370–73). Neither Grimm nor Johst is mentioned in the history.

18. Mosse, *Nationalism and Sexuality*, 19.

19. "The distance in behavior and whole psychical structure between children and adults increases in the course of the civilizing process. Here, for example, lies the key to the question of why some peoples or groups of peoples appear to us as 'younger' or 'more childlike,' others as 'older' or 'more grown-up.' What we are trying to express in this way are differences in the kind and stage of the civilizing process that these societies have attained." Elias, *Civilizing Process*, xiii. Mitterauer (*History of Youth*, 25) confirms this sense of a growing gap between adults and the young, and Aries's famous study, *Centuries of Childhood*, is premised on the increasing importance of it.

20. For Foucault's work on an "internal other," in this case women, see Martin, "Feminism, Criticism, and Foucault," 10.

21. Prümm, "Jugend ohne Väter," 579.

22. Mosse, *Nationalism and Sexuality*, 46.

23. Trommler, "Mission ohne Ziel," 30.

24. Goebbels, *Michael*, 50. Future references will be made parenthetically in the text.

25. See Lamberti, *Politics of Education*.

26. Prümm, "Jugend ohne Väter," 566.

27. Dovetailing with this critique of his own and Hertha's experience at the university is the character of Richard, Michael's academically inclined childhood friend. Richard goes on to finish his dissertation and then joins an esteemed publishing house, a career conveniently coincidental with both bourgeois lifestyle and *Bildung*. After he has abandoned his studies and started his work in the mines, Michael visits Richard one last time, and Richard suddenly tells him that he hates himself and envies Michael. Richard's diminished existence demonstrates how the text targets academic life as one of the core elements of divisive class difference: "That is the horror of it: A wall of arrogance, property, and education stands between the upper and lower classes. We no longer understand one another. We are not a nation" (73).

28. The text also moves quickly to establish a specific generation of soldiers that struggles with returning to civilian life: "there is only one calling for a young German: To stand up for the Fatherland. We did it unprotestingly for four years. It is hard giving it up. That is one of the worst conflicts in the generation of soldiers" (13–14).

29. Mosse, "Two World Wars and the Myth of the War Experience," 495, 497.

30. See Neubauer's study, *The Fin-de-Siècle Culture of Adolescence;* Trommler, "Mission ohne Ziel," 22.
31. Trommler, "Mission ohne Ziel," 20, 26.
32. Prümm, "Jugend ohne Väter," 563.
33. Moeller van den Bruck, *Das Recht der jungen Völker,* 24.
34. Since Goebbels initially submitted the manuscript to two prominent publishing houses that also happened to be owned and run by Jewish publishers, it seems possible that the published text's intermittent but indisputably anti-Semitic comments were added later. The change in the title from a "Man's Fate" to a "German Fate" reflects as well the sociopolitical changes of those crucial years. Finally, though Michael's politicization at the hands of an "inspiring" nationalist orator—clearly meant to invoke Hitler—plays a major role in the text, Goebbels is not confirmed as having encountered Hitler until 1925, so some critics believe these sections were added as well. If these passages were indeed added, Michael's personal and professional turn from bourgeois Hertha would not be galvanized by his hearing Hitler but rather by the shock of her misunderstanding and leaving him.
35. Spengler, *The Decline of the West,* 160.
36. See, for example, Mazower's *Dark Continent,* 130: "Goebbels . . . came from the left wing of the party."
37. For the history and afterlife of the concept, see Schivelbusch, *Culture of Defeat,* 205–10.
38. See Mosse, *Fallen Soldiers;* Lehnert, "'Der gute Krieg ist es, der jede Sache heiligt'" and "Langemarck—Historisch und Symbolisch"; Hüppauf, "Langemarck, Verdun, and the Myth of a New Man."
39. Mosse, *Fallen Soldiers,* 70, Hüppauf, "Langemarck, Verdun, and the Myth of a New Man," 74.
40. Mosse, *Fallen Soldiers,* 71.
41. Unruh, *Langemarck,* 61–69.
42. Hüppauf, "Langemarck, Verdun, and the Myth of a New Man," 76.
43. See De La Maziere, *Captive Dreamer.*
44. "The Lie of Langemarck," quoted in Baird, *To Die for Germany,* 6.
45. See Lothar Kettenacker, "Sozialpsychologische Aspekte der Führer-Herrschaft," in *Nationalsozialistische Diktatur 1933–1945. Eine Bilanz,* ed. Karl Dietrich Bracher, Manfred Funk, Han-Adolf Jacobsen (Bonn: Bundeszentrale für Politische Bildung, 1983), 114. Quoted in Hüppauf, "Langemarck, Verdun, and the Myth of a New Man," 99.
46. Schivelbusch's work *Culture of Defeat* is based on this insight; see also Ketelsen, *Heroisches Theater,* 138; Hüppauf, "Langemarck, Verdun, and the Myth of a New Man," 76–77.

47. Wehner, *Langemarck*, 6.
48. Binding, "Deutsche Jugend vor den Toten des Krieges," 572.
49. In this speech, Heidegger asserts that the student "under the new German reality" is one observing the *Sinnbild* of Langemarck. Schneeberger, *Nachlese zu Heidegger*, 156.
50. *Völkischer Beobachter*, 7 Nov. 1936.
51. Ibid., 10 Dec. 1938.
52. Hüppauf downplays this role of Langemarck past 1933. "Langemarck, Verdun, and the Myth of a New Man," 82.
53. Korfes, "Langemarck."
54. Zerkaulen was the son of a cobbler, apprenticed as a pharmacist, and then volunteered for World War I. He was already quite well known for his 1933 novel, *Der Strom der Väter* which, along with *Musik auf dem Rhein*, lent to his reputation as a mythical, traditional author. His earliest works, including *Wandlung* (1914) and *Insel Thule, Erzählungen aus Deutschlands Notzeit* (1921), confirm his interest in current events and their relation to his search for an *ewiges Deutschland*. For such purposes and for this kind of project—certainly part of a typically folkish-nationalist undertaking during the Nazi time—the myth of Langemarck provided indispensable material.
55. Rühle, *Zeit und Theater*, 750.
56. Vietta and Kemper, *Expressionismus*, esp. 83–95, 176–80.
57. These inherent contradictions dovetail with Kaiser's critique of the war and its relation to industrial production, since the defense industry demands more and more of this lethal product.
58. Deleuze, "Rise of the Social," x.
59. Donzelot, *Policing Families*, 92.
60. The chiasmic intertextual reference—Karl and Franz Moor become Franz Gärtner and Karl Stanz—proves a revealing deviation, since, as with *Gas*, *Youth of Langemarck* invokes basic terms of the canonical dramas but also sublates the earlier plays in its resolution.
61. As with Karl's band of robbers, for which he harbored the highest republican hopes, Gärtner's beloved military turns out to be less than perfect. In *Youth of Langemarck*, bourgeois privilege and self-interest threaten the army and, finally, penetrate the military when a captain appears, at the behest of Franz's powerful family, to pluck him from the ranks and take him home. Echoing Donzelot's description of governing through the family, the text associates decadent values with the bourgeois family, from which it will liberate the young. The scenario is one of the clearest references to *The Robbers*, namely, its "Pater" scene, when a priest (in the text called "Pater," the Latin word for father) comes to Karl and his band of

robbers and invites Karl to give himself up and defuse their putatively inevitable deaths. The chance to return to the family fold and escape death ends up, in both plays, merely reinforcing the decay of the family and the camaraderie of the post- and antifamilial collective. Karl rejects the entreaties of the Pater to remain within his youthful rebellion, and Franz rejects the captain dispatched by his mother to stand by his youthful comrades—both rejections come at the climactic ends of the respective acts and both underscore the generational solidarity at the core of both groups.

62. Rühle, *Zeit und Theater*, 750.
63. Zerkaulen, *Jugend von Langemarck*, 163. Future references will be made parenthetically in the text.

   Rausch, as the impelling force behind the war fever, arose as a key theme in act 1 of the play: Rausch is precisely that which distinguishes Franz from his bourgeois family and home life. In their argument about Franz's departure for the army, his mother insists Franz recognize his duty (*Pflicht*), to which Franz contrasts the Rausch that he thinks and hopes would have affected her, too (155). In contrast to his mother, his love interest, Christa, trusts that there must be "something behind" the ubiquitously celebrated Rausch (154).
64. Jünger, *Der Kampf als inneres Erlebnis*, 57.
65. Other authors likewise suggested that what made Langemarck and its young soldiers special was their susceptibility—or youthful special access—to Rauschen. For instance, in his 1930 speech on Langemarck, "Widergeburt des heroischen Menschen," Hans Schwarz suggests that the Rauschen of the Langemarck youths gave them special insight into the truth, such Rauschen and insight linking them to the German nation's "inner form." Schwarz, *Die Wiedergeburt des heroischen Menschen*. For both Schwarz and Zerkaulen, such Rauschen allows the young to cast away the superficiality of the bourgeois family and achieve a new, "inner" nationalist era. This particular historical break is galvanized above all by youth's special access to collective dreams, thus a specifically generational ecstasy.
66. Many theorists of the nation suggest that, in order to establish the solidarity necessary for a unified identity, nations celebrate their glorified futures with inventions of a mythically shared, localized past. Nations assert a collective project that unifies disparate social elements in the past in order to "progress" to a certain future. Deniz Kandiyoti makes just such a point: "[Nationalism] presents itself both as a modern project that melts and transforms traditional attachments in favour of new identities and as a reflection of authentic cultural values culled from the depths of a pre-

sumed communal past." "Identity and Its Discontents," 378. Saskia Sassen terms this mechanism "national time," a temporal sense both conforming to and confirming the nation and its history. "The time of the national is elusive; its needs excavating. It is constructed of a past filled with nation's founding myths and a future set to inherit the state as the necessary consequence of the nation—that is, the national is a time that looks to the past and inherits the future." "Spatial and Temporalities of the Global," 223.

67. Koselleck, "War Memorials," 297, 308.

68. Baird, *To Die for Germany;* Mosse, *Fallen Soldiers.*

69. See Lane, *Architecture and Politics,* esp. 185–216; Steinweis, *Art, Ideology, and Economics in Nazi Germany,* esp. 22–23.

70. Rentschler, *Ministry of Illusion,* 172, 180, 183.

71. Friedman, *"Ecce Ingenium Teutonicum,"* 190.

72. These two sequences are the focus of some of the other interpretations of *Paracelsus,* but the attention they have garnered seems to indicate the way in which other parts of the plot, including its overall trajectory, are obscured by a few specific aspects of the film. See, for example, Friedman's essay *"Ecce Ingenium Teutonicum."*

73. Koselleck, "Some Questions regarding the Conceptual History of 'Crisis,'" 238.

74. Foucault, "La loi du pudeur," quoted in Stoler, *Race and the Education of Desire,* 141.

75. This shot clearly anticipates the much more discussed sequences of the dance of death or flagellants, which have become the foundation of many scholars' interpretations. The neglect of this shot reflects the general neglect of the film's generational discourse.

76. Giroux celebrates this threat by working-class children and adolescents and takes it as a metaphor for cultural studies as a whole: "As kids, we were border crossers and had to learn to negotiate the power, violence, and cruelty of the dominant culture." *Fugitive Cultures,* 9. In her study "Politicizing Childhood," Polletta states that when the young want freedom, they conceive of its spatially, equate having a space for freedom with having freedom.

77. Mitterauer, *History of Youth,* 8.

78. See Etlin, *Modernism in Italian Architecture,* 439–55.

79. Rentschler, *Ministry of Illusion,* 180.

80. Although she does not label it as such, Stoler highlights this dual and contradictory character of discourse about youth, especially as it regarded sentimentality about children, in her *Carnal Knowledge and Imperial Power,* 119.

Chapter 2

1. Glaser, *Rubble Years*, 95.
2. "Die Ansprache Pastor Niemöllers in der Neustädter Kirche von Erlangen," *Neue Zeitung*, 15 Feb. 1946.
3. "Sieht so die neue akademische Jugend aus? Störungen eines Vortrages von Pastor Niemöller," *Mittelbayerische Zeitung*, 25 June 1946, 2.
4. Kn., "Militaristische Studentenschaft: Die Hochschule ist kein Unterschlupf für arbeitslose Offiziere," *Frankenpost*, 13 Feb. 1946, 3.
5. Blumenfeld, "An Pfarrer Niemöller."
6. "Studentenkrawalle in Erlangen: Leitung der Universität hat bisher keine Untersuchung eingeleitet," *Frankenpost*, 20 July 1946. The article, a DANA (German press service) report that appeared in other newspapers as well, was placed in the *Frankenpost* in the center of page 1. The article recounts how one student said, "We [Germans] ought to pay careful attention to the Nuremberg trials so we know how to pass judgment on the Americans and Russians later" and another: "If I have to hold my mouth now, then someday I'll have these jokers under my control. Then Auschwitz will look like a paradise." There is no evidence in the report that these provocative declarations are in any way representative of general student opinion.
7. Glaser, *Kulturgeschichte der Bundesrepublik Deutschland*, 112–14; Füssl, *Die Umerziehung der Deutschen*.
8. "Von der Kollektivschuld: Zur Ansprache Pastor Niemöllers in Erlangen," *Süddeutsche Zeitung*, 22 Feb. 1946, 1. The article appeared prominently, on the right side of page 1 right under the masthead.
9. The article, "In der Universität Erlangen wurde bis jetzt noch nicht durchgegriffen," *Frankenpost*, 3 Aug. 1946, 1, quotes a professor pointing out that the events in Erlangen reflect attitudes belonging to a very small group of students.
10. "Die Folgerungen, die in den Zeitungsartikeln meistens aus den Vorgängen gezogen werden, kann ich nicht ziehen, wonach die Dissentierenden gewissermassen als verkappte Nazis oder unverbesserliche Militaristen hingestellt werden." Niemöller, "Letter to the Rector," 174.
11. Helmo Baumgärtl, "Not und Hoffnung: Wege der deutschen Jugend," *Süddeutsche Zeitung*, 23 Nov. 1946, 3.
12. Olick regards reeducation as important enough to make it the general rubric for "occupation-imposed memory." See *In the House of the Hangman*, 11. Rupieper similarly suggests that reeducation was the code word for the general project of democratization. *Die Wurzeln der westdeutschen Nachkriegsdemokratie: der Amerikanische Beitrag*, 8.2.
13. As I mentioned in chapter 1, Stephen Brockmann's study of the literary-

cultural public sphere (*German Literary Culture at the Zero Hour*) makes almost no mention of reeducation, while Olick's (*In the House of the Hangman*) foregrounds its centrality in the introduction but then mostly neglects it in the subsequent chapters.

14. Sebald, *Air War and Literature*. Sebald focuses almost exclusively on high literature, a problematic approach in a context where paper shortages and censorship made such publication both difficult and complicated. His approach would be more convincing if he incorporated some study of the discussion of the destruction and reconstruction in the public sphere, where disproportionately much of the paper rations were actually allotted. One example of this lack of attention comes in his short discussion of *Doktor Faustus*, the most discussed novel in the period. Sebald suggests that "few of the readers for whom this novel was originally intended understood [Mann]" without citing any of the innumerable discussions of the novel, many of which did in fact invoke the bombing and widespread destruction (44–45).

15. Educational Minister Grimme, quoted in Weismantel, "Demokratie als Lebensform."

16. Pechel, "Unsere vordringlichste Aufgabe," 45.

17. Foucault, *History of Sexuality: An Introduction;* Donzelot, *Policing Families.*

18. Nandy's seminal study, *Intimate Enemy,* describes a symbolic code, developed in the colonies, that amounted to a symbolic negotiation between ruler and ruled. Nandy shows how the evolution of the concept of the child served this colonial symbolism, rendering colonialism largely a narrative of progress understood as "maturation." In a more deliberately Foucauldian approach, Stoler has applied Nandy's theories to the Dutch colonies; she shifts Foucault's focus on child masturbation to the anxiety around racially other servants' contact with European children. *Race and the Education of Desire,* 136. This argument is the fundamental one that Stoler makes in her fourth chapter, "Domestic Subversions and Children's Sexuality." In her newer work, *Carnal Knowledge and Imperial Power,* Stoler continues this line of inquiry in examining discourse about children of mixed (Dutch and Indo) heritage. Once again, she finds, the child becomes a discursive site at which race, sexuality, and subjectivity in general are negotiated.

19. Tent, *Mission on the Rhine;* Füssl, *Die Umerziehung der Deutschen;* and Rupieper, *Die Wurzeln der westdeutschen Nachkriegsdemokratie: der amerikanische Beitrag* all do a thorough job of tracing how the policies about reeducation emerged and developed.

20. Hocking, *Experiment in Education,* 221. This U.S. educational mission was also covered in the German press: "Die Hoffnung: Neue Wege für die

Jugend," *Süddeutsche Zeitung*, 18 Oct. 1946, 2.

21. *Report of the United States Education Mission*, 19. On p. 16, the report called schools "central to the enterpise" of democratization.

22. This is the argument of Rupieper in *Die Wurzeln der westdeutschen Nachkriegsdemokratie: der amerikanische Beitrag*, but as I note above, it is also made in Olick's *In the House of the Hangman*.

23. Dietrich, *Politik und Kultur*, 40–44. In his well-known and well-regarded history, Norman Naimark is likewise clear about the importance of education to the Soviet's cultural and therefore occupational projects. *Russians in Germany*, esp. 441.

24. Padover, *Psychologist in Germany*, 114; cf. 176.

25. Rempel, *Hitler's Children*, 4: "Recent statistical analysis suggests that the age factor was indeed significant. Both members and leaders in the early party were even younger than had previously been intimated—in their twenties before 1925—and on the whole younger than the Reich population between 1925 and 1932. There was a change in the situation after the establishment of the regime, despite efforts to reverse a familiar institutional phenomenon, which in the case of national socialism meant the average age rose to the middle and late forties by 1942–43. This suggests a lack of a consistent pattern of rejuvenation, and once again points to a different avenue for the expression of youthful energy."

26. Pechel, "Unsere vordringlichste Aufgabe," 45.

27. *Badener Tagblatt*, 13 Apr. 1946.

28. A few examples: Schnog, "Probleme der Jugend"; "Üeber die junge Generation," *Süddeutsche Zeitung*, 15 Feb. 1946, 5; Paarmann, "Das Gesicht der deutschen Jugend"; Böttcher, "Lehrlinge suchen ihren Meister."

29. Here are a few examples in addition to those I discuss below: "Antwort an die Väter," *Suddeutsche Zeitung*, 8 Oct. 1946, 5; "Aus Briefen und Zeitungen," *Frankfurter Rundschau*, 26 Feb. 1946, 4; "Forum der Jugend," *Deutsche Rundschau* 69 (May 1946): 143–45, which includes a series of letters from young officers.

30. "Anfang der Gesundung: Einer der Heimgekehrten schreibt seinem Freunde," *Rheinischer Merkur*, 18 Apr. 1946, 2.

31. *Rheinischer Merkur*, 10 May 1946, 5 July 1946, 30 July 1946, and 13 Aug. 1946.

32. Lambda, "Die Situation der Jugend: Eine Antwort auf zahlreiche Fragen," *Rheinischer Merkur*, 10 May 1946, 3.

33. Such despair features prominently in many articles, for example (besides those mentioned below), Pechel, "Unsere vordringlichste Aufgabe"; Berglar-Schröer, "Die Vertrauungskrise der Jugend."

34. Rosner, "Trostbrief an einen jungen Vater."

35. The part of Frei's book that addresses the notion of "collective guilt" is

entitled "Von deutscher Erfindungskraft" (Of German Inventiveness). Frei, *1945 und wir.*

36. Walter Dirks, "Nicht die Jugend, die Erwachsenen!" *Frankfurter Hefte* 1 (June 1946).

37. "Mütter klagen an: Die Entführung Jugendlicher in der russischen Zone," *Rheinischer Merkur,* 16 Aug. 1946.

38. "Jugend auf schiefer Bahn: Trübe Bilder unserer Zeit: Landstreicher in Kinderschuhen," *Süddeutsche Zeitung,* 1 Mar. 1946.

39. Dietrich, *Politik und Kultur,* 41.

40. Naimark, *Russians in Germany,* 455–56. In his assessment of the program—which received much and laudatory attention in the public sphere—Naimark is skeptical of the actual numbers of workers and farmers introduced to teaching.

41. The Americans dismissed 28,868 teachers out of 42,160 in their zone, while the British, for example, dismissed only 14,079 out of 65,034. Benz, *Deutschland unter allierter Besatzung,* 100.

42. The Zook report was clear about these two separate phases of reeducation. See *Report of the United States Education Mission,* 10.

43. Tent, *Mission on the Rhine,* 114; Schlander, *Reeducation,* 124.

44. Schlander, *Reeducation,* 142.

45. This directive is reprinted in *Germany, 1947–1949.*

46. *Report of the United States Education Mission,* 3.

47. Füssl, *Die Umerziehung der Deutschen,* 60.

48. *Report of the United States Education Mission,* 19.

49. Rupieper recounts the oft-noted dissent of a group of University of Chicago professors who protested plans to restructure the Gymnasium. *Die Wurzeln der westdeutschen Nachkriegsdemokratie: der amerikanische Beitrag,* 116. Schlander does a good job of summarizing the dissenting views within the U.S. ranks. *Reeducation,* 124–29.

50. Benz, *Deutschland unter allierter Besatzung,* 101; Willis, *French in Germany,* 179; Benz, *Deutschland unter allierter Besatzung,* 103; Dietrich, *Politik und Kultur,* 41. This is confirmed as well by contemporary sources. See the report by the Office of Institutional Research of the OSS, "The Program of Reeducation in Germany," Dir Report No. 4237, 3 June 1947, Hoover Institution Archive, Stanford University.

51. Office of Institutional Research of the OSS, "The Program of Reeducation in Germany," 78.

52. An overview of this debate and the tensions around it are recounted in Weismantel, "Demokratie als Lebensform."

53. See, for example, "Humanitisches Gymnasium: Fragen des Bildungsideals unserer Zeit," *Trierische Zeitung,* 24 Jan. 1947; Wenzl, "Vom Sinn der höheren Schulen."

54. Köbelin, "Scharfe Debatte um Dr. Hundhammers Kulturpolitik."
55. That this was Hundhammer's stance was noted by Charles Falk in his memo "Report on Bavarian School Reform Situation," addressed to the director of Education and Cultural Relations Division, 26 May 1948, 1, Hoover Institution Archive, Stanford University. Hundhammer also proclaimed it openly: "In all discussions on school reform, which was ordered by the occupation forces, it has to be considered that even a defeated country has the right to handle affairs of non-military nature by its own [*sic*]." Transcript of Alois Hundhammer's radio speech on school reform, 21 Jan. 1948, Hoover Institution Archive, Stanford University.
56. Allen, "Gardens of Children."
57. See the report by the Office of Institutional Research of the OSS, "The Program of Reeducation in Germany," 75.
58. *Report of the United States Education Mission*, 12.
59. "Mißbilligung für Dr. Hundhammer verschoben," *Münchner Mittag*, 18 July 1947.
60. The importance of the church and Christianity in this context has been long known and is increasingly receiving scholarly attention, as it does in Brockmann, *German Literary Culture at the Zero Hour* and Olick, *In the House of the Hangman*. Füssl details the impact of the church on reeducation. *Die Umerziehung der Deutschen*, 93–95.
61. The report by the Office of Institutional Research of the OSS, "The Program of Reeducation in Germany," 77.
62. Falk, in his memo "Report on Bavarian School Reform Situation," 3, 26 May 1948. See also the report by the Office of Institutional Research of the OSS, "The Program of Reeducation in Germany," 77.
63. Transcript of Alois Hundhammer's radio speech, 2–3.
64. A harsh critique of this pro-Catholic stance can be found, for instance, in "Schule und Leben," *Münchner Mittag*, 11 July 1947, 4.
65. Wiesmantal, *Donau-Kurier*, 21 Feb. 1947.
66. "Hundhammer beschwert sich über die Presse," *Mittelbayerische Zeitung*, 21 Oct. 1947.
67. Transcript of Alois Hundhammer's radio speech, 3.
68. Zink, *United States in Germany*, 210. Another study assessing U.S. influence is Gimbel, *American Occupation of Germany*, 247. The studies of Rupieper (*Die Wurzeln der westdeutschen Nachkriegsdemokratie: der amerikanische Beitrag*), Füssl (*Die Umerziehung der Deutschen*) and, more recently, Jarausch (*Die Umkehr*) revise the negative view of U.S. reeducation a bit and suggest that although the original goals were never met, the long-term political culture of Germany certainly changed and the role of the Allies has been unfairly downplayed.

69. Beddow even has a graph on citations of authors in the postwar literature. Mann and *Doktor Faustus* are far out ahead of any other literary work. *Doktor Faustus*, 97.

70. Both Russell Berman (*Rise of the Modern German Novel*) and Weiner recognize how *Doktor Faustus* drives at the creation of a new community, but they do not recognize how this community is, in part, complicit with Nazism, the clear intent of Mann and a difficult interpretation to dispel. See, for example, Weiner, *Undertones of Insurrection*, 219, 224, 236.

71. Some critics have done their best to shear Zeitblom of this unglamorous career: "Who is speaker here when Zeitblom speaks? If one divests him of his costume of this simple humanist and somewhat plain teacher and instead takes seriously his role as commentator, then Zeitblom is a critic—not only of Leverkühn, but also of life in general." Koopmann, "Docktor Faustus," 19.

72. Though I choose to focus on these two chapters, out of concern for space and symmetry, one finds throughout the novel a reading of Germany's antibourgeois trajectory through the filter of youth. One of the earliest examples comes in Zeitblom's admitting that his sons follow the Führer now, not him—thus, the only literal Nazis the text depicts are young sons who have broken from their father. In Kaiseraschern—the well-known metaphor for Germany—the population's deep irrational streak is linked both to its eccentrics and to the superstitious young people who chase them around (Mann, *Doktor Faustus*, 53). In chapter 10, in which Leverkühn commits to studying theology and departs home for Halle, Leverkühn and Zeitblom debate German character, and Leverkühn asserts typically that Germans are a mixture of "Freiheit und Vornehmheit, Idealismus und Naturkindlichkeit" (116). Much later, in chapter 36, when Zeitblom indulges in a long section about Germany's current state, he writes that he had hoped for Germany's "adult" (*mündig*) and forward-looking progress, but it was not to be (518).

73. Mitterauer, *History of Youth*, 214.

74. Mogge, "Wandervogel, Freideutsche Jugend und Bünde," 175.

75. This implicit critique and negation of modern society is explicitly confirmed by former members of the group. In an important early history of the movement by a former member, Hans Blüher described Wandervogel's basic agenda as "Selbsterziehung in jugendlichen Gemeinschaften": "Die Jugend war ueberlastet, geistig und seelisch verbildet, durch die Schulerziehung und die stuetzenden Gedanken der Eltern im Gemuete verletzt." *Die Wandervogelzeit*, 58.

76. Strachura, *Nazi Youth in the Weimar Republic*, 13.

77. Mann, *Doktor Faustus*, 156. Future references will be made parenthetically in the text. The first citation will be to the English translation by John E.

Woods, with the second citation to the German edition in *Gesammelte Werke*.

78. Mogge, "Wandervogel, Freideutsche Jugend und Bünde," 175.
79. Mitterauer, *History of Youth*, 93.
80. For the politicization and militarization of the movement in the 1920s, see Mogge, "Wandervogel, Freideutsche Jugend und Bünde," 191.
81. See Mann, "Deutschland und die Deutschen," 1133–35, where Mann takes up Luther, his conservative revolution, and its resulting distorted idea of freedom as paradigmatic for German history.
82. Trommler, "Mission ohne Ziel," 18.
83. Dvoretzky, "Thomas Manns *Doktor Faustus*"; Gollnick, "Thomas Mann"; Orlowski, "Die größere Kontroverse."
84. Milch, "Thomas Manns *Doktor Faustus*," 360.
85. Petersen, "Thomas Mann fordert den musikalischen Faust," 52.
86. Sonnemann, "Thomas Mann oder Mass und Anspruch," 639–40.

Chapter 3

1. Just a few examples of such series would include both very short pamphlets as well as long books. For example, *Der Deutschenspiegel: Schriften zur Erkenntnis und Erneuerung* included at least thirty-one volumes ranging from Paul Kluckhorn's slim *Die Idee des Menschen in der Goethezeit* (1946) to Huberta von Bronsart's hefty *Weizen oder Spinat? Der deutsche Landwirt am Scheideweg* (1947); *Europäische Dokumente: Kulturpolitische Schriften*, ed. Rudolf Schneider-Schelde and published by Kurt Desch Verlag in Munich, presented things as diverse as Adolf Weber's *Wohin steuert die Wirtschaft?* (1946) and Peter Scherer's *Wiedergeburt der Menschlichkeit* (1946); not to be outdone, Suhrkamp had its own line, *Beiträge zur Humanität*, which included republications of older pieces like Hermann Hesse's *Der Europäer* (1946) as well as postwar texts like Rudolf Alexander Schröder's *Der Mann und das Jahr: Ein Nachtgespräch/Silvester 1945* (1946).
2. The examples are many. In terms of recent history and what had happened, see, for example: Niekisch, *Deutsche Daseinsverfehlung* (1946), which laments the disaster, says there is hardly any "Volksrechtssubjekt" left, and expects obedience to predominate instead of democracy; Helling, *Der Katastrophenweg der deutschen Geschichte* (1947), which bases the catastrophic path on a long series of counterrevolutions; Harzendorf, *So kam es* (1946), which offers a likewise historical approach, this time based on Prussian militarism. Diagnoses of the present situation include Röpke, *Die deutsche Frage* (1945), which lodges a neoliberal critique against mass politics past and present; Ritter, *Europa und die*

deutsche Frage (1948), which likewise blames the masses for the nation's problems; and Brinkmann, *Geist im Wandel* (1948), which warns of the influence of the masses on today's spirit. For advice, suggestions, and agendas for Germany's future: Ritter, *Geschichte als Bildungsmacht* (1946) sees the past as tragedy and pleads for history as a fortification against future problems; Schwertfeger, *Rätsel um Deutschland* (1948) tries to answer Germany's riddles by emphasizing their common history; and Mitscherlich and Weber, *Freier Sozialismus* (1946) advocates a socialist middle path between the Soviet Union and the United States.

3. Prowe argues that traditional German elites were largely reinstated after World War II as part of an overall "conservative restabilization." See, for instance, his important article "German Democratization as Conservative Restabilization," 308. In his *Divided Memory,* Herf similarly traces "multiple restorations" in the establishment of German democracy (3).

4. A number of scholarly studies have examined the dense discursive context created by the multiplicity of such publications. The two best known and most thorough, Glaser's *Kulturgeschichte der Bundesrepublik Deutschland* and Hermand's *Kultur im Wiederaufbau,* both approach this mass of material along thematically organized lines. As cultural histories these analyses tend—understandably, given their objectives—to subordinate individual texts to their broad topical groupings. In both cases they offer impressively encyclopedic catalogues that favor broad thematic strokes over their more nuanced subtleties or underlying strategies.

5. Dirk van Laak's recent *Gespräche in der Sicherheit des Schweigens* avoids the subordination of one author to the usual postwar thematics by concentrating on Schmitt and the circle around him. It also does an interesting job of highlighting the form of cultural and intellectual activity: small, quasi-secret circles in which conversations between Schmitt and (usually) his disciples took place. He argues, as I have, that intellectual histories too often ignore biographical accidents in intellectual work. A good example is his analysis of "bridges," i.e., the theme of Germany between the East and West, which he traces in its various intellectual and biographical configurations (paying attention to the intellectuals and their profiles) (47–80). Van Laak also shows a sensitivity to the generational question in postwar intellectual history (esp. 19–23) in framing his analysis of Schmitt and his (younger) circle.

6. Glaser deploys Meinecke in exactly this fashion in his history *Kulturgeschichte der Bundesrepublik Deutschland,* 100–103.

7. Wippermann, "Friedrich Meinecke und die deutsche Katastrophe," 102. For Wippermann, the most interesting question about this text is why it became so popular despite its thematic similarity to a great number of other texts. His answer: because it managed to incorporate all the themes

of the other texts.

8. Glaser, *Kulturgeschichte der Bundesrepublik Deutschland,* 100–101 calls the text Meinecke's "Monumentalwerk, das das Geschichtebewußtsein der Nachkriegszeit aufwühlte." Wippermann summarizes the reception as similarly overwhelming. "Friedrich Meinecke und die deutsche Katastrophe," 113. Even in his generally negative assessment of Friedrich Meinecke's politics, Pois features the important reception of the *Die deutsche Katastrophe* in his "Postscript." *Friedrich Meinecke and German Politics in the Twentieth Century,* 148–51.

9. Schildt and Sywottek, *Modernisierung im Wiederaufbau,* 545.

10. Wippermann, "Friedrich Meinecke und die deutsche Katastrophe," 114; Pois, *Friedrich Meinecke and German Politics,* 142 (where he derides Meinecke's nationalistic Goethianism), and Glaser, *Kulturgeschichte der Bundesrepublik Deutschland,* 101–2.

11. English translation modified from Fay's in Meinecke, *The German Catastrophe,* 120; German in Meinecke, *Die deutsche Katastrophe,* 175. Future references will be made parenthetically in the text, with English and then German page number.

12. Various scholars see 1924, the year of publication of Meinecke's *Idee der Staatsräson,* as the crucial turning point in Meinecke's conservative politics, the year of his definitive turn to support for the Weimar Republic. Meinecke no longer saw a harmonious unity between *Ethos* and *Macht*—a synthesis he had formerly located in an idealized state—but rather a hard struggle best fought within a democratic republic. This position was promptly attacked by other historians, making Meinecke's loyalty to this political perspective all the more remarkable. See, for example, Schulin, "Friedrich Meineckes Stellung in der deutschen Geschichtswissenschaft," esp. 28.

13. Much has been made of a statement Meinecke made in support of some kind of "Ceasar" system. Wippermann takes the question head-on and shows that while it was true that Meinecke himself might have supported a Caesar figure before the foundation of the republic, he accepted that the republic could never entertain this form of government. For example, in his 1918 diary, Meinecke wrote: "kommt doch noch ein fähiger Cäsar und ballt ein kleines festes Heer zusammen? Zu wünschen wäre es." Wippermann, "Friedrich Meinecke und die deutsche Katastrophe," 106. But by 1925 he had accepted that "der ganze Geist des deutschen Volks- und Staatslebens" has turned itself "gegen alles, was nach usurpatorischem Cäsarismus schmeckt." This rather regret-soaked concession to the democratic politics of the republic marked various *Vernunftsrepublikaner.*

It is true, however, that throughout the late republic, Meinecke did support the strengthening of the rights and power (*Recht und Macht*) of the Reich president, though this strengthening was to occur within the republic, i.e., to be written into the constitution in order to save the endangered republic. At moments, as late as 1932, Meinecke lobbied for a temporary *Vertrauensdiktatur*, though once again within the frame of the republic. Of course, such a stance does appear inadequate, even absurd, in the hindsight bred of observing where the Reich presidency ended up, but it was not all that uncommon for liberal and conservative supporters of the republic to take this position. For instance, Alfred Weber also argued for such a figure, in his case, for a *plebiszitäre Führerdemokratie*.

14. Hermand discusses Meinecke as a paradigmatic conservative liberal and persuasively reads *Die deutsche Katastrophe* as a paradigmatic symptom of Nazism's assault on liberalism. *Kultur im Wiederaufbau*, 48.

15. Meinecke, *Die deutsche Katastrophe*, 21: "Das heilige Erbe der Goethezeit, das dem deutschen Volke schier wie ein Wunder zugefallen war, vor diesem Drucke der Massen und der damit drohenden Vergröberung und sonstigen Entartung zu bewahren, zugleich aber auch dem, was lebendig und fruchtbar in den neuen Massenwünschen erschien, kräftig zu dienen, das war um die Mitte des Jahrhunderts und darüber hinaus das Hochziel deutscher Kultur überhaupt."

16. In his *Friedrich Meinecke and German Politics*, Pois lodges some legitimate and insightful critiques (particularly in Meinecke's tricky negotiations of the *Kultur* and *Macht* dichotomy), but Pois's reading sometimes de-emphasizes important aspects of Meinecke's texts. For example, in his haste to demonstrate Meinecke's antiquated approach, he completely skips Meinecke's thoroughgoing critique of the German bourgeoisie in *The German Catastrophe*.

17. Giess offers the most severe indictment of Meinecke and has lent secondary scholarship its most popular sound bite by calling Meinecke "a shaman for his class." "Kritischer Rückblick auf Friedrich Meinecke." Like Pois's analysis, Giess underplays Meinecke's quite negative judgment of the German bourgeoisie in *The German Catastrophe*.

18. Pois first highlights this split and then emphasizes it again in his *Friedrich Meinecke and German Politics*, 137, 144–45. See also Wippermann, "Friedrich Meinecke und die deutsche Katastrophe," 114. Hermand, *Kultur im Wiederaufbau*, 49: "Eine "spezifisch deutsche Schuld" konnte Meinecke in dieser Entwicklung nicht erkennen [von der Demokratisierung zur Faschisierung]."

19. A example of another prominent postwar intellectual—this time Swiss—who advocated the teaching of literary classics was Emil Ludwig, who proposed "Goethe, Schiller, and Lessing" as an "antidote against the insane race ideology." Ludwig felt that economy and politics should take

a reconstructive backseat to moral education. See Olick, *In the House of the Hangman*, 57. Jaspers criticized the cult around Goethe in his acceptance speech for the 1947 Goethe prize, which I shall discuss below in my analysis of Jaspers.

20. Sebald, *Air War and Literature*. For a parallel example, Jünger mocks the Allies' attempt at reeducation in his *Strahlungen: Jahre der Okkupation*, his diaries from the beginning of the occupation in April 1945 until 1948. In an entry from 6 October 1945, after a long account of the rapes and kidnappings Russians soldiers were committing in Berlin, he laconically adds that the Allies were also offering café evenings in the new effort at *demokratische Erziehung*. In contradistinction to the Allies' efforts at reeducation, he also takes it upon himself to bring the neighborhood children to the circus, where, he writes, the world-upside-down atmosphere mimics and derides the militarism so prevalent in German society (21 Sept. 1945, *Strahlungen*, 546–48).

21. Meinecke, *Die deutsche Katastrophe*, 153: "Und dieser darf man mit Erfolg entgegenwirken versuchen. Wenigstens hat das die Volkserziehung in allen Kulturländern noch immer, zwar nie absolut, aber doch in hohem Grade zu erreichen vermocht. Der Appell an den anständigen Menschen wird auch in deutschen Herzen immer Widerhall finden. Äußerliche Mittel, selbst solche, die zu einem Zwange sich steigern, sind dabei wie bei jeder Art von Volkserziehung unvermeidlich. Unsere fremden Herren werden sie als mächtige Sieger reichlich anwenden."

22. Jünger, *Strahlungen*, 79. Future references will be made parenthetically in the text with date, volume number, and page.

23. In this context, an overview of texts pro and contra war, one also has to mention the 1939 *Auf den Marmorklippen*, which presented in a highly abstract form a critique of Hitler and his henchmen. After *Auf den Marmorklippen*, Jünger was able to publish *Gärten und Straßen*, the first part of his diaries, before the Nazis discouraged him—without the official ban on writing—from publishing anything else.

After the war, Jünger refused to submit to the Allies' denazification process and was not allowed to publish in Germany as a consequence (though some of his work appeared in Switzerland). After 1949, West Germany was very quick and accommodating with his rehabilitation. *Strahlungen* and *Der Friede* were both officially published for the first time in 1949, though *Der Friede* had been circulating in one form or another since 1944 and with increasing frequency after that.

24. "Das zweite Pariser Tagebuch" refers to the fact that Jünger was assigned during the war to the French Occupation and was almost always between April 1941 and August 1944 based in Paris, where he prepared a few reports for his Wehrmacht superiors and censored mail. The "zweite"

refers to a second diary: he broke his entries in Paris into two separate diaries divided by his 1943 trip to the eastern front.

25. Mendelssohn's review appeared shortly after *Strahlungen* was published in 1949: "Gegenstrahlungen." Mendelssohn had been residing in London during the war and wanted to give a different kind of account than Jünger's, which he found contemptible.

26. For the complexity of Jünger's prewar writings about Jews, see Neaman, *Dubious Past,* 36–37.

27. Loose, *Ernst Jünger,* 78. Before Nevin's study *Ernst Jünger and Germany,* Loose's was the only major Anglophone analysis of Jünger I could find that mentioned *Der Friede.* Loose was completely befuddled by the subtitle and reenacts, as he does here, the recurring ambivalence toward youth.

28. In his *Dubious Past,* Neaman has an entire chapter about *The Peace* and, besides offering important background on its composition, recounts very persuasively its importance for the postwar rehabilitation of Jünger, but there is no mention of the subtitle or its generational context. See esp. chapter 4, "The Pen and the Sword: Last Knights of the Majestic," 122–38.

29. See Bullock, *Violent Eye,* 36. Bullock gives an account of how this abstraction has frustrated critics like J. P. Stern in the long and highly ambivalent reception of Jünger.

30. In his *Der konservative Anarchist,* Schwarz makes clear that Jünger saw *The Peace* as his part, even his participation, in the effort to topple Hitler (173). In *Dubious Past,* Neaman offers an evenhanded account of Jünger's relationship to the various plots of the Wehrmacht to remove Hitler either by arrest or assassination, especially in chapter 4. It may have even been, as Jünger claimed, that the text was to be published after the July assassination with the approval of the conspirators. In May 1944, Rommel read the manuscript and voiced his approval; Neaman even recounts the rumor that reading *The Peace* inspired Rommel to act faster. Soon thereafter, Speidel told Jünger that it would be published in the next months, something conceivable only after the fall, that is, the assassination, of Hitler.

31. Nevin, *Ernst Jünger and Germany,* 210.

32. In his *Violent Eye,* Bullock examines Jünger's implicit and explicit critique of mass society, particularly its devaluation and damage to history and past experience.

33. Jünger, *Werke,* 481.

34. Ibid., 350.

35. Ibid.

36. Jünger had to travel back home to Lower Saxony and even on to Berlin a

number of times in this period because his son Ernst (referred to as Ern-stel in *Strahlungen*) had been arrested and sentenced to several months in prison. Jünger went back at first to try to mitigate the sentence: Ernstel had been arrested for saying, to a group of youths he was leading, that Hitler would have to be hanged for there to be a peaceful end to the war.

37. See, for instance, the introduction to Lüdtke, Marßolek, and von Saldern's *Amerikanisierung*.

38. Sebald, *Air War and Literature*.

39. Neaman, *Dubious Past*, 132–38.

40. Jünger, *Werke*, 144.

41. Bullock, *Violent Eye*, 22: "The wartime diaries are an intimate record of his growing awareness of the horror into which mankind was plunging, seen mostly from an extraordinarily privileged situation." Nevin cites criticism of Jünger's diaries and their callousness and then attempts to defend him against such charges. *Ernst Jünger and Germany*, 211–28.

42. The proximity of the Freikorps to the young is later confirmed in Jünger's analysis of the breakup of the Roßbacher group: "Er selbst schien sich dabei auch nicht wohlzufühlen, denn er löste das Freikorps auf und gründete Spielscharen, mit denen er nach Art des Wandervogels das Land durchzog" (28 Mar. 1946, 2:610).

43. Neaman suggests that *The Peace* was written in 1942–43. *Dubious Past*, 126.

44. Nevin seems particularly struck by these passages on the beginning of the occupation but does not really analyze the passage further. *Ernst Jünger and Germany*.

45. *Jahre der Okkupation*, Jünger's diaries from the occupational years, 11 April 1945–2 December 1948, were published later than the original volume of *Strahlungen* (1949), but are now included in the two-volume *Strahlungen* set.

46. Precisely this basic generational crisis, where adults abrogate the mature role in the family and children step in to fill it, is at the core of the plot of Rossellini's canonical film *Germany, Year Zero*, in which Edmund the son becomes the provider while his father and older brother remain in the (formerly private) house.

47. Hebdige describes how the young were associated with the colonial and racial other: "During the mid-nineteenth century when intrepid social explorers began to venture into the 'unknown continents,' the 'jungles' and the 'Africas' of Manchester and the slums of East London, special attention was drawn to the wretched mental and physical condition of the young 'nomads' and 'street urchins.'" *Hiding in the Light*, 20.

48. Schwarz, summarizing Jünger's *Zeitmauer* text, writes how at the most Jünger saw a temporary usefulness to the church and considered the Bible

not a holy book, but a "useful manual." *Der konservative Anarchist,* 170–71.

49. Jünger, *Der Friede,* 12: "Es muß durch die Vernunft verwirklicht werden, was unklar, doch mächtig in der Sehnsucht ungezählter Millionen lebte, gleichviel in welchem Land der Erde ihr Schicksal sie geboren werden ließ: ein größeres und besseres Friedensreich."

50. Ibid., 13: "Dieser Kampf nicht nur als Wehrgang zwischen Völkern und Staaten, zwischen Nationen und Rassen, sondern in noch weit höherem Maße als einen Weltbürgerkrieg begreift, der den Planeten nichtmals in zwei geheimere, doch um so schrecklichere Fronten spaltete."

51. Ibid., 59: "Europa kann Vaterland werden, doch bleiben viele Mütterländer, bleibt manche Heimat in seinem Raum."

52. Ibid., 17.

53. Ibid., 13.

54. In his analysis, Nevin seems to concur that youth were the "true sufferers" in the catastrophe, but then realizes there's something wrong with this assertion: "Jünger does not forget the true innocent: 'The guilt alleged to the misfortunate was the crimes of existence, the stigma of birth. They fell as sons of their people, their fathers, their race, as hostages, witnesses of inherited belief or bearers of convictions which overnight laws stamped defective.' He avoids Hitler, his henchmen or Jews and others who suffered and died, yet his gift for precision has eloquent moments." *Ernst Jünger and Germany,* 230.

55. Nihilism becomes in this cultural context the opposite of humanism, the mark of the dark (coded as Russian and slightly Asiatic) countercurrent to western European enlightened culture. In a book entitled *Das abendländische Bildungsideal,* for instance, the distorted *Bildungsideal* is seen to have morphed "in den Relativismus, mit dem Historismus und Psychologismus als Sonderformen, und am Ende in den Nihilismus." Burger, "Deutsche Bildungsideale," 27.

Tied redundantly as it is to the youth discourse, the postwar crisis in nihilism—i.e., in this context, apathy and lack of direction—sounds remarkably similar to the complaints about the fabled "Generation X" of the 1990s: "Eine Resignation scheint sich der deutschen Jugend bemächtigt zu haben, die es ihr unmöglich macht, zum Augenblicklichen anders als negativ zu stehen, und die ihr die Loslösung vom Gewesenen verwehrt." Weber, "Die Blaue Blume," 8. For many of the authors, even in their sympathetic depictions, the young seem cynical, detached, blunted: "Von der vor uns stehenden jungen Generation haben wir vor allem den Eindruck, daß sie stumm ist. Stumm und rätselhaft. Mit einem etwas pathetischen Bild: wie eine Mauer. Und tatsächlich: es fliegt uns oft das Gefühl an, daß diese jungen Leute 'alt' sind, älter als wir." Suskind,

"An die Jugend," 60. Of course, these depictions of the young reflect the general ideological fatigue of Germany at the time—they share everything with the depictions of a traumatized masculinity that appear in the rubble film: nihilism was spread throughout the culture, not only among the youth. But again, we find this kind of ideological fatigue projected primarily onto the young. The authors play out national anxieties on the young.

See also Schwarz, *Der konservative Anarchist*, 169 for nihilism's importance in Jünger's thinking and 171 for an interesting nexus of nihilism and child, confirming the confluence of youth and the metaphysical crisis that preoccupied Jünger.

56. Jünger, *Der Friede*, 70.
57. Ibid., 15.
58. Ibid., 59.
59. Along similar lines, in *Strahlungen*'s last section, *Jahre der Okkupation*, Jünger recounts his satisfaction at young people's reading *Der Friede*, being affected by, basically paying homage to, Jünger's word to the young: "Ich habe den Eindruck, daß diese unter allen meinen Schriften am schnellsten bekannt geworden ist, in Wochen, lawinenartig, obwohl keine Presse sie druckte, kein Buchhändler sie verkaufte, keine Zeitung sie besprach. Das Ganze geht auf einige Abschriften zurück, die ich verschenkt habe. Zum Eigentümlichen unserer Lage gehört, daß wir in einen vortechnischen Zustand versetzt wurden. Nichts kann lehrreicher sein" (30 Aug. 1945, 2:525).
60. Schwarz comments that this idea is very similar to those of the resistance circle, the Kreisauer, although he could establish no contact between Jünger and the group. *Der konservative Anarchist*, 297n25. The similarity, I would submit, rests in the ubiquity, currency, and power of the youth discourse in this context.
61. See, for a summary of this group's stance on voting rights, Benz, "Konzeptionen für die Nachkriegsdemokratie." I thank Sean Forner for drawing my attention to this point.
62. This is Nevin's stance in *Ernst Jünger and Germany*.
63. I analyze Bartov's writings on this topic in the introduction. See "Defining Enemies, Making Victims," 788–90.

Chapter 4

1. Stegemann, "Ernst Wiechert," 44.
2. Clark, "Prophet without Honour," 200. Clark recounts how Jaspers, though clearly an opponent of the Nazi regime, never took a public stance

against National Socialism during the regime. According to Clark's account, Jaspers verbally acknowledged Hitler only twice between 1933 and 1945.

3. Jaspers, "Philosophical Autobiography," 66.
4. Clark, "Prophet without Honour," 197.
5. Rabinbach, *In the Shadow of Catastrophe*, esp. his chapter 4 on Jaspers, "The German as Pariah: Karl Jasper's *The Question of German Guilt.*"
6. Jaspers, *Question of German Guilt.*
7. Arendt, "Jaspers as a Citizen of the World," 543, quoted in Rabinbach, *In the Shadow of Catastrophe*, 139.
8. Rabinbach, *In the Shadow of Catastrophe*, 139.
9. "Though Jaspers was far less interested in the formal elements of a new democratic parliamentary system—parties, interest groups, trade unions, and so on—he focused his attention on the moral element, what he believed was the missing element in the German experience." Ibid., 140.
10. Jaspers's inclination to private communication despite his clarion call to public engagement becomes the focus of Rabinbach's chapter in its emphasis on Jaspers's relation to Heidegger. Though Jaspers penned innumerable pages of responses to and critique of Heidegger, he published almost none of it. Despite an emphatic ethic of public political discourse, many of his vehement critiques remained private.
11. Rabinbach, *In the Shadow of Catastrophe*, 140.
12. Remy, *Heidelberg Myth*, 170; Clark, "Prophet without Honour," 208.
13. Two recent examples are Olick, *In the House of the Hangman*, 270–96, and Brockmann, *German Literary Culture at the Zero Hour*, 34–36.
14. Curtius, "Goethe oder Jaspers," quoted in Arendt and Jaspers, *Correspondence*, 714. Originally appeared in the *Zeit*, 28 Apr. 1949.
15. Olick covers this exchange without remarking on its reeducational frame; he focuses instead on its importance for the guilt discussion. *In the House of the Hangman*, 284–85.
16. This is the conclusion in Bolz, "Ansätze zur Universitätsreform," 64.
17. Ritter, "Der deutsche Professor." For testimony to the importance of this article, see Remy, *Heidelberg Myth*, 2.
18. Mannheim, "Die Rolle der Universitäten," 50.
19. "Die Universitäten sind als solche aus dem Geiste der europaischen Entwicklung geboren. Ihre große Bedeutung und Leistung in der deutschen Geschichte wird von niemandem in den angelsächsischen Ländern geleugnet. Im selben Geiste der Achtung für große menschliche Leistung hat man in England und Amerika auch während des Krieges die deutschen Komponisten aufgeführt, die deutschen Dichter gelesen und genau so unentwegt die wirklich bleibenden Leistungen der deutschen Philosophie und Geistesgeschichte diskutiert." Ibid., 50.

20. Arendt to Jaspers, no. 42, 9 July 1946, in Arendt and Jaspers, *Correspondence.*
21. "[Die Universität] wird auch nicht unpolitisch sein, im Gegenteil einen gewichtigen Beitrag zur Legierung von Geist und Politik leisten, aber als Ort der Vorbereitung, nicht des Handelns." Münster, "Die Universität 1946," 9.
22. "die deutsche Universität muß in einem bestimmten Sinne noch nationaler werden als zuvor. . . . National wird die neue Universität sein, da ihr, nachdem des staatliche Gehäuse bedeutend geschwächt ist, die Führung der Nation mehr als je zufallen wird." Mannheim, "Die Rolle der Universitäten," 50.
23. Tent, *Mission on the Rhine,* 84.
24. Ibid., 79.
25. See Wolgast, "Karl-Heinz Bauer"; also discussed in Rabinbach, *In the Shadow of Catastrophe,* 134, 135.
26. Discussed in de Rosa, "Politische Akzente im Leben eines Philosophen," 403–5.
27. "Full frankness and honesty harbors not only our dignity—possible even in impotence—but our own chance. The question for every German is whether to go this way at the risk of all disappointments, at the risk of additional losses and of convenient abuse by the powerful. The answer is that this is the only way that can save our souls from a pariah existence." Jaspers, *The Question of German Guilt,* 10.
28. Olick, *In the House of the Hangman,* 273.
29. Though Remy does tend to Jaspers's lectures and writings on behalf of the university, he does not so much focus on the trajectory of Jasper's thought over the course of these essays, understandably so, since Remy's study (*The Heidelberg Myth*) focuses on the wider context of Heidelberg. For Remy, for instance, it remains a contradiction that Jaspers spoke out on behalf of the university so eloquently but did not really advocate or realize significant change in the university. I argue that it is precisely this contradiction that reading for the discourse about youth can help illuminate: Jaspers argues for the conservation of important aspects of the university with a particular image of the young student.
30. Clark, "Prophet without Honour," 211.
31. For the exculpatory content of many such addresses, see Olick, *In the House of the Hangman,* 276.
32. Jaspers, "Erneuerung der Universität," 96.
33. Jaspers, *The Question of German Guilt,* 65–66.
34. Jaspers, "Erneuerung der Universität," 102.
35. For an illustrative instance related to youth, see von Blanckhagen, "Der Falsche Charakter." Von Blanckhagen attempts to shift the emphasis on

"character" as it was inherited from Nazi propaganda to a postwar focus on *Menschlichkeit.*

36. Jaspers, "Erneuerung der Universität," 103.

37. See Rabinbach, chapter 4, "The German as Pariah: Karl Jaspers's *The Question of German Guilt,*" in *In the Shadow of Catastrophe,* 129–65. See Olick's chapter 12, "The Philosophy of Guilt," in *In the House of the Hangman,* 270–93.

38. Jaspers, "Die Verantwortlichkeit der Universitäten."

39. Ibid.

40. "Thus, while every university is part of a nation, it has its sights set on goals above and beyond nationhood. Differences aside, in this respect, at least, it is akin to the idea of the church. The university proper must not take sides in the conflict between nations, even though as human beings its members have each their national allegiance. Members of the university, whether faculty, deans, or the president himself, abuse their position if they should choose to hold political rallies in favor of either a particular party or of a country as a whole." Jaspers, *Idea of the University,* 134.

41. Jaspers, "Philosophical Autobiography" 40; Jaspers, "Über meine Philosophie," 24, 34.

42. Jaspers, "Volk und Universität," 278.

43. Jaspers, *Idea of the University,* 1.

44. "Das unterscheidet die Hochschule von der Schule: dieses Bewußtsein des Ungenügens Aller, diese Last für jeden Einzelnen, seine Aufgabe frei zu wählen, diese Ablehnung fester Lehrpläne, die nur in den unteren Bereichen des auch an der Universität unerläßlichen Schulbetriebs gelten." Jaspers, "Der lebendige Geist der Universität," 238.

45. For a useful summary of the concept of the "common room," see Young-Bruehl on Jaspers in her *Freedom.*

46. Jaspers, "Europa der Gegenwart," 251, 267, 274. This work was originally a lecture held in Geneva in September 1946 for the Rencontres Internationales, a conference whose other speakers included Lukács; it was first published in German in Jaspers, *Vom europäischen Geist.*

47. Young-Bruehl, *Freedom,* 10.

48. "'European' seems, then, to us to be, first, the depth of human communication between independent individuals, and, second, conscious labor for the freedom of public conditions by means of the forms which shape the will in community. But absolute truth, and with it freedom, is never attained; truth is on the way." Translation from Jaspers's 1946 *Vom europäischen Geist (of European Spirit),* 36. Similarly, Jaspers in *Idea of the University:* "The greatness of our Western history consists of the movements towards freedom which arise *in discussion*" (41).

49. Jaspers, "Philosophical Autobiography," 14, 24.

50. Ibid., 46.
51. "Without mundane concepts, existential communication has no phenomenal medium; without communication, such contents are senseless and void." Jaspers, *Philosophy*, 2:62–64.
52. Jaspers, *Idea of the University*, 41, 104.
53. Rabinbach, *In the Shadow of Catastrophe*, 139–40.
54. Jaspers, *Philosophy*, 1:246.
55. Jaspers, *Idea of the University*, 12–13.
56. Young-Bruehl, *Freedom*, 23.
57. Remy, *Heidelberg Myth*, 8.
58. Jaspers, "Erneuerung der Universität," 227.
59. Ibid., 231.
60. Jaspers, *Idea of the University*, 88: "The reunification of the university . . . cannot simply mean restoring things to their medieval unity. The whole content of modern knowledge and research must be integrated: broadening the scope of the university must initiate a genuine unification of all branches of learning."
61. De Rosa, "Politische Akzente im Leben eines Philosophen," 376.
62. Tent, *Mission on the Rhine*, 83.
63. Naimark, *Russians in Germany*, esp. 444. Though the Soviets trumpeted their efforts to increase the number of students from working-class and farmer backgrounds, the execution of this policy proved much more difficult than anticipated.
64. Adorno, "Zur Demokratisierung der deutschen Universitäten," 334–35.
65. See, for example, Gerst, "Wer darf studieren?" or Dirks, "Wer soll studieren dürfen?"
66. Though he admitted that there were social groups that had long been underrepresented among students, Jaspers characteristically insisted on intellectual "excellence" for students which, he admitted, would favor those families equipped to foster such excellence.
67. See Olick, *In the House of the Hangman*, 276 for convincing detail on the prevalence of this interpretation in the early postwar period.
68. Jaspers, *Idea of the University*, 118.
69. See, for instance, Rommelspacher, "Neuer und alter Geist in der Studentenschaft."
70. Jaspers, *Idea of the University*, 39.
71. Ibid.
72. Jaspers, as has been described in some detail by other scholars, gave a controversial speech upon receiving the 1947 Goethe Prize that criticized not so much Goethe himself as the cult that had grown up around him after the war, one that regarded the reading of Goethe and other classics as a panacea for Germany's cultural and spiritual crisis. See Brockmann, *Ger-*

man Literary Culture at the Zero Hour, 127–29.

73. In his analysis of the denazification of the University of Heidelberg, Remy focuses much more on the struggles between university personnel and the U.S. forces; he does not much address, for instance, the role of Max Bock, the most important labor leader involved in the reform of the university. *Heidelberg Myth.*

74. In terms of basic background on the interesting figure of Penham, both Clark ("A Prophet without Honour") and Remy (*Heidelberg Myth*) offer rich material, though they do not so much feature Bauer's specific reaction to Penham. Bauer certainly implied these kinds of organized attacks by elements outside the university. In February 1946, he sent a memo to Major Crum, the Counter-Intelligence Corps officer responsible for Heidelberg who was investigating Penham's request to reclose the university: after calling the churches and universities cultural/spiritual leaders, Bauer wrote to Crum that "Wir haben viele Beweise für diesen parteipolitischen Kampf gegen die Universität, und es ist kein Zweifel, daß einzelne unruhige Elemente an der Universität Beauftragte von Organisationen außerhalb der Universität sind." After investigating Penham's accusations, Major Crum had Penham reassigned.

75. Remy, *Heidelberg Myth,* 167.

76. See the letters from the summer of 1946 in Jaspers and Bauer, *Briefwechsel,* 43–47.

77. The producer, an anatomy professor at Heidelberg, wrote that the program comprised a lecture by a different professor each week and was intended to win the "trust and understanding" of the wider public. He observed optimistically that university professors were now addressing the people more than before, and "we hope that one hears us more frequently than one did before." The broadcasts included presentations by such prominent professors as Gustav Radbruch ("The Renewal of Law") and K. H. Bauer ("Is Cancer Increasing?"). The lecture series is summarized by de Rosa, *Erneuerung der Universität,* 295–97.

78. Jaspers, in his memoirs, as quoted in de Rosa, *Erneuerung der Universität,* 296.

79. De Rosa reproduces the text in *Erneuerung der Universität,* 449–54.

80. Jasper, "Volk und Universität, 280.

81. For instance: "Die Ablehnung der Parteien durch die junge Generation in Deutschland ist nicht nur mit jugendlicher Unreife, mangelnder Erfahrung und Einsicht zu erklären. . . . Offenbar . . . findet die Jugend im engen Raum der Gegenwart von heute keine Gelegenheit zu einer Politik, wie sie sie täglich vor sich sieht." Böttcher, "Die junge Generation," 761.

82. See Füssl, *Die Umerziehung der Deutschen,* 61.

83. Jaspers to Arendt, no. 35, 12 Mar. 1946, in Arendt and Jaspers, *Correspondence;* Jaspers to Arendt, no. 44, 18 Sept. 46, in Arendt and Jaspers, *Correspondence.*

84. Arendt to Jaspers, no. 47, 11 Nov. 1946, in Arendt and Jaspers, *Correspondence.*

85. In discussing student selection, Jaspers also invoked an "Aristokratie des Geistes" to defend continuing the university admission selection: "Wir stehen gegen die Priviligierung durch Stand, Klasse, Besitz, Parti zugunsten des Rechts aller auf gleiche Chancen. Das heißt nicht, daß wir abschaffen könnten oder wollten: die Aristokratie des Geistes, die jedem offen steht nach dem Maße seiner Begabung und seiner freien Selbsterziehung." "Die Verantwortlichkeit der Universitäten."

86. Jaspers does consider the potential political activities of faculty members in *Idea of the University,* but the resulting highly contradictory statement does not in effect ban party politics among professors, though it would seem to indicate a desire to do so: "Faculty members cannot invoke their constitutional freedom of speech except as private citizens. They cannot expect the university with which they are professionally affiliated to come out in their support when they speak as private citizens. They are entitled to this protection only in matters relating to professional publication, but not in connection with casual political remarks, opinions, or newspaper articles. Academic freedom does not entitle them to special privilege over other citizens" (132).

87. See Wolin, *Heidegger Controversy* for the relevant documents and details. It includes Jaspers's letter to the Freiburg denazification committee (144–51).

88. "Wrecherts schwermütig-grüblerischen Werke, die von der 'magischen ostischen Welt' geprägt sind, zählten zu der im In- und Ausland am meisten gelesenen deutschen Literatur unserer Zeit." Lennartz, *Deutsche Schriftsteller des 20,* Jh. 1866.

89. An MLA database search under "Ernst Wiechert" yielded only eighty-six entries. Eighty-six entries is a pittance for an author with the readership and resonance of Wiechert: for example, a search under "Ernst Jünger" turned up over four hundred and one under "Thomas Mann" turned up over thirty-six hundred.

90. Claude Davis, quoted in Boag, *Ernst Wiechert,* 51.

91. Werner, "Der atomisierte geistige Raum."

92. "Der innere Zwang der vergangenen zwölf Jahre hat aus einem der wenigen Dichter, die diese Zeit innerhalb Deutschlands überstanden, einen Politiker gemacht. . . . Ernst Wiechert meistert die in der jüngsten Vergangenheit so schwer geschändete deutsche Sprache wie nur sehr wenige derer, die von ihr leben. . . . Dennoch wurde die Veranstaltung zur Höhe

einer religiösen Weihestunde erhoben, und die Zuhörer verließen das Theater lautlos, als gingen sie aus einer Kirche." "Ernst Wiechert las in den Münchener Kammerspielen."

93. "Ernst Wiechert als Ankläger."

94. "Nach berühmten Mustern."

95. Alexander Parlach (pseudonym for Erich Kuby), "Die erste und einzige Rede deutscher Jugend an ihren Dichter," *Der Ruf* 2, no. 25, 10, cited in Brockmann, *German Literary Culture at the Zero Hour*, 184.

96. See Boag, *Ernst Wiechert* in his chapter on "The Life," 29: "He could no longer walk under his own trees secure in the knowledge of his own physical safety, for Wiechert had received letters threatening him with physical violence."

97. One does not want to begin the job of judging the severity of someone's time in a concentration camp, but it seems fairly clear that Wiechert's stay was curtailed due to the intervention of friends and that he probably exaggerated his persecution under the Nazis. For instance, after his stay at Buchenwald, he was invited to a poets' conference, and during the entire Third Reich he was able to earn more than enough money from his earlier writings to live comfortably.

98. See, for example, *Wälder und Menschen* (1936) or *Jahre und Zeiten* (1949), two of his memoirs, for these recurring themes.

99. Stegemann calls all the speeches that Wiechert made to the young "Reden an die deutche Jugend," when in fact only one carried that title. "Ernst Wiechert," 44.

100. Boag, *Ernst Wiechert*, 7, 18.

101. Ibid., 11: "Of much greater significance than his first taste of university life was, at this stage of his development, his stay at the home of the old Junker family of Baron Grotthuß. . . . The Grotthuß family possessed what he in his family environment could never have known, 'Wesen und Adel der Kultur.' . . . No experience could have been better calculated to lend substance to Wiechert's growing awareness that man's moral progress was far from being inevitable. The most modern views were not necessarily the best."

102. Stegemann, "Ernst Wiechert," 45.

103. In "Rede an die deutsche Jugend," he says:

> Ja, was sollen wir tun?
> Zweimal, meine Freunde, habe ich versucht Ihnen eine Antwort auf diese Frage zu geben. Das erste Mal im Jahre 1933, das zweite Mal zwei Jahre später. (Wiechert, *Rede an die deutsche Jugend*, 27)

Future references will be made parenthetically in the text.

104. "Aber all diese, meine Freunde, so sehr sie brannten in der Not ihrer Zeit,

erhoben ihre Stimme aus der Ferne. Keiner von ihnen stand auf den Märkten der Zeit, sondern sie standen in der Einsamkeit der Wissenden und der Seher, in einer solchen Einsamkeit, daß zwei von ihnen daran zerbrachen." Wiechert, *Der Dichter und die Jugend,* 37.

105. It is interesting to keep in mind here what purpose youth serves in Thomas Mann's *Doktor Faustus,* in which Adrian's *Durchbruch* in art and into the public is one of the text's undeniable leitmotifs. There as well as in Wiechert's reading of his own life, youth is intimately intertwined with the theme of breaking through from stereotypical German Innerlichkeit to something outside, something bigger.

106. Wiechert, *Der Dichter und die Jugend,* 38.

107. Ibid., 41.

108. I owe this insight to Mark Clark.

109. "[Wiechert] received an invitation in 1935 to address the students at the University of Munich. He was confronted, he claims, with the agonising decision whether or not to omit any reference to the internal political situation in Germany. . . . His sincere love of the individual and distaste for mass movements, his belief in personal inviolability . . . all conspired to force him to adopt a decisive stand against the Nazis and all they represented. Wiechert chose to speak out fearlessly." Boag, *Ernst Wiechert,* 20.

After the 1935 speech, Wiechert remained in trouble with the Nazis, but they tolerated him until 1938, in part because of his popularity. But when Martin Niemöller was rearrested, Wiechert wrote to the party refusing to continue to contribute to the *Winterhilfe* fund, instead sending his contribution to Niemöller's family. Soon thereafter his house was searched, he was arrested, and then he was sent to Buchenwald.

110. Wiechert, "Der Dichter und seine Zeit," 368.

111. Ibid., 369, 370.

112. See Schneider, "Melodie des Leids," which I discuss below as well.

113. Wiechert, "Der Dichter und seine Zeit," 364.

114. Ibid.,

115. Ibid., 376.

116. Stegemann, "Ernst Wiechert," 45.

117. "Kaum eindrucksvoller und grundlegender hätte diese Reihe begonnen werden können als mit dieser Rede, die Ernst Wiechert im November 1945 im Münchner Schauspielhaus gehalten hat. Mit ihr ist der Dichter aus seinem persönlichen Rahmen herausgetreten und hat sich als Mahner und Seelenführer vor sein Volk gestellt." "Ernst Wiechert als Mahner—Rede an die deutsche Jugend. 1945. Europäische Dokumente, H1. Kulturpolitische Schriftenreihe des Zinne-Verlags München," *Neue Zeit* (Berlin), 2 Dec. 1945.

118. Freisel, "Der neue Ernst Wiechert."

119. Wiechert, *Rede an die deutsche Jugend,* 21, 24.
120. Ibid., 13, 14, 20, 23.
121. "Sie [Liebe] aus den Herzen der Jugend zu reißen, war die entscheidend-ste Aufgabe dieser zwölf Jahre, das A und O einer ganzen Weltanschau-ung, verschleiert und verheimlicht, aber im Verschleierten wie Verheim-lichten mit der glühenden Leidenschaft betrieben, mit der der Mörder seinen ersten und letzten Stoß führt." Ibid., 31.
122. Jünger, of course, made precisely this move, i.e., highlighting the youth while downplaying other victims (Jews, political prisoners, Slavs, gays, gypsies, et al.). Cf. ibid., 30.
123. Ibid., 36.
124. Ibid., 32.
125. Ibid., 35.
126. Ibid., 38.
127. Schneider, "Melodie des Leids."

Chapter 5

1. See Rentschler, *Ministry of Illusion;* Hake, *Popular Cinema of the Third Reich;* Koepnick, *Dark Mirror.*
2. The story of the postwar German film market is fascinating, but I shall have to limit my account to German-made feature films made between 1945–49. It is, however, important to keep in mind that these rubble films represent only a fraction of what was being shown in German cine-mas—and an especially small fraction of the overall ticket receipts. By fall 1945, synchronized foreign films were showing all around Germany. Many of these were accompanied by newsreels, either merely synchro-nized (as in the French zone) or cut together and rewritten from other materials (as in the American and Soviet zones). The unsuccessful efforts of the Americans, in particular, to produce documentary films (e.g., *Todesmühlen*) to assist in the reeducation effort around German atrocities is often noted and well described. Finally, many of the cinemas played pre-1945 German films whose release had been approved by the Allies. For instance, the release of Käutner's formerly banned *Große Freiheit No. 7* was a huge hit.
3. Mückenberger and Jordan, *"Sie sehen selbst,"* 34.
4. Ibid., 22.
5. Stalin articulated the theory of "two Germanys" as follows: "It would be absurd to equate the Hitler clique with the German people. The experi-ences of history suggest that the Hitlers come and go, but the German people, the German nation remains." Quoted in Dietrich, *Politik und Kultur,* 15; cf. Pike, *Politics of Culture,* 12.

6. "Within weeks of the war's end, the Communists had started talking about a broad antifascist-democratic consensus; and it soon became routine to speak in terms of a 'mass movement' to argue that considerable segments of the population favored the KPD's policies." Pike, *Politics of Culture*, 14.

7. Many of these films were termed "rubble films." This term was applied derogatorily by film critics to films appearing in the late 1940s that prominently featured the rubble of the current social context. Because so many studios had been destroyed and those remaining were under the tight and usually unyielding control of the Allies, much production was forced (as in Italy) to shoot on location. Even after they were allowed to use the studios, many films continued to highlight the current social context, most conspicuous in shots of rubble.

8. See, for instance, "Filmthema der Zeit," 12–13: "The question of our young people's future and goals is among those themes to which the postwar film has emphatically devoted itself."

9. Heimann, *Künstler und SED-Kulturpolitik;* Brandlmeier, "Von Hitler zu Adenauer," 39.

10. For a contemporary critic's negative evaluation of the recurring and often redundant theme of the Heimkehrer, see E.R.,"Hans Albers in der Trümmerstadt."

11. For these theories, the male, though (as all subjects) lacking and castrated, remains the constructed site of wholeness and plenty through his denial of lack, his compensation for it via his controlling and desiring position as regards gender difference. See Mulvey, "Visual Pleasure and Narrative Cinema," 751. She and other theorists tend to concentrate on the way in which women are voyeuristically or fetishistically objectified to firm up the juggernaut of male subjectivity.

12. Most influential feminist psychoanalytic film theory emphasizes gender difference as the fundamental difference for language and society and subsequently feature film. See ibid. While I would not dispute the superlative nature of these claims, other differences seem pivotal in the construction of patriarchal hierarchies, among them, I am arguing, is generational difference.

13. In her *Male Subjectivity,* Silverman criticizes traditional feminist psychoanalytic theory for its reductive, simplified treatment of the relation between male subjectivity and gender difference in film. In contrast to the active, desiring males posited by such theories, she discusses marginal males who either struggle with or relinquish the usually privileged position of the male subject in the film. She, however, always emphasizes their relation to gender difference in subverting this traditional privilege.

14. Fisher, "Deleuze in a Ruinous Context."

15. See, for instance, Deleuze, *Cinema 1*, 205. For Mulvey and other feminist psychoanalytic theorists, the binary between male and female corresponds unequivocally to the binary between active and passive: "An active/passive heterosexual division of labor has similarly controlled narrative structure." "Visual Pleasure and Narrative Cinema," 751.

16. This inversion of old social as well as specular relations reigns over the first scenes of the first postwar film, *The Murderers Are among Us:* Susanne becomes the actively desiring and productive character, while Mertens's active and effective gaze is consistently undercut. In Susanne and Mertens's initial encounters, *The Murderers Are among Us* inverts the traditional courtship roles by making Susanne the desiring subject and Mertens the preoccupied, tortured, aloof love object. Throughout the film's early scenes, when she looks at him desirously, he averts his eyes: the now-lacking masculine gaze that should be active orients itself inwards, to the damage that prevents him from successfully reintegrating himself into traditional social roles, here the male subject desiring the female.

17. Due to the precarious and carefully controlled condition of the old film studios, many films were shot at least partially on location. In terms of Germany's most famous studio, the studio of Ufa, the dominant production company of the 1920s–1940s, the Soviets did not allow German directors to shoot there until *1-2-3 Corona* (1948). More than an accident, however, the presence of the rubble was thematized by the films in their recurring connection between the rubble of the cities and the rubble inside the men (always the men).

18. In many films, the child also resists socialization by the mother—for example, in *Somewhere in Berlin* and *Before Us Life*. The main conflict in the film, however, usually focuses on the tension between son and father.

19. Their presence and actions signify the lack and castration of the patriarch that film theoreticians Silverman, Studlar, and Shaviro locate in inverted gender relations. I mentioned Silverman above, but Studlar and Shaviro have lodged similar critiques of feminist psychoanalytic film theory. See Studlar, *In the Realm of Pleasure* and Shaviro, *Cinematic Body*.

20. Discussed in Silverman, *Male Subjectivity*, 57–61. Both Studlar and Shaviro emphasize the myopia of locating pleasure only in the sadistic and ego-binding image. Both see cinematic pleasure derived from images that cause the ego pain or dissolution. Studlar elaborates her version of a masochistic cinematic image in her second chapter of *In the Realm of Pleasure*, "Masochism and Visual Pleasure: The Link to the Pre-Oedipal Development," 29–49. In his more direct antagonism of psychoanalytic theory, Shaviro finds it "weird" that "[semiotic and psychoanalytic theory] associates visual pleasure almost exclusively with the illusion of a stable and centered subject confronting a spatially and temporally homoge-

neous world. . . . A wide variety of cinematic pleasures are predicated explicitly on decentered freeplay, the freedom from the constraints of subjectivity." *Cinematic Body,* 42.

21. Many early DEFA films are saturated with such shots of men who, according to Deluze's sensory-motor scheme, should be looking at objects and then dominating them, now look wearily at their surroundings while actually looking into themselves. For example, in *And Once Again 48!* (Gustav von Wangenheim, 1948, DEFA, Soviet license), Ernst Borchert plays another lacking male who sports the same faraway looks as Mertens in *The Murderers Are among Us.*

22. In psychoanalytic theory, the desiring male gaze acts to cover up his lack and castration and shore up his ego. Looking at the woman with desire and then winning her affirms the male ego all the more. Mulvey, "Visual Pleasure and Narrative Cinema," 748; Gledhill, "Recent Developments in Feminist Criticism," 108–9.

23. Deleuze, *Cinema 1,* 201, 214.

24. In this respect, *The Murderers Are among Us* attempts to represent this key duel in the postwar period: the confrontation between those who were more and less guilty of atrocities. In *The Murderers Are among Us* this conflict was already somewhat internalized as a struggle not between Mertens and Brückner but really within Mertens himself; in other early DEFA films, this confrontation disappears altogether. The conflicts, confrontations, duels that might have been created with the past are dissolved into the struggles of the present—the key one of which, I am arguing, was gaining control of one's own children and reconstituting the system of control around children.

25. L.M., "Im Dschungel der zertrümmerten Stadt."

26. Gieschen, "*Irgendwo in Berlin.*" Gieschen emphasizes that despite our not meeting Iller in the first part of the film, he, with his fate shared by millions, is the center of the narrative.

27. Lenning, "*Irgendwo in Berlin.*"

28. Shorter accounts often merely mention the title and the fact that it was the second feature of the postwar period. See, for instance, Rentschler, "Germany," 212. Becker and Schöll, in an entire book on films made in the period 1945–55, mention the film only a couple of times, and cite its most superficial themes of Heimkehrer among the rubble struggling for food. *In Jenen Tagen,* 66.

29. Lamprecht himself spoke of this dual representation of youth in an interview. "In my film, the two main roles are played by children. One boy is a very sheltered child, who is very much rooted in his home. Opposite him is a figure of a neglected boy whose parents have disappeared." "Kulturarbeit nach einem Jahr." Critics likewise underscored this duality:

"Gustav Iller is the brightest and, at the same time, most thoughtful of the boys. . . . the two boys play the lighter and darker sides of life, which they embody, with childish and youthful zeal, adaptability, and wildness." K.D., "*Irgendwo in Berlin.*"

30. Critics picked this figure out as a recurring threatening type from the social context. A.M.U., "*Irgendwo in Berlin.*"

31. Rentschler, "Germany," 213.

32. See Gieschen's review in *Der Morgen Berlin* and Fiedler's in *Neue Zeit,* both of which highlight the general, shared fate of *Somewhere in Berlin*'s Heimkehrer, Iller.

33. In a speech to his friend Kalle, Iller makes this fatigue and loss of faith explicit. He recounts how all during the war he fantasized about coming home only to return and find everything for which he had been pining was destroyed. Once again he informs viewers that nothing seems to matter anymore.

34. For contemporary critics, see, for instance, Ihering, "Mit Sauberkeit der Gesinnung." Modern critics cite the film as exemplary for the postwar rubble- and antifascist film in both Germany and the United States. See, for instance, the entry on early postwar film in the Fischer Press's basic film history: Thiele, "Die Lehren aus der Vergangenheit." For a recent American study, see Silberman, "The Discourse of Powerlessness: Wolfgang Staudte's *Rotation,*" in *German Cinema.*

35. For instance, the wedding scene early in the flashback, with its soundtrack from *The Threepenny Opera,* was cited by contemporary critics as a citation of and a return to the milieu of *Kuhle Wampe.* Joho, "Nicht Originell." Silberman also elaborates the influence of this filmic tradition on *Rotation* in his chapter on the film. *German Cinema,* 102.

36. In recounting his generation of and motivation in the concept of *Rotation,* Staudte cites his own case: he was proud that Hitler refused to take him into service but later recognized that this kind of passive resistance cannot suffice. The film then becomes an exhortation to a more active resistance on the part of the passive acquiescer. "Interview mit Staudte," 15.

37. Even the film's original ending, which Staudte also discusses in the same interview (ibid.), confirms this lack of traditional political activism, this substitution of good parenting and pedagogy for politics. The film's original ending had Hans burning the son's uniform after giving him his old suit and saying, "That was the last uniform you'll ever wear." Though the burning of a uniform would seem to imply a more direct confrontation with politics—like his throwing an ashtray at the Führerbild—the gesture rests primarily in a father mandating what his son wears. He does not even mention refusing the Nazi Party pin he has had on his lapel—Hans after

all never donned a uniform—let alone demand an active participation in collective or public politics.

38. In his chapter for Fischer's *Filmgeschichte*, "Die Lehren aus der Vergangenheit," Thiel discusses all these key themes and even storyboards the cage collage but does not mention the operation of a generational thematic in them.

39. Silberman comes close to this insight near the end of his chapter, but does not end up elaborating it as a theme throughout the film. *German Cinema*, 111–12. It is not only the ending that suddenly associates paternity with politics.

40. The scene seems strangely quiet in large part because the film contains no nondiegetic sound, thus no sound track outside of the action within the frame. The use of only diegetic music adds to the film's realism and permits the blunted sound in this scene to stand out all the more.

41. The graffiti constitute one of the counterdiscourses to the Nazi propaganda machine that the film thematizes. As noted above, various kinds of texts and communicative media—newspapers, graffiti, radio, leaflets, maps—recur throughout *Rotation*.

42. The film protocol for *Rotation,* which describes all major camera movements and sketches the actors' basic gestures, outlines this part of scene 31, shots 86–89: "The camera tilts quickly upward—and happens upon Hans Behnke's face. He looks strangely tense. His facial expression is unreadable, there's something of an incredulous astonishment in it. . . . Hans can't manage to get a word out. It must be something decisive going on—he begins to pace back and forth in the small room, just to get himself together. Finally he finds the first words. . . . Lotte looks up relieved, and her gaze follows Hans as he paces back and forth. He doesn't exactly look angry. But somehow she still does not know what feelings were evoked in him [by the news]." The film protocol also emphasizes the recurring theme of Hans's eyes in moments of crucial decision. Not only does the camera pan to his face and focus on his eyes, but the script dictates that the sound track should have a tenor singing "Deine Augen saugen mir die Seele" at the climactic moments of the scene. Close-ups or pans to Hans's eyes will follow in parallel moments of both his political and parental indecision.

43. For instance, the film protocol makes sure that the scene is shot such that viewers have a sense of Hans's speechlessness, his powerlessness, and his inability to see into the room that is controlled by the midwife: "[Shot] 118. . . . The door opens and Ms. Peschke appears with a bowl in her hands. She closes the door quickly behind her, so that Hans cannot see into the room. . . . [Shot] 119 Hans follows every movement of the midwife speechlessly with his eyes."

44. For the birth scene, the film protocol also calls for symphonic music, which would link it to Helmuth's renunciation of Hans to the tune of Beethoven's Fifth. Though critics often point out the irony of German classical music providing the diegetic background to a Nazi son's renunciation of his dad, they tend not to observe its integration into generational conflicts that anticipate the penultimate betraying one.

45. This theme also recurs in other postwar films like *The Buntkarierten*, in which young Susa is reprimanded for singing along with a Nazi military parade.

46. The importance of this scene has been cited in later scholarship, though it always neglects Helmuth's role in the window action. For instance, "Alte Film neu gesehen: *Rotation*," *Film* 10 (Oct. 1965): 45.

47. Thiel, "Die Lehren aus der Vergangenheit" discusses this proposed intercutting, which was eventually vetoed by Soviet censors because they did not want any footage of Nazis that might have been construed as positive. As noted above, Staudte wrangled for nine months with the Soviet authorities to keep the footage in but eventually had to give in.

48. As Thiel notes in "Die Lehren aus der Vergangenheit," the honor list offers another of *Rotation*'s many texts from the National Socialist context, but it also, I would argue, connects directly to the youth in the classroom.

49. The film protocol calls for more classroom quizzing about countries that the Nazis would eventually try to conquer, a kind of anticipatory geography for the would-be conquerors.

50. The film protocol calls for Helmuth to answer one of the questions, but the film cut out this sequence and so we never actually see Helmuth in the scene.

51. This dueling exchange of generational gazes also recurs in a great many early postwar films. I have already talked about Iller versus his son and then Willi in *Somewhere in Berlin;* Werner the son stares down his father in *And the Heavens Above;* Walter the lost son similarly stares down his father Mauthner in *The Last Illusion;* the same recurs in the generational duels in *Ways into Twilight, And We Find Each Other Again,* and *Before Us Life.*

52. The press materials on the film also emphasize this scene as the film's climax. The summary offered on the back of the *Illustrierter Film-Spiegel: "Rotation"* concludes with: "It is the love for humanity that will guide [Hans's] life and this love finds expression when father and son see one another again and the older one makes a clean break with the inhumanity of the recent past with a lovely gesture [of reconciliation]." With one little gesture, Hans sweeps away history—of course, this marvelous gesture is one of *Versöhnung,* of intergenerational differentiation and recon-

ciliation.

53. The film protocol underscores this sense by connecting Helmuth's inability to read Hans with Lotte's attempt to interpret his reaction in the pregnancy scene.

Chapter 6

1. Käunter, "Demontage der Traumfabrik."
2. One of East Germany's most important critics, Walter Lenning of the *Berliner Zeitung*, published an article in *Neue Filmwelt* dedicated to the issue: "Was heißt Traumfabrik" explains how American films pander to viewers because they see film as a commodity. Lenning argues that even a good film like Billy Wilder's *The Lost Weekend* can be ruined by the inescapable observance of Traumfabrik laws—even a talented Ufa-trained director can be corrupted by Hollywood. Lenning asserts that German films are now at a watershed and must learn to distinguish mere Traumfabrik production from the artistically ambitious. For more articles on the status of the Traumfabrik model after the war, see Reisfeld, "Ende der Traum-Fabrik?"; Ringelband, "Kapitaluation des künstlerischen Films?"; Biermann-Ratjen, "Realste Realistik im Film."
3. N.n., "Quo Vadis Italia?" *Neue Filmwelt* 7, no. 3 (1949): 4–5.
4. See, for instance, Rentschler's analysis of *Glückskinder* in *Ministry of Illusion*, 103–12, which demonstrates what a high profile American cinema retained even after 1933. Welch explains the circumstances under which U.S. films were banned by Goebbels. *Propaganda and the German Cinema*, 256.
5. There is a massive and rich literature on stars within film studies, but I have chosen to highlight two scholars working in this area in part because they both emphasize the wider social field and the stars' ideological function within it. Dyer's study *Stars* was groundbreaking in this endeavor and was recently rereleased in a new edition. McDonald has a supplementary chapter in the new edition of *Stars* entitled "Reconceptualising Stars"; here and in another volume (*Star System*) McDonald extends and deepens Dyer's original project. I shall also be citing other relevant studies that substantially supplement some of Dyer's and McDonald's basic analyses of stars within their social context.
6. Moreover, as outsiders who support the dominant fictions of society, they willfully choose their liminal position: they are outside of their own volition, rather than being forcibly excluded by the context. Dyer points out that they constitute anomalous, rather than alienated or ostracized, individuals: any dissonance with society they might experience is their own doing, not the society's. *Stars*, 52.

7. More than any other scholar, deCordova has analyzed public knowledge of the star's private sphere as constitutive of stardom. For him, the circulation of certain types of knowledge—especially knowledge concerning alleged private lives and "star scandals"—about formerly unnamed actors made the modern star system possible. *Picture Personalities.*

8. McDonald, "Reconceptualising Stars," 197.

9. Of course, there are also stars who adeptly adapt to their roles—are, in short, good actors—but it is revealing that many of the highest-paid stars are notoriously subpar actors. There seems to be something attractive about their transfilmic personas, which the spectator is willing to pay to see poking through the surface of the text, rather than their acting ability. King has analyzed this phenomenon, drawing the distinction between "impersonation" (adapting to and articulating the scripted character) and "personification" (manifesting the star's persona against the scripted character). Barry King, "Articulating Stardom," *Screen* 26 (Sept.–Oct. 1985): 27–50. I shall employ the phrase *transcendent individualism* instead of *personification* because I wish to foreground the function of personification for the contradictory social fantasy the star represents.

10. Some critics, looking back over his career, afforded this element of his "Hans im Glück" career a national importance: "Bis über seinen Tod 1960 hinaus ist er der ewigjunge Hans-im-Glück geblieben. Den einzige, den die Detuschen je besaßen." Merck, "Augen so blau." For his persisting happy-go-lucky attitude in the postwar era, see, for instance: "Schon an [einigen] wenigen Sätzen ist der alte Albers mit seinem unbezwingbaren Lebensmut wiederzuerkennen." "Der 'blonde Hans.'"

11. See, for example, Schümer, "Einmal muß es vorbei sein." In his article "Die Unbekümmertheit des Hans Albers," Harmstein recounts how Albers fought with Goebbels about the terms of his contract for *Große Freiheit No. 7.* Goebbels, who already hated Albers, subsequently banned the film, which was nevertheless shown to soldiers under a different title and went on to become one of the great cult classics of German cinema.

12. A clear statement of such resistance facilitated by a loving fan base: "Mit den Machthabern des 'Dritten Reiches' hat er sich nie eingelassen. Goebbels haßte den Draufgänger. Aber Albers war zu beliebt beim Publikum, als daß ihn der Propaganda-Chef hätte ernstlich gefährden können. Seine Fans wurden so für ihn zum Schutzschild." Kochanowski, "Hoppla, jetzt komm'ich."

13. Jurczyk, in a retrospective of Albers's career on what would have been his hundredth birthday, wrote that his general happy-go-lucky demeanor "gepaart mit seiner ebenso hemmungslosen körperlichen Leinwandpräsenz, wurde ihm absurderweise oft angekreidet, weil er sich damit nicht 'der Bewegung des Films' unterordne. Gleiches könnte dem

nuschelnden Hans Moser, dem dramatischen Richard Burton oder der lasziven Marylin Monroe vorgeworfen werden. Sie alle haben sich dem Gleichmaß und der Harmonie widersetzt, waren verrückt genug, um das seltsame Dasein ins extreme Kameralicht zu setzen. Hollywood nennt solche Sterne respektvoll 'bigger than life.' Ein Übermaß, das nötig ist, um dem Leben auf die Spur zu kommen." Jurczyk, "Findling von der Waterkant." Jurczyk has isolated that feature of the star foregrounded by Dyer and McDonald: the transcendent individualism may come across as bad acting but often it is constitutive of stars' popularity.

14. Barthel reports this anecdote about the chalkboards in his "Hans Albers."

15. In her *Spectacular Bodies,* Tasker analyzes the function of the specifically masculine body in the cinema of the 1980s. The images of such bodies "naturalize" male power and localize it in the body.

16. Silverman points out that, within the prevailing dominant fiction, men generally are not subjected to the gaze and do not generally attain spectacle status. Though I would, on the whole, agree with this assertion, stars seem a very notable exception. The body of even the male star fills the screen more than any other character and sustains lingering shots that are afforded only the most fetishized aspects of the film, usually parts of the woman's body or some longed-for object. For a typical analysis of male lack as spectacle, see, for instance, Silverman, *Male Subjectivity,* 78.

17. McDonald, "Reconceptualising Stars," 181. See Rentschler, *Ministry of Illusion,* 198–200 for a description of Albers's function within the Nazi imaginary.

18. For a study of the deliberate instrumentalization of the star to market material items, see Eckert, "The Carole Lombard in the Macy's Window."

19. "Am Abend legte [Albers] Wert auf Eleganz. Am typischen Albers-Hut erkannte man ihn schon von weitem. Daneben waren Kamelhaarmantel und gelber Kaschmir-Schal seine Markenzeichen." Kochanowski, "Hoppla, jetzt komm'ich." One article related how Albers offered the interviewer a cognac, had one himself, and had one at their second meeting as well, right after breakfast. Miska, "'Herr Albers läßt bitten.'" See, along similar liquor lines, "Ein Otto für den blonden Hans: Drehpause beim "Föhn"-Film in Geiselgasteig." *Heidelberger Abendblatt* 21 (May 1950). The frequent references to his cognac consumption suggest not only Albers's privileged navigation of the material world but also the function of the star's leisure time in the wider economy of the star system. The discourse about stars constantly recount what they do in their leisure time, obviously as part of the fantasy of their negotiation of the economic system but also reflecting the rationalization of leisure. For this second aspect, see Leo Lowenthal, "The Triumph of Mass Idols," in *Literature,*

Popular Culture, and Society (Englewood Cliffs, NJ: Prentice-Hall, 1961), 109–40.

20. In her *Star Gazing*, Stacey explains how the glamour of Hollywood films symbolized overdetermined abundance and affluence in rationed and materially deprived Britain in the mid- and late 1940s. Albers's uninterrupted cognac supply, of course, fit his reputation as an off- as well as onscreen Schieber and Draufgänger type. Albers "handelte noch bei Dreharbeiten 1944 im Hamburger Hafen ungerührt mit geschmuggelten Cognac." Schümer, "Einmal muß es vorbei sein."

21. Albers was "der wahrscheinlich populärste Filmschauspieler in den NS-Jahren." Harmstein, "Die Unbekümmertheit des Hans Albers." Barthel, in his memoirs, recounts this general incommensurability of the star and rubble films. Manfred Barthel, *So war es wirklich*, 32. See, for a contemporary instance, E.R.'s review, "Hans Albers in der Trümmerstadt," which complains that Hans Albers obviously stood *souverän* next to the director and often got his way. The review of *Zwischen Gestern und Morgen* in *Neue Zeit*, 23 Mar. 1948, criticizes both films for mixing the disparate genres. Hembus likewise attacks star vehicles that attempt to take up serious topics. Hembus, *Der deutsche Film*, 70–71.

22. Categories of alterity are often marked by deep contradiction, perhaps the most obvious being that of the simultaneous exclusion and inclusion of the other as socially defining. Likewise, representations of youth are relentlessly contradictory, always representing a tense, often irreconcilable duality that itself articulates fundamental contradictions in the culture. Hebdige, for instance, founds his *Hiding in the Light* on just such a contradiction: "I want to question that puritanical distinction between . . . youth-as-fun and youth-as-trouble" (19). Donzelot also bases his entire approach to the "policing" in families on a similarly contradictory concept of the "protected liberation" of children in the modern family. Youth-as-fun and youth-as-trouble serve as the binary that both Hebdige's work and Donzelot's book serve to collapse: on the one hand youth as the paradigmatic participants in the best society has to offer, and on the other as a threat to the society whose fruits they recalcitrantly seize. *Policing Families*, xxi.

23. The press materials make clear that these images of Hans amid the rubble—even in the case of the relentlessly cheerful Albers—connected his fate to that of thousands. *Illustrierte Film-Kurier: "Und über uns der Himmel"*: "Vor unseren Augen spielt sich die Geschichte eines Heimkehrers ab, ein Schicksal unter vielen Tausenden."

24. In fact, these flashbacks are the only time in which one hears anything about Frau Richter, Werner's mother, from either Hans or Werner. Not much lamenting here in this optimistic world. In the first flashback, Hans

and his future wife are out on a paddleboat, implying their initial courtship. The second flashback fast-forwards to their parenthood, as Hans and she sit at a lakeside café with a cradle next to their table. The third and final flashback writes the mother out of the parenting trajectory altogether, as we see Hans and Werner alone, admiring a monkey at a zoo.

25. "Der 'blonde Hans.'"

26. This series of three shots, cutting cross generationally from the young, to the old, to a middle-aged family, offers the kind of sociological cross section that one also finds in the apartment building subplots of *The Murderers Are among Us, Somewhere in Berlin, Before Us Life,* and *1-2-3 Corona.*

27. "Aber aus dem beschmutzten Antlitz strahlen seine berühmten blauen Augen mit unvermindertem Glanz." Borgelt, ". . . *Und über uns der Himmel.*"

28. See, for instance, E.R.'s review, "Hans Albers in der Trümmerstadt": "Ein neues Gesicht, Heidi Scharf, sehr echt als lebenshungriges Mädchen, künstlerisch aber zu sehr schon auf den Typ festgelegt." In his analysis of the film, Shandley downplays the role of Mizzi. See *Rubble-Films,* 160–67.

29. This figure of an overactive youth provider who threatens the traditionally adult providers—especially the fathers—recurs in just about every film I am discussing in detail or in passing. In *Deutschland Jahre Null* not only his sister but Edmund himself represents this inverted agency that brings home food and coal but also ends up killing the father; in *Somewhere in Berlin* Willi has to feed Gustav's father, Herr Iller; in *1-2-3 Corona* the two gangs end up providing for the injured Corona when social institutions fail them; in *Before Us Life,* the sons of the sailors have to go fishing when their fathers are stranded on land; in *And Someday We'll Find Each Other Again,* Wolfgang and Ulli provide when their teachers fail them; and in *The Sons of Mr. Gaspary,* Günther is left with the task of feeding his ill mother in the absence of his father or her second husband.

30. In the 1920s, Hans Albers made his career as a Schieber type and was a well-known Draufgänger. See Jurczyk, "Findling von der Waterkant." Regarding his Draufgänger status: "Hans Albers war ein simpler, ein eindeutiger Charakter: trinkfester Kumpel, einsamer Draufgänger. Immer ein Kerl mit Anstand im Leib, aber nie sonderlich besorgt um die großen Zusammenhänge." Schümer, "Einmal muß es vorbei sein."

31. This is another of the rubble film's recurring youth types, the angry male adolescent. True to the constructed discourse about youth, this seems to have little to do with actual age. For instance, there is the eleven- or twelve-year-old Kapitän in *Somewhere in Berlin* as well as the upper-twenties Stefan in *Ways into Twilight,* both bitter and aggressive about their postwar lot in life. In *Zugvögel,* Carl Raddatz—who was decidedly mid-

dle-aged at that point—played the same character in Georg, frustrated and resentful about his prospects after the castrating war that ruined his youth and therefore his future.

32. "The kiss is not only the key technique of love-making, nor the cinematic substitute for intercourse forbidden by censorship: it is the triumphant symbol of the role of the face and the soul in twentieth-century love making." Morin, *Stars*, 179.

33. Critics found this duality within Hans of an antisocial worker with a good father irreconcilable. In his review, "Ein moralisches Kuckucksei," Lenning complained that the double moral of a Schieber by day and a good family man by night was too unrealistic.

34. The dissolve recalls that in *Rotation*, when the film dissolves from the son who has denounced his father to the wall at which Hans is staring, which also helps constitute and condition the film's discursive production of youth.

35. This film, like others, emphasizes the peculiar function of the literal sight and metaphorical perspective of the child or son. This child's point of view is invoked often in Italian neorealism as well, as in the end of *Rome Open City*. In her article "The Name of the Child," Ehrlich discusses this phenomenon and its potential for social criticism.

36. Publicity materials deliberately emphasized the power of Werner's view of the rubble after he has his vision restored—the sight of the city and the father before the son is underscored. *Filmpost Programm: "Und über uns der Himmel,"* no. 157: "Werner hat durch eine Operation seine Sehkraft wiedergewonnen. Nix wie heim! Da gibt es kein Halten. Er wartet nicht, bis sein Vater ihn aus der Augenklinik abholt. Erschüttert ist er über das schaurige Bild auf allen Straßen. Überall Trümmer und grauenvolle Oede. Kaum, daß er sich zurechtfindet." *Illustriete Film-Kurier: "Und über uns der Himmel":* Sie fahren in eine Klinik, quer durch das zertrümmerte Berlin, das der Blinde in seiner Erinnerung noch als die von Glanz und Leben erfüllte Weltstadt 'sieht.' Hans verfolgt weiter seinen abschüssigen Weg—Werners Augen sind schließlich wieder geheilt. Zum ersten Male sieht er nun die Stadt in ihrer Not, in ihrem Elend, inmitten der Mühe, die es ihren Menschen macht, Berlin wieder ein neues Gesicht zu geben. Er sieht auch das zweifelhafte Lokal, in dem sein Vater die Geschäfte macht."

37. The same is true in other rubble films, for instance, in *Zwischen Gestern und Morgen*, in which young Kat serves a similar function in a historical mystery. A deep misunderstanding about the past has confused formerly amicable parties, and Kat serves as the pivotal link to the past that resolves the misunderstanding.

38. One can see here a revision of psychoanalysis's work on difference and

hierarchy. In her essay "When the Woman Looks," Williams argues that in an assortment of movies, women are often made literally blind to the social and cinematic conditions under which they suffer. Here, the blindness operates along similar lines, but as much along generational as gender lines.

39. Hans tries to recover by offering Edith's daughter some food, by playing the conventional paternal provider to his new family, but Edith refuses the food, secured on the black market. Hans makes fun of her efforts to work and provide legally, but she reminds him that when he first came back from the war, he still believed in legitimate work. He admits that he believed back then; back then he thought that if one rolled up one's sleeves and went to work, then one could achieve something, but now he knows that's not true. As he recounts his disillusionment, he articulates the most explicit loss of faith in the film, a direct echo of Mizzi's earlier complaint to Walter about the postwar situation. The star's individuating trajectory, in the specific generational logic of this rubble film, invokes the narcissistically juvenile response to the ubiquitous ruins.

40. Barthel relates this anecdote: "Viele haben erlebt, daß er in der Garderobe sein Spiegelbild küßte und Bestätigung heischend fragte: 'Bin ich nicht ein schöner Mensch?'" "Hans Albers." Confirming Albers's emphatic relationship to the mirror, Lädtke recounts a similar rumor: "er soll mit selbstgefälligem Blick in den Garderobenspiegel gerne festgestellt habe: 'Es gibt nur einen Albers, und der bin ich!'" "Der Hans in allen Gassen."

41. "Und während die Restbevölkerung sich ausgemergelt und abgerissen in den Ruinen des zerbombten Berlin zu schaffen macht, sieht man Albers, nachdenklich zwar, aber eben doch in Hut und Mantel—'immer sauber und voll Chic'—durch Schutt und Asche spazieren." "Hans Albers: Meister Des Stilbruchs."

42. "Fröhlich ohrfeigte doch nicht."

43. For the importance of the close-up in the emergence of the star system, see Staiger, "Seeing Stars"; Pearson, *Eloquent Gestures*.

44. Though Klein spends much of his book avoiding the obvious phallic qualities of cigarettes, he does analyze *Casablanca* and Humphrey Bogart in terms of the symbolic phallicity borne by cigarettes. *Cigarettes Are Sublime*, 166–78.

45. When they first approach the clock tower, the youths, especially Stefan, are very impressed by the elaborateness and operation of the *alte Mechanik* of the town clock. The film cuts quickly among gears, cogs, and the swinging pendulum, all humming along productively, in contrast to the youths' antisocial wanderings the day before. Their reverence for the efficient operation of the clock foreshadows their reconciliation to the town pro-

ject and to the dominant fiction generally, though, for the moment, they simply flop down on the floor to sleep.

46. The youths go to work cheerfully and diligently, filmically represented in a collage that invokes the cuts around the mechanics of the town clock.

47. See, for one of the clearest statements of the film's identification with the person Kornter, Hamann, "Fritz Kornters großer Erfolg": "Selten hat vor einem Film mit mehr Berechtigung ein Name gestanden: Ein Fritz-Kortner-Film"—"so sehr vereinigt er Geist, Herz und Kunst eines Mannes. Das Buch ist von ihm, und die Parellele zu seinem eignen Schicksal liegt nahe." See, for similar assertions, "Deutschland Rief Fritz Kortner"; Jaeger, "Kortner kommt nach Berlin." Despite Jaeger's assertion, Kortner was from Vienna.

48. "Deutschland Rief Fritz Kortner."

49. Both Brockmann, in *German Literary Culture at the Zero Hour,* and Olick, in *In the House of the Hangman,* have extensive treatments of this exile issue based on the high-profile and controversial case of Thomas Mann.

50. "I propose the following definition of the nation: it is an imagined political community." Anderson, *Imagined Communities,* 6–7.

51. Stacey, *Star Gazing.*

52. As with much of *The Last Illusion*'s reeducational discourse, the invocation of Goethe here is overdetermined. Goethe was a central figure for the immediate postwar period and for the widespread attempt to restore classical German culture in light of the assault and distortions it had sustained under the Nazis. The controversies surrounding the hundredth anniversary of Goethe's death in 1949 are well known and well described.

53. It is fascinating that the advance publicity took such conspicuous liberty with a key plot development. See *Illustrierter Film im Bild: "Der Ruf"*: "Ebensowenig dachte er daran, daß man ihm, dem gealterten Mann, seine rein freundschaftlichen und wissenschaftlich verankerten Beziehungen zu der Studentin Mary, zugleich seine Sekretärin, die er aus Kalifornien mit zwei weiteren Assistenten und einer Hausangestellten mitbrachte, zweideutig auslegen würde," and *Illustrierte Film-Kurier: "Der Ruf"*: "Walter aber, der nicht ahnt, daß Mauthner sein Vater ist, wird durch die Liebe zu der amerikanischen Assistentin Mary in einen Zwiespalt gestürzt, aus dem er nicht so schnell herausfindet. Als die Gegner des Professors endlich bei einer Feier einen großen Krach inszenieren, verleitet Walter seine falsche Eifersucht, den Professor zu beleidigen."

54. The youthful nature of Mauthner's suspect endeavor is driven home again when an old émigré professor laments that he has not been invited back— he is too old and this reconstructive task is the privilege of youth. As Mauthner considers the invitation back to his home university, the camera

frames him in a conspicuous three-shot between Spencer, the young American, and the old émigré professor—that is, positioned between youth and age. The mise-en-scène and the conversation both suggest that—despite his age and due to his star-based exceptionalness—Mauthner inhabits something of an indeterminate generational zone while in exile.

55. For another example, in one of the film's recurring themes, Mauthner is never able to make a call. At three offices, he is completely frustrated in his attempt to find a telephone. He is called back to Germany but never manages to call himself.

56. Lina has renounced her racial ideas, an abandonment proved in her (rather belated) plan to reveal Walter's true father to him. The only other character with Nazi leanings, the *Privatdozent* Fechner, comes to his hostility to Mauthner only in the postwar period, only through frustration with the denazification process and occupational policies. He makes it clear, and the film offers no grounds to doubt him, that he hated Hitler and refused to consort with him.

57. It is noteworthy that the reviews highlighted how Kortner, a Jewish exile, could articulate love for Germany: the persecuted Jew can manifest nationalism where and when it was otherwise problematic: "'Ja, liebst du denn dieses Land?' fragen [seine Freunde] und [Mauthner] antwortet: 'In meinen besten Augenblicken—ja!' Wir würden diesen Satz aus jeden anderen Munde als nationalistisch tendenziös verdächtig finden, dieser Mann darf ihn sprechen, und wir dürfen ihm dafür danken, aber nicht nur für den einen Satz, sondern für den ganzen Film." Schönfeld, *"Der Ruf."*

58. The editing of the restaurant scene casts Fechner as Walter's false Aryan father via intercutting: the film cuts away from Mauthner demanding to know the identity of the false father to Fechner in the next room. I have noted, since *Hitlerjunge Quex,* the anxiety surrounding false fathers in these films. Serving as false father figures are: in *Somewhere in Berlin,* Birke and Waldemar; in *And the Heavens Above,* Hans's friend Fritz; in *Rotation,* brigade leader Udo. The theme of a false father figure in a pedagogue is especially pronounced not only in *Rotation* but also in *Germany, Year Zero,* with Edmund's teacher, and *And Someday We'll Find Each Other Again,* with "Studienassessor" Paulke.

59. This obscuring of those guilty for Nazi crimes fits the general dispersion of agency Deleuze described in the postwar film. If the social and cinematic context was marked by crises of dispersion, then using the young as the stand-in for Nazi agents added to the deflection and dispersion of that most problematic guilt.

60. Confirming the film's strong reeducational theme, Mauthner's lecture runs almost five minutes, a questionable cinematic choice, underscoring

all the more that the film transpires in the overdetermined realm of reed-ucation. As remarkable a narrative device as it is, the lecture was featured in some of the publicity materials for the film, for instance, in the *Illustri-erte Film-Kurier:* "Bei der Antrittsvorlesung Mauthners beabsichtigen diese jungen Leute einen Skandal zu provozieren, um den Professor zu veranlassen, auf die Lehrkanzel zu verzichten. Sie haben aber nicht mit der Macht seines Wortes gerechnet. Obwohl der Professor die eisige Stimmung fühlt, und nur ein kleiner Teil der Studenten ihm zugetan ist, zwingt er mit seinem Vortrag doch alle Hörer in seinen Bann, so daß wenigstens laute Mißfallensäußerungen unterbleiben." As with its down-playing of the romance between Mauthner and Mary, the summary dis-torts the main message of the scene—that to the surprise of the reverent American students, the German youths reject such an educational effort.

61. Though the scene seemed painfully long and wordy to me, contemporary critics—perhaps attuned to the pedagogical context—praised it. For instance, in his review in *Der Morgen,* E.K. writes: "In seiner Antrittsvor-lesung, in der er die Tugendlehre Platos auf die heutigen Verhältnisse bezieht, legt er ein flammendes Bekenntnis zum Geiste, zu Frieden und Gerechtigkeit ab—in der meisterlichen Diktion Fritz Kortners auch darstellerisch der Höhepunkt des Films."

62. Though, as noted above, the publicity materials attempted to soften Kort-ner's indictment against the majority of the German students—they emphasize how German students were moved by Kortner's speech—con-temporary critics realized that the lecture signifies for Mauthner a peda-gogical failure. See L.M., "Bekenntnis zu Deutschland": "Mauthners Antrittsrede, die den Irrsinn widerlegt, in einem Volk lauter Verbrecher oder lauter Helden zu sehen, wird kühl aufgenommen."

63. "Vor diesem Film erinnern wir uns an betrübliche Vorkommnisse des Jahres 1946. Tatsächlich kam es an westdeutschen Hochschulen damals zu nationalistischen Umtrieben. Tatsächlich traf Kortners Rückkunft auch auf Mißgünstige damals. So schrieb, spielte Kortner ein Stück seiner eige-nen Erfahrung." Mangikamp, "Da reist ich nach Deutschland hinüber."

64. This is the second time that, after being threatened by the dispersive con-text of home, Mauthner is wrapped in a coat by loyal, supporting women. It is almost as if they try to protect his precarious masculinity by shoring it up with the shell of the adult man. One is reminded of Harry Caul and his caul-like overcoat in Francis Ford Coppola's excellent *The Conversa-tion.*

65. Other rubble films also suggest the prevalence of the lacking Heimkehrer's own generational crimes, usually, as in *And the Heavens Above,* an older male acting too juvenilely. For example, in *Between Yes-terday and Today,* initially interested Rott must back off the much

younger, though delightfully flirtatious, Kat. Similarly, in *Ways into Twilight,* Lukas must accept his place as an older man, must abstain from interfering in the affair between his love interest and Stefan, who is more her age. The article "Filmthema der Zeit" explicitly recounts how the older and war-wounded Lukas has to refrain from interfering in love meant for the young.

Conclusion

1. Lenning, "Über ein Jahrhundert hinweg."
2. Link, "Hundert Jahre wie ein Tag."
3. *Neue Filmwoche,* 14 May 1949; Link, "Hundert Jahre wie ein Tag."
4. Naimark, *Russians in Germany,* 441.
5. Pike, *Politics of Culture,* 250.
6. Naimark, *Russians in Germany,* 445–46.
7. Pike, *Politics of Culture,* 359.
8. Tent, *Mission on the Rhine,* 288.
9. Ibid., 289.
10. Ibid., 286–87.
11. Ibid., 288.
12. Ibid., 293.
13. Ibid., 297.
14. Pike, *Politics of Culture,* 394–96.
15. Naimark, *Russians in Germany,* 444.
16. Mückenberger and Jordan, *"Sie sehen selbst,"* 34.
17. Ibid., 22.
18. Naimark, *Russians in Germany,* 445.
19. Ibid., 444.
20. Steinhauer, "Inge von Wangenheim."
21. Boehm, "Der freiheitliche Typus."
22. Menter, ". . . *Und wieder 48!*"
23. Eylau, *"Und wieder 48."*
24. That Mann worked critically but within bourgeois consciousness is one of Lukács's basic points in "Auf der Suche nach dem Bürger," 505–34, esp. 505–9.
25. See, for such a comparison to Joyce, Vaget, "Mann, Joyce, and the Question of Modernism."
26. Ashis Nandy's seminal study, *The Intimate Enemy: Loss and Recovery of Self under Colonialism,* describes a symbolic code that was developed in the colonies but that amounted to a symbolic negotiation between ruler and ruled. Nandy spends a good half of his groundbreaking work on the colonial mechanisms of generation and age. He shows how the evolution

of the concept of the child served this colonial narrative, rendering it a narrative of progress, of "maturation." With this particular discourse of the child, the rulers "telescoped" the theory of social progress onto the individual life cycle in Europe; thus they legitimized their teaching and improvement of the inferiors (5).

Bibliography

Acland, Charles. *Youth, Murder, Spectacle: The Cultural Politics of "Youth in Crisis."* Boulder: Westview, 1995.

Adorno, Theodor. "What Does 'Coming to Terms with the Past' Mean?" In *Bitburg in Moral and Political Perspective*, edited by Geoffrey Hartmann, 115–29. Bloomington: Indiana University Press, 1986.

———. "Zur Demokratisierung der deutschen Universitäten." In *Gesammelte Schriften*, edited by Rolf Tiedemann, 20.1: 334–35. 1977. Reprint, Frankfurt: Suhrkamp, 1997.

Ahonen, Pertti. *After the Expulsion: West Germany and Eastern Europe, 1945–1990.* Oxford: Oxford University Press, 2003.

Allen, Ann Taylor. "Gardens of Children, Gardens of God: Kindergartens and Daycare Centers in Nineteenth-Century Germany." *Journal of Social History* 19 (1986): 433–50.

Althusser, Louis. *Lenin and Philosophy and Other Essays*, translated by Ben Brewster. New York: Monthly Review, 1971.

A.M.U. "*Irgendwo in Berlin.*" *Leipziger Volkszeitung*, 4 Jan. 1947.

Andersch, Alfred. "Getty oder die Umerziehung in der Retorte." *Frankfurter Hefte* 2, no. 11 (1947): 1089–96.

———. "Das Gras und der alte Mann." *Frankfurter Hefte* 3, no. 10 (1948): 927–29.

———. "Das Unbehagen in der Politik: Eine Generation unter sich." *Frankfurter Hefte* 2, no. 9 (1947): 912–25.

Anderson, Benedict. *Imagined Communities: Reflections on the Origin and Spread of Nationalism.* 1983. Reprint, New York: Verso, 1994.

Applegate, Celia. *A Nation of Provincials: The German Idea of Heimat.* Berkeley: University of California Press, 1990.

Arendt, Hannah. "The Aftermath of Nazi-Rule, Report from Germany." *Commentary* 10 (Oct. 1950): 342–53.

———. "Jaspers as a Citizen of the World." In *The Philosophy of Karl Jaspers*, edited by Paul Arthur Schlipp, 539–49. New York: Tudor, 1957.

Arendt, Hannah, and Karl Jaspers. *Hannah Arendt–Karl Jaspers: Correspondence, 1926–69.* Edited by Lotte Kohler and Hans Saner. Translated by Robert Kimber and Rita Kimber. 1985. Reprint, New York: Harcourt Brace Jovanovich, 1992.

Aries, Philippe. *Centuries of Childhood: A Social History of Family Life.* New York: Knopf, 1962.

Bahr, Ehrhard. "Art Desires Non-art: Thomas Mann's Dialectic of Art and Theodore Adorno's Aesthetic Theory." In *Thomas Mann's "Doctor Faustus": A Novel at the Margin of Modernism*, edited by Herbert Lehnert and Peter C. Pfeiffer, 145–60. Columbia, SC: Camden House, 1991.

Baird, Jay. *To Die for Germany: Heroes in the Nazi Pantheon.* Bloomington: Indiana University Press, 1990.

Baker, Mark. "Trümmerfilme": Postwar German Cinema, 1946–48." *Film Criticism* 20, nos. 1–2 (1995–96): 88–101.

Barbu, Eugen, and Andrei Ion Delenau. "Serenus Zeitblom." *Sinn und Form, Sonderheft: Thomas Mann* (1965): 134–43.

Barnouw, Dagmar. *Germany, 1945: Views of War and Violence.* Bloomington: University of Indiana Press, 1996.

———. *The War in the Empty Air: Victims, Perpetrators, and Postwar Germans.* Bloomington: University of Indiana Press, 2005.

Barthel, Manfred. "Hans Albers: 'Bin ich nicht ein schöner Mensch?'" *Berliner Morgenpost*, 4 Jan. 1987.

———. *So war es wirklich: Der deutsche Nachkriegsfilm.* Munich: Herbig, 1986.

Bartov, Omer. "Defining Enemies, Making Victims: Germans, Jews, and the Holocaust." *American Historical Review* 103, no. 3 (1998): 771–816.

———. *Mirrors of Destruction: War, Genocide, and Modern Identity.* New York: Oxford University Press, 2000.

Bauer, Georg. "Jugendamnestie und Spruchkammern: Konflikt zwischen Landesjugendausschuß und Gewerkschaften." *Süddeutsche Zeitung*, 1947, 2.

Bauer, Karl. "Universität Heidelberg und Heidelberger Gewerkschaften." In *Erneuerung der Universität: Reden und Schriften 1945/46*, edited by Renato de Rosa, 455–59. Heidelberg: Lambert Schneider, 1946.

Bauer, Walter. "Der deutsche Jüngling: Zu einer Sammlung von Briefen." *Das innere Reich* (1940): 220–22.

Becker, Wolfgang, and Norbert Schöll. With Heide Becker, Ruth Kayser, and Peter Nowotny. *In Jenen Tagen: Wie der deutsche Nachkriegsfilm die Vergangenheit bewältigte.* Oplade: Leske & Budrich, 1995.

Beddow, Michael. *Mann: "Doktor Faustus."* New York: Cambridge University

Press, 1994.

Behnke, Heinrich. "Universität und Höhere Schulen." *Frankfurter Hefte* 3, no. 1 (1948): 48–58.

Beil, Alfons. "Schuld und Verantwortung." *Frankfurter Hefte* 3, no. 11 (1948): 1058–61.

Benz, Wolfgang, ed. *Deutschland unter allierter Besatzung, 1945–1949/55: Ein Handbuch*. Berlin: Akademie, 1999.

———. "Konzeptionen für die Nachkriegsdemokratie." In *Deutschland nach Hitler: Zukuntspläne im Exil und aus der Besatzungszeit, 1939–1949*, edited by Thomas Koebner, Rolf-Peter Janz, and Frank Trommler, 201–13. Opladen: Westdeutscher Verlag, 1987.

Bergengruen, Werner. "Grabschrift Für ein Kind." *Deutsche Rundschau* 70, no. 10 (1947): 6.

Berglar-Schröer, Hans-Peter. "Filmzensur—Ja oder Nein?" *Frankfurter Hefte* 4, no. 2 (1949): 106–8.

———. "Die Vertrauenskrise der Jugend." *Frankfurter Hefte* 2 (1947): 693–701.

Berman, Russell. *The Rise of the Modern German Novel: Crisis and Charisma*. Cambridge: Harvard University Press, 1986.

Berthold, Will. "Jugend und Wahlen." *Süddeutsche Zeitung*, 24 May 1946, 2.

Beyme, Klaus von. "Karl Jaspes—Vom philosophischen Aussenseiter Zum Praeceptor Germaniae." In *Heidelberg 1945*, edited by Jürgen Hess, Hartmut Lehmann, and Volker Sollin, 130–48. Stuttgart: Franz Steiner Verlag, 1996.

Biermann-Ratjen, Hans. "Realste Realistik im Film," *Filmpress*, 2 Sept. 1949, 9.

Bierner, Otto. "Kalorien für Kinder: Milch und weiße Semmeln für Schulkinder/Nur ein Fünftel ist normal genährt." *Süddeutsche Zeitung*, 22 Oct. 1946, 4.

———. "Kinderwünsche 1946." *Süddeutsche Zeitung*, 21 Dec. 1946, 4.

Biess, Frank. "Pioneers of a New Germany": Returning POWs from the Soviet Union and the Making of East German Citizens, 1945–1950" *Central European History* 32, no. 2 (1999): 153–80.

———. "Survivors of Totalitarianism: Returning POWs and the Reconstruction of Masculine Citizenship in West Germany, 1945–1955." In *Miracle Years: A Cultural History of West Germany, 1949–1968*, edited by Hanna Schissler, 57–82. Princeton: Princeton University Press, 2001.

Binder, Gerhart. *Der Deutschenspiegel: Schriften zur Erkenntnis und Erneuerung*. Stuttgart: Deutsche Verlags-Anstalt, 1946.

Binding, Rudolf. "Deutsche Jugend vor den Toten des Krieges." In *Gesammeltes Werk*, 2:572. Hamburg: Hands Dulk, 1954.

Blackbourn, David. "The German Bourgeoisie: An Introduction." In *The German Bourgeoisie*, edited by David Blackbourn and Richard Evans, 1–45.

London: Routledge, 1991.

Blackbourn, David, and Geoff Eley. *The Peculiarities of German History: Bourgeois Society and Politics in Nineteenth-Century Germany.* New York: Oxford University Press, 1984.

Blanckhagen, P. H. von. "Der falsche Charakter: Zur politischen Haltung der studierenden Jugend." *Wandlung* 1, no. 5 (1946): 377–83.

"Der 'Blonde Hans'—leicht ergraut—nicht gealtert." *Neue Filmwoche* 36 (1947): 149.

Blüher, Hans. *Die Wandervogelzeit: Quellenschriften zur deutschen Jugendbewegung, 1896–1919.* Edited by Werner Kindt. Düsseldorf: Diederichs, 1968.

Blumenfeld, Israel. "An Pfarrer Niemöller." *Frankfurter Rundschau,* 12 Feb. 1946, 4.

Boag, Hugh-Alexander. *Ernst Wiechert: The Prose in Relation to His Life and Times.* Stuttgart: Akademischer Verlag, 1987.

Bodemann, Y. Michal. "Eclipse of Memory: German Representations of Auschwitz in the Early Postwar Period." *New German Critique* 75 (Fall 1998): 57–89.

Boehlich, Walter. "Thomas Manns *Doktor Faustus.*" *Merkur* 2, no. 4 (1948): 588–603.

Boehm, Hans-Joachim. "Der freiheitliche Typus." *Tagesspiegel,* 30 Dec. 1948.

Böhm, Franz. "Entmündigung der Universität." *Gegenwart* 2, nos. 9–10 (1947): 17–20.

———. "Hochschule und Nationalismus." *Gegenwart* 2, nos. 15–16 (1947): 20–22.

Bolz, Rüdiger. "Ansätze zur Universitätsreform." In *Zur literarischen Situation 1945–1949,* edited by Gerhard Hay, 63–85. Kronberg: Athenäum, 1977.

Borchert, Wolfgang. *Das Gesamtwerk.* 1949. Reprint, Hamburg: Rowohlt, 1957.

Borgelt, H. ". . . *Und über Uns der Himmel.*" *Neue Filmwelt* 3, no. 1 (1947): 2–3.

Böttcher, Karl Wilhelm. "Die junge Generation und die Parteien: Bericht über ein Gesprach." *Frankfurter Hefte* 3, no. 8 (1948): 756–61.

———. "Lehrlinge suchen ihren Meister: Zur Berufsnot der deutschen Jugend." *Frankfurter Hefte* 4, no. 12 (1949): 1039–45.

Brandenburg, Hans-Christian. *Die Geschichte der HJ: Wege und Irrwege einer Generation.* Cologne: Verlag Wissenschaft und Politik, 1968.

Brandlmeier, Thomas. "Und wieder Caligari . . . deutsche Nachkriegsfilme, 1946–1951." In *Der deutsche Film: Aspekte seiner Geschichte von den Anfängen bis zur Gegenwart,* edited by Uli Junge, 139–66. Trier: Wissenschaftler Trier, 1993.

———. "Von Hitler zu Adenauer: Deutsche Trümmerfilme." In *Zwischen Gestern und Morgen: Westdeutscher Nachkriegsfilme, 1946–62,* 33–59.

Frankfurt: Deutsches Fimmuseum, 1989.

Braun, Hans. "Die Studenten und die nationalen Ressentiments." *Wandlung* 4, no. 4 (1949): 387–94.

Brinkmann, Albert Erich. *Geist im Wandel.* Hamburg : Hoffmann und Campe, 1946.

Brockmann, Stephen. *German Literary Culture at the Zero Hour.* Rochester, NY: Camden House, 2004.

Bronsart, Huberta von. *Weizen oder Spinat? Der deutsche Landwirt am Scheideweg.* Stuttgart: Deutsche Verlags-Anstalt, 1947.

Bullock, Marcus. *The Violent Eye: Ernst Jünger's Vision and Revisions on the European Right.* Detroit: Wayne State University Press, 1992.

Burger, Heinz Otto. "Deutsche Bildungsideale." In *Das abendländische Bildungsideal,* edited by Gerhard Binder. Stuttgart: Deutsche Verlags-Anstalt, 1946.

Clark, Mark. "A Prophet without Honour: Karl Jaspers in Germany, 1945–1948." *Journal of Contemporary History* 37, no. 2 (2002): 197–222.

Confino, Alon. *The Nation as a Local Metaphor: Württemberg, Imperial Germany, and National Memory, 1871–1918.* Chapel Hill: University of North Carolina Press, 1997.

———. "Traveling as a Cultural Remembrance: Traces of National Socialism in West Germany, 1945–1960." *History and Memory* 12 (2000): 92–121.

Confino, Alon, and Peter Fritzsche, eds. *The Work of Memory: New Directions in the Study of German Society and Culture.* Urbana: University of Illinois Press, 2002.

C.P. "Die Nachkriegswelt der Schule: Bayern lernen schneller Lesen als Preussen/Im Schulzimmer Nr. 8." *Frankenpost,* 17 Apr. 1946, 2.

Curtius, Robert. "Goethe oder Jaspers." *Zeit,* 28 Apr. 1949.

deCordova, Richard. *Picture Personalities: The Emergence of the Star System in America.* Urbana: University of Illinois Press, 1990.

De La Maziere, Christian. *The Captive Dreamer.* Translated by Francis Stuart. New York: Saturday Review Press, 1974.

Deleuze, Gilles. *Cinema 1: The Movement-Image.* Minneapolis: University of Minnesota Press, 1986.

———. *Cinema 2: The Time-Image.* Minneapolis: University of Minnesota Press, 1989.

———. "Rise of the Social." Foreword to *Policing Families,* by Jacques Donzelot, ix–xxvii. New York: Random House, 1979.

"Deutschland Rief Fritz Kortner . . . Er kam und drehte den *Ruf.*" *Film Illustrierte,* 12 Jan. 1949, 5.

Dietrich, Gerd. *Politik und Kultur in der SBZ, 1945–1949.* Bern: Peter Lang, 1993.

Dirks, Walter. "Die Akademie der Arbeit." *Frankfurter Hefte* 2, no. 4 (1947): 326–28.

———. "Dreimail 1848, Dreimal 1948." *Frankfurter Hefte* 3, no. 1 (1948): 5–8.

———. "Nicht die Jugend, die Erwachsenen!" *Frankfurter Hefte* 1, no. 3 (1946): 4–6.

———. "Wer soll studieren dürfen?" *Frankfurter Hefte* 2, no. 5 (1947): 435–37.

Dirks, Walter, and Gerhard Storz. "Konfessionsschulen?" *Frankfurter Hefte* 1, no. 2 (1946): 10–15.

Ditfurth, Hoimar V. "Noch einmal das Problem Ernst Jünger." *Deutsche Rundschau* 71, no. 4 (1948): 50–54.

Doane, Mary Anne. "Film and the Masquerade: Theorising the Female Spectator." *Screen* 23 (Sept.–Oct. 1982).

Döblin, Alfred. *Schicksalreise: Bericht und Bekenntnis: Flucht und Exil, 1940–1948.* Munich: Piper, 1986.

Doetsch, Günther. "Jugend in der Verantwortung." *Frankfurter Rundschau,* 19 Feb. 1946, 4.

Donzelot, Jacques. *Policing Families.* New York: Random House, 1979.

Döring, Magdalene. "Die Schuldfrage und die Generationen." *Deutsche Rundschau* 69, no. 6 (1946): 206–15.

Dörr, Hansjörg. "Thomas Mann und Adorno: Ein Beitrag zur Entstehung des *Doktor Faustus.* In *Thomas Manns "Doktor Faustus" und die Wirkung,* edited by Rudolf Wolff, 2:48–91. Bonn: Bouvier, 1983.

D.P.D. "Niemöllers predigt in Nürnberg." *Frankfurter Rundschau,* 30 Apr. 1946, 2.

Dreyfus, Herbert, and Paul Rabinow. *Michel Foucault: Beyond Structuralism and Hermeneutics.* Chicago: Chicago University Press, 1986.

"Der dritte Spielfilm der Defa: Festaufführung von *Irgendwo in Berlin.*" *Nacht Express,* 19 Dec. 1946.

Dvoretzky, Edward. "Thomas Manns *Doktor Faustus:* Ein Rückblick auf die frühe deutsche Kritik." *Blätter der Thomas Mann Gesellschaft* 17 (1979): 9–24.

Dyer, Richard. *Stars.* London: British Film Institute, 1998.

Echternkamp, Jörg. *Nach Dem Krieg: Alltagsnot, Neuorientierung und die Last der Vergangenheit, 1945–1949.* Zurich: Pendo, 2003.

Eckert, Charles. "The Carole Lombard in the Macy's Window." *Quarterly Review of Film Studies* 3, no. 1 (1978): 1–21.

Ehrlich, Leonard. *Karl Jaspers: Philosophy as Faith.* Amherst: University of Massachusetts Press, 1975.

Ehrlich, Linda. "The Name of the Child: Cinema as a Social Critique." *Film Criticism* 14, no. 2 (1989–90): 12–23.

Eley, Geoff. "Liberalism, Europe, and the Bourgeoisie." In *The German Bourgeoisie*, edited by David Blackbourn and Richard Evans, 293–317. London: Routledge, 1991.

Elias, Norbert. *The Civilizing Process: The History of Manners and State Formation and Civilization.* Translated by Edmund Jephcott. 1939. Reprint, Cambridge: Blackwell, 1994.

Elsaesser, Thomas. *New German Cinema: A History.* New Brunswick: Rutgers University Press, 1989.

Eppenhagen, Karl Andreas. "Bemerkungen zu dem DEFA—Streifen *Rotation.*" *Welt,* 25 May 1950.

E.R. "Hans Albers in der Trümmerstadt." *Volksblatt,* 11 Dec. 1947.

"Ernst Wiechert als Ankläger." *Tagesspiegel,* 20 Feb. 1946.

"Ernst Wiechert las in den Münchener Kammerspielen." *Neue Zeitung,* 15 Nov. 1945.

Etlin, Richard. *Modernism in Italian Architecture, 1890–1940.* Cambridge: MIT, 1991.

Evans, Richard. *In Hitler's Shadow: West German Historians and the Attempt to Escape from the Nazi Past.* New York: Pantheon, 1989.

Eylau, Hans Ulrich. "*Und wieder 48:* Der Revolutions-Gedenkfilm der DEFA im Babylon." *Täglicher Rundschau,* 9 Nov. 48.

Fehrenbach, Heide. *Cinema in Democratizing Germany: Reconstructing National Identity after Hitler.* Chapel Hill: University of North Carolina Press, 1995.

———. "Of German Mothers and 'Negermischlingskinder': Race, Sex, and the Postwar Nation." In *The Miracle Years: A Cultural History of West Germany, 1949–1968,* edited by Hanna Schissler, 164–86. Princeton: Princeton University Press, 2001.

———. "Rehabilitating Fatherland: Race and German Remasculinization." *Signs* 24 (1998): 107–28.

Fetzer, John. *Music, Love, Death, and Mann's "Doctor Faustus."* Columbia, SC: Camden House, 1990.

Fiedler, Werner. "*Irgendwo in Berlin,* Uraufführung des Lamprecht-Films." *Neue Zeit,* 20 Dec. 1946.

"Filmthema der Zeit: Das Bild unserer Jugend." *Neue Filmwelt* 3, no. 2 (1948): 12–13.

Fischer, K. "Neues Leben an den Hochschulen." *Berliner Zeitung,* 9 Feb. 1946, 3.

Fischer, Otto. "Pfadfinder—Jugend baut auf!" *Süddeutsche Zeitung,* 9 Apr. 1946, 2.

———. "Wir Jungen und die Wahlen." *Süddeutsche Zeitung,* 1 Feb. 1946, 2.

Fisher, Jaimey. "Deleuze in a Ruinous Context: German Rubble-Film and Italian Neorealism." In "Gilles Deleuze, Philosopher of Cinema," special issue, *iris* 23 (Spring 1997): 53–74.

Flake, Otto. "Etwas über die Schuldfrage." *Merkur* 1, no. 1 (1947): 140–42.

Flanagan, Clare. *A Study of German Political-Cultural Periodicals from the Years of Allied Occupation, 1945–1949.* Lewiston, NY: E. Mellen, 2000.

Flex, Walter. *Der Wanderer zwischen beiden Welten.* Kiel: Orion-Heimreiter, 1986.

Fontane, Theodor. "Die Alten und die Jungen." *Deutsche Rundschau* 69, no. 1 (1947): 50.

Forschepiepe, Hermann. "Die Jugendherbergen." *Frankfurter Rundschau,* 19 Feb. 1946, 4.

Foucault, Michel. *The Archeology of Knowledge.* Translated by A. M. Sheridan Smith. New York: Pantheon, 1972.

———. *The Care of Self.* Vol. 3 of *The History of Sexuality.* Translated by Robert Hurley. New York: Random House, 1988.

———. *Discipline and Punish: The Birth of the Prison.* Translated by Alan Sheridan. New York: Vintage, 1979.

———. *Foucault Live.* New York: Semiotexte, 1989.

———. *The History of Sexuality: An Introduction.* Translated by Robert Hurley. New York: Random House, 1978.

———. *Language, Counter-Memory, Practice: Selected Essays and Interviews.* Edited by Donald Bouchard. Ithaca: Cornell University Press, 1977.

———. "La loi du pudeur," *Recherches* 37 (Apr. 1976): 77–78.

———. *The Uses of Pleasure.* Vol. 2 of *The History of Sexuality.* Translated by Robert Hurley. New York: Pantheon, 1985.

Franz-Willing, Georg. *Umerziehung: Die De-Nationalisierung besiegter Völker im 20. Jahrhundert.* Coburg: Nation Europa, 1991.

Frei, Norbert. *Adenauer's Germany and the Nazi Past.* Berkeley: University of California Press, 2002.

———. *1945 und wir.* Munich: C. H. Beck, 2005.

———. *Vergangenheitspolitik: Die Anfänge der Bundesrepublik und die NS-Vergangenheit.* 1997. Reprint, Munich: DTV, 2003.

Freisel, Johannes. "Der neue Ernst Wiechert." *Neue Zeit,* 2 Dec. 1945.

Frevert, Ute. *Frauen-Geschichte: Zwischen bürgerlicher Verbesserung und neuer Weiblichkeit.* Frankfurt: Suhrkamp, 1986.

———. *Mann und Weib, Weib und Mann: Geschlechter-Differenzen in der Moderne.* Munich: Beck, 1995.

Friedman, Regine Mihal. "*Ecce Ingenium Teutonicum: Paracelsus* (1943)." In *The Films of G. W. Pabst: An Extraterritorial Cinema,* edited by Eric Rentschler, 184–97. New Brunswick: Rutgers University Press, 1990.

Frisch, Max. "Drei Entwürfe zu einem Brief." *Wandlung* 2, no. 6 (1947): 478–83.

"Fröhlich ohrfeigte doch nicht," *Telegraf,* 27 Feb. 1947.

BIBLIOGRAPHY

Füssl, Karl-Heinz. *Die Umerziehung der Deutschen: Jugend und Schule unter den Siegermächten des zweiten Weltkriegs, 1945–1955.* Paderborn: F. Schöningh, 1994.

Gaddis, John Lewis. *The United States and the Origins of the Cold War, 1941–1947.* New York: Columbia University Press, 1972.

Gallagher, Tag. *The Adventures of Robert Rossellini: His Life and Films.* New York: De Capo, 1998.

Gebhardt, Rudolf. "Über 200,000 Jugendliche entlastet: Staatsminister Dr. Anton Pfeiffer über die Amnestie der Jugend." *Frankenpost,* 21 Aug. 1946, 4.

Germany, 1947–1949: The Story in Documents. Department of State Publication 3556. Washington, DC: Department of State, 1950.

Gersch, Wolf. "Die Anfänge des DEFA-Spielfilms." *Film-und Fernsehkunst der DDR: Traditionen—Beispiele—Tendenzen.* Edited by Hochschule für Film und Fernsehen der DDR. Henschel: Berlin, 1979.

Gerst, Wilhelm Karl. "Friede und Einheit unter der Jugend." *Frankfurter Rundschau,* 30 July 1946.

———. "Jugend trägt schwere Last: so müssen die Alten versorgen." *Frankfurter Rundschau,* 26 Feb. 1946.

———. "Jugend will wandern." *Frankfurter Rundschau,* 16 Apr. 1946.

———. "Neuer Geist—Neues Vertrauen." *Frankfurter Rundschau,* 5 Feb. 1946.

———. "Um die religiöse Erziehung der Jugend." *Frankfurter Rundschau,* 19 July 1946.

———. "Wer darf studieren?" *Frankfurter Rundschau,* 29 Jan. 1946, 5.

Geulen, Eva. "Resistance and Representation: A Case Study of Thomas Mann's "Mario and the Magician." *New German Critique* 68 (Winter 1996): 3–29.

Gieschen, Elizabeth. "*Irgendwo in Berlin* . . . Schicksale unserer Tage—vom Künstler gesehen." *Morgen Berlin,* 20 Dec. 1946.

Giesecke, Hermann. *Vom Wandervogel bis zur Hitlerjugend: Jugendarbeit zwischen Politik und Pädagogik.* Munich: Juventa, 1981.

Giess, Imanuel. "Kritischer Rückblick auf Friedrich Meinecke." *Kritik der bürgerlichen Geisteswissenschaften, das Argument* 70 (1972): 22–36.

Gimbel, John. *The American Occupation of Germany—Politics and the Military, 1945–52.* Stanford: Stanford University Press, 1968.

Giroux, Henry. *Fugitive Cultures: Race, Violence, and Youth.* New York: Routledge, 1996.

Glaser, Herman. *Kulturgeschichte der Bundesrepublik Deutschland: Zwischen Kapitulation und Währungsreform, 1945–1948.* Munich: Carl Hanser, 1985.

———. *The Rubble Years: The Cultural Roots of Postwar Germany, 1945–1948.*

New York: Paragon House, 1986.

Gledhill, Christine. "Recent Developments in Feminist Criticism." In *Film Theory and Criticism: Introductory Readings*, edited by Gerald Mast, 93–114. New York: Columbia University Press, 1997.

Goebbels, Joseph. *Goebbels Diaries: 1942–1943*. Edited by Louis P. Lochner. 1948. Reprint, Westport: Greenwood, 1970.

———. *Michael: A Novel*. Translated by Joachim Neugroschel. 1929. Reprint, New York: Amok, 1987.

Goedde, Peter. *Gis and Germans: Culture, Gender, and Foreign Relations, 1945–1949*. New Haven: Yale University Press, 2003.

Goldhahn, Ernst. "Helft unserer Jugend!" *Frankenpost*, 4 Mar. 1946.

Gollnick, Ulrike. "Thomas Mann—Repräsentant der Nachkriegszeit?" In *Zur literarischen Situation 1945–1949*, edited by Gerhard Hay, 205–26. Kronberg: Athenäum, 1977.

Göttler, Fritz. "Westdeutscher Nachkriegsfilm: Land der Väter." In *Geschichte des deutschen Films*, edited by Wolfgang Jacobsen, Anton Kaes, and Hans Helmut Prinzler, 171–210. Stuttgart: J. B. Metzger, 1993.

Groethuysen, Bernhard. "Über den Kindersinn." *Wandlung* 2, no. 7 (1947): 582–91.

Gromes, Hartwin, ed. *Auf der Suche nach der Stunde Null, Literatur und Alltag, 1945: Eine Ausstellung*. Hildesheim: Frarzbecker, 1991.

Grossberg, Lawrence. *We Gotta Get Out of This Place: Popular Conservatism and Postmodern Culture*. New York: Routledge, 1992.

Grotum, Thomas. *Die Halbstarken: Zur Geschichte einer Jugendkultur der 50er Jahre*. Bad Salzdetfurth: B. Franzbecker, 1991.

Guggenheimer, Walter. "Das Porträt: Alois Hundhammer." *Frankfurter Hefte* 2, no. 11 (1947): 1141–48.

———. "Schulreform und Besatzungsrecht." *Frankfurter Hefte* 3, no. 6 (1948): 488–91.

Günther, Joachim. "Der Dämon und sein Bild." *Deutsche Rundschau* 75, no. 8 (1949): 759–62.

———. "Jaspers, Nietzsche und das Christentum." *Deutsche Rundschau* 71, no. 6 (1948): 254–56.

———. "Jaspers und der philosophische Glaube." *Deutsche Rundschau* 75, no. 6 (1949): 563–65.

Hadeln, Hajo von (Führer der Berliner Studentenschaft). "Student und S.A." *Nationalsozialistische Monatshefte* 5, no. 46 (1934): 25–27.

Hage, Volker. "Vom Einsatz und Rückzug des fiktiven Ich-Erzähler: *Doktor Faustus*—Ein moderner Roman?" *Sonderband: Thomas Mann, Text + Kritik* (1982).

———. *Zeugen der Zerstörung: Die Literaten und der Luftkrieg*. Frankfurt: Fischer, 2003.

Hake, Sabine. *Popular Cinema of the Third Reich.* Austin: University of Texas Press, 2001.

Hallstein, Walter. "Hochschule und Staat: Der Sinn der akademischen Selbstverwaltung." *Wandlung* 2, no. 8 (1947): 706–21.

Hamann, Edith. "Fritz Kornters großer Erfolg." *Neue Film* 3, no. 12 (1949): 7.

"Hans Albers: Meister des Stilbruchs." *Spiegel,* 11 Jan. 1982, 130.

Harmstein, Henning. "Die Unbekümmertheit des Hans Albers." *Neue Zürcher Zeitung,* 13 Apr. 1978.

Hartmann, Geoffrey H., ed. *Bitburg in Moral and Political Perspective.* Bloomington: Indiana University Press, 1986.

Harzendorf, Fritz. *So kam es: Der deutsche Irrweg von Bismarck bis Hitler.* Konstanz: Sudverlag, 1946.

Haurand, Peter Wißhelm. "Wiedergutmachung an den Juden." *Frankfurter Rundschau,* 12 July 1946, 4.

Hausmann, Manfred. "Die Pflichten der Jugend." *Frankenpost,* 1946, 3.

Hay, Gerhard, ed. *Zur literarischen Situation, 1945–1949.* Kronberg: Athenaeum Verlag, 1977.

Hebdige, Dick. *Hiding in the Light.* New York: Routledge, 1988.

Heiber, Helmut. *Goebbels.* Translated by John K. Dickinson. 1962. Reprint, New York: Hawthorn, 1972.

Heidenberger, Peter. "Was Lernen die Studenten? Die meisten studieren Medizin/Amerikaner an der Münchner Universität." *Süddeutsche Zeitung,* 30 Aug. 1946.

Heilbut, Anthony. *Thomas Mann: Eros and Literature.* New York: Knopf, 1996.

Heimann, Thomas. *DEFA, Künstler und SED-Kulturpolitik: Zum Verhältnis von Kulturpolitik und Filmproduktion in der SBZ/DDR, 1945 bis 1959.* Potsdam-Babelsberg: VISTAS, 1994.

Heineman, Elizabeth. "The Hour of the Woman: Memories of Germany's 'Crisis Years' and West German National Identity." *American Historical Review* (1996): 354–95.

———. *What Difference Does a Husband Make? Women and Marital Status in Nazi and Postwar Germany.* 1999. Reprint, Berkeley: University of California Press, 2003.

Heinemann, Manfred, ed. *Umerziehung und Wiederaufbau: Die Bildungspolitik der Besatzungsmächte in Deutschland und Österreich.* Stuttgart: Klett-Cotta, 1981.

Heinzlmeier, Adolf. *Nachkriegsfilm und Nazifilm: Anmerkungen zu einem deutschen Thema.* Frankfurt: Oase, 1988.

Helling, Fritz. *Der Katastrophenweg der deutschen Geschichte.* Frankfurt: V. Klostermann, 1947.

Hembus, Joe. *Der deutsche Film kann gar nicht besser sein.* Bremen: Carl Schünemann, 1961.

Herf, Jeffrey. *Divided Memory: The Nazi Past in the Two Germanys.* Cambridge: Harvard University Press, 1997.

——. *Reactionary Modernism: Technology, Culture, and Politics in Weimar and the Third Reich.* New York: Cambridge University Press, 1984.

Hermand, Jost. *Kultur im Wiederaufbau: Die Bundesrepublik Deutschland, 1945–1965.* Munich: Nymphenberger, 1986.

Hermand, Jost, Helmut Peitsch, and Klaus R. Scherpe. *Literatur im historischen Prozeß: Nachkriegsliteratur in Westdeutschland.* Vol. 2. Berlin: Argument Verlag, 1983.

Herrmann, Klaus. "Die Zwischengeneration." *Deutsche Rundschau* 70, no. 10 (1947): 26–31.

Hesse, Hermann. *Der Europäer.* Frankfurt: Suhrkamp, 1946.

——. "Das feuilletonistische Zeitalter: Ein Rückblick aus dem Jahre 2200." *Süddeutsche Zeitung,* 5 July 1947.

Heukenkamp, Ursula, ed. *Unterm Notdach: Nachkriegsliteratur in Berlin, 1945–1949.* Berlin: Erich Schmidt Verlag, 1996.

Heydecker, Marianne. "Die Jugend in Gefahr: Aus Berichten des bayerischen Innenministeriums." *Mittelbayerische Zeitung,* 12 Feb. 1946.

Hitler, Adolf. *Hitler's Secret Conversations, 1941–1944.* Translated by Norman Cameron and R. H. Stevens. New York: Farrar, Straus and Young, 1953.

Hocking, William E. *Experiment in Education: What We Can Learn from Teaching Germany.* Chicago: H. Regency, 1954.

Hoffmann, Christa. *Stunde Null? Vergangenheitsbewältigung in Deutschland 1945 und 1989.* Bonn: Bouvier, 1992.

Hohlhaase, Wolfgang. "*Rotation:* DEFA." *Start,* 23 Sept. 1949.

Holthussen, Hans Egon. "Die Bewusstseinslage der modernen Literatur." *Merkur* 3, no. 6 (1949): 537–51.

——. "Die Bewusstseinlage der modernen Literatur (II)." *Merkur* 3, no. 7 (1949): 680–89.

——. "Excurs über schlechte Gedichte." *Merkur* 2, no. 4 (1948): 604–8.

——. "Die Welt ohne Transzendenz: Eine Studie zu Thomas Manns *Dr. Faustus* und seinen Nebenschriften." *Merkur* 3, no. 1 (1949): 38–58.

——. "Die Welt ohne Transzendenz: Eine Studie zu Thomas Manns *Dr. Faustus* und seinen Nebenschriften (II)." *Merkur* 3, no. 2 (1949): 161–80.

Holtz, Hannelore. "Erstes DEFA-Filmtheater eröffnet Wolfgang Staudtes *Rotation.*" *Nacht-Express,* 17 Sept. 1949.

Horkheimer, Max. *"Dialektik der Aufklärung" und Schriften 1940–1950.* Vol. 5 of *Gesammelte Schiften.* Frankfurt: S. Fischer, 1985.

——. "Philosophie und Studium." *Frankfurter Hefte* 4, no. 8 (1949):

656–66.

Huber, Heinz J. "Die akademische Jugend baut Brücken." *Süddeutsche Zeitung*, 22 Oct. 1946.

Hupka, Herbert. "Freie Jugend." *Süddeutsche Zeitung*, 19 Nov. 1946.

———. "Studenten in Not." *Süddeutsche Zeitung*, 11 Jan. 1947.

Hüppauf, Bernd, ed. "Langemarck, Verdun, and the Myth of a New Man in Germany after the First World War." *War and Society* 6, no. 2 (1988): 70–103.

———. *"Die Mühen der Ebenen": Kontinuität und Wandel in der deutschen Literatur und Gesellschaft, 1945–1949.* Heidelberg: C. Winter, 1981.

Ihering, Herbert. "Mit Sauberkeit der Gesinnung: *Rotation* in Babylon und in der Kastanianallee." *Berliner Zeitung*, 18 Sept. 1949.

Irving, David. *Goebbels: Mastermind of the Third Reich.* London: Focal, 1996.

Jacobsen, Wolfgang, ed. *G. W. Pabst.* Berlin: Argon, 1997.

Jaeger, Ernst. "Kortner kommt nach Berlin." *Roland von Berlin*, 16 Nov. 1947.

Jarausch, Konrad. *Die Umkehr: Deutsche Wandlungen, 1945–1995.* Munich: Deutsche Verlags-Anstalt, 2004.

Jaspers, Karl. "Bitte um Gerechtigkeit für die Universität." In *Erneuerung der Universität: Reden und Schriften, 1945/46,* edited by Renato de Rosa, 449–53. Heidelberg: Lambert Schneider, 1986.

———. "Erneuerung der Universität." In *Erneuerung der Universität: Reden und Schriften, 1945/46,* edited by Renato de Rosa, 93–105. Heidelberg: Lambert Schneider, 1986.

———. "Europa der Gegenwart." In *Erneuerung der Universität: Reden und Schriften, 1945/46,* edited by Renato de Rosa, 243–74. Heidelberg: Lambert Schneider, 1986.

———. *The European Spirit.* London: SCM Press, 1948.

———. "Geleitwort Zur 'Wandlung.'" *Wandlung* 1, no. 1 (1945): 3–6.

———. *The Idea of the University.* Edited by Karl W. Deutsch. Preface by Robert Ulich. Translated by H. A. T. Reiche and H. F. Vanderschmidt. Boston: Beacon Hill, 1959.

———. "Philosophical Autobiography." In *The Philosophy of Karl Jaspers,* edited by Paul Arthur Schlipp, 3–94. New York: Tudor, 1957.

———. *Philosophy.* 2 vols. Translated by E. B. Ashton. 1932. Reprint, Chicago: University of Chicago Press, 1969–70.

———. *The Question of German Guilt.* Translated by E. B. Ashton. 1946. Reprint, New York: Fordham University Press, 2000.

———. *Rechenschaft und Ausblick: Reden und Aufsätze.* Munich: Piper, 1951.

———. "Thesen über Politische Freiheit." *Wandlung* 1, no. 6 (1946): 460–65.

———. "Über meine Philosophie." In *Erneuerung der Universität: Reden und Schriften, 1945/46,* edited by Renato de Rosa, 17–50. Heidelberg: Lambert Schneider, 1986.

———. "Die Verantwortlichkeit der Universitäten." *Neue Zeitung*, 16 May 1947.

———. "Volk und Universität." In *Erneuerung der Universität: Reden und Schriften, 1945/46,* edited by Renato de Rosa, 275–88. Heidelberg: Lambert Schneider, 1986.

———. *Vom europäischen Geist: Vortrag, gehalten bei den Rencontres Internationales de Geneve, September 1946.* Munich: Piper, 1947.

———. "Vom lebendigen Geist der Universität." In *Erneuerung der Universität: Reden und Schriften, 1945/46,* edited by Renato de Rosa, 215–41. Heidelberg: Lambert Schneider, 1986.

Jaspers, Karl, and K. H. Bauer. *Briefwechsel, 1945–1968.* Edited by Renato de Rosa. Berlin: Springer Verlag, 1983.

Jaspers, Karl, and Fritz Ernst. *Vom lebendigen Geist der Universität und vom Studieren.* Heidelberg: Lambert Schneider, 1946.

Jensdreieck, Helmut. *Thomas Mann: Der demokratische Roman.* Düsseldorf: August Babel, 1977.

Joho, Wolfgang. "Nicht originell, sondern wahr und nötig." *Neues Deutschland,* 18 Sept. 1949.

Jünger, Ernst. *Auf den Marmorklippen.* 1960. Reprint, Frankfurt: Ullstein, 1976.

———. *Der Friede, Ein Wort an die Jugend Europas, Ein Wort an die Jugend der Welt.* Zurich: Verlag der Arche, 1949.

———. *Gärten und Straßen.* Tübingen: Heliopolis, 1950.

———. *Der Kampf als inneres Erlebnis.* 1922. Reprint, Berlin: E. S. Mittler, 1960.

———. *The Storms of Steel.* New York: Fertig, 1986.

———. *Strahlungen II: Das zweite Pariser Tagebuch, Kirchhorster Blätter, die Hütte im Weinberg. Jahre der Okkupation.* Munich: Deutscher Taschenbuchverlag, 1995.

———. *Tagebücher II, Strahlungen—Erster Teil.* Vol. 2 of *Werke.* Stuttgart: Ernst Klett, 1960.

Jurczyk, Günter. "Findling von der Waterkant: Hans Albers' Geburtstag jährt sich zum 100. male." *Tagesspiegel,* 22 Sept. 1991.

Ka. "Militaristische Studentenschaft: Die Hochschule ist kein Unterschlupft für arbeitlose Offiziere." *Frankenpost,* 13 Feb. 1946, 3.

Kadow, Hermann. "Aussichten der deutschen Filmwirtschaft." *Frankfurter Hefte* 2, no. 3 (1947): 303–6.

———. "Kino von Innen und Außen." *Frankfurter Hefte* 1, no. 5 (1946): 6–8.

Kaes, Anton. *From Hitler to Heimat: The Return of History as Film.* Cambridge: Harvard University Press, 1989.

Kandiyoti, Deniz. "Identity and Its Discontents: Women and the Nation." In *Colonial Discourse, Postcolonial Theory,* edited by Francis Barker, Peter

Hulme, and Margaret Iversen, 376–91. New York: St. Martin's Press, 1994.

Kater, Michael. *Hitler Youth.* Cambridge: Harvard University Press, 2004.

Käunter, Helmut. "Demontage der Traumfabrik." *Film-Echo,* no. 5 (June) 1947: 170.

K.D. *"Irgendwo in Berlin:* Uraufführung des zweiten Spielfilms der 'Defa' in der Staatsoper." *Neues Deutschland,* 19 Dec. 1946.

Keller, Marion. "Kinder vor der Kamera." *Filmwelt* 12 (1949).

Kerenyi, Karl. "Thomas Mann und ein Neuer Humanismus." *Merkur* 1, no. 4 (1947): 613–15.

Ketelsen, Uwe-K. *Heroisches Theater: Untersuchungen zur Dramentheorie des Dritten Reichs.* Bonn: Bouvier, 1968.

———. *Literatur und Drittes Reich.* Schernfeld: SH-Verlag, 1992.

Ki. "Das Schul-und Erziehungswesen bei uns und den Anderen." *Berliner Zeitung,* 20 Jan. 1946.

Kirchner, Engelbert. "Amerikanische Hochschulen." *Frankfurter Hefte* 4, no. 12 (1949): 1074–77.

Kirkbright, Suzanne. *Karl Jaspers, a Biography: Navigations in Truth.* New Haven: Yale University Press, 2004.

Kittel, Manfred. *Die Legende von der "zweiten Schuld": Vergangenheitsbewältigung in der Ära Adenauer.* Berlin: Ullstein, 1993.

Klein, Richard. *Cigarettes Are Sublime.* Durham: Duke University Press, 1993.

Klönne, Arno. *Jugend im Dritten Reich: Die Hitler-Jugend und ihre Gegner.* Köln: PapyRossa, 1999.

Klose, Werner. *Die Generation im Gleichschritt: Die Hitlerjugend, ein Dokumentarbericht.* Oldenburg: G. Stalling, 1982.

Kluckhorn, Paul. *Die Idee des Menschen in der Goethezeit.* Stuttgart: Deutsche Verlags-Anstalt, 1946.

Kn. "Auf Hundert Schüler kommt ein Lehrer: Sorgen um die Unterbringung der Hofer Volksschulen—Hilfslehrkräfte müssen heran." *Frankenpost,* 20 Feb. 1946, 2.

Knopp, Guido. *Hitler's Children.* Translated by Angus McGeoch. Stroud, UK: Sutton, 2002.

Köbelin, K. "Scharfe Debatte um Dr. Hundhammers Kulturpolitik." *Süddeutsche Zeitung,* 19 July 1947, 1.

Koch, H. W. *Hitler Youth: Origins and Development, 1922–1945.* 1975. Reprint, New York: Stein & Day, 2000.

Kochanowski, Bodo. "Hoppla, jetzt komm'ich." *Berliner Morgenpost,* 22 Sept. 1991.

Koebner, Thomas, Rolf-Peter Janz, and Frank Trommler, eds. *"Mit uns zieht die neue Zeit": Der Mythos Jugend.* Frankfurt: Suhrkamp, 1985.

Koebner, Thomas, Gert Sautermeister, Sigrid Schneider, eds. *Deutschland nach*

Hitler: Zukuntspläne im Exil und aus der Besatzungszeit, 1939–1949. Opladen: Westdeutscher Verlag, 1987.

Koepnick, Lutz. *The Dark Mirror: German Cinema between Hitler and Hollywood.* Berkeley: University of California Press, 2002.

Kogon, Eugen. "Die deutsche Revolution: Gedanken zum zweiten Jahrestag des 20. Juli 1944." *Frankfurter Hefte* 1, no. 4 (1946): 17–26.

———. "Das deutsche Volk und der Nationalsozialismus." *Frankfurter Hefte* 1, no. 2 (1946): 62–70.

———. "Das Jahr der Entscheidungen." *Frankfurter Hefte* 3, no. 1 (1948): 16–28.

———. "Juden und Nichtjuden in Deutschland." *Frankfurter Hefte* 4, no. 9 (1949): 726–29.

———. "Kritik: 'Der Teufels General.'" *Frankfurter Hefte* 3, no. 2 (1948): 183–85.

———. "Politik der Versöhnung." *Frankfurter Hefte* 3, no. 4 (1948): 317–25.

———. "Schon wieder Mythos der 'Kriegsgeneration'?" *Frankfurter Hefte* 2, no. 5 (1947): 520–22.

———. "Die Währungsreform." *Frankfurter Hefte* 3, no. 6 (1948): 504–6.

Koopmann, Helmut. "*Docktor Faustus:* A History of German Introspection." In *Thomas Mann's "Doctor Faustus": A Novel at the Margin of Modernism,* edited by Herbert Lehnert and Peter C. Pfeiffer, 17–31. Columbia, SC: Camden House, 1991.

———. *Thomas Mann: Konstanten seines literarischen Werks.* Göttingen: Vandenhoeck & Ruprecht, 1995.

Korfes, General O. "Langemarck—Wahrheit und Legende." *Freies Deutschland,* 5 Nov. 1944.

Koselleck, Reinhart. "Some Questions regarding the Conceptual History of 'Crisis.'" In *The Practice of Conceptual History: Timing History, Spacing Concepts,* 236–47. Stanford: Stanford University Press, 2002.

———. "War Memorials: Identity Formation of the Survivors." In *The Practice of Conceptual History: Timing History, Spacing Concepts,* 285–326. Stanford: Stanford University Press, 2002.

Kr. "Erziehung neuer Menschen." *Berliner Zeitung,* 6 June 1946, 2.

Krabbe, Wolfgang, ed. *Politische Jugend in der Weimarer Republik.* Vol. 7 of *Dortmunder Historische Studien.* Bochum: Brockmeyer, 1993.

Krauss, Werner. "Die deutsche Universität zwischen Tradition und Demokratie." *Frankfurter Rundschau,* 23 July 1946, 4.

Kreimeier, Klaus. *Kino und Filmindustrie in der BRD: Ideologie und Klassenwirklichkeit nach 1945.* Kronberg: Scriptor, 1973.

Kröhnke, Friedrich. *Literatur und Wirklichkeit.* Edited by Karl Otto Conrady. Vol. 22 of *Junge in schlechter Gesellschaft: Zum Bild des Jugendlichen in deutscher Literatur, 1900–1933.* Bonn: Bouvier, 1981.

"Kulturarbeit nach einem Jahr: Gespräch mit Gerhard Lamprecht." *Sonntag Berlin,* 1 Sept. 1946.

Kurzke, Hermann. *Thomas Mann: Epoche—Werke—Wirkung.* Munich: Beck, 1991.

Laak, Dirk van. *Gespräche in der Sicherheit des Schweigens: Carl Schmitt in der politischen Geistesgeschichte der frühen Bundesrepublik.* Berlin: Akademie, 1993.

Lädtke, Manfred. "Der Hans in allen Gassen." *Berliner Morgenpost,* 16 Jan. 1982.

Lamberti, Marjorie. *The Politics of Education: Teachers and School Reform in Weimar Germany.* New York: Berghahn, 2002.

Laurien, Ingrid. *Politisch-Kulturelle Zeitschriften in den Westzonen, 1945–1949: Ein Beitrag zur politischen Kultur der Nachkriegszeit, Europäische Hochschulschriften.* Frankfurt: Peter Lang, 1991.

Lehnert, Herbert. "'Der gute Krieg ist es, der jede Sache heiligt': Das innere Reich, Langemarck und moralische Konsequenzen." In *Im Dialog mit der Moderne: Zur deutschsprachigen Literatur von der Gründerzeit bis zur Gegenwart,* edited by Roland Jost and Hansgeorg Schmidt-Bergmann Host, 311–21. Frankfurt: Athenäum, 1986.

———. Introduction to *Thomas Mann's "Doctor Faustus": A Novel at the Margin of Modernism,* edited by Herbert Lehnert and Peter C. Pfeiffer. Columbia, SC: Camden House, 1991.

———. "Langemarck—Historisch und Symbolisch." *Orbis Litterarum* 42 (1987): 271–90.

Lennartz, Franz. *Deutsche Schriftsteller des 20: Jahrhunderts im Spiegel der Kritik.* Vol. 3. Stuttgart: Kröner, 1984.

Lenning, Walter. "*Irgendwo in Berlin* Uraufführung des neuen DEFA-Films in der Staatsoper." *Berliner Zeitung,* 20 Dec. 1946.

———. "Kortner auf der Leinwand: Uraufführung des Films *Der Ruf* im 'Mamorhaus.'" *Berliner Zeitung,* 21 Apr. 1949.

———. "Ein moralisches Kuckucksei: . . . *Und über uns der Himmel* in der Neuen Scala." *Berliner Zeitung,* 10 Dec. 1947.

———. "Über ein Jahrhundert hinweg: *Und Wieder 48* im Babylon uraufgeführt," *Berliner Zeitung,* 7 Nov. 1948.

———. "Was heißt Traumfabrik?" *Neue Filmwelt* 1, no. 3 (1949): 3–5.

Lenz, Friedrich. "Alfred Weber." *Deutsche Rundschau* 71, no. 2 (1948): 144.

Lewalter, Christian, and Hans Paeschke. "Thomas Mann und Kierkegaard: Ein Briefwechsel über den *Dr. Faustus* und seine Kritiker." *Merkur* 3, no. 9 (1949): 925–36.

"The Lie of Langemarck: A Crime of the High Command—No Deed of Heroism." *Vorwärts,* 11 Nov. 1929.

Lifton, Robert Jay. Preface to *The Inability to Mourn: Principles of Collective*

Behavior, by Alexander Mitscherlich and Margarete Mitscherlich, ii–xiii. 1967. Reprint, New York: Grove, 1975.

Lindemann, Helmut. "Ernst Jünger." *Deutsche Rundschau* 75, no. 9 (1949): 859.

———. "Die Schuld der Generale." *Deutsche Rundschau* 75, no. 1 (1949): 20–26.

Link. "Hundert Jahre wie ein Tag: Wie Wangenheims Film *Und Wieder 48* entsteht," *Berliner Zeitung,* 28 Mar. 1948.

L.M. "Bekenntnis zu Deutschland: Kortners Film *Der Ruf* im Marmorhaus." *Volksblatt,* 21 Apr. 1949.

———. "Im Dschungel der zertrümmerten Stadt: Der neue DEFA-Film *Irgendwo in Berlin* uraufgeführt." *Volksblatt,* 20 Dec. 1946.

Lommer, Horst. "Die Situation der Jugend." *Frankenpost,* 11 Dec. 1946, 3.

Loose, Gerhard. *Ernst Jünger.* New York: Twayne, 1974.

Lübbe, Hermann. "Der Nationalsozialismus im deutschen Nachkriegsbewusstsein." *Historische Zeitschrift* 236 (1983): 579–99.

Lüdtke, Alf. "'Coming to Terms with the Past': Illusions of Remembering, Ways of Forgetting Nazism in West Germany." *Journal of Modern History* 65 (Sept. 1993): 542–72.

Lüdtke, Alf, Inge Marssolek, and Adelheid von Saldern. *Amerikanisierung: Traum und Alptraum.* Stuttgart: Steiner, 1996.

Luft, Friedrich. "*Irgendwo in Berlin,* Eine DEFA-Uraufführung." *Tagesspiegel,* 20 Dec. 1946.

Lukács, Georg. "Auf der Suche nach dem Bürger." In *Deutsche Literatur in zwei Jahrhunderten,* vol. 7 of *Werke,* 505–34. Berlin: Hermann Luchterhand, 1964.

Maase, Kaspar. *Bravo Amerika: Erkundungen zur Jugendkultur der Bundesrepublik in den fünfziger Jahren.* Hamburg: Junius Verlag, 2000.

———. "Establishing Cultural Democracy: Youth, Americanization, and the Irresistible Rise of Popular Culture." In *The Miracle Years: A Cultural History of West Germany, 1949–1968,* edited by Hanna Schissler, 429–50. Princeton: Princeton University Press, 2001.

Maier, Charles. *The Unmasterable Past: History, Holocaust, and German National Identity.* Cambridge: Harvard University Press, 1988.

Mangikamp, Fritz. "Da reist ich nach Deutschland hinüber." *Neue Film,* 20 Oct. 1948, 2.

Mann, Thomas. "Deutschland und die Deutschen" (1945). In *Gesammelte Werke in Einzelbänden. Frankfurter Ausgabe,* vol. 11, edited by Peter de Mendelssohn, 1126–48. Frankfurt: Fischer, 1980.

———. *Doctor Faustus: The Life of the German Composer as Told by a Friend.* Translated by John E. Woods. New York: Knopf, 1997.

———. *Doktor Faustus: Das Leben des deutschen Tonsetzters Adrian Leverkühn erzählt von einem Freund.* Vol. 11 of *Gesammelte Werke in Einzelbänden. Frankfurter Ausgabe,* edited by Peter de Mendelssohn. Frankfurt: Fischer, 1980.

———. *Die Entstehung des Doktor Faustus: Roman eines Romans.* 1949. Reprint, Frankfurt: Fischer, 1995.

———. *Gesammelte Werke in dreizehn Bänden.* 1960. Reprint, Frankfurt: Fischer, 1974.

———. "Goethe als Repräsentant des bürgerlichen Zeitalters" (1932). In *Ein Appell an die Vernunft: Essays, 1926–1933,* 307–42. Frankfurt: Fischer, 1994.

———. "Nietzsches Philosophie im Lichte unserer Erfahrung" (1947). In *Meine Zeit: Essays, 1945–1955,* 56–92. Frankfurt: Fischer, 1997.

———. *Tagebücher: 1933–1934.* Edited by Peter de Mendelssohn. Frankfurt: Fischer, 1977.

———. *Tagebücher: 1944–1946.* Edited by Inge Jens. Frankfurt: Fischer, 1977.

Mannhardt, Johann Wilhelm. "Politik und Hochschule." *Deutsche Rundschau* 69, no. 1 (1946): 37–43.

Mannheim, Karl. "Die Rolle der Universitäten: Aus einer deutschen Sendung der Londoner Rundfunks." *Neue Auslese* 1, no. 4 (1945): 49–53.

Martin, Biddy. "Feminism, Criticism, and Foucault." *New German Critique* 27, no. 9 (1982): 3–30.

Mathes, Willi. "Probleme um die Jugend (die Jugend-Gemeinschaft)." *Mittelbayerische Zeitung,* 4 July 1947.

Mazower, Mark. *Dark Continent: Europe's Twentieth Century.* 1998. Reprint, New York: Vintage, 2000.

McDonald, Paul. "Reconceptualising Stars." In *Stars,* by Richard Dyer, 177–200. London: British Film Institute, 1998.

———. *The Star System: Hollywood's Production of Popular Identities.* London: Wallflower, 2000.

Meinecke, Friedrich. *Die deutsche Katastrophe: Betrachtungen und Erinnerungen.* Wiesbaden: Eberhard Brockhaus, 1946.

———. *The German Catastrophe: Reflections and Recollections.* Translated by Sidney B. Fay. Cambridge: Harvard University Press, 1950.

"Meinecke revidiert unser Geschichtsbild." *Süddeutsche Zeitung,* 1 Oct. 1946, 2.

Meister, Max. "Noch Etwas über die Schuldfrage." *Merkur* 1, no. 2 (1947): 292–94.

Mendelssohn, Peter. "Gegenstrahlungen." *Monat* 14 (1949).

Menter, Leo. ". . . *Und wieder 48!*" *Weltbühne* 46 (1948): 1458–59.

Merck, Nikolaus. "Augen so blau, so blau: Hans Albers wäre morgen 100 Jahre alt geworden." *Tageszeitung,* 21 Sept. 1991.

Merritt, Richard L. *Democracy Imposed: U.S. Occupation Policy and the German*

Public, 1945–1949. New Haven: Yale University Press, 1995.

Milch, Werner. "Thomas Manns *Doktor Faustus*," *Sammlung* 3, no. 6 (1948): 360.

Miller Lane, Barbara. *Architecture and Politics in Germany, 1918–1945.* 1968. Reprint, Cambridge: Harvard University Press, 1988.

Minssen, Friedrich. "Europa und die deutsche Jugend." *Merkur* 1, no. 4 (1947): 605–8.

———. "Notizen von einem Treffen junger Schriftsteller." *Frankfurter Hefte* 3, no. 2 (1948): 110–11.

———. "Der Widerstand gegen den Widerstand." *Frankfurter Hefte* 4, no. 10 (1949): 884–88.

Miska, Peter. "'Herr Albers läßt bitten . . . ': Interview Von Peter Miska." *Film (für Sie und Ihn)* 12, no. 2 (1949): 3–4.

Mitchell, Maria. "Materialism and Secularism: CDU Politicians and National Socialism, 1945–49." *Journal of Modern History* 67 (1995): 278–308.

Mitscherlich, Alexander, and Margarete Mitscherlich. *The Inability to Mourn: Principles of Collective Behavior.* 1967. Reprint, New York: Grove, 1975.

Mitscherlich, Alexander, and Alfred Weber, *Freier Sozialismus.* Heidelberg: L. Schneider, 1946.

Mitterauer, Michael. *A History of Youth.* Oxford: B. Blackwell, 1992.

Moeller, Robert. "Germans as Victims? Thoughts on a Post–Cold War History of World War II's Legacies." *History and Memory* 17, nos. 1–2 (2005): 147–94.

———. *Protecting Motherhood: Women and Family in the Politics of Postwar West Germany.* Berkeley: University of California Press, 1993.

———. *War Stories: The Search for a Usable Past in the Federal Republic of Germany.* Berkeley: University of California Press, 2001.

Moeller van den Bruck, Arthur. *Das Recht der jungen Völker.* 1919. Reprint, Berlin: Verlag der Nahe Osten, 1932.

Mogge, Winfried. "Wandervogel, Freideutsche Jugend und Bünde: Zum Jugendbild der bürgerlichen Jugendbewegung." In *"Mit uns zieht die neue Zeit": Der Mythos Jugend,* edited by Thomas Koebner, Rolf-Peter Janz, and Frank Trommler, 174–98. Frankfurt: Suhrkamp, 1985.

"*Die Mörder Sind Unter Uns:* Der Erste deutsche Spielfilm in Berlin uraufgeführt." *Frankenpost,* 23 Oct. 1946.

Morin, Edgar. *The Stars.* 1957. Reprint, New York: Grove, 1960.

Mosberg, Helmuth. *Reeducation: Umerziehung und Lizenzpresse im Nachkriegsdeutschland.* Munich: Universitas, 1991.

Mosse, George. *Fallen Soldiers: Reshaping the Memory of the World War.* New York: Oxford University Press, 1991.

———. *Nationalism and Sexuality.* Madison: University of Wisconsin Press, 1985.

———. "Two World Wars and the Myth of the War Experience." *Journal of Contemporary History* 21 (1986): 491–513.

Mückenberger, Christian, and Günther Jordan. *"Sie sehen selbst, Sie hören selbst. . . .": Die DEFA von ihren Anfängen bis 1949.* Marburg: Hitzeroth, 1994.

Mühl-Benninghaus, Wolfgang. "Vom antifaschistischen Aufbruch zum sozialistischen Realismus: Die Anfänge der DEFA." In *Der deutsche Film: Aspekte seiner Geschichte von den Anfängen bis zur Gegenwart,* edited by Uli Jung, 215–31. Trier: Wissenschaftler Trier, 1993.

Mühlberg, Walther. "Jugend bedroht von Nihilismus." *Frankfurter Rundschau,* 9 Apr. 1946, 4.

Mulvey, Laura. "Visual Pleasure and Narrative Cinema." In *Film Theory and Criticism: Introductory Readings,* 4th ed., edited by Gerald Mast, Marshall Cohen, and Leo Braudy. New York: Oxford University Press, 1992.

Münster, Clemens. "Humanistische und realistiche Bildung." *Frankfurter Hefte* 2, no. 2 (1947): 209–10.

———. "Problem Nummer Eins: Der Mensch." *Frankfurter Hefte* 3, no. 3 (1948): 202–4.

———. "Die Universität 1946." *Frankfurter Hefte* 1, no. 1 (1946): 7–9.

"Nach berühmten Mustern: 500. Rede an die deutsche Jugend nach Ernst Wiechert." *Berlin Kurier,* 2 Mar. 1946.

Naimark, Norman. *The Russians in Germany: A History of the Soviet Zone of Occupation, 1945–49.* Cambridge: Harvard University Press, 1995.

Nandy, Ashis. *The Intimate Enemy: Loss and Recovery of Self under Colonialism.* New York: Oxford University Press, 1983.

Neaman, Elliot Y. *A Dubious Past: Ernst Jünger and the Politics of Literature after Nazism.* Berkeley: University of California Press, 1999.

Neckar, W. "Akademische Freiheit? Mutige und ängstliche Universitäten." *Frankenpost,* 30 Oct. 1946, 6.

Nelson, Cary, Paula A. Treichler, and Lawrence Grossberg. "Cultural Studies: An Introduction." In *Cultural Studies,* edited by Cary Nelson, Paula A. Treichler, and Lawrence Grossberg, 1–22. New York: Routledge, 1992.

Neubauer, John. *The Fin-de-Siècle Culture of Adolescence.* New Haven: Yale University Press, 1992.

Nevin, Thomas. *Ernst Jünger and Germany: Into the Abyss, 1914–45.* Durham: Duke University Press, 1996.

Niekisch, Ernst. *Deutsche Daseinsverfehlung.* Koblenz: D. Folbach, 1946.

Niemöller, Martin. "Letter to the Rector of the University of Erlangen." in *Als der Krieg zu Ende war: Literarisch-politische Publizistik, 1945–50,* edited by Gerhard Hay, Hartmut Rambaldo, and Joachim W. Storck, 174–75. Stuttgart: Ernst Klett, 1973.

Niven, Bill. *Facing the Nazi Past: United Germany and the Legacy of the Third Reich.* New York: Routledge, 2002.

Nothingale, Alan L. *Building the East German Myth: Historical Mythology and Youth Propaganda in the German Democratic Republic, 1945–1989.* Ann Arbor: University of Michigan Press, 1999.

Olick, Jeffrey K. *In the House of the Hangman: The Agonies of German Defeat, 1943–1949.* Chicago: University of Chicago Press, 2005.

Orlowski, Hubert. "Die größere Kontroverse: Zur deutschen 'nichtakademischen' Rezeption des *Doktor Faust* von Thomas Mann (1947–1950)." In *Erzählung und Erzählforschung im 20. Jahrhundert,* edited by Rolf Kloepfer und Gisela Janetzke-Dillner, 245–55. Stuttgart: Kohlhammer, 1981.

Paarmann, Heinz. "Das Gesicht der deutschen Jugend." *Deutsche Rundschau* 70, no. 9 (1947): 189–94.

Padover, Saul. *Psychologist in Germany.* New York: Foreign Policy Association, 1951.

Paetel, Karl O. *Jugend in der Entscheidung, 1913–1933–1945.* Bad Godesberg: Voggenreiter, 1963.

Pearson, Roberta. *Eloquent Gestures: The Transformation of Performance Style in the Griffith Biograph Films.* Berkeley: University of California Press, 1992.

Pechel, Rudolf. "Unsere vordringlichste Aufgabe." *Deutsche Rundschau* 69, no. 1 (1946): 45–49.

———. "Der 20. Juli." *Deutsche Rundschau* 69, no. 3 (1946): 67–68.

Petersen, Jürgen. "Thomas Mann fordert den musikalischen Faust." *Nordwestdeutsche Hefte* 1, no. 5 (1946): 52.

Peterson, Edward Norman. *The American Occupation of Germany: Retreat to Victory.* Detroit: Wayne State University Press, 1977.

Peukert, Detlev. *Inside Nazi Germany: Conformity, Opposition, and Racism in Everyday Life.* London: Batsford, 1987.

———. *The Weimar Republic: Crisis of Classical Modernity.* London: Penguin, 1991.

Pike, David. *The Politics of Culture in Soviet-Occupied Germany, 1945–49.* Stanford: Stanford University Press, 1992.

Pleyer, Peter. *Deutscher Nachkriegsfilm, 1946–1948.* Vol. 4 of *Studien zur Publizistik.* Münster: C. J. Fahle, 1965.

Poiger, Uta. *Jazz, Rock, and Rebels: Cold War Politics and American Culture in a Divided Germany.* Berkeley: University of California Press, 2000.

Pois, Robert. *Friedrich Meinecke and German Politics in the Twentieth Century.* Berkeley: University of California Press, 1972.

Polletta, Francesca. "Politicizing Childhood: The 1980 Zurich Burns Movement." *Social Text* 33 (1992): 82–102.

Pringsheim, F. "Erziehung zum Recht: Auszug aus einer Ansprache an deutsche Studenten: Aus der 'Neuen Zürcher Zeitung.'" *Neue Auslese* 3, no. 1

(1948): 63–69.

Pronay, Nicholas, and Keith Wilson. *The Political Re-education of Germany and Her Allies after World War II.* London: Croom Helm, 1985.

Proske, Rüdiger. "Kritik: Jugend im Chaos." *Frankfurter Hefte* 3, no. 11 (1948): 1056–58.

———. "Das Porträt: Dr. Chaim Ben Ozer Weizmann; Vater des staates Isreal." *Frankfurter Hefte* 4, no. 4 (1949): 345–47.

———. "Die vereinigten Staaten von Europa: Idee und beginnende Wirklichkeit." *Frankfurter Hefte* 3, no. 1 (1948): 72–77.

———. "Ein Weg zur Verständigung." *Frankfurter Hefte* 2, no. 4 (1947): 324–26.

Proske, Rüdiger, and Walter Weymann-Weyhe. "Wir aus dem Krieg: Der Weg der Jüngen Generation." *Frankfurter Hefte* 3, no. 9 (1948): 792–803.

Prowe, Diethelm. "German Democratization as Conservative Restabilization: The Impact of American Policy." In *American Policy and the Reconstruction of Germany, 1945–1955,* edited by Axel Frohn, Jeffrey M. Diefendorf, and Hermann-Josef Rupieper, 307–30. New York: Cambridge University Press, 1993.

———. "'The Miracle' of the Political-Culture Shift: Democratization between Americanization and Conservative Reintegration." In *The Miracle Years: A Cultural History of West Germany, 1949–1968,* ed. Hanna Schissler, 451–58. Princeton: Princeton University Press, 2001.

Prümm, Karl. "Jugend ohne Väter: Zu den autobiographischen Jugendromanen der späten zwanziger Jahre." In *"Mit uns zieht die neue Zeit": Der Mythos Jugend,* edited by Thomas Koebner, Rolf-Peter Janz, and Frank Trommler, 563–89. Frankfurt: Suhrkamp, 1985.

Prutti, Brigitte. "Women Characters in *Doctor Faustus.*" In *Thomas Mann's "Doctor Faustus": A Novel at the Margin of Modernity,* edited by Herbert Lehnert and Peter C. Pfeiffer, 99–112. Columbia, SC: Camden House, 1991.

Pütz, Karl-Heinz. "Business or Propaganda? American Films and Germany, 1942–1946." *Englisch-Amerikanische Studien* 2, no. 3 (1983): 394–415.

Rabinbach, Anson. *In the Shadow of Catastrophe: German Intellectuals between Apocalypse and Enlightenment.* Berkeley: University of California Press, 2000.

Radku, Joachim. "Die singende und die tote Jugend: Der Umgang mit Jugendmythen im italienischen und deutschen Faschismus." In *"Mit uns zieht die neue Zeit": Der Mythos Jugend,* edited by Thomas Koebner, Rolf-Peter Janz, and Frank Trommler, 97–127. Frankfurt: Suhrkamp, 1985.

r.d. "Fritz Kortner diskutiert über *Der Ruf.*" *Neue Filmwoche,* 14 May 1949.

Regenbogen, Otto. "Humanistische Halbbildung." *Merkur* 3, no. 9 (1949): 920–25.

Reimann, Viktor. *Goebbels.* Translated by Stephen Wendt. Garden City, NY: Doubleday, 1976.

Reisfeld, Bert. "Ende der Traum-Fabrik? Krise und Wandel in Hollywood." *Neue Film* 11, no. 2 (1948): 1.

Reithinger, Anton. "Die Bedeutung des amerikanischen Wiederaufbaupro-gramms für Europa." *Merkur* 3, no. 2 (1949): 180–85.

Rempel, Gerhard. *Hitler's Children: The Hitler Youth and the SS.* Chapel Hill: University of North Carolina Press, 1989.

Remy, Steven P. *The Heidelberg Myth: The Nazification and Denazification of a German University.* Cambridge: Harvard University Press, 2002.

Rentschler, Eric. *The Films of G. W. Pabst: An Extraterritorial Cinema.* New Brunswick: Rutgers University Press, 1990.

———. "Germany: The Past That Would Not Go Away." In *World Cinema since 1945,* 208–51. New York: Ungar, 1987.

———. *The Ministry of Illusion: Nazi Cinema and Its Afterlife.* Cambridge: Harvard University Press, 1996.

———. *West German Filmmakers on Film: Visions and Voices.* New York: Holmes & Meier, 1988.

Report of the United States Education Mission to Germany. Department of State Publication 2664, European Series 16. Washington, DC: Department of State, 1946.

Reuth, Ralf Georg. *Goebbels.* Translated by Krishna Winston. 1990. Reprint, New York: Harcourt Brace, 1993.

Riebau, Hans. "Thomas Mann und die Nazis." *Süddeutsche Zeitung,* 17 July 1947.

Ringelband, Wilhelm. "Kapitulation des künstlerischen Films?" *Neue Film* 18, no. 2 (1948): 1.

Ritter, Gerhard. "Die aussenpolitischen Hoffnungen der Verschwörer des 20. Juli 1944." *Merkur* 3, no. 11 (1949): 1121–38.

———. "Der deutsche Professor im 'Dritten Reich.'" *Gegenwart* 1, no. 1 (1945): 23–26.

———. *Europa und die deutsche Frage.* Munich: Münchner Verlag, 1948.

———. *Geschichte als Bildungsmacht.* Stuttgart: Deutsche Verlags-Anstalt, 1946.

Rodowick, D. N. *Gilles Deleuze's Time Machine.* Durham: Duke University Press, 1997.

Roger. "Emigranten-Erfahrungen: *Der Ruf.*" *Berliner Film Blätter,* no. 9 (1949).

Rommelspacher, Franz. "Neuer und alter Geist in der Studentenschaft: Eine Ansprache und ein Bericht." *Frankfurter Hefte* 1, no. 2 (1946): 52–61.

Rompe, Dr. "Der Zustand der Berliner Universität." *Berliner Zeitung,* 9 Feb. 1946, 2.

Röpke, Wilhelm. *Die deutsche Frage.* Erlenbach-Zurich: E. Rentsch, 1945.

Rosa, Renato de, ed. *Erneuerung der Universität: Reden und Schriften, 1945/46.* Heidelberg: Lambert Schneider, 1986.

———. "Politische Akzente im Leben eines Philosophen: Karl Jaspers in Heidelberg, 1901–1946." In *Erneuerung der Universität: Reden und Schriften, 1945/46,* edited by Renato de Rosa, 301–423. Heidelberg: Lambert Schneider, 1986.

Rosenbaum, Jonathan. "Ruiz Hopping and Buried Treasures." *Film Comment* (Apr.–May 1997). Reprinted in *Essential Cinema: On the Necessity of Film Canons,* 215–31. Baltimore: Johns Hopkins University Press, 2004.

Rosner, Karl. "Dämonie als Macht: Ein parapsychologischer Versuch." *Deutsche Rundschau* 71, no. 5 (1948): 111–16.

———. "Trostbrief an einen jungen Vater." *Deutsche Rundschau* 69, no. 6 (1946): 236–39.

Ross, Kristin. *Fast Cars, Clean Bodies: Decolonization and the Reordering of French Culture.* 1995. Reprint, Cambridge: MIT University Press, 1999.

Rüdiger, Jutta. *Die Hitler-Jugend und ihr Selbstverständnis im Spiegel ihrer Aufgabengebiete.* Preussisch-Oldendorf: Deutsche Verlagsgesellschaft, 1999.

Rühle, Günther. *Zeit und Theater: Diktatur und Exile, 1933–1945.* Vol. 3. Berlin: Propyläen, 1974.

Rupieper, Hermann-Josef. *Die Wurzeln der westdeutschen Nachkriegsdemokratie: der amerikanische Beitrag, 1945–1952.* Opladen: Westdeutscher Verlag, 1993.

R.W. "Wer darf studieren? Die Akademie der Arbeit soll wieder errichtet werden." *Frankfurter Rundschau,* 28 Mar. 1946.

Saalmann, Dieter. "Fascism and Aesthetics: Joseph Goebbels's Novel *Michael:* A German Fate through the Pages of a Diary (1929)." *Orbis Litterarum* 41 (1986): 213–28.

Sabais, Heinz-Winfried. "Die Situation der Jungen Dichtung." *Deutsche Rundschau* 69, no. 7 (1946): 76–81.

Santner, Eric. "History beyond the Pleasure Principle: Some Thoughts on the Representation of Trauma." In *Probing the Limits of Representation: Nazism and the "Final Solution,"* edited by Saul Friedländer, 143–54. Cambridge: Harvard University Press, 1992.

———. *My Own Private Germany: Daniel Paul Schreber's Secret History of Modernity.* Princeton: Princeton University Press, 1996.

———. *Stranded Objects: Mourning, Memory, and Film in Postwar Germany.* Ithaca: Cornell University Press, 1990.

Sassen, Saskia. "Spatial and Temporalities of the Global: Elements of a Theorization," *Public Culture* 12, no. 1 (2000): 215–32.

Scherer, Peter. *Wiedergeburt der Menschlichkeit.* Munich: Kurt Desch Verlag, 1946.

Schildt, Axel, and Arnold Sywottek, eds. *Modernisierung im Wiederaufbau: Die westdeutsche Gesellschaft der 50er Jahre.* Bonn: Dietz, 1993.

Schissler, Hanna, ed. *The Miracle Years: A Cultural History of West Germany, 1949–1968.* Princeton: Princeton University Press, 2001.

Schivelbusch, Wolfgang. *The Culture of Defeat: On National Trauma, Mourning, and Recovery.* Translated by Jefferson Chase. New York: Henry Holt, 2001.

———. *Disenchanted Night: The Industrialization of Light in the Nineteenth Century.* Translated by Angela Davies. Berkeley: University of California Press, 1995.

———. *In a Cold Crater: Cultural and Intellectual Life in Berlin, 1945–1948.* Translated by Kelly Barry. Berkeley: University of California Press, 1998.

Schlander, Otto. *Reeducation—Ein politisch-pädagogisches Prinzip im Widerstreit der Gruppen.* Bern: Peter Lang, 1975.

Schneeberger, Guido. *Nachlese zu Heidegger: Dokumente zu seinem Leben und Denken.* Bern: Buchdrückerei, 1962.

Schneider, Eugen. "Münchner Universität und die Kohlen." *Süddeutsche Zeitung,* 1 Feb. 1947, 3.

Schneider, Reinhold. "Melodie des Leids/Zu Ernst Wiecherts sechzigsten Geburtstag am 18. Mai 1947." *Süddeutsche Zeitung,* 17 May 1947.

Schnog, Karl. "Probleme der Jugend." *Frankenpost,* 6 Nov. 1946.

Schönfeld, Friedrich. "*Der Ruf.*" *Kirche und Film,* no. 10 (1949): 1.

Schrenck-Notzing, Caspar von. *Charakterwäsche: Die Politik der Amerikanischen Umerziehung.* Frankfurt: Ullstein, 1994.

Schröder, Edward. "Ernst Jünger und die Maßstäbe." *Frankfurter Hefte* 4, no. 9 (1949): 799–802.

———. "Politik in der Schule." *Frankfurter Hefte* 4, no. 3 (1949): 202–4.

———. "Das Porträt: Hermann Hesse." *Frankfurter Hefte* 3, no. 9 (1948): 841–45.

Schröder, Rudolf Alexander. *Der Mann und das Jahr, Ein Nachtgespräch/Silvester 1945.* Frankfurt: Suhrkamp, 1946.

Schulin, Ernst. "Friedrich Meineckes Stellung in der deutschen Geschichtswissenschaft." In *Friedrich Meinecke Heute,* edited by Michael Erbe, 25–49. Berlin: Colloquium, 1981.

Schulte-Sasse, Linda. *Entertaining the Third Reich: Illusions of Wholeness in Nazi Cinema.* Durham: Duke University Press, 1996.

Schümer, Dirk. "Einmal muß es vorbei sein: Gedenkblatt zum hundertsten Geburtstag von Hans Albers." *Frankfurter Allgemeine Zeitung,* 21 Sept. 1991.

Schütte, Elisabeth. "Ruf der Welt an die deutsche Jugend." *Süddeutsche Zeitung,* 1 July 1947, 1.

———. "Zwischen Gestern und Morgen: Der erste Münchner Film-Aufnahmen im Regina-Hotel." *Süddeutsche Zeitung,* 29 Apr. 1947, 3.

Schwarz, Egon. "Jewish Characters in *Doctor Faustus.*" In *Thomas Mann's "Doctor Faustus": A Novel at the Margin of Modernity,* edited by Herbert Lehnert and Peter C. Pfeiffer, 119–40. Columbia, SC: Camden House, 1991.

Schwarz, Hans. *Die Wiedergeburt des heroischen Menschen: Eine Langemarck-Rede vor d. Greifswalder Studentenschaft am 11. Nov. 1928.* Berlin: Verlag des Nahen Ostens, 1930.

Schwarz, Hans-Peter. *Der konservative Anarchist: Politik und Zeitkritik Ernst Jüngers.* Freiburg: Rombach, 1962.

Schwertfeger, Bernhard. *Rätsel um Deutschland.* Heidelberg: C. Winter, 1948.

Sebald, W. G. *Air War and Literature: Zurich Lectures.* In *On the Natural History of Destruction,* translated by Anthea Bell, 1–104. New York: Random House, 2003.

Seelmann-Eggebert, Ulrich. "Die deutsche Filmgestaltung zwischen Gestern und Morgen." *Wochenpost* 36 (1948).

Sell, Friedrich. "Ein Kommentar zu Thomas Manns *Doktor Faustus.*" *Wandlung* 3, no. 5 (1948): 403–18.

Shandley, Robert R. *Rubble-Films: German Cinema in the Shadow of the Third Reich.* Philadelphia: Temple University Press, 2001.

Shaviro, Stephen. *Theory Out of Bounds.* Vol. 2 of *The Cinematic Body.* Minnesota: University of Minnesota Press, 1993.

Silberman, Marc. In *German Cinema: Texts in Contexts.* Detroit: Wayne State University Press, 1995.

Silverman, Kaja. *Male Subjectivity at the Margins.* New York: Routledge, 1993.

Sonnemann, Ulrich. "Thomas Mann oder Mass und Anspruch." *Frankfurter Hefte* 3, no. 7 (1948): 625–40.

Spengler, Oswald. *The Decline of the West.* Vol. 1. 1918. Reprint, New York: Knopf, 1932.

Stacey, Jackie. *Star Gazing: Hollywood Cinema and Female Spectatorship.* London: Routledge, 1994.

Stadelmann, Rudolf. "Das Jahr 1848 und die deutsche Geschichte." *Deutsche Rundschau* 71, no. 5 (1948): 99–110.

Staiger, Janet. "Seeing Stars." *Velvet Light Trap* 20 (Summer 1983): 10–14.

Staudte, Wolfgang. "Interview mit Staudte." In *Die Mörder sind unter uns— Ehe im Schatten—Die Buntkarierten—Rotation. Filmerzählungen,* edited by Ellen Blauert. Henschel: Berlin/DDR, 1969.

Stegemann, Herbert. "Ernst Wiechert." *Deutsche Rundschau* 71, no. 4 (1948): 44–49.

Stein, Gottfried. "Ernst Jünger." *Frankfurter Hefte* 3, no. 5 (1948): 443–54.

Steinhauer. "Inge von Wangenheim." *Neue Filmwelt* 7, no. 2 (1948): 25.

Steinweis, Alan. *Art, Ideology, and Economics in Nazi Germany: The Reich*

Chambers of Music, Theater, and the Visual Arts. Chapel Hill: University of North Carolina Press, 1993.

Stern, Fritz. *The Politics of Cultural Despair: A Study in the Rise of the German Ideology.* Berkeley: University of California Press, 1974.

Sternberger, Dolf. "Aspekte des bürgerlichen Charakters." *Wandlung* 4, no. 5 (1949): 474–86.

———. "Begriff des Vaterlands." *Wandlung* 2, no. 6 (1947): 499–501.

———. "Bürgerlichkeit." *Wandlung* 3, no. 3 (1948): 195–99.

———. "Herrschaft der Freiheit." *Wandlung* 1, no. 7 (1945–46): 556–71.

———. "Zweimal in Kino." *Wandlung* 3, no. 2 (1948): 99–105.

Stoler, Ann. *Carnal Knowledge and Imperial Power: Race and the Intimate in Colonial Rule.* Berkeley: University of California Press, 2003.

———. *Race and the Education of Desire: Foucault's History of Sexuality and the Colonial Order of Things.* Durham: Duke University Press, 1995.

Strachura, Peter D. *The German Youth Movement, 1900–45: An Interpretative and Documentary History.* London: Macmillan, 1981.

———. *Nazi Youth in the Weimar Republic.* Santa Barbara: Clio Books, 1975.

Studlar, Gaylyn. *In the Realm of Pleasure: Von Sternberg, Dietrich, and the Masochistic Aesthetic.* New York: Columbia University Press, 1988.

Suskind, W. E. "An die Jugend." In *Die Frage der Jugend,* edited by Rudolf Schneider-Schelde. Munich: Kurt Desch, 1946.

S.Z. "Die Amnestie für Jugend." *Süddeutsche Zeitung,* 8 July 1946, 3.

———. "Die Schule auf neuen Wegen." *Süddeutsche Zeitung,* 1947, 2.

Tasker, Yvonne. *Spectacular Bodies: Gender, Genre, and the Action Cinema.* London: Routledge, 1993.

Tent, James. *Mission on the Rhine: Reeducation and Denazification in American-Occupied Germany.* Chicago: University of Chicago Press, 1982.

Thiele, Jens. "Die Lehren aus der Vergangenheit: *Rotation* (1949)." In *Fischer Filmgeschichte,* vol. 3 of *Auf der Suche nach Werten,* edited by Werner Faulstich and Helmut Korte, 126–47. Frankfurt: Fischer Taschenbuch, 1990.

Tipton, Frank B. *A History of Modern Germany.* Berkeley: University of California Press, 2003.

Trevor-Roper, Hugh. *The Last Days of Hitler.* New York: Macmillan, 1947.

Trommler, Frank. "Mission ohne Ziel." In *"Mit uns zieht die neue Zeit": Der Mythos Jugend,* edited by Thomas Koebner, Rolf-Peter Janz, and Frank Trommler, 14–49. Frankfurt: Suhrkamp, 1985.

Unruh, Karl. *Langemarck: Legende und Wirklichkeit.* Koblenz: Bernard & Graefe, 1986.

Vaget, Hans. "Mann, Joyce, and the Question of Modernism in *Doctor Faustus.*" In *Thomas Mann's "Doctor Faustus": A Novel at the Margin of Modernity,* edited by Herbert Lehnert and Peter C. Pfeiffer, 167–92.

Columbia, SC: Camden House, 1991.

Vietta, Silvio, and Hans G. Kemper. *Expressionismus.* Munich: DTV, 1975.

Visarius, Karsten. "Hans-Albers-Reihe im Fernsehen: Vom gewissenlosen Verführer zum Held." *Frankfurter Allgemeine Zeitung,* 15 Feb. 1982.

Weber, Adolf. "Deutschland und Europa: Zugleich eine Betrachtung des Ruhrstatuts." *Wandlung* 4, no. 2 (1949): 99–111.

———. "Student und Politik: Ein Vortrag." *Wandlung* 2, no. 4 (1947): 283–94.

———. *Wohin steuert die Wirtschaft?* Munich: Kurt Desch Verlag, 1946.

Weber, Alfred, and Wilhelm Röpke. "Deutschland, Europa und die Welt." *Frankfurter Hefte* 3, no. 5 (1948): 461–66.

Weber, Carl August. "Die Blaue Blume." In *Die Frage der Jugend,* edited by Rudolf Schneider-Schelde, 49–54. Munich: Kurt Desch, 1946.

Weel, Edith. "Die Sorgen der Mütter: *Irgendwo in Berlin,* zu dem neuen DEFA-Film, der in der Staatsoper uraufgeführt wurde." *Für Dich,* 29 Dec. 1946.

Wehner, Josef Magnus. *Langemarck: Ein Vermächtnis.* Munich: Albert Langen & Georg Müller, 1932.

Weiner, Marc. *Undertones of Insurrection: Music, Politics, and the Social Sphere in the Modern German Narrative.* Lincoln: University of Nebraska Press, 1993.

Weiner, Susan. *Enfants Terribles: Youth and Femininity in the Mass Media in France, 1945–68.* Baltimore: Johns Hopkins University Press, 2001.

Weise, Dr. Gerhard. "6300 Studenten in München: Übersicht über die neuen deutschen Hochschulen." *Frankenpost,* 12 Oct. 1946.

Weismantel, Leo. "Demokratie als Lebensform—Eine Erziehungsaufgabe." *Münchner Mittag,* 11 July 1947.

Welch, David. *Propaganda and the German Cinema, 1933–1945.* 1983. Reprint, New York: I. B. Tauris, 2001.

Wenzl, Alois. "Vom Sinn der höheren Schulen: Bemerkungen zur Schulreform." *Süddeutsche Zeitung,* 17 May 1947.

Werner, B. E. "Der atomisierte geistige Raum." *Athena* 2, no. 6 (1947–48): 95–96.

Weyer, Adam, ed. *Reden: Reden an die deutsche Jugend im zwanzigsten Jahrhundert.* Wuppertal-Barmen: Jugenddienst-Verlag, 1966.

Wiechert, Ernst. *Der Dichter und die Jugend.* Zurich: Die Arche, 1946.

———. "Der Dichter und seine Zeit." In *Sämtliche Werke in zehn Bänden,* 10:368–80. Vienna: Kurt Desch, 1957.

———. *Jahre und Zeiten, Erinnerungen.* 1949. Reprint, Erlenbach-Zurich: E. Rentsch, 1951.

———. *Missa Sine Nomine.* Munich: Kurt Desch, 1952.

———. *Rede an die deutsche Jugend.* Berlin: Aufbau, 1947.

———. *Wälder und Menschen: Eine Jugend.* Frankfurt: Ullstein, 1967.

Wieruszowski, Helene. "Gespräche mit deutschen Studenten." *Wandlung* 4, no. 1 (1949): 82–91.

Willett, Ralph. *The Americanization of Germany, 1945–49.* New York: Routledge, 1989.

Williams, Linda. "When the Woman Looks . . . " In *Re-Vision: Feminist Essays in Film Analysis,* edited by Mary Ann Doane, Pat Mellencamp, and Linda Williams, 83–99. Frederick, MD: AFI-University, 1984.

Willis, Roy F. *The French in Germany.* Stanford: Stanford University Press, 1962.

Wilms, Wilfried. "Taboo and Repression in W. G. Sebald's *On the Natural History of Destruction.*" In *W. G. Sebald: A Critical Companion,* edited by J. J. Long and Anne Whitehead, 175–90. Seattle: University of Washington Press, 2004.

Wippermann, Wolfgang. "Friedrich Meinecke und die deutsche Katastrophe." In *Friedrich Meinecke Heute,* edited by Michael Erbe, 101–21. Berlin: Colloquium, 1981.

Wolff, Rudolf. *Thomas Mann: Dr. Faustus und die Wirkung.* Bonn: Bouvier, 1983.

Wolgast, Eike. "Karl-Heinz Bauer—Der erste Heidelberger Nachkriegsrektor: Weltbild und Handeln, 1945–46." In *Heidelberg 1945,* edited by Jürgen Hess, Hartmut Lehmann, and Volker Sollin, 107–29. Stuttgart: Franz Steiner Verlag, 1996.

Wolin, Richard. *The Heidegger Controversy: A Critical Reader.* New York: Columbia University Press, 1991.

Wollenberg, H. H. *Fifty Years of German Film.* 1948. Reprint, New York: Arno, 1972.

Wood, Robin. *Personal Views: Explorations in Film.* London: Gordon Fraser, 1976.

Young-Bruehl, Elisabeth. *Freedom and Karl Jaspers's Philosophy.* New Haven: Yale University Press, 1981.

———. *Hannah Arendt: For Love of the World.* New Haven: Yale University Press, 2004.

Zahn, Peter von. "Verrat an der deutschen Jugend." In *Die Frage der Jugend: Aufsätze, Berichte, Briefe und Reden.* Munich: Kurt Desch, 1946.

Zerkaulen, Heinrich. *Jugend von Langemarck: Ein Schauspiel in drei Akten und einem Nachspiel* (1933). In *Zeit und Theater,* edited by Günther Rühle, 3:141–94. Berlin: Propyläen Verlag, 1974.

Zink, Harold. *The United States in Germany.* Princeton: Princeton University Press, 1957.

Index

361

Rentschler, Eric, 48, 188, 214,
287nn70, 79, 311n1,
314–15nn28, 31, 318n4,
320n17
resocialization, 178, 183, 227
responsibility: and adult guilt, 253;
collective responsibility, 167; in
film, 181; for Nazi crimes, 123;
political, 196, 211; youth assuming, 269
restoration: of education, 152; of a
former unity, 144; of freedom,
105; of *Geist*, 93; of German
democracy, 90, 138, 295n3; of
the individual, 105; of paternal
hierarchy, 169, 255; of social
order, 184
revolution. *See* Nazi revolution; youth
revolution
Riefenstahl, Leni, 202
right: extremism, 94; liberal tradition,
96; political, 5, 37, 99, 110, 159,
282n16
Rilke, Rainer Maria, 93
Ringelband, Wilhelm, 318n2
Rittau, Gerhard, 182
Ritter, Gerhard, 134–35, 294–95n2,
303n17
Röhm, Ernst, 22
Rommelspacher, Franz, 306n69
Ross, Kristin, 3, 275n4
Rossbach, 44
Rossellini, Robert, 224, 300n46
rubble film. *See under* film
rubble woman. *See Trümmerfrau*
rule of law: youth fleeing the, 240
Rupieper, Hermann-Josef, 63,
280n48, 288–92nn12, 19, 22,
49, 68

SA (storm troops), 22, 43
Sachsenhausen camp, 59, 103
safety of silence (*Sicherheit des
Schweigens*), 295n5
Santner, Eric, 6, 8, 277n15
Sassen, Saskia, 287n66

Scherer, Peter, 294n1
Schildt, Axel, and Arnold Sywottek,
295n9
Schiller, Friedrich, 42–43, 93,
297n19
Schirach, Baldur von, 19–23,
280–81nn1, 2
Schivelbusch, Wolfgang, 38,
284nn37, 46
Schlieffen plan, 35
Schneider, Reinhold, 171,
310–11nn112, 127
Schneider-Schelde, Rudolf, 294n1
Schröder, Rudolf Alexander, 294n1
Schuld. See guilt (*Schuld*)
Schümer, Dirk, 319n11,
321–22nn20, 30
Schwarz, Hans, 286n65,
299–300nn30, 48, 55, 60, 302
science: natural, 136, 144; occult, 99;
political, 136; pseudoscience, and
the humanities, 142; and the
search for truth, 142–43; social,
72
Sebald, W. G., 6, 8, 9, 63–64, 106,
112, 277–78nn14, 15, 23,
289n14, 298n20, 300n38
S.E.D (Socialist Union Party), 177,
262
self-determination, 71
shame, 38, 121
Shandley, Robert, 9, 278n27, 322n28
Shaviro, Stephen, 182, 313
shortage: of coal and housing, 89; of
food, 89; of medical care, 137; of
paper, 289; of teachers, 70
Silberman, Marc, 315–16nn34, 35,
39
silence, postwar, 5–11, 63–64,
277–78nn14, 23, 29
Silverman, Kaja, 179, 182,
312–13nn13, 19, 20, 320n16
Social Democratic Party (SPD), 73,
159
social discourse, 15, 37
social hierarchies, 2